Dramatic Criticism

Dramatic Criticism
A History

by
Charles W. Meister

McFarland & Company, Inc., Publishers
Jefferson, North Carolina, and London

Library of Congress Cataloging in Publication Data

Meister, Charles W., 1917–
  Dramatic criticism.

  Bibliography : p.
  Includes indexes.
  1. Dramatic criticism—History. 2. Drama—History
and criticism. I. Title.
PN1707.M45   1985   801'.952   84-43222

ISBN 0-89950-155-9 (alk. paper)

©1985 Charles W. Meister. All rights reserved.

Printed in the United States of America.

McFarland & Company, Inc., Publishers
Box 611, Jefferson, North Carolina 28640

Preface

Modern drama finds new followers every day. Inevitably, as we become absorbed in the conflicts and resolutions of the characters of a play, we begin to make evaluations and comparisons of the sorts of dramatic art that we prefer. This book is designed to help stimulate and organize the varying reactions we all have toward the art.

Several assumptions underlie this book. One is that the questions a playgoer might ordinarily raise about a play are similar to or address the problems faced by the playwright, the critic, or the serious student. A discussion, therefore, of many of the key questions that arise in dramatic criticism will help us appreciate the achievements of drama. No doubt it should likewise alert us to the meretricious.

Another assumption is that the various dramatic media have sufficient similarity to benefit from a common consideration of what it basically takes to make a good play. Allowances must be made for the specific limitations and strengths of each medium, but the desirability of a broad knowledge of dramatic effects suggests that cross-pollination might mutually enrich the media. It might also enable us to accept certain inescapable limitations as inherent in the medium, and thus not ask drama to be something it cannot be.

As entertainment, drama in its various forms can provide pleasant escapism. As literature, drama can be a vivid and imaginative art form, acquainting us with both linguistic and pictorial beauty. As food for thought, drama raises profound questions about the meaning and purpose of life. Great masters like Sophocles,

vi Preface

Shakespeare, and Chekhov give us representations of the human predicament in dramatic form that is at once entertainment, literature, and food for thought.

The enjoyment of drama is one of mankind's sublimest diversions. So deeply rooted in human nature is the mimetic urge that no society has been known that did not employ drama in some form. At its best, of course, drama often merges with religion to represent sacred themes or to help preserve traditional values. In this book many of the most penetrating drama critics, ancient and modern, offer the reader the challenge to return constantly to drama to find fresh beauties, fresh insights and joys.

An annotated bibliography provides a summary of 225 of the leading books in the history of dramatic criticism. Many books not mentioned in the text are summarized here. This format permits additional information, without interfering with the narrative flow of the text. In the summaries, mention is usually made of both the names of notable critics and dramatic concepts and terms as they have evolved.

If, for example, the reader wishes to discover what John Dryden said in the field of dramatic criticism, he would do well to consult both indexes. Likewise, if he is pursuing what critics have said on tragedy, both indexes are useful. Please note, however, that reference numbers in the Index to Text are to *page* numbers, whereas reference numbers in the Index to Bibliography are to *entry* numbers.

If the reader of this book broadens or deepens his knowledge of the field of dramatic criticism, the purpose of the book will have been served.

Table of Contents

Preface v

1. Beginnings 1
2. Greek and Roman Criticism 5
3. Medieval Criticism 15
4. Renaissance Criticism 21
5. Spanish Criticism 37
6. 17th Century French and English Criticism 42
7. 18th Century French and English Criticism 55
8. Shakespearian Criticism 66
9. German Criticism 73
10. 19th Century French and English Criticism 84
11. American Criticism Before 1920 97
12. Russian Criticism 115
13. 20th Century European Criticism 142
14. The Theater of the Absurd 158
15. American Criticism Since 1920 176
16. Motion Picture Criticism 202
17. The Achievements of Dramatic Criticism 230

References 249
Bibliography 265
Index to Bibliography 295
Index to Text 301

1. Beginnings

The cave man who grinned approvingly at his wife, as she flapped her arms to imitate a bird, probably started it all. Ever since then, men and women have been interested in expressing their reactions to the art of mimesis. When we find a dramatic representation that pleases us, there are few thrills that can rival our exultation. But when we witness drama that we do not care for, new and creative depths of invective are likely to be plumbed. What have been some of the more significant contributions to the art of dramatic criticism?

As soon as primitive peoples had taken care of their food, shelter, and security, they turned to the dance as a religious ritual and as a means of self-expression. The dance frequently employed masks for symbolization and role-playing, and in time the dramatic element outweighed the dance itself.

Since most early drama seems to have had a religious function, criticism of it was tantamount to criticizing the group's religion, a practice not allowed in most primitive tribes. Since the ritual-dramas were not written down, and their performance sometimes lasted several days, the dancer-actors performed prodigious feats of memory not only in recalling their lines but also in knowing at what precise point the music and dance steps change. Visitors to the American Southwest, for example, are still amazed at the precision and stamina of the Hopi dancers.

Because the ritual-drama was related to the religious needs of the tribe, errors were almost sacrilegious. A boy undergoing initiation rites was learning the highly guarded secrets of his tribe and was thus expected not to err, lest the divine message be lost. Sheldon Cheney reports that "among the Maoris if even a single word is dropped or incorrectly spoken in certain rituals, the mistake is believed to presage the death of the performer. In other cases a mistake is actually punishable by death."[1] "Civilized" dramatic criticism has never reached this point, although some bilious critics in advanced countries have been tempted at times to suggest this strict a punishment!

In contrast, however, is the fact that many primitive peoples have a well developed sense of humor. Ritual-dramas enacting a hunting or battle scene may burlesque someone who failed ludicrously. Many tribes have clown characters who intentionally fail, like the Apache Devil-Dancer. In the preliterate cultures more criticism is directed at acting than at creative composition in words. The Aztecs, we are told, had developed the art of acting to a high degree of perfection before the Spaniards arrived. Moreover, "in savage communities practically the only amusement of the children consists in imitating the more serious acts and experiences of their parents."[2]

As ritual began to involve audience considerations it started to evolve into an art form. As the archeologist Jane Harrison stated, "It is in this new attitude of the spectator that we touch on the difference between ritual and art; the *dromenon*, the thing actually done by yourself has become the *drama*, a thing also done, but abstracted from your doing."[3]

Perhaps the earliest extant dramatic criticism is that contained in the testament inscribed at Abydos about 2000 B.C. by the Egyptian actor, I-kher-nefert, "giving a personal impression of the Passion Play of Osiris, which he himself produced."[4] A somewhat similar record is found in Herodotus (Book II, Chapter 63), where he describes the ritual drama at Papremis as it was staged in the fifth century B.C.

The Bible contains many references to dancing but few to drama. *Job* and *The Song of Solomon* are often considered to be dramatic in form, and the passages such as the one describing the exhibition of Samson in the Philistine temple at Gaza certainly have much dramatic force. The complete history of Christ is of course re-enacted symbolically in the mass. But little dramatic criticism emerges from the early Judeo-Christian background.

Nor is the Orient very rich in dramatic criticism. Yet several interesting things can be learned from looking at the theater in India. The divinely inspired sage Bharata received the art of the drama from heaven, it is believed, and the dramatic canons associated with his name became the high authority for subsequent Sanskrit playwrights. Scarcely ever has a body of drama had such a strict set of rules—and little great drama has resulted.

For one thing, Hindu drama tended to appeal to the Brahmins, and was thus too intellectual for broad acceptance. In addition, Indian critics set up rigid categories of plays based upon the caste of the characters, the supernatural elements, the style of writing, the intensity of emotion, and numerous other criteria. Initially there were ten types of "higher" drama and eighteen types of "lower." Thus the rigid formalization of drama in India paralleled the caste system, and by forcing playwrights to conform to ironclad rules, may have had a lot to do with stultifying Hindu dramatic art.

Sanskrit theorists concentrated not upon the emotions which inspire the dramatist but rather the emotions, or *rasas*, aroused in the audience by his work. There were nine possible *rasas*: love, anger, heroic ardor, disgust, laughter, pathos, wonder or admiration, fear, and tender affection. If a play mingles several of these, one must always remain dominant, so as not to confuse the audience. It was believed that in a great play, the audience lost itself in the *rasa* it was experiencing. "In this area of Sanskrit critical thought the truly significant concepts are the recognition that these 'poetic relishes' are limited, and that an audience must be directed towards one or another if complete satisfaction is to be attained."[5]

A comment from the prologue to Kalidasa's first play, *Malavik-agnimitra* (c. A.D. 400), offers a pragmatic warning to critics:

Wise men approve the good, or new or old;
The foolish critic follows where he's told.[6]

In China the first glimpses of drama are seen in pre-Confucian religious dances. Classical scholars after Confucius objected to the drama as undignified, and it was not until the Mongol invasions that drama in China received a great forward impetus. In the eighth century A.D. the Emperor Ming Huang formed the first Chinese dramatic company, which came to be called after the stage in his pear garden, the Pear Garden School of Acting. There has never been as much interest in the script of the drama as in the accompanying stage spectacle, which is done in brilliant symbolic colors to the constant accompaniment of music. Chinese plays are traditionally considered to be of two sorts: military plays based upon history, and civil plays dealing with humorous matters in everyday life. Since there seems to be no rich body of Chinese drama, there has been little Chinese dramatic criticism of note. Japanese drama had the traditional origin in religious ritual. The Shinto priest Kwanami crystallized the form of the No-play, which is the classical Japanese drama form, in the fourteenth century. Since then tradition has largely governed the development of the No-play, which uses ghosts as its chief characters. The popular drama in Japan, the Kabuki theater, fuses music, dance, and acting in a form somewhat like our musical comedy. Japan has a rather extensive body of drama, but little of its dramatic criticism has attracted attention outside of Japan.

One result of recent wars has been to acquaint many Westerners with Oriental drama, and a number of competent scholars are now bridging the gap between Eastern and Western drama. Outstanding among these scholars have been Ezra Pound, Arthur Waley, A.E. Zucker, Stark Young, Faubion Bowers, and Donald Keene. Periodic visits to the United States of troupes of Oriental actors have helped the West to understand Eastern drama.

In summary, then, little outstanding dramatic criticism seems to have been produced in primitive or Oriental cultures. Until a culture has a body of written drama sufficient for study and reflection, it seems to produce little dramatic criticism of any lasting merit.

2. Greek and Roman Criticism

Parody, said Professor George Saintsbury of Edinburgh University, is "criticism in the rough,"[1] and thus always precedes genuine criticism. At any rate, some of the earliest Greek criticism is found in parody form in the Greek tragedies. The occasional tendency for Sophocles to parody the style of Aeschylus gave rise to complaints from later Greek and Roman critics that the writing of Sophocles was "frigid" and "uneven." Euripides, of course, ridicules Aeschylus for the improbability of the recognition scene in *Choephori*. In *The Suppliant Women*, Euripides also makes fun of the technique of awkward dramatic narration.

Euripides, in turn, is belabored by Aristophanes for his skepticism, sophism, and tedious narratives. In *Thesmophoriazusae* Aristophanes has Euripides condemned by the women for treating them poorly in his plays. In *Frogs* Dionysus chooses Aeschylus over Euripides on intuitive and impressionistic grounds: it is the older dramatist "in whom the soul of Dionysus delighted." The charges levied against Euripides are these: he constantly uses unpleasant stories; his style is affected and sophistical; by introducing blind beggars into high tragedy he detracts from the majesty appropriate to the gods; he too often employs tiresome preliminary explanations and interpolated narratives; and he innovates too freely in education and politics.

Nevertheless Euripides is praised by Aristophanes for his use of dialogue by all characters, his realistic scenes of everyday life, and his clarification of the overall design of tragedy. For twenty years,

Saintsbury says, the campaign of Aristophanes against Euripides was consistent, being based upon "a reasoned view of art and taste as well as of politics and religion."[2] Although he did not formulate a large body of systematic criticism, Aristophanes did show a sane and perspicacious awareness of certain excesses to be avoided.

Emile Egger, in his *History of Greek Criticism* published in Paris in 1887, reveals that, aside from Aristotle, little dramatic criticism of lasting worth appears to have been written during the classical Greek period. There are a few fragments from Theophrastus and Simylus, but most of the criticism was contained in the comedies, which are almost all lost. While comparing tragedy and comedy, Antiphanes humorously suggests that it is easier to write tragedy than comedy, for the plots, being prescribed by convention, call for no imagination on the author's part. The variety of treatment given one plot by the great tragedians, however, seems to gainsay this view.

Plato, in *Phaedrus*, defines tragedy not in terms of gifted individual speeches but in their relationship to one another and to the whole effect. In *The Republic* he goes on to attack tragedians for stirring emotions that are not in accord with reason. Most of Plato's remarks, however, are given as adjuncts to his philosophy rather than as specific dramatic evaluations. Following Plato and Aristotle came the Scholiasts, chiefly grammatical critics whose comments on the plays were for the most part superficial and pedantic.

Greek dramatic criticism remains important, nevertheless, solely because of the contribution of one man, Aristotle. So significant have his views been that much of subsequent dramatic comment consists of re-affirmation or attack upon the principles laid down in his *Poetics*. The *Poetics* is at once a judicious appraisal of Greek dramatic achievement and a skeleton for a whole philosophy of the drama. Although Aristotle concentrates his emphasis upon tragedy (and Sophoclean tragedy at that, for H.D.F. Kitto warns us against using Aristotle's standards in evaluating the plays of Aeschylus and Euripides), his insights can be used in appreciating many other art forms. Saintsbury's sentence stands: "He is the very Alexander of criticism, and his conquests in this field, unlike those of his pupil in another, remain practically undestroyed, though not extended, to the present day."[3]

Aristotle's life is often divided into three periods: (1) for twenty years he was a student of Plato at Athens; (2) for twelve years he lived at Assus, Lesbos, and Pella—during eight of these years he tutored Alexander; (3) from 335-323 B.C. he ran the Peripatetic

School in Athens. He left Athens in 323 because of the chaos following Alexander's death, and died the following year in Chalcis.

In the *Poetics*, Aristotle finds the origin of all literature in two traits of human nature: man's instinct for representing things ("imitation"), and man's instinctive pleasure in recognizing a good imitation. He also feels that man's deep-seated feeling for rhythm and harmony contributed to the origin of "poetry" (literature). He recounts the historical rise of Greek drama, for he wishes to differentiate one poetic species (tragedy) from another (comedy). Serious-minded writers, who wished to deal with noble actions and characters, wrote what developed into tragedies; the "meaner sort" of writers wrote invective that tended to produce the comedy as a literary form. Homer occupied a significant place in both forms, Aristotle believed. Just as *The Iliad* and *The Odyssey* were the forerunners of tragedy, so was Homer's *Margites* an improvement over the older form of invective comedy, for it dealt with the general ludicrous rather than with personalized attack. Comedy, Aristotle contends, deals with persons below average in one respect—the ridiculous, which he defines as a mistake or deformity not productive of pain or harm to others.

Much dramatic criticism through the ages has concerned itself with whether plays observe the Three Unities of time, place, and action. This means, of course, that the play should contain but one main action, taking place within one day's time in one setting. Ultimately the interpretation of setting was broadened to permit one city to be the locale of the play. To attribute the constraint of the Three Unities to Aristotle is obviously unjust. He did believe in unity of action, but he never mentioned unity of place. While differentiating the relatively short dramatic form of tragedy from the longer narrative form of the epic, he did state that tragedy endeavors as far as possible to keep "within a single circuit of the sun, or something near that."[4] Kitto points out that adherence to the unities of time and place were accidental, not fundamental, in Greek drama. It was inconvenient to move the chorus about, so the scene tended not to change. Originally, Greek drama depicted not so much action as thought and feeling about action, so it was not natural for the chorus to attempt to pursue actions. When changes in setting were made necessary and probable, as in the *Eumenides* of Aeschylus and the *Ajax* of Sophocles, they were made without hesitation.

So, too, with the unity of time. Time, in Greek drama, is a convention, not a measured regularity. When intervals of time are needed, as between battle scenes, it is sufficient that *some* time interval be allowed, not necessarily the calendar-and-clock interval. *The Suppliant Women* by Euripides occupies nearly a week of time. Aristotle, basing his critique upon actual stage productions rather than upon mere theory, records a general practice rather than an esthetic need. Neoclassical critics of course had lost this sense of practicality when they tried to fit entirely different dramatic needs and staging opportunities into the mold of the Three Unities.

Our version of the *Poetics* is probably in the cryptic form of lecture notes. This terse form keeps the treatise from full consideration of the great philosophical ideas underlying tragedy. But at least one merit of the *Poetics* is conspicuous. Through careful definition and extension, Aristotle placed criticism on a systematic basis, so that the shifting standards of impressionism no longer need be employed. His definition of tragedy is time-honored: "A tragedy, then, is the imitation of an action that is serious and also, as having magnitude, complete in itself; in language with pleasurable accessories, each kind brought in separately in the parts of the work; in a dramatic, not in a narrative form; with incidents arousing pity and fear, wherewith to accomplish its catharsis of such emotions."[5]

Since a play exists to show an action, the plot is the most important part of a tragedy. Francis Fergusson points out that Aristotle uses plot in two senses: most importantly, it is the formal cause, the "soul," of the tragedy, the touchstone into deep religious feelings assumed by the Athenian playwright. Less importantly, the plot, conceived of as a final cause, is a series of incidents connected through necessity and probability, existing for the purpose of diverting an audience. Gilbert Murray, studying tragedy in the light of Greek ritual, shows how parts of the ritual seem to correspond to parts of the plot, such as recognition and suffering scenes, mentioned by Aristotle. Unfortunately, in Fergusson's view, we have lost "the idea of a theater" that the Greeks and the Elizabethans had. In other words, our theater does not serve as a focal point of our culture, bringing into one vista the inter-related values and insights of the culture. Hence it is difficult for us to conceive of how the plot serves as the "soul" of the tragedy, triggering deep-felt religious emotions in something like the way T.S. Eliot's "objective correlative" functions, but in a grander and more significant realm of associations.

Since Aristotle could assume the ritualistic background on the part of the Athenian audience, he turns most of his discussion of plot to the second consideration, that of a series of incidents representing an action. A good plot is one that is of the proper magnitude, with unity, probability, and universality. An artistic plot has beginning, middle, and ending, so that a sense of esthetic wholeness is left with the audience. Omission of any one of these three requisites would leave a truncated emotional reaction. Moreover, plot incidents should be so ordered that change of any of them will dislocate the entire plot. Plot incidents are most interesting when they are unexpected, but connected through necessity. Complex plots may also employ a sudden reversal of fortune's wheel, a discovery (a change from ignorance to knowledge on someone's part), and suffering, or pathos. Reversals and discoveries Aristotle called "the most powerful elements of attraction" in tragedy. He stated that the most effective discoveries are not due to birthmarks or outer signs, but grow out of inherent character relationships in the play.

The six "parts" of tragedy mentioned by Aristotle—plot, character, thought, language, melody, and spectacle—are not quantitative parts, but are inseparable in the finished work. Like the ingredients of a cake, they combine and fuse to form a new object. They are separable in the writer's mind, while planning the work, and they can be evaluated separately by an audience, but always with the thought of their contribution to the overall effect.

Character ranks second to plot, in the *Poetics*. Aristotle says that tragedies can be written without character, but not without plot. Character, he feels, is that which reveals the moral purpose of the person represented. It can thus best be revealed by placing the person in a position of choice wherein the alternatives are not obvious—the person's choice will reveal his character.

The tragic hero, according to Aristotle, is a person above average in morals, but possessed with some tragic flaw in his character that inevitably leads to his undoing. He is not near-perfect, or his fall to misery would be odious to us; he is not vicious, or his rise to fortune would be resented and his fall to sorrow would be deserved, and thus not pitiable. Pity grows out of undeserved misfortune: a disproportion exists between a man's character and his deserts. Characters in a tragedy, Aristotle felt, should be moral, appropriate, lifelike, and consistent. If the person represented is an inconsistent person, then make him consistently inconsistent. The actions of the characters should always be necessary or probable; if they did something improbable, omit the improbability in the representation, as Sophocles did with Oedipus' failure to use a murder he had committed as a clue to discovering the murderer of his father, Laius.

Aristotle gives little attention to thought, which he calls the power of saying what is appropriate to the occasion. He feels that this element falls under the arts of politics and rhetoric. That part of language dealing with manner of speaking he similarly believes subject to the criticism of professors of elocution. Language is best when it is unusual yet clear. Most of his discussion of language deals with grammatical and metrical analysis. He says little about music and spectacle, for he feels that they, particularly spectacle, are more properly the concern of the stage manager than the playwright.

The *Poetics* distinguish four types of tragedy: the complex tragedy, using reversals and discoveries; the tragedy of suffering; the tragedy of character; and the tragedy of spectacle. Aristotle felt that the chorus should be an actor in the play, as in Sophocles, and not an outside commentator, as in Euripides. The final part of the *Poetics* differentiates tragedy from the epic.

Here, then, was a solid foundation for future critics. A system of terms was adopted that admitted of more than purely impressionistic whimsy, and concrete examples were quoted of what Aristotle meant by excellence or lack of it in dramatic art. He was not captious, but generous in his praise—something future critics could well note. He grounded his judgments not only on esthetic theory, but on the collective judgment of many playgoers.

Most of the unduly confining influence of Aristotle upon subsequent drama and dramatic criticism grew out of misapplications of his approach. His concept of "imitation" was sometimes construed as meaning photographic representation, and his stress upon ethical considerations may have led future commentators into moral didacticism rather than esthetic appraisal. But on the whole it is extraordinary that so much insight and wisdom could be contained within one treatise, even when written by the man universally considered to be "the father of dramatic criticism."

As was true in Greece, some of the earliest dramatic criticism in Rome was embodied within plays by leading dramatists. Plautus, for example, defends *Amphitruo* as a tragicomedy, an early example of defense of a mixed genre; and he and Terence satirize such things as stereotyped lovers, stock characters, and the constant use of Athens as a setting. Terence, of course, was charged with "contamination" for uniting scenes from several Greek plays to serve a new purpose in his plays. Several of his comments, nevertheless, have been abiding ones. His rejection of an expository prologue on the grounds that exposition should be incorporated within the play itself is one of these, and another is his defense of expropriation of former playwrights' language: "There is nothing now said that has not been said before."[6]

Aristotle's influence upon Latin dramatic criticism was surprisingly slight. Cicero mentions that Aristotle was not popular with the Romans, but in his own writing on comedy Cicero seems to be following the Stagirite. Comedy, he says, grows out of "ugliness or deformity which is pointed to as something offensive, but in an inoffensive manner."[7] Aware of the social function of comedy, Cicero states that neither great vice nor great misery is fit subject for ridicule, for crime should be fought by laws and misery derided is always unpleasant. Cicero differs with Maetius ("our professed critic," as he is described by a contemporary) who defended the lavish Roman spectacles. "What pleasure could it afford to a judicious spectator," asks Cicero, "to see a thousand mules prancing about the stage in the tragedy of Clytemnestra, or whole regiments accoutered in foreign armor in that of the Trojan Horse?"[8] Such shows may captivate vulgar eyes, he goes on to say, but can never please anyone with taste. More specifically than Aristotle, Cicero indicates types of characters suitable for dramatic genres, saying that comedy should employ the morose, the superstitious, the suspicious, the boastful, and the foolish. He differs with Plautus in at least one regard: he believes that there should be no mixture of comedy and tragedy.

Cicero could have been influenced also by the *Tractatus Coislinianus*, first century B.C. document that Lane Cooper believed to be the lost work on comedy by Aristotle. In a somewhat wooden parallel to Aristotle's definition of tragedy, comedy is defined as "an imitation of an action that is ludicrous, unfortunate, and of an adequate magnitude in embellished language, the several kinds of embellishment being separately found in the several parts of the play; presented by persons acting and not in the form of narrative; through pleasure and laughter effecting the purgation of the like emotions."[9] Why purge pleasure, and should comic language be "embellished"? Nevertheless, the *Tractatus* contained one of the earliest extant inquiries into the nature of comic effects. Laughter, it says, comes from either "diction" or "things done"; then both categories are handled at length. "Diction" laughter comes from puns, degrading synonyms, garrulity, grammatical blunders, and similar sources, whereas "subject matter" laughter arises from deceptions, degrading comparisons, impossibilities, surprises, incongruous actions, or distorted characters with exaggerated defects.

The only complete example we have of Roman dramatic criticism is Horace's *The Art of Poetry* (also called *Epistle to the Pisos*), which has been very influential upon subsequent drama critics. "Critical activity in nearly all the countries of western Europe seems to have been ushered in by the translation of Horace's *Ars Poetica* into the vernacular tongues,"[10] said Professor Joel Spingarn of Columbia University.

Few Romans were familiar with Aristotle's works. "In the *Ars Poetica* of Horace," says Marvin Herrick, "there are superficial traces of Greek theory, but these are remote from Aristotle, who, as Cicero tells us, was not popular with the Romans."[11]

Based upon a no longer existing treatise by Neoptolemus of Parium, *The Art of Poetry* follows the three-fold division into content, technique, and poet that was typical of critical works of the period. It is so brilliantly phrased that many of its lines have become commonplaces of criticism. Yet this very terseness led to later formal frigidity as interpreters followed Horace slavishly.

The function of literature, Horace says, is to entertain or to enlighten. A play that does both is of the highest kind. The first requisite in the dramatist is for him to have "good sense." Patriotism, family values, friendship, and a description of how government works are all good subjects for plays, since they have universal audience appeal. The highest type of literature serves a moral purpose, such as reinforcing religion, bolstering sexual morality, or establishing codes of proper conduct.

The dramatist should stick to his strengths. He should reflect long on his subject, and then choose his words carefully, eliminating all thoughts except those germane to his theme. Skilled in language, he should be able to use common words in uncommon contexts. For this the audience will applaud him, Horace promises, provided he does not innovate too frequently.

Within twenty-three short lines (lines 178-201) Horace announced the principles that chained many neoclassical playwrights and critics: a play must have five acts; nothing violent, disgusting, or incredible should be staged; the chorus should keep to its business of voicing moral sentiment. Since it is hard to invent new plots, a new treatment should be given the Greek plots. The plot should open quietly, in the midst of complications. No *deus ex machina* solution should be used, unless a difficulty occurs worthy of such a deliverer. Tragedy and comedy should not be mingled, and no more than three characters should speak in any one scene. Decorum must be observed in characters, who should embody normal traits appropriate to the four stages of life: playful childhood, unstable youth, ambitious adulthood, and reminiscent age. Horace recommends careful mingling of action and narration, and the use of iambic verse in both tragedy and comedy, for the quick recurrence of its marked beat makes it easily heard in noisy assemblies. Language should be differentiated and appropriate to the age, sex, country, social status, and temporary mood of the speaker.

Horace's desultory judgments were hardly able to bear the authoritative status given them. Besides being arbitrary and conservative guides to dramaturgy, these rules tended to shackle genius down to mediocrity.

It is difficult to imagine a Hamlet or an Iago growing out of observance of this advice: "Above all, be like the best of your predecessors, stick to the norm of the class, do not attempt a perhaps impossible and certainly dangerous individuality."[12] As Saintsbury pointed out, the false *mimesis*—imitation of previous art—was mixing itself up more and more with the true *mimesis*—representation of nature. But Horace's vivid phrases possibly helped crystallize dramatic terms so that chaotic anarchy would not prevail in drama.

Following Horatian precepts of decorum, probability, and verisimilitude, Plutarch clearly prefers Menander to Aristophanes. Plutarch surprisingly finds no cleverness or genius in Aristophanes, but merely vulgar and theatrical use of puns, jingles, and tasteless antitheses. In an ethical vein, Plutarch shows how Menander's graceful satire avoids bitterness and spite, whereas Aristophanes seems to try to represent humanity at its worst. Like the rhetorician Quintilian, Plutarch believes that Menander is more instructive, sensible, and "normal" than Aristophanes. Aside from this early misuse of such concepts as decorum and verisimilitude, this criticism suggests that if we had more than mere fragments of Menander's plays, perhaps we would value him more highly.

Julius Caesar paid Terence the compliment of calling him "half a Menander," and a grammarian of Alexandria, a certain Aristophanes, asked: "O life and Menander, which of you two imitated the other?"[13] Gellius, a second-century grammarian, devoted a whole chapter to showing why he preferred Menander over the Roman comic writer Caecilius for superior plot invention, expression, wit, and variety of emotion.

Quintilian similarly prefers Menander to the three great Greek tragedians, viewed from the standpoint of models for the study of oratory. Menander's virtues are seen to be the presentation of character, eloquent speeches, and "criticism of life." Quintilian regarded the Latin writers Marcus Pacuvius and Lucius Accius as the greatest tragedians of antiquity, for their dignity of thought, forceful language, and impressive characters. There are other occasional references to Roman drama in the writings of Livy, Juvenal, Martial, Lucian, and Petronius.

In his treatise *On the Sublime*, Longinus stressed the artistic conception of drama more than did his contemporaries. Longinus also put great stress upon sincerity on the part of the dramatist and the critic alike. His defense of drama served well during the attacks upon the theater by church fathers such as Tertullian and Augustine.

Unfortunately not more influential in their day were the comments of Dio Chrysostom, who unerringly went to the heart of dramatic criticism, finding the quintessence of a dramatist's genius. Dio contrasted the plays of the three Greek tragedians chiefly from the standpoint of plot. Although Aeschylus used improbability, his direct handling of myth and his grandeur of concept and phrase are applauded. Euripides is praised for his keen intellect and his ability to revise plots so as to achieve the maximum rhetorical color. Sophocles is found superior in sweetness, elevation, and human charm, and thus is preferred over the two others in his handling of the tragedy of Philoctetes.

Ironically, Roman critics were more influential than Greek critics in shaping the creed that came to be known as "classicism." Although Aristotle had provided guidelines for a critical credo that incorporated esthetic principles within an eclectic framework, for many centuries critics and playwrights preferred the Horatian version of classicism, which recommends the regular over the unusual, adherence to safely established traditions, and use of types and generalizations rather than eccentric or highly individualized characters.

3. Medieval Criticism

As is well known, the church played a vital role in all aspects of medieval life. Consequently the chief factor in the development of medieval dramatic criticism was the attitude of the church. After all, the Roman theater had been the source of much of the derisive attack upon the early Christian church. Thousands of Roman spectators in amphitheaters laughed at parodies of the rites of this little-known Nazarene sect. As Benjamin Hunningher observes, "even the most tolerant Christian could not really swallow theatrical representations of bishops as grotesque ithyphallic characters and of the sacrament of baptism as a dunking-party in a tub, from which the fool was finally fished up a baptized Christian."[1]

Thus, shortly after his conversion to Christianity, about A.D. 198, Tertullian wrote his famous treatise *Of Public Shows*, which set the tone for persistent church hostility toward drama. Tertullian calls the theater "the shrine of Venus," and he describes Satan taking over the souls of playgoers. To answer the charge that drama can be a useful school of morality, he replies: "The moral good induced was only a drop of honey, mixed with the poison of toads."[2]

St. John Chrysostom agreed that stage plays were deceitful in nature, and thus to be avoided. In the fourth century Athanasius attacked Arius of Alexandria for bringing into the church music that Athanasius said came from "ungodly mimes." The efforts of Arius to erect a Christian theater to combat the lewd pagan theater were stifled when he was excommunicated for his heretical doctrinal views.

In his early days at Carthage, Augustine wrote a tragedy that won a prize. Later, however, he opposed the theater, on the one hand for its dedication to pagan gods, and on the other because it moves viewers towards immoral behavior. He did believe, however, that "genuine tragedy and comedy" can be "honest and liberal studies,"[3] especially when compared to the offensive use of filthy language in other kinds of plays.

Augustine applauded Plato for banishing poets from the ideal state, since poets tend to trust their wild fancies more than religious tradition. Augustine also commended Cicero's approval of the Roman death sentence penalty for a person found guilty of composing a satire designed to bring infamy or disgrace on any person. Augustine supported the Roman law which prevented any living person from being either praised or blamed on the stage.

Despite church opposition, drama continued to exist, particularly in the Near East. A fourth-century Galician noblewoman, Aetheria, describing her pilgrimage to the Holy Land, mentions plays performed at Christmas and Easter by Christian congregations in Palestine. Records also indicate that mimes (actors and entertainers) existed throughout the history of the Byzantine empire. In the eighth century John of Damascus attacked common people's veneration of mimes, and contrasted the mimes' lewd performances with the solemn mass. People spent so much time in diversion, he said, that they had no time left for the church. At the court of Charlemagne, strict Alcuin, as counselor to the emperor, did everything he could to oppose the love for the mime which his colleague Angilbert showed.

In the tenth century Hrosvitha, a Benedictine abbess at Gandersheim in Saxony, finding herself a great admirer of the style of Terence's plays, undertook to provide a Christian alternative to them by writing six plays modeled on Terence but dealing with Christian subjects. One of her plays tells of Thaïs, the Egyptian courtesan, who was converted by the monk Paphnutius when he posed as her lover. For penance she was required to live in a small brick enclosure for a period of five years. In her confinement she lived in bliss in the Presence of Christ, and died when the five-year term ended. Anatole France, much later, added the alternative ending of having Paphnutius lust after her beauty, and it is France's version that was used in the opera by Massenet.

Hrosvitha also wrote some brief comments on her plays. At about the same time *The Passion of Christ* appeared, now important chiefly because it incorporates several hundred lines of plays by Euripides, including some passages found nowhere else. By this time medieval clergy were beginning to show at least a modicum of interest in classical drama.

It is common to consider European drama as having evolved out of medieval church drama. About the year 970 St. Ethelwold of Winchester describes the Easter trope *Quem Quaeritis? (Whom Do You Seek?)*, which is often regarded as the forerunner of Western drama, for it used dialogue by several persons.

Hunningher, however, in *The Origin of the Theater*, feels that Western drama had its origin in the secular mimes that also influenced church drama. It is certainly true that the humorous element was getting much more evident in religious plays through the eleventh and twelfth centuries. The Feast of Fools and the Feast of Boys were jocular take-offs on religious rituals. These feasts grew out of the church, seeming to serve as safety valves for lower clergy and laity.

As might be expected, church leaders attacked these licentious rites. In the twelfth century Gerhoh of Reichersberg went so far as to condemn everyone who interested himself in dramatics. He reproved the monks of Augsburg, who used the refectory only for dramatic representations, which he felt always led to conviviality. He said that those who portray Anti-Christ in the church become Anti-Christ!

Shortly thereafter Herrad, abbess of Hohenburg, made a more reasonable protest. She said that church plays were originally well intended to deepen faith, but that subsequently so much buffoonery and disorder had come into them that they should be prohibited. She particularly objected to the slapstick and profanity of the ranting Herod in Christmas plays. As a substitute she recommended a return to the symbolic ceremony of the liturgy itself.

Glynne Wickham has recently shown that medieval drama, like medieval life, was very close to nature. In *The Medieval Theatre* Wickham devotes a section to "theatres of recreation," in which he includes such activities as festivals, mummery, and sworddances.

Wickham also shows how Christianity took over rituals and customs that were originally Celtic, Norse, Teutonic, or Roman, and incorporated them into the church calendar. Medieval Christians could thereby retain their time-honored customs since now the Christian meaning superseded the original one. As Wickham states, "The Sun-King that conquered winter and ruled in summer is still to be descried behind St. George of the Mummers' Play and Robin Hood of the May-game, the one owing his place to Christianity, the other to romantic songs and ballads."[4]

In 1207 Pope Innocent III finally banned popular plays from the church, although reverential liturgical plays were still permitted. In fact, Karl Young indicates that church authorities consistently differentiated between the church's own religious drama and secular plays given by entertainers on church property. The steady tendency was to encourage the first but suppress the latter.

St. Thomas Aquinas said that the object of play acting is "to cheer the heart of man. If man cannot have intellectual pleasures, the pleasures of the spirit, he will seek the pleasures of the flesh."[5]

As a counter offense to the rising secular drama, the church began to encourage miracle plays and mystery plays. In the words of E.K. Chambers, "such opposition to the religious drama as can be traced after the thirteenth century came not from the heads of the Church but from its heretics."[6] Thus the vehement *Treatise Against Miracle Plays* of the late fourteenth century is considered by Young to be a Wycliffite document. This impassioned sermon, one of the earliest extensive pronouncements on English drama, refutes the alleged virtues of plays, stating that a stage representation of Christ's miracles is a desecration of a sacred subject. Drama was said to arouse false emotions which were due to mere play-acting and not to a consciousness of sin. But by now, of course, the Western world was getting ready for a brilliant outburst of dramatic activity, and the embittered religious opposition to the stage was somewhat subdued until the Puritans came into power in England.

From the standpoint of dramatic theory, the chief concern of a thousand years of medieval critics was to distinguish comedy from tragedy. It is shocking how imperfect a job was done with this chore, considering the energy expended on it. Much medieval comment on comedy and tragedy deals with the narrative as well as with the dramatic form.

The fourth century grammarian Diomedes stated that comedy concerns the harmless actions of persons in private or public life. Donatus, another grammarian, wrote more extensively on comedy and tragedy. He quotes Cicero's definition of comedy as "a copy of life, a mirror of custom, a reflection of truth."[7] He goes on to define comedy as a story "treating of various habits and customs of public and private affairs, from which one may learn what is of use in life, on the one hand, and what must be avoided, on the other."[8]

This definition scarcely differentiates comedy from tragedy. One of the chief topics developed by Donatus is the description of dramatic costumes. On this ground he divides comedies into three groups: the *palliata*, in which actors wear Greek costumes; the *togata*, in which the actors wear togas; and the *atellana*, which he simply says is full of witticisms and jokes. Colors also epitomize character types: old men wear white, young men wear a variety of colors; slaves wear thick shawls, "either as a mark of their former poverty, or in order that they may run the faster."[9] A girl wears a foreign robe, a procurer wears a robe of many colors, and a courtesan wears a yellow robe, symbolizing greed. Although Donatus provided little incisive criticism, he ultimately influenced both Giraldi Cinthio and Lope de Vega.

Isidore of Seville in the seventh century adds little new insight into comedy. In fact, his division of comedy into two parts seems rather odd: old comedy consists of Plautus and Terence and new comedy of Horace, Persius, and Juvenal. Most writers agreed with the later John of Salisbury and John of Garland, who stated that comedy began in adversity and ended in joy. On this basis, of course, Dante called his masterpiece a comedy. Dante's *Epistle to Can Grande* goes on to state that his language, being Italian, is proper for comedy for it is "careless and humble, the vulgar tongue in which even housewives hold converse."[10] Meanwhile, the mistaken explanation of how the plays of Terence had been acted in Roman times offered by Hugutius about the year 1200 shows that medieval knowledge of classical drama left much to be desired.

The medieval definition of tragedy was no better than that of comedy. Diomedes, following Theophrastus and Suetonius, calls tragedy the story of the fortunes of heroic characters in adversity. Isidore simply designates it the "sad story of commonwealths and kings."[11] By the thirteenth century John of Garland does a little better, defining tragedy as a work in the grand style, treating of shameful and wicked deeds, beginning in joy and ending in grief. In 1286 Johannes de Balbis perpetuated these usual distinctions between tragedy and comedy. By this time, however, the Moorish philosopher Averroës had added a commentary to his abridged version of Aristotles's *Poetics*, so criticism was preparing for a revival of consideration of some of the more important concepts of classical criticism.

On the whole, then, medieval dramatic criticism was undistinguished. It consisted chiefly of moral diatribes by churchmen or repetitious and uninspired definitions of comedy or tragedy. The lack of knowledge about classical times, the unsettled conditions in Europe, and the dearth of interest in drama and in culture generally, kept any advance from being made in this field of activity, as in many others.

As the medieval period was drawing to a close, one important feature of medieval drama was being lost, in the opinion of William Tydeman. This was the closeness to the people that characterized medieval plays. Mystery plays had been staged by craft guilds, and even miracle plays often involved the laity. But with the coming of the professional theater, this close link to the common people was sacrificed. Tydeman feels that the leasing of land for the Globe Theater by James Burbage in 1576 marked the end of an era: "As commercial considerations came to dominate, no longer did hard work, time, talent, and monetary levy weld together people and presentation; no longer was a public dramatic performance the result of widespread communal activity. Now an invisible wall had sprung up between the paid actor and the paying audience. It has still to be demolished."[12]

4. Renaissance Criticism

Italy, as is well known, led Europe into the Renaissance. The only European country with a fully developed vernacular language, Italy had long been the cradle of the humanistic study of the classics. Italian critics found little, save Dante, in their medieval literature to study, and they were proud of their Roman forebears. These are among the reasons that led to the appearance of a number of literary and dramatic critics in sixteenth-century Italy. Modern criticism may be said to have begun here, for these scholars organized and defined criticism as a separate discipline.

The rediscovery of Aristotle's *Poetics* also added new life to dramatic discussion in Italy. A Latin translation by Giorgio Valla appeared in 1498, the Aldine edition of the Greek text in 1508, Allesandro de' Pazzi's version of the Greek original together with a revised Latin text in 1536, Francesco Robortello's Latin translation with the first full commentary in 1548, and an Italian translation, the first in any modern tongue, was published by Bernardo Segni in 1549.

Aristotle's terse comments required amplification and clarification, a task that scores of Italian critics were all too eager to do. It is only natural that many of their interpretations were given in the light of current Italian theatrical conditions.

In addition to commentators on Aristotle and Horace, there were many Italians who produced an "art of poetry" that echoed the classical critics. Marco Girolamo Vida published *The Art of Poety* in 1527. This long critical poem echoed Horace: Follow the ancients, especially Seneca; shun novelty; always use five acts; adhere to the

Three Unities. After Lodovico Dolce translated Horace in 1535, Bernardino Daniello came out with his *Poetics* the following year. This work, the most ambitious piece of criticism since antiquity, was also the first important dramatic criticism in the Italian tongue. Besides echoing Horace on literature's function being to delight and to teach, Daniello bravely states that tragedy should employ mean or humble language when appropriate, just as comedy may use grandiloquence upon occasion. While outlining the duties of the tragic chorus as furthering morality and favoring those who are wrongly oppressed, Daniello comments that the chorus in comedy has been replaced by jesters and musicians.

By 1536 the great influence of Aristotle was beginning to be felt. That year there appeared two editions of the famous Greek critic, one by de' Pazzi and a Greek text by Trincaveli. A few years later the editions of Robortello and Segni were published. In 1550 Vincenzo Maggi furnished explications similar to those of Robortello.

Benedetto Varchi's *Lezzioni* in 1553 also followed Aristotle's precepts, and Francesco Vettori printed a Latin commentary on Aristotle's *Poetics* in 1560. By this time the more important critics—Cinthio, Minturno, Scaliger, Castelvetro, and Guarini—were beginning to lay the basis for an extensive addition to the field of dramatic criticism.

Francesco Robortello published his commentary on Aristotle at Florence in 1548. To Robortello the three bases of dramatic pleasure are imitation (in Aristotle's sense), "difficulty overcome," and admiration. "Difficulty overcome" is our delight in seeing an almost impossible task done well; thus, tragedy can surpass other genres, for a dramatist who can please through presenting sad and unpleasant incidents is attaining the highest reaches of his art. Admiration, the most recurrent source of dramatic pleasure, is the feeling of wonder or amazement which comes from the unexpected or the marvelous. Unfortunately, Robortello and many of his successors twisted Aristotle's original stress on drama as an art form into an evaluation according to rhetorical or moral persuasion, and thus drama as an artistic creation lost its most basic critical principle.

The novelist Giraldi Cinthio published his *Discourse on Comedy and Tragedy* in 1554. Like most Italian critics of his day, Cinthio follows Aristotle and Seneca on tragedy, and Plautus and Terence on comedy. In one sense he was more formal than Aristotle—he is said to have invented the unity of time. But his regard for authority is curiously mingled with independence. He sets aside Aristotle's strictures against a double plot in tragedy, adding lip-service by the phrase, "always remembering the reverence due to Aristotle."[1] He states that Aristotle does not demand rigid adherence to his precepts when conditions have changed. So Cinthio recommends a happy ending in tragedy, provided the catharsis of pity and fear is accomplished. And his attitude toward new dramatic genres is refreshing: "Kinds which the ancients knew not, are free from the ancients' laws."[2]

Cinthio defends the Italian dramatic practice in his day on the grounds of its growing realism. Thus, dramatic theory would seem to parallel the Renaissance painter's search, through perspective, for the "science of illusionism." The ultimate development of this "picture frame" stage practice was the super-realism achieved by the Moscow Art Theater around 1900. Some of Cinthio's preferences, because of their greater realism, include: separation of the prologue from the play proper; division of the play into acts and scenes; large casts of characters, where needed; realistic language; and women characters who are as intelligent as men characters.

The origin of a new dramatic form was heralded by Gianmaria Cecchi in the prologue to his play *La Romanesca* (1574): "The *Farsa* is a new third species between tragedy and comedy. It enjoys the liberties of both, and shuns their limitations; for it receives into its ample boundaries great lords and princes, which comedy does not, and ... welcomes the vilest and most plebeian of the people, to whom Dame Tragedy has never stooped.... It accepts all subjects—grave and gay, profane and sacred, urbane and crude, sad and pleasant. It does not care for time and place."[3]

Plautus had used the term tragicomedy to describe a comic plot containing persons of high estate, and several Greek plays, like *The Eumenides* of Aeschylus and *Alcestis* of Euripides, had mingled serious and light effects. Following Cinthio, Italian critics tended to use the term to designate a tragic plot with a happy ending. The phrase was also used to apply to any play of medieval origin which had at least a partly classical form and a happy outcome.

The chief spokesman for the new form was Giambattista Guarini, whose pastoral tragicomedy *The Pastor Fido* attracted great attention in going through twenty editions between 1585 and 1602. Guarini repeatedly refers to the spirit of Aristotle's *Poetics* to justify his venture in the new genre. To justify his mingling of pity and laughter, Guarini shows that the two are not inharmonious, as long as fear has not been aroused by the drama, for fear is exclusively in the domain of pure tragedy. Mixtures exist in nature, he says, quoting as examples a mule, bronze and other alloys, painting's colors, music's notes, and government, a mixture of rich and poor. He thus defines tragicomedy as a stage imitation of "an action that is feigned and in which are mingled all the tragic and comic parts that can coexist in verisimilitude and decorum, properly arranged in a single dramatic form, with the end of purging with pleasure the sadness of the hearers."[4] Just as the form is mixed, so is the language a mingling of the magnificent with the polished — humble language is considered inappropriate, since tragicomedy generally employs heroes of high rank. Guarini calls tragicomedy the highest form of drama, for it not only follows nature most closely but it avoids the excesses of pure tragedy and pure comedy. It "does not inflict on us atrocious events and horrible and inhuman sights, such as blood and deaths,"[5] he says, and yet it "does not cause us to be so relaxed in laughter that we sin against the modesty and decorum of a well-bred man."[6] Thus did this bold Italian playwright answer the charge against "contaminating the genres" even before neoclassical critics could formulate the rule.

Antonio Sebastiano, called Minturno, took time out from his affairs as Bishop of Ugento to produce a Latin *De Poeta* in 1559, and an Italian *Arte Poetica* in 1563. To Minturno, drama should not only teach and delight but also "move" — that is, "transport" in a Longinian sense. Minturno's discussion of dramatic theory was the fullest up to his time: he has nearly 100 pages on tragedy, and even more on comedy, stressing types of comedy as well as discussing the ludicrous and its sources. His clerical interest is perhaps revealed in a long section on "sentences," that is, philosophic statements on grave subjects by wise persons. It may also be discerned in what he felt to be the didactic value of tragedy. Since anyone, even a person in lofty place, is liable to a sudden reversal of fortune, we should learn to cope with adverse circumstances by watching the way tragic actors endure their fate. It should be observed that, just as there was a Renaissance revival of interest in Greek and Roman gods, so did the Renaissance concept of Fortune resemble the awe in which the Greeks held fate and the Romans the goddess Fortuna. Minturno's sound and independent comments were widely influential abroad at a comparatively early date, and his stress on drama's inciting "admiration" may have helped contribute to the movement during the following century to raise "admiration" to the level of pity and fear as desiderata in drama.

Julius Caesar Scaliger, a philosophic pedant, published his *Poetics* in 1561. Though his outlook was wide and his tendency to use comparative dramatic criticism was somewhat broadened by years of residence at Lyons, his taste was unfortunately defective (he preferred Musaeus to Homer, for example). His work shows the topics in dramatic criticism then considered most fruitful: the relative importance of action and character, the parts of tragedy, the chorus, and the meters most suitable to the stage. Scaliger often differed with Aristotle. He did not believe that all tragedy effected catharsis of pity and fear, and he believed that comedy was the original and pure form of literature, since its matter was wholly invented by the writer. His division of the tragic plot also differs from Aristotle's; Scaliger recognized four parts: introduction, main action, climax, and plot resolution. Like Minturno, he stressed stately speeches and moral teaching, and thus he liked the plays of Seneca. In what he felt was being true to the Aristotelian tradition, he tried to evolve a standard of perfection for each genre. His vigorous stress on verisimilitude helped lead to the doctrine of the Three Unities. Only his common sense kept Scaliger's dogmatism from being unsufferable.

Two years later, in 1563, the two concluding books of Giangiorgio Trissino's *Poetica* were published posthumously. They contained one important doctrine: a theory of comedy compounded of Aristotle, Cicero, and Lucretius, based upon the ludicrous, and ultimately responsible for Hobbes' comic theory of the "passion of sudden glory." Trissino knew Aristotle well, and had he published his material in 1529, when much of it seems to have been written, he would have been the first to have introduced Aristotle's *Poetics* in a vernacular European language.

Probably the most influential of the great Italian dramatic critics in the Renaissance was Lodovico Castelvetro. Once again, it was a shame that some of his weakest contributions were those most treasured. For example, it was chiefly his formulation and defense of the Three Unities of time, place, and action that led to frigid French adoption of them as a veritable strait jacket. His translation and commentary on Aristotle's *Poetics* which appeared in 1570 were based largely on the fact that plays were written to be staged, not read. He felt that a play should be adjusted, in action, space, and time, as nearly as possible to the actual capacity of the stage and the actual duration of the performance. He was thinking of the theater of his day, but had he been more familiar with medieval mystery plays — which ranged from Heaven to Hell, took weeks to act, and covered millennia in their action—he might never have gravitated toward the doctrine of the Three Unities. Since the stress on audience appeal was the first consideration of a dramatist, Castelvetro believed that physical comfort of the audience would limit the play to three or four hours, that elemental passions and interests of mankind would be the only themes broad enough to appeal to a variegated crowd, and that poetry would serve admirably to allow the actors to raise their voices without losing dignity or naturalness. The weak point of Castelvetro's basic approach, of course, was that drama might degenerate into superficial sensationalism while trying to pander to unimaginative audiences. Had Shakespeare composed his plays purely in accordance with Castelvetro's canons, he would probably have been long since in oblivion.

At any rate, Castelvetro was at least independent in judgment. His rejection of Aristotle's view that there can be tragedy without character has been repeated by more modern critics, and he disavowed purely moral catharsis, which makes us better persons, as not a necessary part of esthetics. Nor was it a slavish adherent of Aristotle who dared ask: "What do beginning, middle, and end matter in a poem, provided it delights?"[7] Although he is here moving away from the tendency to consider drama as an adjunct to ethics, as Minturno and Scaliger had done, he lamentably views "delight" in its lowest sense of entertaining any sort of crowd. Castelvetro further shows his independence from Aristotle in his views on imitation and probability. He makes a distinction between the creative writer's imitation and the imitation practiced by an average person. The latter is done unthinkingly, but the former is a carefully planned effort. To Castelvetro, dramatic probability is life's probability—there is no esthetic probability, covering the play's special frame of reference. Nevertheless, his emphasis on a knowledge of theater conditions helped both dramatist and critic to descend the ivory tower of theory into a practical fusion of theater art and dramaturgy. With Castelvetro, reason was always the highest criterion—neither custom, precedent, nor authority has an ultimate sanction, he said. It cannot be assumed that the tendency toward narrow classicism and strict adherence to dramatic rules in France ever was universal or uncontested. Certainly it must be granted that there are early evidences of classicism in France. Jodocus Badius, for example, has introductions and commentaries to his editions of Terence and Seneca (1504-14) in which he repeated the views of classical critics as restated by Donatus and Diomedes. Lazare de Baïf, one of the first translators of Sophocles and Euripides, repeated the classical view that tragedy deals with the great calamities that befall persons in high place.

The very status of French drama at the time, however, legislated against any quick adoption of classical dramatic canons. The old French morality plays ran several days and employed multiple stage settings. The Italian *commedia dell'arte* was growing in popularity, and it of course was based upon anything but classical improvisation. That curious medley of genres, the Spanish *Celestina*, went through five rapid translations.

In addition, at least five genres were recognized as intermediate between classical comedy and tragedy: the satyr play, the pastorale, tragicomedy, morality, and farce. Jean Bouchet's classification of drama in 1526 included the satyr play, which the Greeks had used as a ribald afterpiece to tragedy. The pastorale was a genre using characters disguised as shepherds in an idyllic Arcadian setting. Tragicomedy received its greatest impetus from the work of Alexandre Hardy. Even Thomas Sebillet in his *Art of Poetry* (1548) illustrates the tragedies of antiquity largely by noting parallels to the morality play. He states that neither morality nor farce is a "pure" form, for they are mixed to produce a hodge-podge. The farce he sees as unlike Latin comedy but similar to the Latin *Mime*, in which every license is permitted as long as more laughter is obtained. "To tell the truth," he says, "the acts and scenes of Latin comedy would result only in a tiresome prolixity."[8] Sebillet is the first French critic to show significant influence of both Aristotle and his Italian commentators. He is also in a sense the dramatic spokesman for the *Pléiade*, who had little to say on drama, despite their importance in other forms of French literature.

The opposition to neoclassicism was considerable. In the preface to his play *The Death of Caesar* (1562), Jacques Grévin repudiated Seneca and classical criticism, stating that a chorus of song at a tragedy is not true to life, and that "different nations require different ways of doing things."[9] By 1598 Pierre de Laudun d'Aigaliers objected both to the Three Unities and the classical "law" concerning the number of acts. His *Art poétique* listed five arguments against the unity of time: moderns need not be bound by the ancients; observance of this law would either limit the embellishments now permitted or require the introduction of improbabilities; the ancients themselves did not always observe the unity of time; one day is insufficient to bring about all that a tragedy is supposed to accomplish; and finally, tragedies which observe the rule are no better than those that do not. Laudun is here doing some of the things for French criticism that Cinthio had earlier done for Italian.

But perhaps Alexandre Hardy performed the most important task, by getting tragicomedy accepted as a recognized form. Plautus, of course, had used the term, but more immediately the genre had the medieval *detritus* as a forerunner. Sixteenth-century critics were following Cinthio in using tragicomedy to denote a tragic plot with a happy ending. During the latter half of the century the term was frequently employed for any play of medieval origin which had a happy denouement and at least a partly classical form, so that even miracle, mystery, and farce came under this heading. Hardy, following Robert Garnier, developed a form of tragicomedy distinct from the pastorale. Working with the stage setting of the Hotel de Bourgogne, which represented several localities at once, Hardy ignored the unities of time and place, gave up the chorus, increased the number of characters, and in general strove for more realistic stage presentation. "Everything," he said, "which is approved by usage and public taste is legitimate."[10] If support was needed for this heresy against the classics, Spanish writers were generally quoted.

It should be borne in mind that the "classical" French plays of the following century owed as much to Hardy as to the more "pure" forms of tragedy and comedy written in Greek and Roman times. Finally, the revolt against classical laws culminated in François Ogier's famous preface to *Tyr et Sidon* (1628), a tragedy converted into a tragicomedy by Ogier: "To separate the comic and tragic elements in the same play is to ignore the condition of men's lives, of whom the days and hours are often intermingled with laughter and tears, with contentment and affliction."[11] Ogier goes on to attack classical drama as an offense to nature, with improbability as his chief point. After questioning the verisimilitude in *Agamemnon* and the unity of time in *Antigone*, he asks how old Athens and Rome can give final and prohibitive rules to modern France. His bold and independent spirit is refreshing, on the eve of the *Cid* controversy, but his acknowledgement that his stand is somewhat heretical indicates that neoclassicism was already well developed by this time.

The first French tragedy, *Cléopâtre* by Etienne Jodelle (1552), had formulated a "unity of time," derived and developed from Aristotle. The *Art poétique* of Jacques Peletier du Mans (1555), a full exposition of dramatic theory based largely on Horace, Donatus, and Diomedes, incorporated many of the views of the *Pléïade*. Joachim du Bellay's famous *Defense of the French Language* (1549) urged dramatists to follow the practice of the ancients. Pierre de Ronsard agreed that the great masters of tragedy and comedy imposed a twenty-four hour limitation on the duration of the action represented. A very significant document was Jean de la Taille's *Art de la tragedie* (1572), based on Aristotle, Horace, and the Italian critics. It was de la Taille's borrowing of the Three Unities from Castelvetro that brought that ironclad dogma into France. De la Taille, a practicing playwright as well as a theorist, was particularly influential in formulating the third unity, that of place. Since the prevailing conception of French drama was more lyrical than dramatic—few tragedies of the time were performed—de la Taille pleads for the "purity of the French language," which he feels can be abetted by an unmixed form following classical precedents. Occasions for lyrical expression were being increased through the use of monologues, long moralizing speeches, and choral roles. Since the plays contained little action, special attention was being given to stylistic expression.

The last important orthodox figure was Vauquelin de la Fresnaye, who published his *Art poétique* in 1605. He follows Horace and Seneca, although Aristotle, Vida, and Minturno also influenced his views. He includes tragicomedy in his discussion of comedy, and he asks for plays on Christian subjects. In general, he may be said to summarize the formal criticism of the *Pléiade*, that group of nationalistic poets led by Pierre de Ronsard.

It is generally known that great drama in England preceded great dramatic criticism. At a time when even second-rate dramatists were writing memorable plays, criticism is nothing more than a scant reflection of Aristotle, Horace, Donatus, Minturno, and Scaliger. As Vernon Hall, Jr., states, "When the English critics were not borrowing from across the sea, they were borrowing from each other."[12]

The paucity of Renaissance dramatic criticism in England can be accounted for on several scores. First of all, Elizabethan drama itself was a late, sudden flowering, and it was only when there was a significant body of drama that critics started to analyze the plays. The first theater opened in London in 1576, about the same time that actors gained a new status. The Puritans and others interested in moral problems immediately responded with an attack upon the theater. Then, too, Elizabethan playwrights, an empirical group on the whole, were more impressed by dramatic models from Italy and classical times than by dramatic theories.

Virtually the only dramatic criticism produced by the earlier humanists was to be found in introductions to academic plays, in educational treatises or pamphlets, and ultimately in plays themselves. These views were chiefly moralistic, as for example Sir Thomas Elyot's defense of comedy as showing how to avoid vice, in his *Governour* (1531). Most of Elyot's contemporaries couched their views in Latin rather than in the "vulgar" English. Sir Thomas More's *Utopia* objected to mingling comic and tragic elements, and John Palsgrave, in his notes on his translation from the Dutch of Fullonius' *Acolastus*, gave extensive directions on such stylistic matters as meter, figures of speech, and rhetorical devices.

Many plays were produced in response to the request for a "Christian" drama. Some of these plays contain accompanying dramatic comment of some interest. Nicholas Grimald, in his dedicatory epistle to *Christus Redivivus* (c. 1540), shows an independent spirit similar to that later displayed by Cinthio and Ogier. He cites *Captivi* by Plautus as his authority for violating the unity of time, and he feels the success of his mixture of tragic and comic effects justifies his departure from Cicero's rule. John Christopherson shows the influence of medieval schoolmen, while commenting on his Greek play, *Jephtha* (1546). Christopherson feels that tragedy's greatest glories come from a grand style heightened by philosophic and moral "sentences," as well as from the grave theme of the fall of great men.

Roger Ascham's scattered references to Aristotle's dramatic principles in *Schoolmaster* (1570) are the first in English, although Roger Bacon had made a passing comment to Aristotle's *Poetics* in his *Compendium Studii Theologiae*. Ascham follows Aristotle in considering tragedy the leading literary form, and he shows a preference for Greek plays over Seneca's tragedies, which were better known than the Greek in sixteenth-century England.

It was not only the Puritans who opposed the theater on moral grounds. Some of the early attacks upon the English stage were translations of continental works. An early English protester was the Bishop of Exeter, who in 1571 condemned plays among other "wanton books." John Northbrooke's treatise of 1577 was perhaps the first systematic attack upon the theater, though it is largely a restatement of the conventional moral viewpoint.

The plague in London in 1577 intensified the attack upon the stage. Reverend T. Wilcocke on November 3, 1577, preached at St. Paul's Cathedral: "The cause of plagues is sin, and the cause of sin is plays; therefore, the cause of plagues is plays."[13] Shortly afterward a schoolmaster from Tonbridge, John Stockwood, said from the same pulpit: "Will not a filthy play, with the blast of a trumpet, sooner call thither a thousand, than a hour's tolling of a bell bring to the sermon a hundred?"[14]

In 1579 Stephen Gosson, who had been an actor and playwright, published *School of Abuse*, in which he used invective, racy anecdotes, and choice allusions to attack the stage. He freely confessed past sins: "If any man ask me why myself have penned comedies in time past and inveigh so eagerly against them here, let him know I have sinned and am sorry for my own fault."[15] In *Plays Confuted in Five Actions* (1582), Gosson described drama as a distortion of life rather than as a representation of it.

Thomas Lodge immediately answered Gosson's first polemic with his *Defense of Poetry* (1579), which defends comedy on the ground that it censures vice. A more significant response was Sir Philip Sidney's *Defense of Poesy*, written about 1583 and circulated in manuscript until it was posthumously published in 1595. Although few of the moralistic attacks upon the theater contained dramatic criticism of any merit, the same cannot be said of Sidney's inspired defense. In many ways, this document may be said to inaugurate dramatic criticism in England. Although it must be admitted that there are few original ideas in it, and that it betrays an almost slavish regard for the Italian critics, still the work has an impassioned purity that qualifies it as literature, as well as important early criticism.

The Aristotle that Sidney introduced English readers to was largely the one known to recent Italian commentators. Sidney approves of Scaliger's emphasis on stately speeches and moral teaching in the Senecan manner. He follows Minturno in seeing the office of tragedy as the arousing and catharsis of "admiration and commiseration" rather than Aristotle's "pity and fear." And perhaps most grievous of all, he accepts Castelvetro's formulation of the Three Unities, which of course was not an Aristotelian requirement. Although he correctly states Aristotle's position that tragedy is subject not to the laws of history but the laws of poetry, he scarcely seems ready to accept the Stagirite's dictum that in drama "a convincing impossibility is always preferable to an unconvincing possibility."

Sidney's comments concerning comedy are interesting. He differentiates laughter from delight, stating that the two can exist separately, but that the proper combination of the two produces true comedy. His opposition to tragicomedy is on two grounds: the ancients had not favored it, and he had never seen an example of a good one. His general approach to drama would have outlawed Shakespeare for irregularity, but at least he deserves credit for having produced the first serious dramatic criticism in England.

The state of English drama before 1590 accounts for some of the vehement protests against it. During the first few decades of Elizabeth's reign, there was an overwhelming vogue of comedy, much of which steadily degenerated into farce. Even plays on traditionally serious themes were often being infiltrated with buffoonery and horseplay. Nicholas Udall, in his prologue to *Ralph Roister Doister* (1553), issued one of the first challenges for a comedy free from scurrility and abuse.

Another type of popular Elizabethan drama was the pseudo-chivalric tale, which seems to have had the dramatic art of a modern Space-Man serial. Describing two surviving specimens—*Common Conditions* (1568) and *Sir Clyomon and Sir Clamydes* (c. 1579)—J.W.H. Atkins writes: "Both are stories of wanderings in strange lands where dwelt crafty enchanters, flying serpents, and other monsters, and where whole pirate-crews were dispatched by valiant knights single-handed."[16] George Whetstone's dedication to *Promos and Cassandra* attempts to arraign some of these crudities. "Your Englishman," he says, "first grounds his work on impossibilities; then in three hours he runs through the world, marries, gets children, makes children men, men to conquer kingdoms, murder monsters, and bringeth gods from heaven and fetcheth devils from hell."[17] Whetstone not only called for dramatists to differentiate dialogue in their characters, but also recommended an observance of character "decorum," which meant that human beings were divided into distinctive categories or types, with a pattern of conduct fixed for each type.

Decorum, variously interpreted, proved to be an important concept to many Elizabethans. Among other things this meant that kings spoke as kings, commoners as commoners. Ben Jonson's comedy of humours demanded strict observance of decorum in character. A writer who kept decorum would not mix people of different classes together in the same scene. Decorum also referred to not mixing comedy and tragedy, and adhering to the unities. It often entailed a love of order and a distrust of emotion that would have banished such romantic works as Christopher Marlowe's *Tamerlane*.

Opposition to Marlowe's free-flowing imaginative approach to drama was a rallying point for a number of playwrights who wrote criticism. The most widely held Renaissance theory concerning the imagination was that developed by Pico della Mirandola, who held that the workings of the imagination were a form of mental aberration. Thomas Nashe thus ridicules the "swelling bombast" of "vainglorious tragedians" like Marlowe and Thomas Kyd. Joseph Hall similarly protests against "thundering threats" issued in "big-sounding sentences," and warns that current tragedy all too frequently falls into melodrama.

Much Elizabethan criticism is contained in playwrights' comments on plays by themselves and by other writers. In *Old Wives' Tale* (1595), George Peele satirizes chivalrous melodrama by interspersing realistic rustic characters with fantastic language and actions of magicians, Furies, and similar characters. The mock-heroic *Knight of the Burning Pestle*, by Beaumont and Fletcher, continues to ridicule the pseudo-chivalric play, at the same time castigating the crude taste of city playgoers, who are held responsible for the far-fetched plots and forced situations of that type of play.

Like most dramatists of his day, John Lyly also shows more empirical than theoretical tendencies. His chief contribution lies in the field of comedy. Refusing to recognize genre boundaries as definitely fixed, he does not classify his plays as comedies, tragedies, or anything else, but opens the door to a free development of dramatic forms. He bases his departure from classical rules on the change in audience, and thus lays the basis for a consideration of the audience as a prime factor in dramatic creation. He strips comedy of moral aims by stating that its proper function is to give pleasure and amusement. His final important contribution is seen in his recognition of "wit" as one of the chief ingredients of high comedy. "It is wit that allureth," Lyly states, "when every word shall have his weight, when nothing shall proceed but it shall either savour of a sharp conceit or a secret conclusion"[18] — foreshadowing the witty Restoration comedy.

As was true in France, several new dramatic genres were beginning to gain notice. John Fletcher, introducing *The Faithful Shepherdess* in 1610, tried to gain acceptance for his tragicomedy by explaining that it "is not so called in respect of mirth and killings, but in respect it wanteth deaths, which is enough to make it not tragedy, yet brings some near it, which is enough to make it no comedy."[19] Nashe praised another new form, the historical drama, for inculcating civic virtues: "They show the evils of treason, the fall of those who mount too quickly, the miserable end of usurpers, the misery of civil strife."[20]

This "didactic heresy," that drama's function is primarily moral, was led by Ben Jonson and was supported by a number of Elizabethan playwrights. George Chapman stated that the purpose of tragedy was to offer "elegant and sententious excitement to virture," and the closing words of Beaumont and Fletcher's *Philaster* (1610) state that from the play "princes should learn to rule the passions of their blood."

In 1612 Thomas Heywood defended his profession in *An Apology for Actors*. The author of 220 plays, Heywood argued that the subject of "this harmless mirth" called comedy was "to show others their slovenly and unhandsome behavior that they may reform. There is neither tragedy, history, comedy, moral or pastoral, from which an infinite use cannot be gathered."[21]

Not all dramatists, however, succumbed to the "didactic heresy." John Marston in the prologue to *The Dutch Courtezan* (1605) bluntly states: "We strive not to instruct but to delight." Thomas Dekker's dedication to *The Shoemaker's Holiday* (1599) states that in the play "nothing is purposed but mirth." Shakespeare too, in such places as the epilogues to *As You Like It* and *The Tempest*, states that his aim is merely that of giving pleasure. His famous statement in *Hamlet* on the function of drama is worth mentioning: "To hold, as 'twere, the mirror up to nature; to show virtue her own feature, scorn her own image, and the very age and body of the time his form and pressure."[22]

Although there is some moral stress here, there is more concern for drama as a reflection of human nature and life. As Atkins observes, it is ironic that Shakespeare uses the figure that Plato had employed to attack poetry, since the mirror of literature, in Plato's *Republic*, produced only unsubstantial images and distortions. Shakespeare, of course, felt that stage representations which did not promote the use of the audience's imagination were mere mockeries. The active imagination helped make the play a living structure. Less gifted playwrights, like Thomas Dekker and Thomas Heywood, hesitant about leaving much to inference, employed a chorus to explain plot exposition, but honestly confessed that they were merely stating in their own person what should have been worked into the texture and grain of the action.

This inartistic employment of the chorus to cover up unstageable improbabilities was one of the charges levied against the drama of his time by the greatest critic of his day, Ben Jonson. Jonson is not only the first English dramatist to give criticism a prominent place in his plays, but he is also the first to expound consciously his critical principles of evaluation. Nature made him a critic, and a judicious one—many of his comments are still pregnant with suggestiveness. Convinced that most contemporary drama lacked art, he set out, in scholarly comments on his plays and others, to rectify the situation. There is almost as much criticism in *The Poetaster* as in *The Frogs*. He first published a definitive edition of plays, in his Folio of 1616, for which he wrote new critical material. Here, then, was finally a critic who not only knew the classics intimately, but who also saw the need for creatively deviating from classical patterns.

For Jonson was no servile sycophant to the classics. Although it is true that he follows Sidney in lamenting unnecessary violation of the unities of time and place (for example, in the prologue to *Every Man in His Humour*), still he can follow inner instinct to violate the "rules," when the dramatic necessity demands. He confessed to such violation in *Every Man Out of His Humour*, stating that he knew that his play lacked Terence's division of acts and scenes, the chorus, the proper number of actors, and the observance of the unity of time. These things he saw as "too nice requirements," which dramatic license should permit him to set aside. He further admitted that his *Sejanus* (1605) was irregular, if judged by classical standards, since it lacked both the unity of time and a proper chorus. But he recognized that the nature of contemporary audiences had to be taken into consideration, and thus classical canons would need modification.

Jonson's *Discoveries*, a commonplace book published posthumously in 1641, show his ultimate critical position. When the ancients led the way, he avers, they opened the gates as guides not as commanders. Although Aristotle is the best philosopher and the truest judge, he is not to be slavishly revered. "Nothing is more ridiculous," he states, "than to make an author a dictator, as the schools have done Aristotle.... Let Aristotle and others have their dues; but if we can make farther discoveries of truth and fitness than they, why are we envied?"[23]

Jonson's interpretation of Aristotle largely follows that of Daniel Heinsius, the great Dutch critic who helped restore Aristotle's original view that the one necessary unity was unity of action. Following Heinsius, Jonson misquotes Aristotle, however, as calling laughter, "a fault in comedy, which depraves some part of a man's nature." Jonson goes on then to build his theory of comedy on serious grounds. This concept follows in the realistic vein of Udall, Dekker, and others, but adds the idea of "humour," an idiosyncrasy of behavior that becomes a prevailing passion, and undoes the balance of common sense and reason. It is thus a human folly, and since it can lead to human suffering, it needs to be purged out of one's behavior. Thus comedy serves a social purpose, for the "time's deformity" should be "anatomized in every nerve and sinew," so that correctives would be applied. There develops in the humour character then the opportunity for comedy's own type of catharsis, which Jonson called "the physic of the mind."

Jonson's approach to tragedy is similarly moral, seeming to follow Seneca and Sidney more than Aristotle. Thus a tragedy is expected to be realistic and have a didactic purpose of showing us what to avoid. His own tragic plots tend to follow the medieval concept of tragedy—the sudden fall from prosperity to adversity. Although he inveighed against "fine speeches," he recognized the need for elevated diction where appropriate, and he believed that figurative language could be employed structurally, for it frequently said things that unadorned diction could not say.

Jonson, then, was England's first great critic of drama. He summarizes earlier views but adds some insights of his own. His temperament, which blended creative with critical attributes, was excellent for his office as judge of the drama of his time. In a period when most creative writers were too busy writing plays and poetry to take time for critical evaluation, he, along with Sidney, ranks as a striking exception and as a landmark in the evolution of the art of dramatic criticism.

5. Spanish Criticism

Spain has produced few outstanding dramatic critics. Despite Dryden's surprising statement that "he got more from the Spanish critics alone than from the Italian and French and all others together,"[1] there have been relatively few fresh dramatic insights that originated in Spain.

Spanish dramatic criticism, like all of Spanish literature, has been relatively free of outside influence. Geographical and cultural isolation characterized Spain until late in the Renaissance, and the body of indigenous drama that had been produced is not very classical in form. In this respect, early Spanish drama resembles Elizabethan drama in England.

As H.J. Chaytor has observed, the conventions governing early drama in Spain were more social than literary. Thus the play was expected to help further incipient nationalism, perhaps by referring to military successes; it should also show respect for woman, for family pride, and for loyalty to the church. The style often employed extravagant language, with bombastic passages and far-fetched figures of speech. The play could also depict the *hidalgo* fraternizing with the lower classes, for class distinctions in Spain were nothing like as rigid as those in France at that time.

Since literary matters were relatively unimportant compared to their position in France, Spanish literary critics were not very influential. With little attention paid to drama, it is easy to see why few outstanding drama critics were produced in Spain. One significant early tendency is a large amount of writing defending tragicomedy, a form which was under attack in other countries once the influence of the Italian Aristotelians spread throughout Europe.

The earliest Spanish dramatic criticism appeared in the writings of Enrique de Villena and the Marquis de Santillana about 1434. Spain's first important drama critic was Torres Naharro, who defined some dramatic terms in the prologue to his collection of poetry, *Propaladia*, in 1517. Naharro follows Dante in differentiating comedy from tragedy by comedy's use of a happy ending. Naharro likes the five-act structure, and claims to have invented the term *jornada*. His reference to Italian terms suggests that his plays were probably staged originally in Italian, for educated Italians commonly spoke Spanish in the sixteenth century.

The influence of the Italian Aristotelians is finally seen by the end of that century. Alfonso López protested in 1596 against the current "irregular drama." Luis Alfonso de Carvallo wrote in 1602 on some technical definitions in drama. A transition figure between old and new Spanish drama, Juan de la Cueva, published his *Exemplar Poetico* in 1606. Cueva pretended to have introduced many things that actually antedate him, but he did innovate in the use of Spanish legends as dramatic material.

Another type of attack upon Spanish drama at that time was based on the grounds of morality. In fact, Spanish theaters were closed twice, from 1597 to 1598 and from 1644 to 1649, because they were thought to contribute to lewdness among actors, writers, and audiences. Many church people, particularly the Jesuits, favored the closing of the theaters. Juan de Mariana wrote treatises in 1599 and in 1609 charging the stage with immorality.

Such were conditions, then, when Lope de Vega published his famous essay, *The New Art of Writing Plays*, in 1609. This essay, certainly the most influential work of Spanish dramatic criticism, aroused immediate and prolonged reaction. For many years afterward the easiest way to describe a critic was to find out whether he was pro–Lope or anti–Lope.

The New Art of Writing Plays has been called "the first classic of box-office criticism."[2] Although Lope drew upon Donatus, Robortello, and possibly Castelvetro, he based most of his sentiments upon his practical experience in writing many hundreds of plays. Since the crowd pays the bill, he says, they call the tune. Satisfy the desires of the audience, he recommends: "Give plenty of variety, let women wear men's costumes, keep up the suspense and mystery to the last scene, and don't bore your audience with pregnant silences."[3]

For subject matter Lope de Vega recommends honor and virtuous deeds, since they have universal appeal. Comedy, which is fiction, and tragedy, which is historical, should be mixed; this mixture follows nature, and through such variety comes beauty. Each one of the three acts should be confined to twenty-four hours' duration, he feels. The last act, containing the denouement, should trick expectation, for the audience likes the unexpected. Plays should not exceed two hours in length, for after that the crowd loses interest. Dialogue should be simple for everyday affairs and elevated for persuasive passages, but playwrights should avoid both quotations and "exquisite" words.

Among others, Miguel de Cervantes seems to have been influenced by Lope's argument. In Chapter 48 of *Don Quixote*, Part One, Cervantes had inveighed against the violation of the unities and of decorum, as practiced by contemporary Spanish playwrights. His strictures sound as formal as those of Sidney in England.

But in his play, *El Rufián Dichoso*, published in 1615, Cervantes reverses his position and defends Lope's principles. Perhaps another reason for the change in Cervantes' attitude was his own experience as a playwright, for on the whole his plays are of the same "loose" sort he had condemned in 1605. Chaytor has another explanation of the earlier Cervantes position. He says that both Cervantes and his fellow dramatist Lupercio Leonardo de Argensola were disappointed playwrights, "and were inclined to attribute their failure rather to the debased nature of the public taste than to defects in their own capacities or methods."[4]

Among the classicists who attacked Lope de Vega were Cristóbal de Mesa and Cristóbal Suarez de Figueroa, both in 1618, and Diego de Colmenares in 1630. The gist of their approach was that tragicomedy was a hybrid which violated the rules of art, nature, and classical authors.

Lope's defenders tended to carry the day. Ricardo de Turia and Carlos Boyl appeared in his behalf as early as 1616. Boyl, who wrote chiefly about poetry, divided Spanish drama into two types: the comedy of intrigue, for salon audiences, and religious plays for popular audiences. The defense was continued by Julius Columbarius in 1618 and Francisco de la Barreda in 1622.

The most vigorous defender, however, was the playwright Tirso de Molina, who, in his *Ciggarales de Toledo* (1624), said with some justification that Lope de Vega had modestly confessed to pandering to public taste when in reality he had reformed comedy in their day by valid statements that no dramatist could afford to ignore. Could an entire love match—meeting, involvement, difficulties, resolution—be consummated within twenty-four hours? May not comedy present to the eye what history presents to the understanding—much in little? With these and other comments, de Molina helped fortify the "new art."

Even Gonzales de Salas, in an Aristotelian treatise published in 1633, admitted: "You are not bound to follow the ancients. Time and taste may improve and alter art."[5] Although the Spanish approach was fraught with danger signs in the direction of vulgar conformity to mediocre taste, it was too bad that it had so little influence a few miles to the north, where a French audience at Racine's comedy *Les Plaideurs* was afraid that it had not laughed "according to the rules."[6]

As Spanish drama waned, so did its criticism. The eighteenth century witnessed the inevitable battle between neoclassical rule-makers and believers in the freer approach. By now some French influence was discernible, especially in the *Poetics* of Ignacio de Luzán, who in 1737 announced that his purpose was to make Spanish literature conform to "rules prevailing among the cultured nations."[7] Luzán's views show the influence of Aristotle, Nicolas Boileau, and recent Italian critics. Other neoclassicists included Blas de Nasarre, Montiano y Luyando, Nicolas Fernández de Moratín, and Sebastian y Latre.

Much of the attack on the rules continued the defense of Lope de Vega and his approach. Writers criticizing French rules included José Carrillo and Juan de Zabeleta. The popular dramatist who introduced Shakespeare to Spain, Ramón de la Cruz, also attacked formal proscription in his preface to *Teatro* (1786–91). His version of *Hamlet* appeared in 1772.

Another admirer of Shakespeare, Leandro Fernández de Moratín (son of Nicolas, above), wrote a number of plays and pamphlets in favor of an independent method. As in other European countries, the rise of Shakespeare in critical favor accompanied a decline in neoclassical critical orthodoxy.

Spanish literature and criticism were also getting better known beyond the Pyrenees. Besides Dryden's statement of indebtedness to Spanish critics, Gotthold Lessing knew quite a bit about seventeenth century Spanish drama and was also familiar with Lope de Vega's broadside. Friedrich von Schelling and August and Friedrich von Schlegel also showed interest in Spanish views on drama.

The nineteenth century saw more drama than important dramatic criticism appearing in Spain. There was, to be sure, the Spanish version of the Romantic period, which tended to reinforce the followers of freedom-loving Lope against neoclassical canons. Agustín Durán extolled the native Spanish dramatists in *The Golden Age* (1828). A new note was added during this period in that the revolt against the classics now included the right to revolt against society, something not countenanced in the time of Lope.

The plays of José Echegaray y Eizaguirre show the connection between Spanish drama and its European counterparts. On the one hand he wrote many plays of melodramatic action similar to Scribe and Sardou in France. On the other hand his later realistic plays based upon social problems suggest the influence of Ibsen. In neither case, however, was there a critic who attempted to write an explanation of the changing developments.

At the end of the century, when Spain lost her colonies, a nationalistic renaissance was initiated by the "Generation of '98." Leading playwright of this movement was Jacinto Benavente, who has been called the originator of Spanish fantastic comedy, a blend of fantasy and realism. Benavente also contributed to the most original trend in modern Spanish drama, the peasant play. This movement originated with the Catalan playwright Angel Guimerà, and culminated in the poetic tragedies of Federico García Lorca, who died at the age of 37 in the Spanish Civil War.

Although Spain has produced little memorable criticism, it has remained remarkably free from the artificial restraint of rule-makers. The plays of Lope de Vega and Pedro Calderón de la Barca in the earlier period and of Benavente and Lorca more recently are testimony of how a good body of dramatic literature can be built outside the classical tradition. From the standpoint of criticism, perhaps the ideal critic would combine the stage-worthiness of Lope de Vega with the classical knowledge and background of Gotthold Lessing.

6. 17th Century French and English Criticism

In 1636 Pierre Corneille published *The Cid*, a tragicomedy that set off one of the most heated controversies in the history of dramatic criticism. A rival of Corneille's, Georges de Scudery, early the next year published his *Observations on the Cid*, stating that the play's subject was worthless, poorly handled, and stolen from the Spanish, the dialogue was poor, and the play violated the chief rules of drama.

Vituperative pamphlets ensued pro and con until late in 1637, when the newly formed French Academy issued an opinion on the subject that was written largely by Jean Chapelain. To Chapelain the Three Unities were the highest tests of a play, and so for the most part he supported Scudery, finding the plot improbable but complimenting Corneille for certain forcefully written passages.

Chapelain, who lacked the intuitive insight of a great critic and who was being goaded into attacking *The Cid* by Cardinal Richelieu, was the culmination of a movement toward regularity and reason in dramatic criticism. Misapplying Aristotle, he judged that the spectator should be moved by the actions of a play just the way he would be moved by historical fact. Aristotle's important distinction between poetic and historic truth was being lost.

In a posthumously published *Summary of a Poetic of the Drama*, Chapelain added several new insights. He struggled against previous rules to finally permit more than three characters on stage during the last act, arguing that the resulting confusion tended to make the denouement more elaborate and more interesting. He also quoted classical drama as examples of deviation from the close *liaison des scènes* that was beginning to be prescribed by some French critics. Finally, he called attention to the need for motivating the entrances and exits of characters.

The controversy concerning *The Cid* had several important results. It not only bolstered the authority of the French Academy but also popularized the practice of dramatic criticism in France. Scudery followed with a series of pamphlets; his play *Tyrannical Love* would have been in Aristotle's *Poetics* had it been on hand then, one friend insisted.

Pseudo-Aristotelian regularity came to be the order of the day. In 1639 Jean-François Sarasin published a formal treatise founded on Aristotelian precepts, *Discourse on Tragedy*. The following year La Mesnardière came out with an ultra-classical work, *The Art of Poetry*, which chastised Spanish and Italian critics for not following Aristotle closely enough. It is hard to conceive that this amount of formalizing was occurring a scant dozen years after Ogier's fervent plea for greater dramatic license.

The most ponderous tome of classical orthodoxy was produced by François Hédelin, the Abbé d'Aubignac, whose *The Practice of the Theater* appeared in 1657. This work, devoted more to theatrical criticism than to dramatic, was the greatest defender of classical rules. The Three Unities, decorum, verisimilitude, and all the other sacred terms were here given laborious justification, with no glance toward the *je ne sais quoi* that René Rapin was later to acknowledge. For d'Aubignac there was only one court of higher authority than the ancients, and that was reason. Classical drama was best, he averred, because it best followed reason; where it failed to, it erred. The only exception he made to this criterion was for the sake of patriotism. Thus Euripides in *The Suppliants* properly sacrificed art for the glory of his country. Similarly, in choosing a subject the playwright should consult contemporary audiences as much as ancient examples. Greek tragedy accordingly could deal with the downfall of cruel kings because democracy was in vogue at that time, but current French love of their monarchs outlawed such depiction of court life. Many seventeenth century French critics were clerics, in whom a tendency toward authority and obedience might be expected. D'Aubignac spoke with pontifical éclat in his France, and "there is reason to suspect a much greater indebtedness to d'Aubignac among English critics than they have seen fit to acknowledge."[1]

A general acceptance of the Italian critics' versions of Aristotle was now taking place. Saintsbury felt that unlike any other period, there was now a growing consensus of what constituted a good play: "Take a dozen critics of different countries of the seventeenth century in Europe, ask them to enunciate some general laws of criticism, and the results would be practically the same."[2]

Some understanding of the French formulation of neoclassical rules can be obtained by observing the stage conditions of the time. Chapelain had followed Castelvetro in arguing that the primary consideration of dramatic technique is that of stage representation. *Vraisemblance*, or verisimilitude, demanded that the plays should be proscribed by the stage settings available, as well as by the duration of the presentation. This was not Aristotle's conception of verisimilitude, of course, for he had said that convincing improbability was preferable to unconvincing probability.

The stage area at the Hotel de Bourgogne at that time was quite restricted, so that the actors were confined to the part of the stage on which the set was located. Shakespeare, faced by similar limitations, used poetic fancy to embody lush settings. Corneille and Jean Racine, bound by physical confinements as well as by critical judgment, found their solution by replacing external action with inner emotional climaxes. Thus the Three Unities and other laws were not felt to suppress the emotions but rather to concentrate and focus them. The result was a body of drama peculiarly expressive of its time, sometimes achieving great success because of the rules, and sometimes soaring into great art despite them.

Corneille, for example, refused to sacrifice a good subject to the demands of external rules. He "found a way out of this difficulty by making the drama psychological, through the substitution of the external action by an inner one, often in defiance of verisimilitude."[3]

Corneille's stormy experience with *The Cid* illustrates his constant attention to dramatic theory. Also, his practice of prefixing an *examen* to each of his plays, showing how he tried to reconcile dramatic theory with dramatic practice, bolstered a tradition which John Dryden and many subsequent critic-dramatists tended to follow. In his preface to *La Suivante* (1634), Corneille showed the independent spirit that led to the controversy over *The Cid*: "To know the rules and to understand the secret of skillfully adjusting them to our stage are two different sciences," he observed. "And perhaps," he went on, "to make a play succeed nowadays it is not enough to have studied the books of Aristotle and Horace."

Nevertheless, he publicly confessed his irregularity after Chapelain's judgment was given, and he proudly pointed to *Horace* (1640) as a "regular" play that observed all the rules. Understanding as little about Aristotle as did his critics, Corneille sometimes ate humble-pie for his irregularity and sometimes quoted Italian critics in defense of dramatic license.

The striking thing about Corneille is that his ultimate submission to the Three Unities seems to have been based upon a genuine conviction that a stricter conformity to them kept his errant fancy from straying from art. Hence his three essays on dramatic art, published in 1660 in reply to d'Aubignac's criticism, defend the Three Unities, although he admits that in practice it is difficult to define their bounds. Even here, however, he asks theoretical critics to write ten or twelve plays before formulating rules which hamper the dramatist's inventiveness and outlaw possible beauties.

Unlike Corneille, Racine did not have an inner struggle regarding whether to follow the ancients. Constantly defending the single simple plot, Racine says that a dramatist's question should ever be: "What would Sophocles say if he saw this scene?"[4] For those who said that a simple plot betrayed lack of invention on the author's part, Racine replied: "On the contrary, an author's invention is most severely put to test in making something out of nothing."[5] Racine felt that to crowd a multitude of happenings into a single day's action was not true to life and hence should be avoided. Racine also believed that plays should follow the classical example of serving a moral purpose.

Molière wrote relatively little dramatic criticism, but he also envisaged the stage as a powerful corrective medium. "To expose vices to the ridicule of all the world is a severe blow to them," he said in the preface to *Tartufe*. "People do not mind being wicked," he observed, "but they object to being made ridiculous." Nevertheless, Molière's chief dramatic tenet was that plays are written in order to please an audience. The cardinal error in drama to him was to be dull.

A logical successor to d'Aubignac was Nicolas Boileau-Despréaux. A law-giver was the critic's office at that time, and few critics responded as readily as Boileau. His doctrine was chiefly Horatian—he had few original ideas. He recommends: a short introduction; observance of the unities; no improbability; character decorum; no superfluity. His one critical principle, good sense, would virtually legislate imagination out of drama. His writing is largely negative, telling dramatists what to avoid rather than what to do. Charles Sainte-Beuve felt that Boileau's greatness as a critic lay in the acutely perceptive intuition that he showed in his critical judgments, but his censure of Corneille and his virtual disregard of Molière raise some question about Sainte-Beuve's accuracy here. Since "nature" had by Ogier's day been seen as irrefutably necessary in a work, Boileau justifies the ancients on the grounds that they best followed nature. If Boileau was to become a French Dryden (and he was followed sanctimoniously), then like Dryden he should have left safety valves for the dramatic genius too mighty for the narrow channels of dramatic rule.

Spingarn sees Boileau as the epitome of neoclassical criticism, which had gone through three distinct stages. First, Vida had said that the first essential of all literature is to imitate the classics. Scaliger had gone on to say that the poet creates another nature as if he were a sort of god. Boileau caps this development by his synthesis of nature and art. In his view, nothing is beautiful that is not true, and nothing is true that is not in nature.

Thus had the neoclassical dramatic canons evolved. Saintsbury has fairly well summarized neoclassical critical procedure, in a paragraph that could have described nearly any leading critic in a European country in the seventeenth century:[6]

> To submit himself frankly to the effect of the work and judge it as he would a prospect or a picture, a vintage or a face, was forbidden him. It was his duty, in the first place, if the author openly classed his work in any kind, to decide whether it really belonged to this or to another; if the author had omitted that ceremony, to determine the classification sedulously for himself. Then he had to remember, or look up, the most celebrated ancient examples of the kind, or those modern ones which had obtained the credit of being most like the ancients; and to decide whether the resemblance was sufficient in general. And then he had to descend ... to particulars,

to see if every little part was in accordance with the rules. If everything checked out all right, he was free to enjoy the work. It must be assumed that a well-trained neoclassical critic would keep these standards in mind almost subconsciously, so that by the end of his reading he could have a final verdict ready with relatively little reflection.

Another neoclassical lawgiver, René Rapin, went a step or two beyond Boileau. As Austin Warren has pointed out, Rapin performed the final codification of neoclassicism in his synthesis of the doctrines of the three leading contemporary critical schools:

classicism, with its imitation of the ancients; rationalism, stressing adherence to nature, reason, and common sense; and the cult of taste, which acknowledged a certain *je ne sais quoi* in creative work. This last addition, necessary as it was, was of course the fatal addition that largely led to the downfall of neoclassical criticism. Rule-following would never supplant genius, said Rapin: "There are no precepts to teach the hidden graces, the insensible charms, and all that secret power of poetry which passes to the heart."[7] Although such persons as Corneille, J.B. Bossuet, and Charles de Saint-Évremond found it hard to understand how Aristotelian catharsis operated, Rapin evolved an interpretation of the concept that became widespread, chiefly among eighteenth-century sentimentalists. This interpretation avers that the chief tragic pleasure lies in the "agitation of the soul moved by the passions." Rapin said that when the soul was shaken by such "natural" and "humane" emotions as pity and fear, the impressions become delightful—"its trouble pleases." Thus, "tragedy rectifies the passions by the passions themselves, calming by their emotion the troubles they excite in the heart."[8] Rapin was highly regarded not only by such orthodox English neoclassical figures as Dryden, Pope, and Addison, but also by the more eccentric Rymer.

Criticism flowed as freely as wine in seventeenth-century France. Besides the major figures already mentioned, there were countless other commentators. Jean de la Bruyère, comparing Molière with Terence, shows discriminating taste in accounting for the excellencies of each. Terence is praised for polish, elegance, and exactness to rule, while Molière is applauded for power, exact imitation of manners, and his "scourge of ridicule." André Dacier, a pedantic Aristotelian, largely concerned himself with the functions of the chorus and the nature of the tragic hero. Saint-Évremond, with a catholic background and a delicate taste, summed up the best features of neoclassicism, without succumbing to its unduly narrowing effects. He joined Corneille and Boileau in helping reintroduce "admiration" as one of tragedy's proper emotions, and his writings on opera are still among the best literary treatments of the subject. During his forty-odd years' residence in England he was one of the best and most influential critics in that country. His insight into English comedy preceded and surpassed that of any contemporary. His independent judgment and historical-relativistic approach make him one of the most penetrating writers on drama that had yet appeared. It is fortunate that an era of such rigidity found a graceful, open-minded critic, who knew both "rules" and their limitations.

English drama, meanwhile, instead of battling neoclassical critics was struggling to survive the Puritan onslaught against the stage. In 1632 William Prynne published *Histriomastix: The Scourge for Actors*. Neither as lively as Gosson before or Jeremy Collier later, Prynne nevertheless summed up the Puritan attitude toward the theater. "Stage plays," said Prynne, "the very pomps of the Devil, which we renounced in baptism, are sinful, heathenish, lewd, ungodly spectacles, condemned in all ages as intolerable mischiefs to churches, republics, and the soul of men. The professions of play-poets and stage-players are unlawful and misbeseeming Christians."[9]

Prynne was pilloried and had his ears cut off because his attack upon "women actors" was construed as a reference to a performance by Queen Henrietta Maria in a court masque. S.R. Littlewood, a later English critic, said, "To my thinking, he deserved the treatment equally for having turned out a book so sour and unhelpful and merely destructive."[10]

Dramatic criticism, like drama, was at a stalemate during the Commonwealth period. Between Ben Jonson and John Dryden, little more than John Milton's Aristotelian introduction to *Samson Agonistes*, colored by the Italian critics' insistence on the Three Unities, was noteworthy. Milton shows the clearest conception of catharsis in tragedy of all Englishmen up to his time. One is purged of pity and fear, Milton believed, by seeing an artistic representation of these emotions; hence, the purgation is more psychological than ethical.

Milton compiled a list of 93 subjects for tragedies, of which 60 came from the Bible and 33 from British history. He planned to gain his dramatic inspiration not from "vapours of wine" or from an invocation to pagan gods but by prayer to the Holy Spirit. And why not, asks Littlewood. "The theatre," he says "was popular enough when it was offically a Temple of Venus. No one objected to it then on the score of its being religious. Why should it not be regarded, under Christian auspices, as a Temple of the Holy Ghost? This is a very vital question for any who wish to take dramatic criticism seriously."[11]

Upon the re-opening of the theaters in 1660, a number of burning questions arose concerning drama. Chief among these were: Should a playwright follow the simple French plot-pattern or the complex Elizabethan one? Was rhyme, blank verse, or prose the most suitable style for drama? What role should wit play in comedy? Was the recent introduction of scenery a good thing for the English stage?

Richard Flecknoe, Sir Robert Howard, Thomas Shadwell, and of course Dryden were among the leading spokemen for drama at this time.

In his *Short Discourse on the English Stage* (1664), Flecknoe, an Irish priest, shows a preference for French simplicity over the long and intricate Elizabethan plays. He welcomes scenery as an improvement over the barren stage, seeing it as an aid to the spectator's imagination. He also defends wit, defining it not as puns and word jingles, but as "pleasant and facetious discourse" acquired only by culture and refinement.

Howard, Dryden's brother-in-law who appears as Crites in the latter's famous *Essay of Dramatic Poesy*, took exception to some of Flecknoe's views. Howard prefers English plays to French on several grounds: they contain more action and less narration, and they tend to use blank verse rather than rhyme, which is stilted and unnatural in dialogue. He shows typical English independence of categorical neoclassical rules. In ridiculing the Three Unities, he shows that even employing them, complete verisimilitude is impossible, so why should certain conventions not be employed? Taste was to Howard the sole arbiter of dramatic art. How would Boileau, his contemporary, have responded to the pronouncement by Howard that to like or dislike by the rules of others was like believing, not what one must, but what others were directing him to believe?

Shadwell was more of a traditionalist than Howard was, and thus saw little to criticize in the Three Unities. Shadwell shows a preference for Ben Jonson's comedy of humours. He objects to the "bawdy profaneness" of Restoration comedy, and asks instead for ridicule of the vanities and artificial fopperies displayed at court. Satirical representation of everyday characters called for keen observation and selective judgment which, Shadwell said, was in Thomas Hobbes' opinion the very essence of wit.

These men were scarcely first-rate dramatic critics. In John Dryden, however, England produced one of the greatest of all critics. "He established (let us hope for all time)," said Saintsbury, "the English fashion of criticizing, as Shakespeare did the English fashion of dramatizing—the fashion of aiming at delight, at truth, at justice, at nature, at poetry, and letting the rules take care of themselves."[12] The dialogue form, which he used in his *Essay of Dramatic Poesy* (1668), not only permits a parallel airing of contrasting views but gives the strongest arguments for them, so that a reader can choose the one he desires. Since his own prose style was clearer and more fluent than any before his time, Dryden could defend his ideas with great brilliance. In a sense, Dryden was a compromise between the somewhat artificial neoclassicism of Italy and France and the native romantic elements of England.

After permitting spokesmen in his *Essay of Dramatic Poesy* to bring out the values of classical, Elizabethan, and French drama, Dryden voiced his own views in the person of Neander. Neander admires the "regularity" of French plays, but thinks they lost the depth of sub-plots and the variety of pleasing contrasts. He quotes Corneille to the effect that strict observance of rules banishes many potential beauties. He here defends tragicomedy, stating that if our eyes can pass quickly from pleasant to unpleasant objects, surely our soul can also. In general, his test is Nature—what is natural is desirable in drama. He dislikes long speeches because they are not lifelike, but in this essay Dryden favors rhyme in tragedy, saying that it disciplines an errant imagination. Though some of his argument seems forced, he brings out as many arguments against blank verse as he can muster. He defines tragedy as "a representation of Nature, but Nature wrought up to a high pitch."[13] Then, since rhyme is considered the noblest form of poetry, it alone is worthy of the exalted language required in tragedy. Using blank verse is following Nature on foot: "You have dismounted him from his Pegasus."[14] Later, of course, in his preface to *All for Love* (1678), he reluctantly admits that blank verse better serves his purpose in that tragedy.

Some of Dryden's other views are also significant. In his defense of witty Restoration comedy, he paved the way for Congreve's later achievements. His preface to *The Mock Astrologer* attacks farcical buffoonery, at the same time indicating a dissatisfaction with the Jonsonian comedy of humours. The latter avoided the conversation of gentlemen to deal with "the follies and extravagancies of Bedlam," and since he considered polite repartee to be "the greatest grace of comedy," he felt that he and his contemporaries were adding further to the refinement of the English language, as used in drama. He had earlier tried to sharpen the critical terminology of the time by defining "wit." "Wit active" he calls the poetic faculty, or the imagination of the playwright; "wit written" is the written product, or the play which embodies "delightful imagining of persons, actions, passions or things," and is not the result of word-play or purple passages.

Dryden was scarcely at his best in defending heroic drama. The Duke of Buckingham and others had satirized the "unnatural" exaggerations of this form, in *The Rehearsal*, where Dryden is lampooned as Bayes. Specific charges against the heroic play were that it used rhyme, dull wit, strutting heroes, and an awkward mix of tragicomedy.

In *The Conquest of Granada*, Dryden defended heroic drama, stating that the times demanded the epic grandeur of historical spectacle. Heroic drama permitted the dramatist to use the supra-natural to give wider scope to his imagination, Dryden insisted. He went on to argue that just as his age excelled previous ones in courtliness and gallantry, so the language of serious drama should be more polished and polite. Here Dryden seems to be engaged in special pleading; the death of the form shortly thereafter ended that particular exchange of views.

Like any good critic, Dryden merged originality and taste with a knowledge of previous drama and criticism. Discussing charges of plagiarism levied against the great Elizabethans, he defended borrowed material, as long as the dramatist breathed new life into it. "The price (or value) of a work of art," he felt, "lies wholly in the workmanship."[15] He was one of the first not only to acknowledge Shakespeare's greatness, but to account for it in some detail. He knew Horace first-hand, but his Aristotle came largely through Rapin, Le Bossu, André Dacier, and Corneille. Like Corneille, he sometimes felt the cramping effect of the Three Unities. Perhaps his most important critical contribution was to help formulate the character of the tragic hero. He need never have apologized for "sailing in a vast ocean without other help than the pole-star of the ancients and the rules of the French stage,"[16] for he charted a course for English criticism that, on the whole, led to sanity and perspicacity. By far the greater number of his judgments remain sound and penetrating today, and his style is as readable as it was nearly three hundred years ago. All in all, he might justly be called the "Aristotle of English criticism."

If Dryden is the English Aristotle, Thomas Rymer is the English d'Aubignac. Rymer thought the ancients never erred. For a man of wide learning, he attacks Shakespeare blindly; his insistence upon character decorum (which states, for instance, that all soldiers should be bluff and hearty, with never a dissimulating Iago) was an atavism that shrewder critics were already discarding. Nevertheless, T.S. Eliot said that he has never seen Rymer's vituperative attack on *Othello* repudiated. It was Rymer who gave the name to poetic justice, supplying critics with a term for the age-old moral purpose of drama. His most significant gift was the application of Aristotelian terms in a minute analysis of a play. Lamentably his taste did an injustice to his thoroughness.

John Dennis, unlike Rymer, could view drama in its historical light. Thus, when Dennis answered Rymer in *The Impartial Critic* (1693), he pointed out that changing conditions now made love a proper subject for drama and made the use of a chorus obsolete. Most of Dennis' rebuttal was taken from Dacier. Dennis, noting the emphasis on the supernatural in Longinus' *On the Sublime*, combined that stress with Aristotle to ask for pity and fear heightened by religion, and thus he asked for "Christian tragedy." Ironically, the older Dennis grew, the closer his views paralleled those of his old adversary, Rymer. He finally upbraided *Julius Caesar* for lacking poetic justice, and he remodeled *The Merry Wives of Windsor* because it had three actions, and because Falstaff does nothing but talk!

Coffee-houses bred contention, and so a number of critical battles waged around the end of the seventeenth century. Gerard Langbaine, in *An Account of English Dramatic Poets* (1691), brought charges of plagiarism against Dryden, who had fallen somewhat into eclipse after the exodus of James II. Langbaine's contribution was more to demonstrate the possibilities of exhaustive scholarship in buttressing an issue of dramatic controversy than to show as new something that Dryden had earlier dealt with candidly and ably. Another argument concerned the use of a chorus. The chorus was not widely used in drama of the period, but classical critics had insisted on it. Moreover, it was said to further moral instruction, and drama was under attack on grounds of immorality. French critics like Chapelain, Dacier, and Boileau had favored the chorus, and Milton had used it in *Samson Agonistes*. Rymer, who had praised the French for their "regularity," felt that his joy was complete when he heard they were considering restoring the chorus, for "the chorus was the root and original, and is certainly always, the most necessary part of tragedy."[17] Opposed to the chorus were not only critics like Dennis, Charles Gildon, and Samuel Butler, but also dramatists like Corneille, Jonson, Webster, and Dryden. These dissenters insisted that the chorus was superfluous, unnatural, and awkward, detracting far more from the playgoer's pleasure than it contributed.

In the rivalry between ancient and modern comedy, those who opposed the chorus favored modern comedy. They were joined in this set-to by such lovers of the classics as Rymer and Sir William Temple.

The consensus was that comedy, especially of the humour variety, was most congenial to the English temperament. Even over the term "humour" there was disagreement, however. Dryden applied the concept to extravagant habits, ridiculous customs, and artificial fopperies, but he felt that wit was more important to comedy than humour. Most critics, though, agreed with Dennis that humour is more important than wit in comedy, for humour encourages more vivid character delineation and contains the instructive part of comedy. Congreve, who also preferred humour, defined it as a bias of mind which twists our wills and actions in a certain direction.

Although farce was popular with the seventeenth-century public, the critics were virtually unanimous in condemning it. D'Aubignac disliked its "dishonest words" and "impudent actions." Dryden said its "forced humours and unnatural events" appealed only to the fancy, and was enjoyed only by those who do not understand nature. In his preface to *Plautus* (1694), Echard said that farce presents men more vicious, covetous, and foolish than they really were. In general, farce was considered an injudicious mixture of the reasonable and the unreasonable, with the latter predominating.

The growing elaboration of stage settings and costumes, partly influenced by the innovation of Italian opera, drew the wrath of such neoclassical critics as Rymer, Dennis, and Addison. Even plot, stated by Aristotle to be the most important ingredient in tragedy, was under attack. Restoration drama featured comedy, and comedy stressed wit, humour, repartee, and character more than plot. Oldmixon argued for "irregular" comic plots in 1699, and George Farquhar and Henry Pemberton joined in the attack on plot. Comedy was believed to aim more at pleasure than at instruction, and thus the plot, as the chief instructive element, was not so important. Pemberton said, in a twentieth-century vein, that the audience derives more pleasure from vivid characterization than from a well-constructed plot.

On the whole, then, it is clear that English dramatic criticism never felt the yoke of the "rules" to the extent that French criticism did. Although it is true that works appeared which followed Boileau in codifying "rules" for dramatists—such as the Earl of Mulgrave's *Essay upon Poetry* (1682)—more typical was Samuel Butler's satire of Rymer in his essay, *Upon Critics who judge of Modern Plays precisely by the Rules of the Ancients* (1678). Although many playwrights and critics alike seemed confused at whether to give in to the rules or be original, it certainly can be said that England, like

Spain, seemed relatively free from the strait jacket of neoclassicism that engulfed France and, to a lesser extent, Italy. The large body of rules-free drama produced in Elizabethan England no doubt was one leading reason for this condition.

7. 18th Century French and English Criticism

George Farquhar's *A Discourse upon Comedy* in 1702 continued the protest against the rules. Aristotle is a poor judge of drama, Farquhar says, because he never wrote a play. Since the creative dramatist is too wise to hamper genius by conforming to artificial regulations, Farquhar depicts a dull scholar writing a dull play, in obedience to university critics. Probably his success with *The Beaux' Stratagem*, however, did more than his essay did to discredit pedantic criticism.

The final years of the seventeenth century saw a vigorous outburst of attack upon the theater on moral grounds. Court life under William and Mary scarcely resembled the profligacy of the Restoration court, and so reform was in the air. Sir Richard Blackmore capped a series of protests with *Satire upon Wit* (1700), a direct attack upon current drama.

More famous was Jeremy Collier's *Short View of the Immorality and Profaneness of the English Stage* (1698), which contained much dramatic criticism as well as moral censure. Using Rymer's method, Collier assiduously indicates the indecent elements in Restoration drama, at the same time finding structural blemishes in the plays of Dryden, Sir John Vanbrugh, Thomas D'Urfey, and others. Collier objected to offensive handling of clergymen, as well as to the triumph of vice and the lack of character decorum in depicting persons of high estate. Although he tended to ignore merit while berating lewdness, his influence helped lead to two prevailing characteristics of eighteenth century drama: morality and mediocrity.

After the attacks upon the stage by Collier and others, sentimental comedy came into its own. Although this tragicomic mixture was distasteful to classicists like Joseph Addison, the implicit assumption of sentimental comedy about the native goodness of man was widely current. "The writers of sentimental comedy were not so much interested in a mixture of tragic and comic happenings as in presenting happenings that aroused pleasant and sad emotions at the same time."[1]

Instead of ridiculing foibles in other people, sentimental comedy endeavored to purge ludicrous behavior by depicting it within oneself, and thus it was gentle rather than invidious in its approach. Later in the century psychologists worked out their theory of mixed sensations, in which one emotion stimulated its contrary. David Hume, especially, in his *Essay on Tragedy* (1742), accounted for the paradox of pleasure growing out of tragic events happening to good persons by stating that the painful emotions originally aroused receive a new direction and are reinforced by the beauty and eloquence of the representation. Thus the peculiar pleasure of tragedy is produced by mixed feelings, with artistic excellence transforming distress into tempered delight. Edmund Burke went beyond Hume to assert that all emotions, even the feeling of terror excited by tragedy, are delightful, and thus the more realistic the tragic representation, the more it arouses emotion and thus pleases.

Most of Addison's dramatic criticism is found in *The Spectator*. He felt that modern tragedies surpassed the classics in plot development but fell short in moral thoughts. Some of the things that Addison opposed in drama were rhyme, poetic justice, long speeches, and elaborate staging effects. Though elements of neoclassicism are evident in his criticism, he deplores the critic who "never dares praise anything in which he has not a French author for his voucher."[2]

Addison also helped define the controversial term "wit." He felt that Dryden's version of wit as "propriety of words and thoughts adapted to the subject" was too broad, and so he started with John Locke's definition: "the resemblance and congruity of ideas giving pleasure to the fancy," to which he added that, since the pleasure should involve ingenuity and surprise, the ideas should not be closely similar. This, of course, resembles recent views of wit, which contain components of delight, facetiousness, and the unexpected.

Addison was by no means alone in opposing tragicomedy. William Warburton, Bishop of Gloucester, tracing the rise of tragicomedy to an inartistic blend of religious mystery and farce, said that the result was a "mongrel species, unknown to nature and antiquity, called tragicomedy."³ Charles Gildon, who began by opposing Rymer's narrow veneration of the ancients, followed Dennis in ultimately fostering the "regularity" of the classics and the purity of genres against the "Gothic" chaos of Richard Steele and other writers of sentimental comedy.

The rise of the newspaper provided a medium for rapid and regular dramatic criticism. An important theorist of sentimental comedy, "Richard Steele is the first important journalistic critic of the drama."⁴ Unlike Addison, Steele accepted tragicomedy. Most of their contemporaries preferred the open-hearted naïveté of Steele to the trenchant irony of Addison.

The elasticity of neoclassical English criticism toward the rules continued throughout the century. Joseph Trapp granted that domestic tragedy had a legitimate function, albeit lower than that of classical tragedy. Henry Fielding, though he could observe Aristotle's precepts on occasion, wrote a satirical burlesque on heroic tragedy and neoclassical stiffness in *The Tragedy of Tragedies, or the Life and Death of Tom Thumb the Great* (1730). This play not only parodies such critics as Dennis, Richard Bentley, and Lewis Theobald, but it also arraigns much contemporary dramatic practice. Melodramatic and improbable plot incidents, fantastic and crude characters, trite and plagiarized language, a denouement of wholesale slaughter — all are ridiculed in their turn. Writers of heroic tragedy, such as James Thomson and Nathaniel Lee, were not spared Fielding's sharp satire. "The whole work — preface, play, and elaborate notes — is the keenest of satire, not so much upon particular playwrights of the heroic school as against the school itself, and the unbending standards of neoclassical drama."⁵

A number of factors contributed to the breakdown of neoclassicism. English common sense revolted against the idea that dramatic art was subject to harsh law, particularly since the great Elizabethans had seemed to demonstrate the contrary. Despite the eighteenth century's high opinion of reason, there was a growing recognition of the importance of feeling and emotion. Literary reflections of this are seen in Edward Young's stress on originality in creative literature, the popularity of Longinus as a critic, and Edmund Burke's interest in the sublime as a literary effect. In addition, of course, there was the whole rising movement of romanticism, seen in the Graveyard poets, the Gothic movement, and the early romantic poets.

Thomas Gray felt that a chorus had actually hampered classical drama, and that it was inappropriate, confining, and moralistic in current plays. Joseph Warton objected to petty rules, which either debilitated dramatists' natural powers or caused them to write from the head rather than from the heart. England, which understood the rules, he said, was now producing "uninteresting though faultless" tragedies.

The struggle to free oneself from airtight canons is further illustrated in the writings of Richard Hurd, Bishop of Worcester. Hurd began by stoutly defending the purity of genres. The literary kinds are fixed, said he, "founded in nature and the reason of things," and therefore "not to be multiplied at pleasure."[6] But, after accepting comedies of high life as well as tragedies of low life, he is led to approve an intermediate species, the tearful comedy, which had been advanced by Bernard de Fontenelle. After all, Hurd said, Terence had demonstrated that ridicule was not vital to comedy, so a gentler sort of comedy was deemed possible.

At the same time James Beattie published his *Essay on Laughter and Ludicrous Composition*. Beattie reviewed the theory of comedy, rejecting Aristotle's concept of laughter arising from harmless faults, Hobbes' theory of a "sudden glory," and Francis Hutcheson's view that comedy grew out of the contrast of dignity and meanness. Instead, Beattie saw comedy as a combination of incongrous, sudden, and surprising incidents; so broad a definition scarcely differentiates comedy from tragedy.

The theater was being recognized as having divergent appeals which no one play, however well written, could satisfy. The great actor David Garrick had a habit of turning to each segment of the audience as he said:

> *You* relish satire (to the pit), *you* ragouts of wit (to the boxes),
> *Your* taste is humour and high-season'd joke (to the first gallery),
> *You* call for hornpipes and Hearts of Oak (to the second gallery).[7]

The death-knell to the rules in England seems to have been sounded by Samuel Johnson. He disavows imitation of the classics, stating that great works require originality of design or execution. He doubts that all drama can be conveniently grouped into distinct "kinds," since the imagination seemed to him to be a rather lawless faculty. He noted the many unsatisfactory attempts to define genres, and finally recommends a definition of comedy based upon its psychological effects: "a dramatic representation of human life calculated to excite mirth."[8]

At the opening of the Drury Lane Theatre in 1747 Johnson showed acute awareness of the public's role:

> Ah, let not censure term our fate our choice,
> The stage but echoes back the public voice;
> The drama's laws the drama's patrons give,
> For we that live to please must please to live.[9]

Johnson recommends observance of some fundamental dramatic principles, such as unity of action and the need for a strong central character with whom spectators can empathize. Secondary principles, based on custom rather than nature, may be altered in accordance with changing dramatic needs. Thus there is no longer a need to confine the cast to a total of three, or for a play to have five acts. Destroying the unity of time, he said that it is rare that "minds not prepossessed by mechanical criticism feel any offense from the extension of the intervals between the acts."[10]

Consistent with his theory is Johnson's approach to tragicomedy. Since the stage mirrors life, what is more natural for drama, he asks, than the mingling of great and trivial matters so characteristic of life? His praise of Dryden as a critic and Shakespeare as a playwright shows that he was far from being negative in his approach. He remains a unique blend of neoclassicism, common sense, and independence, with the latter predominating.

Lord Kames continued the attack against classicism. Kames would have nothing to do with fixed "kinds." "Literary compositions run into each other precisely like colors,"[11] he stated. In an effort to clarify critical terminology, he distinguished between the ludicrous and the ridiculous—the former produced only laughter, whereas the latter produced laughter plus scorn. Humour he feels results when an author affects to be serious, but so handles his material as to produce mirth. Wit consists of expressions which are ludicrous, and which cause surprise by their singularity and unexpectedness.

In *The Rosciad* (1761), Charles Churchill attacked not only most actors of his time but also most critics. Like Addison, Churchill believed that current critics had fallen far from the role played by ancient critics. Former critics, he said, had good sense and good judgment, confining themselves largely to pointing out hidden beauties. Modern critics prefer to spitefully find fault.

Several playwrights were vocal during the latter half of the century. Oliver Goldsmith, after accounting historically for the rise of sentimental comedy, calls it a "bastard tragedy." Goldsmith felt that pure comedy should return to the stage, bringing with it the humour and laughter which had been lost in "tearful comedy." Richard Brinsley Sheridan, the other outstanding playwright of the century, wrote *The Critic* (1779) as a satire against the inferior dramaturgy of his time. Besides disparaging sentimental comedy, Sheridan attacks a host of practices: inept exposition, unrelated double plots, inappropriate love scenes, asides, improbable denouements, and melodramatic stage effects, such as the playing of soft music to accompany the entrance of the heroine.

More sympathetic to the use of music to enhance dramatic effects was James Moor, who broadened the concept of catharsis to define it as a purgation of all human sufferings, not just the emotions of pity and fear. Thomas Percy and Thomas Hawkins wrote histories of the drama, Hawkins recognizing Shakespeare's drama as a new form which was not subject to ancient rules. In their translations of Aristotle's *Poetics*, Henry James Pye and Thomas Twining differed as to the artistic importance of spectacle; Pye was sure that had the Greek seen Garrick play Lear he would have evaluated spectacle more highly.

To a great extent, then, the chief concern of eighteenth century English dramatic criticism was to establish its independence from neoclassical rules. Although neoclassicism undoubtedly served a two-fold purpose of calling attention to earlier wisdom regarding playwrighting and to considering drama as an art form, the general tenor of the century was away from the "rules." More important than the casting off of neoclassical precepts was the establishment of new ideas and insights regarding drama. The century's peculiar blend of reason and imagination led to more stress being placed upon, at times, common sense, and at times, inspiration. Both qualities were to be needed subsequently as drama moved slowly from its doldrums toward modern spontaneity and inventiveness.

Recognized as an era of mediocre drama in France, the eighteenth century is scarcely more memorable for the quality of its dramatic criticism. As in England, the chief characteristic of the period in France was the battle between neoclassical rules-lovers and nonconforming individualists. Charles Perrault's attack upon the ancients had precipitated the famous war between Ancients and Moderns. At the same time, a series of moralistic attacks upon the theater paralleled those of Jeremy Collier in England. Written by such persons as Jacques Bossuet, Pierre Nicole, and the Prince de

Conti, these works contained even less original criticism than Collier's polemic. The spirit of the time, thus, was contentious and more narrow-minded than we might expect from an era of enlightenment.

Voltaire and Denis Diderot are the two principal dramatic critics in the France of their time. Voltaire was his century's peculiar blend of traditionalism and rationality. Although he thought that Boileau was obstinate not to recognize the superiority of the moderns over the ancients, he castigated the Baron de la Motte for installing unity of interest in place of the revered Three Unities. To Voltaire taste was the ultimate arbiter, and style was the surest guide to ultimate fame. Language became the leading literary ingredient; verse, necessary for tragedy, constituted its chief artistic beauty. Voltaire grew out of a French culture that was copied in Russia, envied in Germany, and admired in Italy, and thus perhaps his literary nationalism can be somewhat understood and pardoned. To Voltaire, Shakespeare was a "writer of monstrous farces called tragedies,"[12] whose "pieces can please only at London and in Canada."[13]

When Shakespeare is recognized internationally, it will be time enough to see whether he has any permanent claim to greatness. Shakespeare had genius and sublimity, Voltaire admitted, but not a spark of good taste, nor acquaintance with a single rule. Thus his monstrous farces, miscalled tragedy, are the ruination of the English drama. *Hamlet*, in Voltaire's opinion, was "a coarse and barbarous piece which would not be tolerated by the lowest rabble of France and Italy."[14] "One would suppose this work," said Voltaire, "to be the fruit of the imagination of a drunken savage."[15] Above all, Voltaire liked Racine, for his style, clarity of plot, and adherence to the Three Unities, those great safeguards against improbability. In criticizing Corneille's plays, Voltaire attacked preciosity as a vice, for clarity is always a supreme requisite of great writing. His famous statement that "any verse or any sentence which requires explanation does not deserve to be explained" is more severe on poetry than on drama. Voltaire also liked the classical distinctions of language into three levels: natural, elegant, and elevated. Style is a touchstone of genius, he believed. Since all persons have relatively the same ideas, the way of expressing the ideas distinguishes the great writers from the hack.

Rules, thus, though important to Voltaire, are secondary to the cultivation of taste. Rules such as the Three Unities are to be observed because they are "good sense," but mere local customs, or *bienseances*, need not be followed. Love, he believed, was the supreme tragic passion, provided the love interest was central in the plot. The stage should never be empty, and each character's entrances must be motivated. Though Shakespeare's plays were a necessary step as drama progressed through barbarism into art, there was no good comedy until Molière, he felt. "Shakespeare is not at all comparable to Molière," Voltaire said, "either for art or for the representation of manners."[16]

Voltaire thus seems to have been imprisoned by his milieu. He made vigorous nationalistic utterances, perhaps aware that the great French dramatists of the previous century no longer found their counterparts in such drama as Voltaire and his contemporaries were writing. He seems to have taken it upon himself to uphold French aristocratic breeding during a time when it was being threatened by bourgeois democracy. But at least in his plea that drama should inspire a horror of fanaticism we see a reflection of the great rationalistic mind in the age of the *philosophes* and Encyclopedists.

A number of critics tended to follow Voltaire. Abbé Batteux, like Voltaire, used "taste" as a measure of when to apply the rules; when the rules seem too numerous or too confining, they could be reduced to a useful minimum by seeing if the play was an imitation of the "best" nature: "If the rules are too narrow and precise, taste holds them open; if taste shows any signs of getting lawless, the rules bring it to its bearings."[17] Jean-François Marmontel blended rationalism and imagination in something like Voltaire's manner. Marmontel tried to explain drama and literature scientifically; he wished to examine the conditions which produced the flowering of great art. To him, unity meant not only the traditional Three Unities, but also that of design, tone, and style. His distrust of metaphor was typical of what modern critics have subsequently called the "dissociation of sensibility," or the separation of thought and feeling. At times Marmontel was exceedingly rules-bound, but at other times he spoke in defense of genius, enthusiasm, and imagination.

Another disciple of Voltaire was Jean-François de la Harpe. Although he possessed the critical ability to analyze specific dramatic ingredients such as plot probability and character drawing, La Harpe now seems outdated in his preference of Voltaire's verse over Shakespeare's or the *Oedipe* of Voltaire to Sophocles' original play. Most of La Harpe's strictures against Shakespeare echo Voltaire's: clowning in serious scenes, quibbling, and coarse passages that violate good manners.

Two Encyclopedists aired contrary views over drama. Jean Le Rond d'Alembert, at the instigation of Voltaire, had criticized the Geneva authorities for their law prohibiting stage plays. Rousseau replied with a puritanical treatise that quoted the long-heard charge that the theater was an immoral place. Rousseau also attacked the "sterile pity" of sentimental drama of his day, for it had never led to "the least act of humanity." He also questioned that only certain specific emotions could be aroused in a play; he believed that since "all passions are sisters," to arouse one would be to arouse many other nearly related ones. Probably Rousseau's chief importance lay in his stress on primitivism in general — whatever is natural is good, he preached.

Like Rousseau, Diderot thought that the drama of civilized society was too divorced from primitive emotions to be deeply moving. Especially in his early writings, Diderot asks for emotional intensity bordering on sensationalism. In place of the weak sentiments of modern times, use as a model the mother who bares her bosom and appeals to her son by the breasts which have nursed him, Diderot recommends. The Greeks could afford simplicity and dignity, he felt, because of the civic importance and spectacular staging of their plays, but French tragedy unwisely stripped itself of more elaborate stage effects.

As he aged, Diderot found certain neoclassical views supplanting his early preference for sensational emotionalism. He condemned tragicomedy for mingling genres separated by a natural barrier. Filling a legitimate gap between tragedy and comedy, however, was *drame bourgeois*, or domestic tragedy, which answered the need of his day. This new genre differs from tragedy in tone and subject matter, and in its lack of heroic passion. For this genre he advocated subjects from everyday life, prose style, and frequent use of pantomime, tableaux, and other aids to action. This, then, was an extension upon the *comedie larmoyante* as written by Nivelle de la Chaussée, and a movement in the direction of nineteenth century realism.

Another shift that took place in Diderot's outlook was in reference to his faith in the theater as an agency of moral reform. At first the theater seemed designed to arouse emotions against evil, both personal and social. Thus Diderot praised George Lillo's *London Merchant* and Edward Moore's *The Gamester*, a play attacking gambling. In fact, both Diderot and Bernard Saurin wrote French adaptations of *The Gamester*. As the years passed by, however, and

French morals seemed no better despite the didactic plays designed to improve them, Diderot showed less reliance upon drama's moral use, stating that the playgoer could well afford to be compassionate because it cost him not a sou to feel magnanimous. By now he ceased asking for violent emotional effects, but preferred acting which employs restraint, caused by the actor's following the interior model of the character which he has formed in his mind.

Though Diderot considered Shakespeare a crude genius, he is less harsh on him than was Voltaire. Diderot admired Aeschylus and Sophocles, and preferred Terence's bourgeois comedy to the political satires of Aristophanes. On the whole, he is independent, perhaps impressionistic in outlook — a transitional figure between crumbling neoclassicism and nineteenth century romanticism.

Like Voltaire, Diderot had his followers, too. Friedrich Grimm was one of these, though it seems likely he also influenced Diderot in turn. In the variety of hybrid forms that included the *philosophe* comedy of propaganda, the *comedie larmoyante*, and the *comedie serieuse*, Beaumarchais appeared, in theory and practice, with the genre of "serious drama," also called the *drame*. When the public showed its disinterest in this genre and its preference for his *Barber of Seville* and *Marriage of Figaro*, Beaumarchais cynically concluded that a "middle" drama was impossible — the only possible theater was "ridiculous citizens and unhappy kings." His dedicatory letter to *The Barber of Seville* shows his impatience with neoclassical conventions, and his disgust with public taste:

> I had the weakness once, monsieur, to present to you at different times, two sad dramas; monstrous productions, as everyone knows! because no one fails to recognize that there is no middle ground between comedy and tragedy; that point is decided. The master has said it, and the school retains it, and I am so completely convinced, that if today I wanted to put into the theatre a distressed mother, a betrayed wife, a distracted sister, a disinherited son, I should, in order to present them decently to the public, begin by supposing for them a fine kingdom where they would have reigned wisely — in some far archipelago or some such corner of the world; certain after that, that the improbability of the fable, the enormity of the deeds, the bombast of the characters, the exaggerated ideas and the buffoonery of the language, far from imputing reproach to me, would insure my success.
>
> Present men of middle condition dejected and in sorrow? Fie

upon it! That is worthy only of being laughed at. Ridiculous citizens and unhappy kings—there is your existing and possible theatre, and I content myself with saying, it is done, and I don't want to quarrel with anyone.[18]

Sebastien Mercier did not give up so easily, however. Echoing the egalitarian sentiments of the Revolution, he called for a middle-class drama that would link man to man through the victorious unity of compassion and pity. Foreshadowing Tolstoy, he asks for a tragedy so moving and so virtuous as to change the bad politics of a kingdom. En route, Mercier condemns the unities, and purity of the genres, and the shocking morals of many classical plays. One important result of the *drame* was its influence on the art of acting, causing a decline in declamatory phrasing and a toning-down of gesture.

Nor was Mercier alone in his attack. Pierre Brumoy had earlier shown that conditions were so different in classical Athens and modern France that comparisons were difficult, and common dramatic laws impossible. Kurt Wais, in a recent study, describes a whole stream of French writers toward the end of the century, constituting a French *Sturm und Drang* movement. Revolutionary ideas were in the air, and dramatic criticism seemed for a time to be taking its cue from politics. The collapse of the *ancien regime* was scarcely more profound than the ultimate destruction of the neoclassical "laws" of the drama.

8. Shakespearian Criticism

Attention to Shakespeare's rise in critical esteem is merited not only by the worth of the plays themselves but also by the light it sheds on changing standards of dramatic judgment. Many reasons account for the growing interest in Shakespeare's plays. For one thing, the critical battle that raged throughout the seventeenth century tended to rank Ben Jonson's plays ahead of those of Shakespeare, albeit not without some sturdy minority protests to the contrary. Vehement detractors of Shakespeare, like Rymer and Voltaire, tended to cause scholars to re-examine the plays to see what was actually there. The garbled texts, however, plus the distorted acting versions staged around 1700, pointed up the need for considerable editorial work before the plays themselves could be examined critically. Dryden and his contemporaries had raised criticism to the rank of reputable scholarship, so a new generation of critics and editors were on hand to do their necessary jobs. Three results ensued: the gradual evolution of texts of the plays more nearly representing what Shakespeare had written; a great deal of new insight into the artistic merit of the plays; and a changing regard for what constitutes dramatic excellence, in view of Shakespeare's success despite disregard of neoclassical rules.

Shakespeare's steady popularity even during the seventeenth century can be attested by the fact that he alone, among Elizabethan dramatists, had four folio editions of his plays published by 1685. Jonson himself, in the preface to the First Folio (1623) had ranked Shakespeare with the greatest of the ancients, finding his work both universal in scope and permanent in appeal. Young John Milton, in verses appended to the Second Folio (1632), found that Shakespeare had built himself "a live-long monument," a tomb for which kings might wish to die. Dryden, speaking through Neander in his famous *Essay*, although commending Jonson's *Silent Woman* as an exemplary play, finally calls Shakespeare "the largest and most comprehensive soul of all modern, and perhaps ancient, poets."[1] Dryden went on to say that Shakespeare "is always great when some great occasion is presented to him."[2] Thus, by the end of the century, Jonson's supremacy was under persistent serious attack.

Nicholas Rowe in 1709 produced the first of a long line of eighteenth century editions of Shakespeare. Rowe defended Shakespeare from Rymer's invective, stating that the Elizabethan had lived in an age of "universal license and ignorance" of classical laws, and thus had written in the light of Nature alone. Acquaintance with dramatic rules might have improved the defective plots, Rowe felt, but might also have fettered the creative imagination that bodied forth some of the greatest characters ever invented.

Alexander Pope based his edition of Shakespeare's plays upon Rowe's text, which in turn had relied upon the inaccurate Fourth Folio. In addition, Pope, disliking "the dull duty of an editor," followed current practice in "improving" the plays in accordance with eighteenth century taste. As Lewis Theobald appropriately remarked, Pope thereby frequently inflicted a wound where he intended a cure. Pope disliked Shakespeare's choice of subjects, his forced and bombastic expressions, and his far-fetched incidents, but, like Rowe, he defended Shakespeare's right to be free from Aristotle's rules. To so measure Shakespeare, Pope believed, was "like trying a man by laws of one country who acted under those of another."[3]

Shakespeare, in Pope's opinion, knew the world and human nature intuitively; thus he excelled in originality, characterization, and the power to move our emotions. Likening "correct" current drama to a neat eighteenth century building, Pope goes on to prefer the majestic Gothic architecture of Shakespearian drama, with its greater variety and much nobler apartments, although he conceded that we are often led to them by dark, odd, and uncouth passages.

John Upton, though a professed follower of Horatian rules, in 1746 defended Shakespeare from charges of indecorum and Gothic irregularity that had been advanced chiefly by Rymer, Dennis, and Voltaire. Dennis had strongly praised Shakespeare for his skillful characterization and his masterly blank verse, but had pointed to certain anachronisms and indecorous use of mob scenes in the tragedies. Theobald, whose contribution was chiefly textual, felt that the anachronisms could be accepted as poetic license. William Warburton, in the preface to his edition of Shakespeare in 1747, agreed that nature and common sense were better foci for evaluating the plays than watered-down neoclassical canons.

A further reflection of this rise of independent judgment is seen in the approach of Joseph Warton. Warton had little use for "general criticism" of Shakespeare, whose plays he felt "must be accompanied step by step, and scene by scene, in his gradual developments of characters and passions, and whose finer features must be singly pointed out, if we would do justice to his beauties."[4] Recalling how Horace had shown the difficulty of creating a truly original character, Warton pointed to Caliban as a convincing portrait of someone beyond ordinary human nature. His careful examination of details of plotting and his psychological analysis of Shakespeare's characters both constituted a real advance in Shakespearian criticism in his day.

Another important defender of Shakespeare was Lord Kames, whose *Elements of Criticism* employed Shakespeare's plays as examples of the literary taste the work was written to advance. Stating that too much attention had been paid to sheer mechanical matters—the unities, historical accuracy, and mingling of comic and tragic effects—Kames makes a case for Shakespeare based upon the dramatist's extraordinarily intimate acquaintance with the nuances of human personality. Kames pointed out how Shakespeare reveals character by actions and words, in artistic fashion, rather than by the artificial declamation and description often used by French dramatists.

Shakespeare's knowledge of human emotions surpassed that of all philosophers, Kames asserted. For example, a person could be shown under the agitation of several conflicting emotions at once. The penetrating psychological insight of the soliloquies, the propriety of dialogue to the speaker, and the sureness of choice in selecting verse and prose in appropriate places are all praised. Though Kames felt that sometimes Shakespeare's high-flown language degenerated into mere surface ornamentation, he praised the Elizabethan for setting aside the artificial unities of time and place in order to achieve freer and more profound beauties. Kames' influence spread to the continent, and eleven editions of his work appeared by 1840.

David Garrick also did much to popularize Shakespeare. Between 1747 and 1776 Garrick produced twenty-four Shakespearian plays at Drury Lane. Sometimes he adapted texts to suit his needs, but frequently he ignored Restoration versions and went back to original texts. He thus helped demonstrate the stageability of many plays heretofore considered solely as poetry.

It was Samuel Johnson, however, who pronounced the final liberating decision. Using a judicious, pro-and-con method of weighing virtues and blemishes (a technique disliked by William Hazlitt but praised by T.S. Eliot), Dr. Johnson settled once and for all the question of Shakespeare's irregularities. The strict approach to decorum in character and swift scene changes he called "the petty cavils of petty minds."[5] His judgment has been called by Nichol Smith "a conclusive summing up by a strong, wise, and impartial mind, of a prolonged discussion."[6] We read it in *Rambler* #156: "It ought to be the first endeavour of a writer to distinguish nature from custom, or that which is established because it is right from that which is right only because it is established; that he may neither violate essential principles by a desire of novelty, nor debar himself from the attainment of beauties within his view by a needless fear of breaking rules which no literary dictator had authority to enact."[7]

Johnson's preface to his edition of Shakespeare appeared in 1765. In this landmark of Shakespearian criticism Johnson warned against the dangers of editorial emendation. Speaking from experience, he said that the more he employed conjecture, the less he trusted it. "An emendation is wrong," he said, "that cannot without much labor appear to be right."[8] He ascribed much of the confusion over the text of Shakespeare's plays to the fullness of the dramatist's imagination. A second idea crowded into his mind before the first idea had been clearly revealed, Johnson felt. Though sometimes gross jest, tiresome quibble, or bombastic passion resulted, Johnson recommended a close study of the language and customs of Shakespeare's day before a final decision be rendered regarding his language. Johnson felt that such historical insight did away with most of the complaints of Rymer and Voltaire.

Johnson's proof of Shakespeare's greatness lay in the Longinian test, the "length of duration and continuance of esteem." Thus, he says, "the stream of time, which is continually washing the dissoluble fabrics of other poets, passes without injury by the adamant of Shakespeare."[9] The chief reason for this is Shakespeare's unerring representation of the fundamental aspects of human nature common to all ages. Shakespeare knew not only how human beings behaved, but how they would behave in crises to which they could not be exposed. No one but Homer had done so much for literature, Johnson felt, stating that the form, the language, and the characters of English drama all originated with Shakespeare.

Shakespeare's flaws were likewise noted by Johnson. The tragic scenes were often labored, the plots loosely formed, and there was all too often a sacrifice of virtue to convenience. But the rules received notice to quit, once and for all; since Corneille's day they "had given more trouble to the poet than pleasure to the auditor."[10] The basis of pleasure is variety, Johnson said. If pleasure is outlawed by criticism, "there is always an appeal open from criticism to nature."[11] Shakespeare's plays, neither tragedies nor comedies in the classical sense, did not have to conform to classical precepts. Shakespeare did, however, "instruct by pleasing," for out of "the chaos of mingled purposes" that constituted life, he had originated a new kind of drama in which every walk of life was represented. In this manner did the eighteenth century arbiter of literary taste put a capstone to the battle of "Shakespeare versus the rules." Not only did Shakespeare emerge a winner, but also the entire field of literary and dramatic criticism was further opened to independent development, with room for attention to new points of discussion.

One of these new fields of inquiry was the matter of Shakespeare's sources. In 1748 Peter Whalley, following Gildon, Upton, and others, had argued that Shakespeare must have relied heavily upon a knowledge of classical literature, because there were a striking number of passages in his plays that closely paralleled classical sources. Charlotte Lennox pioneered in the study of Shakespeare's sources, but Richard Farmer did more than that. In his *Essay on the Learning of Shakespeare* (1767), Farmer showed how much of Shakespeare's work could have come out of English translations of the classics. Because of his wide reading in Elizabethan literature, Farmer made a deep impression on the scholars of his time. Instead of detracting from Shakespeare's genius, Farmer quoted Dryden's view that those who accused Shakespeare of little learning really thereby gave him the greater commendation.

In 1773 Thomas Hawkins wrote *The Origin of the English Drama*, in which he argued that current drama, being anything but a revival of classical drama, was thus subject to its own criteria for excellence. "Therefore criticism of Shakespeare for his neglect of the rules," Hawkins concluded, "is completely beside the point."[12]

Another critical battle raged over Voltaire's views on Shakespeare. Early inclined to favor Shakespeare's plays, Voltaire later came to describe the tragedies as monstrous farces, the work of "a savage with a spark of genius." Voltaire had his followers in England, such as Edward Taylor, but the *Zeitgeist* was against him and he suffered much censure.

Perhaps his chief adversary was Elizabeth Montagu, who not only questioned his critical judgment and his knowledge of English but who also brought out several dramatic points in defending Shakespeare and attacking French dramatists. Her objection to French plays was that they too frequently contained artificial courtly diction and passages of declamation, that their characters were all courtiers, not men, and that their plots showed a wooden observance of obsolete rules. On the other hand, Shakespeare's genius was seen to lie in his sensitive characterization and his several dramatic innovations. Among the latter Mrs. Montagu enumerated the history play, the discovery of the supernatural as a source of unknown terror, and the use of ghosts and fairies grounded in national traditions and customs. Her occasional inaccuracies did not keep Mrs. Montagu from calling attention to several hitherto unexplored facets of Shakespeare's dramaturgy.

Edward Capell in 1768 and George Steevens in 1773 produced important editions of Shakespeare in which their texts incorporated careful collation of the quartos as well as the folios. Edmond Malone published a chronology of the plays in 1778 and later he produced a biography and other scholarly aids.

Stress was upon character among late eighteenth century critics of Shakespeare. Thomas Whately provided the first detailed analysis of Shakespeare's characters in 1770; William Richardson and Elizabeth Griffith followed shortly thereafter, stressing the characters as moral and ethical models.

In 1777 came Maurice Morgann's essay on Falstaff, which A.C. Bradley considered to be the best piece of Shakespearian criticism he had ever seen. Morgann's originality came in his recognition of the need for "entering into the inward soul" of the characters, seeing them as totalities. Thus, although Falstaff seemed on the surface to be a coward, actually the "inner impression" we have of him is quite different, for we are saddened at Hal's final ingratitude toward him. Morgann found Shakespeare's characters to be presented "in the round," forever having unplumbed recesses and forever being capable of growth.

Perhaps Morgann's most important contribution was his faith in the overall impression that a play made despite its external logical facts. The proper approach to drama as indeed to all literature, he felt, was to trust the effect, not necessarily to try to define it. For in creative appreciation of all art, he believed, some other faculty than logical prosaic understanding is needed. In this way Morgann was preparing the way for Coleridge's later work on the imagination.

Esteem for Shakespeare was also growing on the continent. Lessing, in his *Hamburg Dramaturgy* in 1767, had praised Shakespeare highly, and in 1770 Johann Herder opened up Shakespeare to Goethe. As a matter of fact, the entire *Sturm und Drang* period was favorable to the "irregular genius" of Shakespeare. The French too were following the trend. By 1800 Madame de Staël admitted that the age of Voltaire was over and that Shakespeare and Schiller were now the models for France. Chateaubriand also valued Shakespeare highly, as did Victor Hugo in his scathing destruction of the rules.

It can thus be concluded that Shakespeare's rise in critical esteem paralleled the decline of neoclassical rigidity concerning the rules of drama. The chief stages of eighteenth century Shakespearian criticism were his ultimate ranking over Jonson, elaborate textual study, a discussion of his works as literature more than as drama, and finally, extensive comment on his marvelous creations of character.

9. German Criticism

German dramatic criticism, like the German nation, made its appearance only relatively recently. When it did arrive, however, it made considerable impact.

Sixteenth century scholars who wrote literary treatises containing some dramatic criticism were Johann Sturm, Georgius Fabricius, and Jacobus Pontanus. More important was the *Book of German Poesy* (1624) by Martin Opitz, which inspired much original German literature of all sorts. In the subsequent battle over the rules, Philip von Zesen and Augustine Buchner took the familiar neoclassical position, while Andreas Gryphius, the leading dramatist of the period, and Erdmann Neumeister showed a preference for the freedom of English drama.

Johann Gottsched was the most influential early drama critic. A faithful follower of Boileau and other French neoclassical critics, Gottsched prescribed careful formulas for the composition of tragedies and comedies in his *Essay on a Critical Creative Literature for Germans*, published in 1730. Re-interpreting the dicta of Horace, Gottsched preferred the useful over the beautiful. He wrote several plays on classical principles, including an adaptation of Addison's *Cato*. His collaboration with the actress Karoline Neuber led to the establishment of the "Leipzig school" of acting and criticism. Gottsched's influence declined after 1740, under the attack of the Swiss critics Johann Bodmer and J.J. Breitinger, who demanded that the creative imagination of the dramatist should not be shackled by external rules.

Johann Elias Schlegel, uncle of the two more famous critics, was the early pioneer of Shakespeare in Germany. Moses Mendelssohn later continued the drive to use Shakespeare as a model for the rising German drama. The poet Friedrich Klopstock wrote several lyrical plays and was a general inspiration to Goethe and others in the *Sturm und Drang* movement in German literature.

Gotthold Lessing stands as the greatest drama critic of the eighteenth century. Jules Isaac felt that Lessing in his *Laokoon* (1766) "gave so powerful a thrust and so rigid an integrity to critical procedure as to earn him a position second to none but Aristotle."[1] J.G. Robertson pointed out that although others had depicted the limitations of rules-bound French classical drama before Lessing, "none was able to dethrone it so effectively as he, with his brilliant reduction of the plot of *Rodogune* to absurdity."[2]

Partial to drama, perhaps because he himself wrote plays, Lessing composed in the *Hamburg Dramaturgy* a brilliant if uneven theory of drama that is comprehensive and elucidatory. Although many of his views are not original and much of his writing is confined to plays enacted at the Hamburg theater, Lessing showed how an eclectic viewpoint can produce a penetrating insight into dramatic effects. His vigorous style, his dependable judgment, and his catholic range make him still readable on such issues as plot, character, unity, and catharsis.

Lessing's limitations grew largely out of his Gallophobia, his intruding moralism, and the journalistic pressure of reporting daily on what were often mediocre plays. Though he confessed great indebtedness to Diderot, Lessing had little use for French neoclassical rules of drama. Even a pleasing hybrid he accepts with more gusto than a correct cold play by Racine.

Probably his most original contribution was Lessing's approach to tragedy. Tragedy, he says, by creating a world analogous to the real one, is a justification of the ethical in the world, even of God. To achieve the purgation of serious emotions one must find the golden mean of pity and fear: those who feel too much must learn to feel less, and those who feel too little must learn to feel more. On the whole, despite its didacticism, the work of Lessing remains that of a first-class critical mind summing up the eighteenth century concept of the drama.

In the *Sturm und Drang* of the 1770's, the term "genius" became synonymous with complete rejection of discipline and tradition, as well as implicit faith in creative spontaneity. Lessing worked out an interesting reconciliation of genius and rules. In his view, the rules simply explained what genius had accomplished, and thus came after them rather than prior to them. Mechanical rules do not matter, but the dramatist must develop the "hidden organization" of his plot in order to achieve the "inner probability" necessary for empathy with the tragic protagonist. Thus a great play is seen to be a product of orderly judgment as well as of intuitive talent.

The whole *Sturm und Drang* movement gave a forward impetus to German culture. It had many tributaries. In opposition to Gottsched's predilection for French neoclassicism, it stressed a return to native German roots. Particularly in Herder, who was deeply influenced by Scottish critics, is there visible a nationalistic search for folk elements, albeit as a stepping stone toward world literature.

Prussia was growing under Frederick the Great, and the usual literary revival was under way. Shakespeare, under vigorous attack in France, was accepted in Germany as the apex of dramatic genius. Heinrich Gerstenberg wished to destroy all systems of classification that tended to qualify Shakespeare's art. In these plays, Gerstenberg said, one finds everywhere a designed whole, with appropriate proportions and with intentionally contrasting characters and groups. Herder, who felt that a critic should be "a servant of the author, his friend, his impartial judge," not only helped bury neoclassical standards but also laid the foundation for a new romantic criticism based upon imagination, spontaneity, and genius.

Herder's influence on the young Goethe is well known. After their association at Strasbourg in the winter of 1770-71, Goethe shared Herder's enthusiasm for German folk literature, for James Macpherson's Ossian, and for Shakespeare. Of Shakespeare he said, "The first page I read of him made me his own for life."[3] Goethe felt that he must now desert the popular theater as well as the limitations of the Three Unities.

After discarding neoclassical canons of form, however, Goethe realized that some principle of organization is needed in drama. Hence he derived his concept of "inner form," based upon nature, imagination, and genius, and found in slightly altered form in the writings of the third Earl of Shaftesbury. This "inner form" of a work is the hidden unity that is more important than external plot form. The creative process is described as being imbedded in the unconscious mind of the author. Mere subjectivity, which he called "the general disease of the age," he eschewed in favor of a profound identity of subject and object, of writer's mind with the facts of the external world. He also prizes the organic principle of totality of impression, as seen in Wilhelm Meister's conception of what Hamlet's character was like before his father was murdered. While he deplored the mixture of genres, Goethe realized how inevitably the process went forward.

At times Goethe laments undue concentration on audience reactions, feeling it will undermine dramatic art; elsewhere he forgives Shakespeare's slips because they would quickly slide past an audience and be forgotten. He rejects Aristotle's approach to tragedy largely because it depends too much on the patrons' response. But he likes the "largeness of soul" of Greek tragedy, and finds the "Greek armor" too heavy to be carried by the classical "little Frenchmen." Although he realizes that drama has moral consequences, he thinks it ruinous for a great artist to write with a didactic intent. Perhaps his most important creed was that the critic must have no ironclad creed.

Friedrich von Schiller, under Immanuel Kant's influence, was a philosopher of the esthetics of drama. He sees tragedy as producing a peculiar pleasure, brought on by the victory of a higher moral law over a lower one. He praises the theater as a great civilizing force. When we see Man's freedom struggling in a tragedy, he says, we resign ourselves to the mystery of the universe and are inoculated against unavoidable fate. Schiller follows the general preference for Greek drama over Roman drama that was common after Johann Winckelmann had published that view in an essay on classical culture. In his preface to *The Bride of Messina* in 1803 Schiller wrote his reasons for attempting to reestablish the dignity of the classical chorus as used in the play.

Echoing Lessing, Schiller felt that tragic pity needed to achieve a certain mean: if it is too weak, we remain cold, and if it is too strong it becomes painful and hence ceases to be art. Schiller, like Goethe, combines classicism and romanticism; the former strain is seen in his praise for "naïve imitation of nature" (by which he meant idealized human nature). The latter strain, never as fully developed as in Goethe, is seen in his search for a reconciliation of the "naïve" and the "sentimental." He was willing to recognize that the tired businessman and the worn-out scholar craved for mere recreation and amusement in drama. He was unfortunately never successful in his search for a form that would satisfy both popular taste and the connoisseurs.

Friedrich von Schlegel, the younger of the two brothers, was the more original critic of the two. Though he himself varied his reports with pleasant impressionistic outbreaks, he pointed out the dangers of sheer impressionism—if all standards are discarded, soon "I'll be damned!" would be the best judgment on the greatest work.

Friedrich von Schlegel introduced the term "irony" into modern criticism. Since the world is basically paradoxical, he said, only an ironic ambivalence can grasp its perennial contradictions. He also evolved a three-stage history of tragedy: first came mere depiction of nature, next came the delineation of the riddle of man's existence, and finally (with Calderón) came the solution of the riddle, in the spiritual transfiguration of the hero. Although he had little use for Aristotle, he admired Greek drama and was ahead of his time in recognizing the greatness of Aristophanes. With his brother he popularized the new concept of "romanticism" as a modern successor to classicism. The brothers epitomized Goethe's search for a world literature, since their catholic range extended even to the Orient.

Friedrich's brother August Wilhelm was the more influential of the two critics. August Wilhelm was the chief diffuser and popularizer of the new romanticism. He appreciated the role played by the audience in drama; he knew that the theatric and the dramatic are inextricably interwoven. He felt that the audience provided the equivalent of the playwright's comment: "The effect produced by seeing a number of others share in the same emotions is astonishingly powerful."[4]

Like Goethe, whom he admired, August Wilhelm stressed organic unity in a work and disliked mixed genres. He postulates a comic mood as a basis for comedy, a viewing of imperfections in a playful light. He sees realistic comedy and comedy of manners as too close to seriousness to be pure comedy; therefore he prefers the comedy of fantasy and caprice. Thus Molière's plays are attacked as lacking humor and as having insufficient universality and probability. Besides translating seventeen plays of Shakespeare's, he wrote much sensitive and sympathetic criticism of the plays. His lack of fairness toward French drama and criticism was one of his few weaknesses.

A flood of German critics now seemed to discover classical Greek drama. Johann Süvern showed the importance of the historical setting in understanding Greek tragedy. Karl Solger wrote a highly praised review of August Wilhelm von Schlegel's *Lectures on Dramatic Art and Literature*. The review placed irony at the center of dramatic art; irony was the product of the reconciliation of opposites: conscious and unconscious, universal and particular, divine and human.

Believing that textual criticism must go hand in hand with exegesis, Gottfried Herrmann worked hard to recover original Greek texts. His philosophy as an editor was "to explain the individual words, elucidate the historical references, set forth the author's aim and the general scheme of his work with its merits and its defects."[5]

August Boeckh went far beyond textual criticism, asking such questions as the extent to which Greek actors introduced their own wording into tragedies in which they performed. Boeckh's criticism of *Antigone* was printed in his edition of the text, together with a free translation, "the publication of which in 1843 was prompted by the first performance of the play with Mendelssohn's music in Berlin in 1841."[6]

Not every German critic praised Shakespeare. Christian Grabbe in 1827 said that "the German nation wants the greatest possible simplicity and clearness in language, form, and plot. In the comic scenes it demands not peculiar turns or witticisms, which except for the form of expression have nothing witty in them, but sound common sense."[7] Finding little in Shakespeare in line with this theory, Grabbe wrote a series of plays that have long since been forgotten.

Following the suppression of the Paris revolution of 1830, a group of writers calling themselves Young Germany sought to express the revolutionary call for a liberal democracy. In technique they called for realism rather than escapism. Their models were Victor Hugo, the elder Alexander Dumas, and Eugène Scribe. Their esthetic spokesman was Ludolf Wienbarg, who asked for an emotional portrayal of the rights of the common man. Heinrich Heine and the critic Ludwig Börne had prepared the way for this kind of drama.

Leading playwrights in the movement were Karl Gutzkow and Heinrich Laube. Although their plays used melodramatic effects and exaggerated characters, "the influence of this thoroughly superficial but ever graceful and entertaining drama reaches down into the present,"[8] wrote Georg Witkowski at the turn of the century.

The greatest drama critic of the period was Ludwig Tieck, who was dramaturg at the Dresden theater from 1825 to 1842. Tieck produced Shakespeare in an Elizabethan manner, and also inaugurated the modern study of early German drama. In an effort to keep the leading actor in the "star system" from mugging so as to destroy the chief effects of plays by Goethe, Schiller, and Shakespeare, Tieck recommended entirely new staging techniques, which were opposed because of their novelty. "When one reads the criticisms of Tieck and

Ludwig Börne, one is astonished at the lack of critical judgment against which they had continually to fight."[9]

Tieck sought for greater intimacy in drama, in the modern manner of Thornton Wilder. He advocated a stage of several levels, using naturalistic acting in plays of middle-class realism. Eric Bentley says of Tieck, "In his demand for a more intimate theater and a more experimental leadership, for more natural acting and careful enunciation, he is a great pioneer of modern theater."[10]

Meanwhile Adam Müller argued for a return to religious drama. Müller also bravely defended French regularity on the grounds of its aiming at a unified, almost oratorical effect. He likewise recommended a return to greater audience appeal by such means as destroying the dramatic illusion, drawing the spectator into the action by chorus, fool, or prologue figures.

Hermann Hettner, in *The Modern Drama*, a book that influenced Henrik Ibsen after it appeared in 1850, wrote that family life itself could produce the soul-searching probing of struggles between morals and fate, out of which "pure" tragedy could be produced. Hettner felt that the playwright Friedrich Hebbel had invented a new kind of play in his thesis play about middle-class life.

German philosophers also wrote on the drama. Arthur Schopenhauer, for example, said that tragedy gave us a peculiar elevation by showing us that life, being frustration, cannot satisfy us and so we negate our will to live. He thus contrasts markedly with Lessing's optimistic defense of God's order as revealed through tragedy. Schopenhauer ranked an interesting plot beneath the beauty of ideas, and he felt that the curtain in comedy must fall rapidly on a moment of joy, lest we see what comes afterward.

Georg Hegel defined tragedy as a conflict of legitimate moral forces that must somehow be reconciled. Thus Antigone and Creon in Sophocles' play are exclusively dedicated to their respective loyalties of family and state. Both suffer, but there is a final resolution of the disparate views. Crediting Ben Jonson with the invention of realistic comedy, H. Ulrici said of Jonson: "Where he combats folly, vice, and senselessness, he forgets his learning, he warms up, everything is full of life and energy."[11]

Richard Wagner endeavored to restore music in opera to its Greek role as a contributing effect to the music-drama rather than as an end in itself, as it tended to be in Italian opera. He thus was searching for a unification of art forms. "Like Hebbel he desired to make the drama the image of the inner world of the poet and the receptacle of the loftiest and deepest impulses of the present, to combine philosophical, political, and social purposes."[12] Wagner imbued the stage with the fervor of religious pageantry. His influence can be measured by the fact that "talented and imaginative scene designers such as Adolphe Appia, Gordon Craig, and Vsevolod Meyerhold attempted to bring about the complex union of the arts which Wagner had envisaged."[13]

Friedrich Nietzsche originally favored Wagner's approach, for he felt that the Greeks had overcome life's pessimism through their dramas in celebration of Dionysian rituals. Later, of course, Nietzsche broke with Wagner's more Christian tendencies, to put his hope in more Dionysian (romantic) and less Apollonian (classical) art tendencies.

Several playwrights also wrote treatises on drama. Gustav Freytag, in *The Technique of the Drama*, dealt at some length with advice, chiefly theatrical, gleaned from the practice of Sophocles, Shakespeare, Lessing, Goethe, and Schiller. The Austrian Franz Grillparzer called himself "that middle thing between Goethe and Kotzebue which the times need."[14] His critical approach was refreshing. Discarding theory, he analyzed each play in terms of what seemed to flow out of its nature. His comments on Beaumont and Fletcher, Shakespeare, and Spanish drama are especially incisive. He praised Goethe highly but had little use for Lessing.

Though they were rivals, Otto Ludwig and Friedrich Hebbel agreed with Schiller's contention that dialogue is the essence of the dramatist's art. Also, both Ludwig and Hebbel argued for a modern drama of ideas. Ludwig, who believed that drama consisted of a fusion of the arts of poetry and acting, asked for tragedy dealing not only with the passing hour but with "the whole complex of actual life." Ludwig said that "the play should be one catastrophe motivated by characters and situations; its exposition and dialogue generally should be analytic, that is, should carry forward the action and acquaint us with the preliminary facts at the same time."[15] Ludwig was here giving a foreview of Ibsen's later bourgeois tragedy.

Hebbel tried to achieve in his plays what he gave Shakespeare credit for mastering: "To disclose the roots of morality in the grandest possible manner by cutting away the weeds that cover them up."[16] Witkowski believed that "Hebbel penetrates deeper than earlier dramatists into the mysterious origin of personality and discovers features there which at first strike one as irregular and willful."[17] Witkowski found that Hebbel's *Mariamne* resembled the plays of Racine: "Just as in the great French tragedy writer, so here there is united with strict forms borrowed from the classical writers, a sympathetic, thoroughly modern sentiment and a deep subjectivity."[18]

Hebbel as a critic went beyond Ludwig in demanding a new theater of dialectic. Influenced by Hegel, Hebbel stated that great drama occurred during periods of great historical change. In Greek times, the great tragedies expressed the shift from a belief in gods to a belief in fate. Thus the conflict depicted is one between man and Idea (Hegel's term for society's institutions). The second great crisis of Western civilization was the shift from medieval collectivism to Renaissance individualism; at this point the dramatic conflict is within man himself.

Now, in the third crisis of Western culture, with man evolving toward some "new form of humanity," the conflict is within the Idea, that is, drama must permit radical questioning of the fundamentals of our political, religious, and moral institutions. Hence "the playwright as thinker," as Eric Bentley has requested for our time, is called for in Hebbel's approach.

Just as Georg Büchner first discovered the tragedy of "little" people in *Wozzeck*, so did Hebbel establish a dialectic for middle-class tragedy, upon which Ibsen and Eugene O'Neill could build. Hebbel united Lessing's stress on bourgeois tragedy with Schiller's emphasis on poetic treatment to lay the basis for such differing modern dramatic techniques as the problem plays of Ibsen and Shaw's plays of intellectual discussion.

In 1859 the Duke of Saxe-Meiningen had been impressed by the ensemble effects achieved by Charles Kean in a series of Shakespearian plays in London. He accordingly founded a company of actors devoted to ensemble acting, which from 1874 to 1890 gave 2591 performances of 41 plays in Germany and other countries. Opposing the "star system," their success was due to one principle: "Everything to be subordinated to the purposes of the poet and these to be realized by summoning all the devices of dramatic art and of modern stage technique."[19]

The Meiningen Players had a direct effect upon the development of such new theaters as the Moscow Art Theater and the Freie Bühne in Berlin. These new theaters, in turn, were of great importance in modern drama. Some of their achievements were that "the limits of the permissible were extended, new subjects had been introduced, careful observation took the place of conventional characterization, and the technique of author and actor endeavored to arrive at complete illusion."[20]

Situation comedies prevailed in the German theater of the 1890's. These comedies, said Witkowski, always have two main ingredients: "The comic of situation at all costs and empty play on words, both of which aim merely at exciting peals of laughter. Wherever they hold sway, all regard for a connected plot and for characterization vanishes, all trace of an idea is lacking and at most the semblance of proper feelings is awakened by the aid of false sentimentality."[21]

Naturalism in modern drama found its most complete expression in the plays of Gerhart Hauptmann. Naturalism in Germany was a compound of the materialism of the philosopher Ernst Haeckel, the positivism of Auguste Comte, Darwin's theory of evolution, and the environmental determinism of Hippolyte Taine and Émile Zola. Hauptmann added to these an almost classical sense of form and an instinct for ensemble effect acquired from the Meiningen Players. When his sensitivity was brutalized by modern life, Hauptmann responded with a restrained but emotional cry of protest. *The Weavers*, for example, shows not only individualized characters but also "a coherent structure, derived from rhythmic waves of mounting tension and from the interweaving of the *Leitmotif* of the weavers' song."[22]

Expressionism also found a cordial reception among German dramatists. The Swedish playwright August Strindberg virtually created expressionism in a series of "dream" plays which intentionally distort external reality in order to reveal an irrational, often frenzied, underlife. Although Georg Kaiser and Ernst Toller were the best known dramatists in this movement, they derived their impetus from Frank Wedekind, "whose unmasking of instinctive animal forces revealed the anarchy and chaos beneath the surface of 'civilization'."[23]

The leading critic of expressionism, Reinhard Sorge, summarized its main points as follows: It is subjective; it avoids external reality in order to express the inner man, the unconscious; it seeks the spiritual and the divine; it works by lyricism and music; and it asserts the importance and the dignity of the individual in the face of the forces that would crush him.

Eric Bentley found Bernhard Diebold's *Anarchy in Drama* (1925) to be an excellent analysis of modern expressionism. Diebold, says Bentley, "writes the best things obtainable on the art of Strindberg and Wedekind."[24] Other recent German drama critics recommended by Bentley include Julius Bab, Herbert Ihering, Alfred Kerr, and Egon Friedell, whose book *Cultural History of the Modern Age* contains "some of the best commentary ever written on the plays of Goethe, Schiller, Ibsen, and others."[25]

On the whole, then, Germany has been well represented in the field of dramatic criticism during the several centuries since her critics began to receive general notice. In fact, Germany seems to be one country in which dramatic criticism has flowered more abundantly than has the art of drama itself.

10. 19th Century French and English Criticism

It seems odd that for a time, at least, a nation of political rebels remained dramatic conservatives. As Irving Babbitt said, "Men who had toppled over altars and beheaded a king were ready to kneel down superstitiously in the little Temple of Taste."[1] Népomucène Lemercier in 1817 said that tragedy must fulfill twenty-six rules, comedy a mere twenty-two. Napoleon himself had given official sanction to neoclassicism. But its standards were as surely doomed as Napoleon's regime. Lemercier, who had begun historical comedy in France with his *Pinto* in 1800, went on in an independent manner to slight the unities and admire Shakespeare. Stendhal, defending Shakespeare while attacking Racine and Molière, said in 1823: "Romanticism is the art of giving people themselves pleasure, Classicism that of giving them what pleased their grandfathers."[2]

The essence of the romantic revolt against neoclassicism was basically the same in France as in the rest of Europe. Much of it, in fact, could have or did come from Samuel Johnson. Setting aside rules in favor of spontaneity and genius; mixing genres; following emotion rather than observing decorum — all of these critical issues were once again rehearsed.

Madame de Staël was the most refreshing of the early romantic critics. Although she felt that each nation had to develop its own characteristic type of drama, she was by nature a cosmopolite, taking some of her views from Johnson and some from A.W.

Schlegel. She by no means slavishly copied German viewpoints; she prized free expression and spontaneity on her own grounds. For example, she differed sharply from the Schlegels in preferring Schiller to Goethe. She gave her considerable influence toward shifting criticism away from examination of small details and toward broader questions of cultural history.

Victor Hugo's preface to *Cromwell* in 1827 is generally considered the spearhead of the French revolution against neoclassical criticism. Although he had predecessors, none of them carried the day with so comprehensive an attack as did Hugo. Moreover, he was no idle theorist, but a writer of plays that incorporated his views. His inspired rhetoric rose to the need of freeing French playwrights from the cramping confines of superficial conformity. He advocated mixing dramatic forms with the epic or with lyrical forms; he followed Diderot in stating that rules are an impediment to genius, and he saw legitimate need for only one unity, that of action.

Hugo also developed an interesting theory of the "grotesque." Since man's nature is dual, drama should reflect this fact—hence, there should be a mingling of tragic and comic, beautiful and ugly, bad and good. "Everything that is in nature is in art,"[3] Hugo said. He cited, as examples of the grotesque, Gothic architecture and Shakespeare's alternations of buffoonery with high tragedy. As an esthetic principle, this approach clearly foreshadows much of what is contained in modern art forms. Like the early Dryden, however, Hugo still recommended verse for serious drama. In his later years, Hugo's most important critical contribution appeared in his book on Shakespeare. Here Hugo enunciated a theory of character types, that a type sums up and concentrates under one human form a whole family of characters and minds. Hugo's views at this point presage Jung's later interpretation of literature as the creation of archetypal patterns.

Stendhal supported Hugo's cry for a new form of drama, though he preferred prose to such an extent that he disliked Hugo's own poetic dramas. The second part of Stendhal's *Racine and Shakespeare* attacked the French Academy for its action against the rising tide of romanticism. Stendhal disavowed German influence, for he wished to show that romanticism was not necessarily mystical and Teutonic. Stendhal writes of comedy in terms of Hobbes' theory of "sudden glory," the unexpected realization of our superiority over another person. Stendhal was more attracted by English critics—Johnson, Francis Jeffrey, and William Hazlitt—than by the

Germans. He rejected Molière as neither moral nor comic, and was ultimately led to conclude, like S.N. Behrman in our time, that a serious age could produce no genuine comedy.

It must not be imagined that neoclassicism was completely dead after the romantic critics fired their opening guns. Julien-Louis Geoffroy, for example, whose *Course of Dramatic Literature* was published posthumously in 1818, was scarcely an advance over Voltaire. Geoffroy interpreted the rise of bourgeois drama as a counterpart of the growing political vulgarity of his age; he confines his approach chiefly to moral rather than artistic criticism. In Vicomte de Chateaubriand, too, the neoclassic generally overshadows the romantic. After grudgingly acknowledging Shakespeare's great insight into human nature, Chateaubriand concludes that his plays are decidedly lacking in dignity and taste. Chateaubriand had the emotional intensity of a romantic: he describes how he prefers Homer's description of a storm at sea to his own experience while crossing the Atlantic. But he generally gravitated toward the rules; even late in his career he admits that he accepts completely the precepts enunciated by Aristotle, Horace, and Boileau. Désiré Nisard also wrote a study of French romanticism which considers it a reflection of decadence in French culture.

Charles Sainte-Beuve, a greater literary than dramatic critic, early was an enthusiastic supporter of Hugo and the romanticists, but later he attacked their excesses, as well as the excesses of naturalism. He used close biographical and psychological studies of writers to determine their predominating interests and their "essential vices." The later Sainte-Beuve can praise Racine above Hugo, despite more powerful passages in Hugo, because Racine perfects the whole, and the parts in relation to the overall effect. Sainte-Beuve's criticism is admired because it is clear, readable, cosmopolitan, and free from dogmatism. His acquaintance with history also gave him concrete support for his particular views.

That insightful political analyst, Alexis de Tocqueville, had little optimism for the future of drama in a democracy. He believed that in a democratic society plays are watched but seldom read, and thus are never carefully examined. All that is required in a play is an evening's amusement. Under these conditions drama was destined never to evolve into a very high level, he felt. Possibly he overlooked the fact that sensitive and well-informed critics provide that necessary close scrutiny that democratic playgoers shun doing.

Francisque Sarcey is the Aristotle of the "well made" play.

"Dramatic art," said Sarcey, "is the ensemble of conventions, universal or local, by the aid of which the playwright, representing human life in a theatre, gives to the audience an illusion of truth."[4] To Sarcey, the only requirement for a play is an audience, and thus all laws of the theater should be drawn up in recognition of this one fact. True to his belief, he supported the rising thesis plays of Eugène Scribe, the younger Dumas, and Victorien Sardou. Scribe's plays deal with social problems, generally in a four-act formula of exposition, complication, crisis, and resolution. Though his plays are contrived and artificial, Scribe paradoxically influenced such greater artists as Ibsen and Wagner. The younger Dumas had insisted that a play should be socially useful, exposing evils and correcting vices in society. Sarcey accepted this, but set up certain dramatic absolutes based upon theatrical considerations. He stressed the "art of preparations," the unity of impression, a great deal of action, and especially the *scène à faire*, or the requirement that the central plot situation must be represented on the stage. Despite the dangers obviously inherent in his approach, he frequently framed sound and stimulating criticism.

Ferdinand Brunetière, a latter-day Boileau, was a classical lawgiver in drama who fought both romanticism and naturalism with the weapons of neoclassicism: reason, universality, and morality. Applying Darwinian principles to drama, he traces the evolution of genres from simple, undifferentiated forms to complex, transfigured entities. By using Darwin's technique in his criticism, "Brunetière forges the final link between nineteenth-century science and literature. It is true that such a genre as classic tragedy will seem to accomplish an evolution, because of the perpetual changes operated on the form and the desire for novelty felt alike by artists and public."[5] Brunetière's famous "law of the theater" was that drama required a conscious will encountering conflict; genres were defined by seeing what kinds of obstacles were opposed to this will. Although the idea of a tragic struggle is as old as Aristotle, Brunetière shifted the emphasis from conflict to conscious will, and thus started a discussion of dramatic effect that engaged many English and American critics.

It is striking how rapidly romantic drama passed away in favor of modern realism and naturalism. In his preface to *Thérèse Raquin* in 1873, Émile Zola stated that the great romantic plays of the 1830's had done their job in destroying the artificiality of neoclassical drama, but now they were themselves as insincere as their predecessors. The only salvation for modern drama he found in applying the scientific spirit realistically to human problems.

In 1887 André Antoine founded the Théâtre Libre for the express purpose of staging the new naturalistic plays, and Jean Jullien became one of the leading expositors of this "slice-of-life" approach to drama. Alfred de Vigny had earlier pleaded for a "drama of thought," in his preface to *Chatterton*. Vigny's mention of "the spiritual man stifled by a materialistic society" parallels the "superfluous man" found at that time in Alexander Pushkin and Alexander Griboyedov, and later represented in the plays of Ivan Turgenev and Anton Chekhov. Henry Becque, a naturalistic dramatist, also wrote in defense of his technique, which was to portray sordid problems realistically. Becque felt that the universities were the only possible breeding-ground of great modern dramatists. On the whole, the "well made" play as practiced by Scribe, Sardou, and the younger Dumas was an even greater bane to the naturalists than was the romantic play of the Hugo era.

Maurice Maeterlinck, on the other hand, infused a spirit of poetry into modern drama. Maeterlinck wrote a type of "static" drama similar to Chekhov's, but he refused to be doctrinaire about his achievement. He suggests certain subconscious elements in his approach to drama, which combines symbolism with artful atmospheric effects. Maeterlinck insisted that everyday life of common people contained elements as dramatic as the lives of kings. He also used repetitious dialogue and pregnant silences structurally.

The poet Stéphane Mallarmé had meanwhile formulated the goals of symbolist drama in a series of "Notes on the Theatre" that appeared in the *Revue Independante* in 1886-87. Attacking the mediocrity and vulgarity of current drama, Mallarme said that plays should express a "soul state," an inner condition rather than external action. He cited *Hamlet* as the epitome of drama.

As the century ended, the impressionistic Anatole France issued two descriptive warnings: "The good critic is he who relates the adventures of his own soul among masterpieces," and "Objective criticism has no more existence than objective art."[6]

In summary, then, a good deal was accomplished in this century by French critics. At least three distinctive schools of dramatic criticism are apparent. The final vestiges of neoclassicism are exemplified in critics as far apart in time as Geoffroy and Brunetière. The brilliant romantic revolution headed by Victor Hugo, after playing its role as the formidable opponent of neoclassicism, was itself finally engulfed in the naturalistic avalanche that was led by Zola. Nitze and Dargan, in their history of French literature, say that half of all the literary criticism penned in France was written during the nineteenth century. A similar ratio might well prevail for the exclusively dramatic criticism. At any rate, it was during this period that France overcame its time-lag in assessing earlier drama and criticism freshly. As a result, French critics, as well as French dramatists, once again began to be extremely influential upon the rest of the Western world.

It is interesting that at a time when English drama was in its doldrums, a striking number of stimulating dramatic critics flourished. The romantic critics, as they are known, included such figures as Samuel Taylor Coleridge, Charles Lamb, William Hazlitt, and Leigh Hunt. Sir Walter Raleigh, speaking in 1907 of the romantic critics, said: "They love to lose themselves in *O altitudo*. When they are inspired by their divinity they say wonderful things; when the inspiration fails them their language is maintained at the same height, and they say more than they feel. You can never be sure of them."[7] Nevertheless, at a later date T.S. Eliot could testify: "It is impossible to understand Shakespeare criticism to this day, without a familiar acquaintance with Coleridge's lectures and notes."[8]

Though much of Coleridge's approach was borrowed from the Germans, a good deal of it was original with him. "He agrees with Lessing, from whom he probably took a good share of his admiration for Aristotle, that Shakespeare's plays come much closer to the principles laid down in the *Poetics* than do most of the 'regular' dramas."[9] Coleridge's most important contribution was the formulation of the working of the imagination as the creative shaping power that mediated between reason and understanding—at once a unifier and an empathic force. No critic strikes better sparks of fire from reading a work, inspired flinders of insight into the play.

Coleridge felt that drama's essence was a will struggling with fate, and that the deepest effect is produced when fate is represented as "a higher and intelligent will," and the individual's opposition springs from a defect. Plot interest he valued less than organic unity, also called "homogeneity," "proportionateness," or "totality of interest." Like Goethe, there is no pre-established Procrustean critique; sometimes Coleridge disparages genres, and sometimes he seeks for perfection within a genre. He generally accepts tragicomedy, for he believes that opposites illustrate each other's nature.

Though his scholarship concerning Shakespeare is sometimes inaccurate, Coleridge's interpretations are often creative and significant. He felt, for example, that Shakespeare turned the paucity of stage settings into a blessing, by producing drama which is between "recitation and representation," and thus more stirring to the sensitive imagination. Unlike Johnson, the romantic critics did not feel it necessary to find faults in Shakespeare before praising him. Intuitively sympathetic towards him, they give interpretations rather than judgments. The chief danger of this method is that sometimes the critic reads himself into the work. Nevertheless, Coleridge was an important bridge of German romanticism, and as René Wellek wisely concludes, he "carries enough of the Aristotelian and empirical tradition to make the idealistic elements palatable."[10]

Wellek goes on to show how Charles Lamb and William Hazlitt brought three new techniques into nineteenth century criticism. These are the use of evocation of an author's style or quality, metaphor coined to capture the writer's quintessence, and personal reference or impression. Lamb's *Specimens of English Dramatic Poets* (1808) called attention to the powerful language employed by some of Shakespeare's contemporaries. A lifelong friend of Coleridge, Lamb confessed that as a critic he had been desultory and unsystematic, "suggestive merely, and content with fragments and scattered pieces of truth."[11]

S.R. Littlewood, however, felt that Lamb's essays, particularly "The Old Actors" and "On the Artificial Comedy of the Last Century" had possibly "made more people love the theatre than any criticism that has ever been written."[12] Edmund Blunden, moreover, felt that Lamb was the most "perceptive, bold, and appropriate" critic of the Elizabethan playwrights up to his day, and Brander Matthews considered it naïve to accept at face value Lamb's comment "that the plays of Shakespeare are less calculated for performance on a stage than those of almost any other dramatist whatever."[13] For example, Lamb's fervent recollections of many playgoing experiences belie the fact that he championed closet drama solely. Matthews also interpreted Lamb's praise of Restoration comedy as due to humorous exaggeration, a view that might have forestalled Thomas Babington Macaulay's moralistic attack on Lamb's acceptance of Congreve and Wycherley. Lamb's statement that Shakespeare's plays are much better read than acted suggests his appreciation of the great poetic content of the plays, as well as the poor status of stage representation in Lamb's day.

William Hazlitt, like Lamb, showed insight into Restoration comedy, which he preferred to Shakespearian comedy because it was less serious and more satirical and ridiculous. He differentiated wit from humour, and also endeavored to account for three stages of comic effect. The first, the laughable, arises out of an incongruity between one's expectation and the actual event. The next stage, the ludicrous, employs an incongruity accompanied by a deformity or inconvenience that is contrary to custom. The highest stage, the ridiculous, is a heightened effect of the previous two, violating not only custom but also common sense and reason.

Hazlitt believed that a critic's job was to communicate his personal feelings with gusto. Taste to him was subjective. Just as there are people who cannot enjoy olives, he said, he could not relish Ben Jonson. The danger of this method of impressionistic criticism is that an inspired critic who lacks taste can err badly. Also, this personalized approach does not permit an incremental growth from critic to critic until an entire body of critical thought is produced. But there is more system in Hazlitt's criticism than one might expect in a journalistic critic. He concerns himself with emotion, imagination, and symbolism as we would expect a romantic critic to do. His concern is at this point more on the equipment of the creative writer, however, than on the work itself. Despite heavy reliance on A.W. Schlegel, Hazlitt's treatment of Shakespeare shows considerable feeling for character and language. He is one of the first critics, for example, to bring out Shylock's argument in sympathetic light. Hazlitt's method is to go round and round a subject, always unveiling a little more, until finally the whole is revealed.

Like Hazlitt, Leigh Hunt concentrated much of his attention upon acting. According to William Archer, Hunt was "the first writer of any note who made it his business to see and report upon all the principal theatrical events of the day."[14] Hunt wrote a scathing satire on the venality of the critics of his day in *Rules for Theatrical Critic* (1807), where he said that reviews gave more attention to the boxholders' apparel than to the play itself, and gave most plaudits to the actors who furnished the finest dinners.

Contemporary English critics seemed to be strangely unaware of the critical revolution proceeding in the name of French romanticism. In 1831, for example, Leigh Hunt praised an adaptation of Hugo's *Hernani*, without knowing the author's name or what a challenge he had given to neoclassicism in his plays as well as in his criticism.

This condition soon changed. In 1843 Parliament, goaded by Edward Bulwer-Lytton, passed the Theatres Act, which broke the time-honored patent monopoly enjoyed by three London theaters. Within a generation London had twenty theaters, in addition to vaudeville stages and music halls. There was an instant market for more plays, more dramatists, and more critics. The absence of a copyright agreement made it economical to use adaptations of continental plays. Soon London was flooded with European drama.

Meanwhile the first important woman drama critic in England had made her appearance. Aphra Behn had written dramatic criticism in the seventeenth century, but none of it contained original ideas. Elizabeth Inchbald, on the other hand, made some real contributions. Her background as actress, dramatist, editor, and critic gave her a rich perspective for her work. In 1806-09 she edited a collection of old plays called *The British Theatre*. Her plays show her to be a not unworthy follower of the social comedy of Goldsmith and Sheridan. In criticism she is chiefly remembered for having edited *Collection of Farces*, a series of eighteenth century farces of character. Her biographer, S.R. Littlewood, says that "it was no mere accident that Dickens in his youth devoured Mrs. Inchbald's farces, and confessed afterwards how much he owed to them."[15]

By now the "rules" had received their death-blow in England. This was agreed to by such different persons as Francis Jeffrey, Sir Walter Scott, Cardinal Newman, and Robert Browning. Jeffrey chided Lord Byron for his claim that he observed the Three Unities in *Sardanapalus*. Said Jeffrey: "We have had a considerable contempt for those same Unities, ever since we read Dennis's criticism of *Cato* — except, indeed, the Unity of Action."[16] In his *Essay on the Drama* Scott similarly rejects the rules-yoked French for the independent Spaniards and Englishmen.

Browning, in *Aristophanes' Apology* (1875), discusses dramatic theory and practice and argues in favor of tragicomedy, which he says can move pity and fear as much as can tragedy. Browning postulates Shakespeare as the one ideal writer of tragicomedy. Herrick felt that John Henry Newman, especially in *Poetry, with Reference to Aristotle's Poetics* (1829), had produced as sane an interpretation of Aristotle as anyone in the nineteenth century. Instead of interminably quarreling over the relative merits of epic and tragedy or over drama's proper moral, "Newman has caught the investigative spirit of Aristotle,"[17] Herrick said, and thus applies this spirit sensitively to individual plays.

Only Matthew Arnold endeavored to resist the changing tide. Arnold wanted to restore the chorus, and he argued that Greek tragic laws, while not exhaustive, at least were "prophecies of the improbability of dramatic success under any other conditions."[18] George Meredith contrasted comedy with irony, farce, and satire. Meredith developed the idea that comedy is the corrective tool of common sense for combating vanity, egotism, and sentimentality.

Little new significant Shakespearian criticism appeared after the great romantic critics. Thomas Carlyle and Algernon Swinburne heaped extravagant praise upon Shakespeare. Edward Dowden traced Shakespeare's creative growth into four distinct periods. J.O. Halliwell-Phillipps worked mainly on Shakespeare's biography as revealed by contemporary records, and F.J. Furnivall evolved a chronological order of the plays in order to better perceive the oneness of Shakespeare.

George Henry Lewes, the common-law husband of George Eliot, wrote on topics as varied as philosophy, science, and drama. Besides a book on *The Spanish Drama* (1845), he wrote *On Actors and the Art of Acting* (1875). In the latter work he warned that "the drama in Europe and America is rapidly passing from an art into an amusement, just as of old it passed from a religious ceremony into art."[19] Lewes felt that the only hope to retain drama as an art form would be to have specialized theaters where the serious playgoers could see their fare, while permitting the popular theaters to appeal to the masses.

The acting of Henry Irving, in Shakespearian as well as other roles, elicited much criticism in the latter half of the century. Irving was primarily a romantic actor, highly original and with a magnetic personality, but with mannered speech and stage movement. The critic Clement Scott attacked his portrayal of Bulwer-Lytton's Richelieu, ignoring, in Littlewood's opinion, the limitations of the play itself.

An article called "To a Fashionable Tragedian" in *Fun* in 1875 accused Irving of canonizing murderers (in depicting them on stage) and in having a hireling press to praise him. "If your performance of Othello be trumpeted by the gang of time-serving reporters in your employ," the article stated, "you will increase the epidemic of wife-murder one hundred-fold."[20] Irving sued for libel and won an apology.

Irving's acting, in Littlewood's opinion, was "a standing refutation of the very false adage that 'all great acting is a return to nature.' Irving's acting was never a return to nature. The imaginative mask was never cast off,"[21] said Littlewood, but the audience was made to feel life's adventure in either hero or villain idealized by the power and the charm of the actor's personality.

Ibsen and the advent of modern drama set off a wholly new school of journalistic critics. William Archer translated and championed Ibsen's plays, though he himself, following Sarcey, was willing to let audience appeal measure a play's effectiveness. Having what H.G. Wells called "unscrupulous integrity," Archer helped introduce English audiences to the new, largely continental drama that became influential shortly before 1900. Besides his successful melodrama *The Green Goddess*, Archer wrote such critical works as *English Dramatists of Today* (1882), *About the Theatre* (1886), *Playmaking* (1912), and *The Old Drama and the New* (1923). Although he credits Sarcey with the first extensive use of the term *scène à faire*, or obligatory scene, it was Archer who developed the concept most fully. "An obligatory scene," says Archer, "is one which the audience foresees and desires, and the absence of which it may with reason resent."[22] He goes on to show how dramatists err in failing to stage scenes which are demanded by exigencies of the plot, by character growth and development, or by history, legend, theme, or the author's unconscious build-up toward such scenes. Archer also feels that Brunetière is mistaken: crisis, and not conflict, is the chief requirement of drama.

At this point Henry Arthur Jones, the playwright, offered his services as referee of the critical disagreement between Brunetière and Archer. Jones felt that Archer had shown satisfactorily, in such great plays as *Agamemnon*, *Oedipus*, and Ibsen's *Ghosts*, that Brunetière's dramatic law of conflict as the essence of drama seemed inadequate. But Jones also believed that when Archer admitted that "crisis" was too broad a term to account for dramatic effects (since some crises were undramatic), the crises which were dramatic were those accompanied by conflict, and so Jones felt he had reconciled the two viewpoints by synthesizing them.

Another playwright, Sir Arthur Pinero, felt that Robert Louis Stevenson failed as a dramatist because he refused to exert the intense effort and concentration required to get the peculiar compression without falsification that drama demands.

The new drama, particularly Ibsen's, had a stormy reception for years. Clement Scott, who liked Sardou and romantic melodrama, called *Ghosts* "a lazar-house with all its doors and windows open."²³ Despite Ibsen's valorous champions, his plays were not staged in the popular theater in England for years. Even Max Beerbohm quickly tired of Ibsen: "That is the dangerous thing about new ideas: they are old so soon."²⁴ But Beerbohm liked Shaw, and he wanted a drama of modern fantasy, of which he considered *The Admirable Crichton* the forerunner.

Ibsen's defenders included the four men called by S.R. Littlewood "the pioneers of modern dramatic criticism in England." These four are Archer, J.T. Grein, A.B. Walkley, and George Bernard Shaw. Grein was an indefatigable laborer for a public for sincere dramatic art. As founder of the Independent Theatre, he gave many new plays their first English audience. It was "in response to Grein's appeal for a native drama of contemporary relevance that Shaw turned from criticism to the theatre."²⁵ Walkley was a light-hearted opportunist who was more content to follow, than to lead, audience reaction. Walkley said that before assessing the merit of a play, the critic should consider the special conditions under which the dramatist worked, such things as the "peculiar psychology of the crowd he is addressing"²⁶ and the stage conditions of his theater. This caveat would keep critics from expecting the playwright to show conformity to external signs of modernity, Walkley felt. Shaw's regular stint as a dramatic critic came in the 1890's when his early plays (along with Ibsen's) were considered immoral, and so, as critic for *The Saturday Review*, he set himself the task of reforming public taste. Since Shakespeare was the "holy of holies," he decided that the new Temple of Taste could not be erected until the old one was destroyed. His vigorous polemics shocked many people, but at least he served to arouse many out of apathy. His chief targets, besides Shakespeare, were the "well-made" play and romantic melodrama. Littlewood concluded that "the success of Shaw's escapade as a dramatic critic has undoubtedly encouraged smaller people, without his qualifications or excuse, to get notoriety by reckless abuse."²⁷

Shaw felt that since Wagner had fused music and drama, the only future for drama without music lay in the "problem play" or the social drama. To him the theater was a means, not an end—it was the means for society's discussion toward improvement. Paradoxically, though Shaw thus agreed with Tolstoy on drama's social utility, he felt that the greatest dramatist (after himself) was Chekhov, a great artist of dramatic effect but scarcely the author of "problem plays."

The century also produced a number of lesser critics. Some of them, along with their works, are: William Hayley, *Dramatic Obser-*

vations (1811); Edward Mayhew, *Stage Effect* (1840); Percy Fitzgerald, *Principles of Comedy and Dramatic Effect* (1870); Theodore Martin, *Essays on the Drama* (1874); Morris Mowbray, *Essays in Theatrical Criticism* (1882); and Dutton Cook, *On the Stage* (1883).

On the whole, nineteenth century criticism in England started strongly, waned into mediocrity near mid-century, and then ended in a fresh demonstration of new life as modern drama began to appear. Scarcely any one statement of summary will adequately survey the period. The early decades witnessed intuitive flashes of insight that are still brilliant, if sometimes not wholly reliable, contributions to contemporary criticism. The romantic critics seem to have drawn their inspiration from two main sources, Shakespeare and German criticism. Later in the century French drama and criticism, particularly in connection with the "well made" play, made a deep impression. Finally, as Ibsen and other moderns began to appear, a healthy closeness of critic and playwright began to be evident. Many of the leading critics were also dramatists of some repute. By 1900 it was evident that the revolutionary nature of modern drama was straining Aristotelian formalistic criticism, even as modified by Lessing, Coleridge, and others, almost to the breaking point.

11. American Criticism Before 1920

American dramatic criticism, like American drama, can be said to be roughly two hundred years old by now. In 1714 the first play was published in America, *Androboros*, a satire written by Governor Robert Hunter of New York as an attack upon his political foes. The earliest kind of critical reaction toward drama, that voiced during colonial times, is negative. When Thomas Otway's *The Orphan* was performed at a coffee house in Boston in 1750, "Massachusetts authorities immediately passed a law forbidding any form of theatrical entertainment and establishing a schedule of fines to be levied against actors and owners of buildings where plays were performed."[1] To escape such censorship, David Douglass employed various disguises. For example, in Newport, Rhode Island, in June 1761 Douglass put on "a series of moral dialogues in five parts depicting the evil effects of jealousy."[2] This, of course, was really Shakespeare's *Othello*!

Douglass had merged two early American companies when he married the widow of another pioneer producer, Lewis Hallam. "With her as leading lady, with eighteen-year-old Lewis Hallam, Jr., as leading man, and with himself as manager, promoter, diplomat, builder, and actor, David Douglass became theatrical king of North America for almost twenty years."[3]

The three collaborators on *Ye Beare and Ye Cubb* in Virginia in 1665 were prosecuted for immorality, but ultimately acquitted. During the Revolutionary War, the Continental Congress several times introduced resolutions recommending the prohibition of public theatrical performances. On October 20, 1774, the Continental Congress passed a recommendation that the colonists discontinue "horse racing, gaming, cock fighting, plays, and other expensive diversions and entertainments."[4] Immediately Douglass and his company left for the West Indies. For the most part it appears as if the wishes of the Continental Congress were respected. Drama continued to be performed in British-occupied America. Both sides, of course, employed plays of political propaganda during the war.

Periodical criticism of drama existed as early as 1757 in *The Pennsylvania Gazette*. Philadelphia was an early dramatic center, not only because it was larger than New York City, but also because the latter city, being a major port, was the haven for many European theatrical people, and thus American actors and playwrights gathered in a place more likely to support them. Absence of copyright protection also flooded early America with foreign imports. The first copyright law offering dramatists protection against piracy was passed in 1856, and the international copyright law was finally adopted in 1891.

The first American comedy, *The Contrast* by Royall Tyler, elicited fairly sophisticated critical response. Signing himself "Candour," a reviewer in *The Daily Advertiser* for April 18, 1787, said that although "the characters are drawn with spirit and the dialogue is easy and often witty, the soliloquies are conducted so as to wound probability."[5] Colonel Manly's patriotic effusions are forced and unnatural, Candour feels, and would have been much more effective if worked into the dialogue sequence.

A group of New York City playgoers in 1796 began writing drama reviews in order, said William Dunlap in *A History of the American Theatre*, "to correct the abuses existing in the costume, demeanor, and general conduct of the actors on the stage."[6] These writers included Charles Adams, the son of President John Adams, and Peter Irving, the older brother of Washington Irving.

William Dunlap's contributions as scene painter, playwright, manager, producer, and drama historian were so profound as to cause Garff Wilson to label him "Father of the American Drama."[7] Among other things Dunlap wrote or adapted at least 56 plays. Although he knew Adams, Irving, and the other early critics, Dunlap objected to their technique of reporting. The group met after a play, each contributing a reaction, and all the last-name initials were signed to the review. In addition, a "D" was added, as if Dunlap were a member of the clique, which he was not. The group accused managers of employing claques or hired applauders. Severe in their dramatic expectations, the group asked for a national drama to express the new sentiments of democracy.

In the 1802–03 season a large amount of dramatic criticism began appearing in American periodicals. At that time Peter Irving published *Letters of Jonathan Oldstyle, Gent.*, in which his brother Washington, writing in Addisonian style, satirized the crudeness, pretense, and pomposity of the current drama. In 1807 Washington Irving founded *The Salmagundi*, in which he continued his satirical writing. He also wrote dramatic criticism for other periodicals. On the whole he was one of the most reliable drama critics of his time.

Written mostly by professors and scholars, the criticism of this period was highly moralistic. The editor of the *Theatrical Censor* wrote in 1806 that "the stage must refine our manners, enlarge our minds, and ennoble our hearts, or it must degrade and debase."[8] Some ministers called the theater "Satan's Synogogue." Lyman Beecher preached that the theater was "the center of the valley of pollution."[9]

These critics generally drew their views about drama from such neoclassical critics as Ben Jonson, John Dryden, and Samuel Johnson. Their style tended to follow that used by Joseph Addison and Richard Steele in their periodical writing.

As a town grew in size it would be a mark of achievement to form a resident stock company to stage plays. Various methods were used to persuade critics to give favorable reviews. Reporters and editors were given free season passes. Play managers often wrote paid press releases, called puffs, concerning their plays. Stage directors began to hire full-time publicity agents. At the Bowery Theatre in 1826 a "cold-cut room" offered the press food, beverages, and writing materials.

A drama critic uninfluenced by such bribery was Edgar Allan Poe. Poe quoted Calderón: "A man who has never seen the sun cannot be blamed for thinking that no glory can exceed that of the moon."[10] Then Poe added: "It is the business of the critic so to soar that he shall see the sun."[11]

Since he generally did not find the sun, Poe attacked most plays as being inartistic. He wanted verisimilitude, not stage conventions. He inveighed against asides, stage whispers, and soliloquies for being unnatural. He persistently pressed for esthetic rather than ethical standards. He believed that "conveying what is absurdly termed a moral should be left to the essayist and preacher."[12]

Mrs. Anna Cora Ritchie Mowatt was a playwright and actress whose play *Fashion*, a satire upon women's taste, was put on in New York City in 1845. Reviewing it for *The Broadway Journal*, Poe found it theatrical but undramatic because of its lack of verisimilitude. He found the influence of Elizabethan drama to be pernicious to the American theater. Attacking "the preposterous soliloquizing and the even more preposterous asides,"[13] Poe stated that "we must discard all models. We need principles of dramatic action drawn not from the 'old dramatists,' but from the fountain of a Nature that can never grow old."[14]

Finding flaws in Shakespeare, Poe wants to know "why there is so very, very much which he has utterly failed to accomplish."[15] What we need, says Poe, is to electrify mankind by a play which would synthesize tragedy, comedy, farce, opera, melodrama, and spectacle. One wonders whether similar calls issued later by Richard Wagner and Antonin Artaud would have pleased him. Even if all other arts should pass away, Poe said, man would still need drama because it is the highest of the arts, being their synthesis.

As editor of *The Brooklyn Daily Eagle* from 1846 to 1848, Walt Whitman attacked the vulgarity of New York theaters. He castigated writers of puffs, saying that five of every six reviews were written before the performance! He called upon the American theater to rid itself of slavish dependence upon British plays, actors, and directors. He preferred the Americans, Charlotte Cushman and Henry Placide, to the English actors then touring America, Charles Kean and his wife, Ellen Tree.

Although Whitman deplored "the miserable state" of the American theater, he defended drama as an institution: "The drama has been, and still must be, a great element in the amusement and instructive agencies of civilized life."[16] To him the American theater was a school for democracy. Whitman's quarrel with Shakespeare is that "he stands entirely for the mighty esthetic sceptres of the past, not for the spiritual and democratic, the sceptres of the future."[17] Shakespeare's comedies, in Whitman's opinion, "are altogether nonacceptable to America and Democracy, made for the divertisement only of the elite of the castle and from its point of view."[18] To achieve its high mission, drama required impartial and independent criticism. He thus felt that the young nation should take pains to develop trained drama critics who could exercise their office responsibly.

By mid-century changes were occurring in theatrical conditions. Improvements in transportation, especially the railroad and the steamboat, made it possible for dramatic companies to travel with their casts and sets. Before long there were 100 traveling companies taking plays throughout the land. Several results ensued. The quality of resident companies declined under the competition. Traveling companies developed the star system, taking nationally famous stars to outlying communities, letting the resident companies provide the minor roles. Periodicals now started offering dramatic criticism for a national audience. This, in turn, encouraged newspapers and magazines to develop specialists in the art of writing play reviews.

One such specialist was J.W.S. Hows, professor of elocution at Columbia, who was drama critic for *The Albion* in the 1840's. A believer in the classical style, Hows denounced the American tragedian Edwin Forrest for over-acting. Hows is credited with helping the actress Anna Cora Mowatt eliminate artificial and declamatory elements from her acting style.

From 1846 to 1859 Richard Grant White wrote drama criticism for the *New York Courier Enquirer*. As an editor of Shakespeare, White was the first American to prepare an edition of Shakespeare compiled from original sources. Like Hows, White wrote basically as a moralist trying to reform the American theater.

Controversy over acting styles could lead to bloodshed in nineteenth century America. The masses had grown to prefer the baroque declamation of Edwin Forrest and the forceful masculine style of Charlotte Cushman. The upper-class theatergoers appreciated more fully the polished and intellectual style of the English actor William C. Macready. On May 10, 1849, occurred the Astor Place Riot, pitting the followers of Forrest against the proponents of Macready. Twenty-two lives were lost as the interior of the theater was destroyed, and the professional reputations of both men were stained. Macready, in fact, never again acted in America.

Two new actors benefited from the vacuum. Edwin Booth launched a successful career with a style of acting, according to Tice L. Miller, "more graceful and dignified than Forrest's, but with more passion and power than Macready."[19] Matilda Heron electrified the audience as the sensational Camille, the virtuous "fallen woman" of Victorien Sardou's melodrama adapted from the novel, *The Lady of the Camelias* by the younger Alexander Dumas. Unlike Booth, Heron's popularity was short-lived.

The French influence upon American drama became very marked in the 1850's for several reasons. First was the vivid theatricality of French plays. Next was the fact that many French plays used risqué themes, even daring to represent characters of questionable sex habits. Finally, the plays were easily pirated because of inadequate copyright laws.

In 1855 the French actress, Mlle. Rachel, toured the United States playing *Camille* as well as plays by Corneille, Racine, and Eugène Scribe, and many French romantic melodramas. The Irish-born actor, playwright, and director Dion Boucicault made a living out of Anglicizing French plays. *Les Pauvres de Paris* had instant appeal as *The Poor of New York*, *The Poor of Boston*, or the poor of whatever town in which the melodrama was staged.

Playwright and director Augustin Daly was responsible for forty-four adaptations of French plays from 1865 to 1900. Cynical Ambrose Bierce defined a dramatist as "one who adapts plays from the French."[20]

Another order of drama also appeared at this time. Taking his plot from Dante, George Henry Baker wrote the verse tragedy, *Francesca da Rimini*, which appeared in New York and Philadelphia in 1855. Arthur Hobson Quinn said that "the art with which the medieval Italian life is depicted, the music of the verse, and the noble conception of Lanciotto, the wronged husband and brother, lift this tragedy to its deserved place in the first rank of verse dramas written in the English language during the nineteenth century."[21]

By 1855 a group of New York City critics who considered themselves bohemians met regularly at Charlie Pfaff's Restaurant and Bier Saloon at 647 Broadway to discuss plays and their reactions to them. Their common opposition to Boston Brahminism gave them a unity that transcended their individual quirks and preferences. They championed French drama and French criticism in spirited, impressionistic reviews. They were noted for individuality, aggressiveness, and subjectivity. Led by Henry Clapp, Jr., the group included Charles B. Seymour, drama critic of the *New York Times* and Edward H. House, drama critic of the *New York Tribune*. Others who attended were Thomas Bailey Aldrich, George Arnold, Fitz-James O'Brian, Edward G.P. Wilkins, and William Winter. Blue-stocking members included feminist Ada Clare and actress Adah Isaacs Menken. Walt Whitman, William Dean Howells, and Artemus Ward occasionally dropped by for conviviality and inspiration. Howells considered the gathering at Pfaff's to be the brightest new literary life in the city. The Civil War pretty well dispersed the group, and by 1865 they had no more than their individual identities.

Having lived for several years in the Latin Quarter of Paris,

Henry Clapp, Jr., brought credentials as a bohemian that other group members envied. His best criticism he wrote under the signature Figaro for *The Leader* from 1861 to 1869, as well as his work for the *New York Weekly Review* in 1865 and for the *Saturday Press* in 1865-66.

Clapp founded the *Saturday Press* in 1858 as a rival to the *Atlantic*, and it was one until its collapse in 1860 due to faulty business procedures. Later he revived it for a short period.

Clapp's position was that drama should appeal to more than simply the intellect. Thus to him ballet, pantomime, music — in fact, everything that appeals to the senses — was a legitimate part of drama. He espoused the French melodrama, especially *Camille*. He praised Charles Kean for his natural style of acting, which achieved greater emotional depth by deliberately holding back some of the gestures. He liked Forrest more than Booth, because of Forrest's virility and long experience in the theater, but he found Booth promising in such Shakespearian roles as Hamlet and Richard III. In Clapp's opinion Joe Jefferson had no equal as an eccentric low comedian.

Clapp's last years were tragic. Penniless, he turned to drink and ended up in the New York City asylum on Wards Island. He who had been a radical temperance writer died an alcoholic. But his influence upon American writers was profound. Among the rising young authors he helped were Whitman, Mark Twain, Howells, Artemus Ward, Thomas Bailey Aldrich, and many others.

Edward G.P. Wilkins had the most promise of all of the bohemian critics. From 1853 to 1861 he was dramatic editor of the *New York Herald*. Since his editor, James Gordon Bennett, hated England and admired the South, Wilkins never does justice to British plays or actors, and never mentions racially-oriented drama like *Uncle Tom's Cabin* or Dion Boucicault's *The Octoroon*. Since the *Herald* was America's largest newspaper, Wilkins was the most widely read critic of his time.

To show how Wilkins tailored his criticism to please his boss, one can contrast his praise of Charlotte Cushman in the *Herald* for her fire and emotional depth with his attack on her "awkward poses" and "vulgar gestures" in *The Leader*. Wilkins disliked the star system and hence the star, Cushman. "He seemed less enraged by her style of acting," says Tice L. Miller, "than by her lack of artistic development and her selfishness towards the rest of her profession."[22]

Wilkins also wrote plays, chiefly satires on the *nouveau riches*. His criticism of three versions of *Camille* is an accurate mirror of the taste of his time: Jean Davenport's version seemed inconsistent to him, since it omitted all reference to her sexual improprieties. Matilda Heron's version he attacked as a "deification of prostitution"; "it is morally impossible," he said, "that such a person as she represents could have made such a sacrifice."[23] Laura Keene's version was the one Wilkins preferred, for by making the sex scenes a dream it kept the play "fresh, natural, unconventional, and vigorous."

Despite his professed rejection of New England puritanism, Wilkins had an underlying moral tone in his critical reviews. But he continually merged three strains into some of the best criticism of his time: the French critical approach, popular journalistic style, and Yankee common sense. Unfortunately he died of pneumonia at the age of 31.

Probably the most influential nineteenth century drama critic in America was William Winter. In his reviews for the *Saturday Press*, Winter used the meat-axe on plays he disliked. Later he mellowed and was more even tempered. His law degree perhaps gave him the ability to see more than one side of an issue.

Winter's background in dramatic criticism was excellent. He knew the works of Aristotle, Samuel Johnson, Coleridge, Lamb, and Hazlitt. He was also widely read in contemporary theater reviews. His style, however, was somewhat pedantic, lacking the verve of Wilkins.

Winter considered acting to be the primary art of the theater. The actor's chief requisite was personal integrity, he felt. Thus, after admitting Forrest's talent, attractiveness, and strength, he said Forrest fell short of greatness because of lack of character. At first Winter found Edwin Booth to be an uncouth genius, but in later years he applauded Booth for personal magnetism and controlled power.

Winter gave special notice to Charlotte Cushman. "No woman in the theatre of this period," he said, "shows the inspirational fire, the intellect, the dominant character and the abounding genius—rising to great heights and satisfying the utmost demands of great occasions—that were victorious and imperial in Charlotte Cushman."[24]

Cushman often played Romeo opposite her sister Susan's Juliet. At the age of 21 Charlotte played Romeo in New York City but only after she had made a hit in other roles in London eight years later did Winter find that "her performance elicited in England fervent admiration."[25]

When the popular press condemned the stage for the actor John Wilkes Booth's assassination of Lincoln, Winter fervently defended the theater as a bastion of morality. As a matter of fact, Winter advanced this view in his attack upon French plays involving sex. "The stage is not a place for the analysis of moral ulcers," he stated. "The sole refuge of this age is art, and that should be kept pure and beautiful. What we need on stage is what will cheer, and comfort, and strengthen!"[26]

Winter's outlook was standard for his period. Ralph Waldo Emerson stated that the office of the poet is to inspire. William Dean Howells said that the novelist should confine himself to "the smiling aspects of life." Longfellow, a close friend of Winter, wrote the sort of poetry embodied in this artistic credo.

As a spokesman for newspaper drama critics, Winter defended his coterie against attacks levied by Dion Boucicault in 1889. Boucicault accused critics of being both corrupt and detrimental to the theater. He said they were generally incompetent and biased. Newspapers, said Boucicault, had usurped the public's rightful role as drama's judges.

Winter conceded that neither the press nor the public showed very good judgment in evaluating plays, but he argued that newspapers were not corrupting public taste since they had little influence upon their readers. He believed that newspapers play their role properly if they stimulate their readers, help them clarify their views, and aid them in a growing appreciation of dramatic art.

The new drama of the late nineteen century was too frank for Winter. He abhorred the plays of Ibsen, Shaw, Pinero, and Sudermann. "It is not the province of the stage to photograph the surfaces of actual life," he said. "Art implies selection."[27]

Ibsen's *Ghosts* Winter called "unmitigated filth," and Shaw's *Candida* he labeled "reckless, mischievous, conceited, and vicious sophistry." When the American actor Arnold Daly was acquitted in a trial for immorality for having staged Shaw's *Mrs. Warren's Profession* in New Haven in 1905, Winter disagreed with the verdict, saying, "No right-minded, well-bred person introduces an indelicate, not to say foul, subject for conversation in a drawing room."[28] Sentiment, said George Hellman, played a great part in the writings of this "brave antagonist of all the blatant and insidious influences which drag down the art of a nation."[29] All told, Winter wrote over fifty books, many of them on the theater. Included were biographies of such figures as Richard Mansfield and David Belasco as well as stage reminiscences, studies of Shakespeare, and collections of his reviews. In his long career he served the theater faithfully if not always wisely. Harrison Grey Fiske, the editor of *Dramatic Mirror*, probably summarized the views of most of his contemporaries when he accused Winters of "hopelessly confusing the duties of the reviewer with those of the moralist."[30]

Another critic who had been trained in law was Stephen Ryder Fiske, who was also a playwright. Managers liked to produce plays written by critics, since it tended to get critics on their side. Critics generally needed the money, and could earn up to ten times their weekly salaries by adapting or translating plays. Boucicault would permit a critic to insert a couple of lines in one of his plays just so he could copyright the play under both their names. This assured Boucicault of at least one favorable critical review! Fiske attacked Boucicault for this practice. In general, Fiske felt that writing plays and criticizing them made for a bad mixture, since fellow critics were placed in an awkward position, and managers who did not stage his play might suffer retribution from the rejected critic.

Like Winter, Fiske attacked the new drama. He considered Zola's *Thérèse Raquin* to be false to both art and nature. "American girls will not go to a theatre," he said, "to see a hussy and her paramour murder her husband and then undress themselves and sit by the fire and talk about it. No father will take his daughters, no lover will escort his sweetheart to look at this sort of unveiled vileness."[31]

A controversy raged in the 1880's over whether an actor needed to deeply feel an emotion in order to portray it. A translation of Diderot's *The Paradox of Acting* fed the fire of the negative side of the issue. In 1888, however, William Archer's *Masks or Faces? A Study in the Psychology of Acting* supplied ammunition for those supporting this assumption.

Fiske felt that actors were but a small part of the play's effect. Theirs was an imitative rather than a creative art, he felt. He also attacked actors as being poor citizens—they seldom attend church or pay taxes, they usually do not vote, and they are not very patriotic, he believed.

He did, however, praise the English actor and manager, Henry Irving. Irving, he said, produced good new plays, revived worthy old ones, took an active interest in all of the arts, and improved the social position of actors. In fact, he said, Irving did more to give the American theater dignity and importance than any American.

Two big interruptions to the theater year were the circus and Lent. Each spring Barnum's Circus emptied the theaters in many towns. It bothered Fiske that certain churchgoers boycotted the theater but not the opera during Lent. "Fashion," he said, "not religion, has decreed that for forty days and forty nights 400 persons may go to the opera to hear how Wagner's heroes married their own sisters, but must not go to the wicked theatres."[32]

Fiske suggested a compromise, which worked at least in the year 1897. Theaters were open in Lent except for Ash Wednesday and Good Friday; attendance was good in the intervening period.

Just as in American industry, the movement towards combination of theaters led to a virtual monopoly of American theaters by a syndicate. In 1896 a theatrical syndicate tried to control all theatrical booking. By 1903 seventy of the largest theaters were owned by the syndicate, which also had indirect control, through booking contracts, of an additional 700 theaters. Much good was accomplished by the syndicate, such as eliminating double bookings, broken engagements, and road shows going bankrupt. But since the ultimate criterion was dollar profit, little consideration was given a play's merit.

Most critics attacked the syndicate, but Fiske did not. He said that the syndicate offered the public "more theatres and better theatres; more new plays, more new stars, more performances, and in some respects better performances than we ever had before."[33]

Fiske approached the theater not so much as an art form but as a kind of mass entertainment. A shrewd judge of public taste, he knew the public's needs, wants, and fears. Unlike most of his contemporary critics, he demanded that the theater be run in a thoroughly professional manner. Arthur Hornblow in the *Dramatic Mirror* called Fiske "a reliable prophet concerning the fate of a new play." Lewis Rosenthal of the *New York Telegram* said that Fiske's critical comments were "acute, crisp, and trenchant."

Andrew C. Wheeler was the chief drama critic for the *New York World* in the 1880's when its circulation made it America's largest newspaper. Since his paper appealed largely to the working class and small businessmen, Wheeler tried to appeal to their interests. He also wrote plays; his most successful (written with E.M. Alfriend) was *The Great Diamond Robbery* in 1895.

Wheeler drew heavily upon such French critics as Mme. de Staël, Sainte-Beuve, and Hippolyte Taine. Whereas William Winter tended to follow the English romantic critics, Wheeler liked the

French emphasis on the importance of nationality, epoch, and milieu. Wheeler felt that his more scientific approach judged an artistic work by its intended effect rather than on how it fit into some preconceived theory.

Wheeler differed with Winter in judging *Camille*. Because the courtesan's degenerate life came to a pitiful death Wheeler called it "one of the most moral of plays." He did, however, consider *Rip Van Winkle* to be an immoral play because a lazy drunkard was rewarded more than his industrious wife. Scientific approach or not, Wheeler apparently felt that literary justice must prevail.

Wheeler recommended the French plays, because they dealt with modern problems. He did not see drama as something to elevate or inspire mankind. Like the newspapers, it should keep up with the latest trends. "What we want is more nowness in the serious drama,"[34] he wrote in 1886. He attacked the Genteel movement in American literature, saying that Genteel writers substituted sentimentalism for passion and cold intellectuality for emotion. Paradoxically, Wheeler had no use for Ibsen's drama. He scored Ibsen for such alleged faults as didacticism, slow moving plots, and pessimism.

Wheeler felt that Richard Wagner's stress upon ensemble effect and a synthesis of the arts led to downgrading acting into an inferior role. But Wheeler praised Eleanora Duse for tenderness, sincerity, and lack of clichés in her acting. Duse, he felt, *was* the character she portrayed.

In his final years Wheeler did an about face. After the death of his first wife he married the young actress, Jennie Pearl Mowbray. Since she was very religious, he became so too. He even took her maiden name and wrote under the pseudonym of J.P. Mowbray. He quit the theater and wrote popular novels, nature tracts, and religious pamphlets. "He sadly deplored the loss of simple faith and hope which allowed civilization as well as individual man to enjoy life more,"[35] wrote Tice L. Miller. "The new idolatry is Brains," Wheeler said, "but what has become of the Peace that passeth understanding?"[36]

In his final years Wheeler even deplored newspaper critics, because he felt that they ignored what is true for what is current. Years of "superficial chronicling," he said, had devaluated dramatic art until now the stars were mere "playthings of the public."

While the newspaper critics were pounding out their regular reactions to stage fare, more academic persons were also trying to elevate the popular taste for drama. Perhaps most important of these was the poet, essayist, and diplomat James Russell Lowell. As a critic, Lowell never quite lost his early impressionism. He confessed that he always looked first for certain qualities in a writer, such as naturalness, simplicity, sincerity, and humor, without which no great work could be achieved.

To prepare himself to give a series of lectures at Harvard, Lowell in 1854 made a serious study of literary art. Two results ensued: Harvard placed Shakespeare into its regular curriculum, and Lowell developed a very conscious sense of what constituted organic form in literature.

Lowell's critical position derives from Aristotle, Coleridge, and the Germans, especially Goethe. Like Aristotle, he based his comments on actual plays rather than on purely theoretic grounds. "It is the Greeks," said Lowell, "who must furnish us with our standards of comparison."[37] He felt that the successful critic needed sensitivity, historical awareness, and combined esthetic-ethical judgment. Although Shakespeare may have written with no avowed moral purpose, "yet, with a temperament so just, an insight so inevitable as his, it was impossible that the moral reality, which underlies the poet's vision, should not always be suggested,"[38] Lowell felt. And Shakespeare's humor and satire are never destructive, said Lowell, because of his light touch — puffing away foibles with the breath of a clown, or "shivering them with the light laugh of a genial cynic."[39]

Another academic critic, George William Curtis, answered Wheeler's charge that Rip Van Winkle was an immoral character. Curtis, editor of *Harper's Weekly* and later of the "Easy Chair" department of *Harper's Magazine*, said that Joe Jefferson so charmed viewers with his depiction of the lazy Rip that we find his shrewish wife objectionable. No matter how wretched or lowdown a person may be, said Curtis, there is an inherent human dignity about him that demands that he be given a certain amount of respect.

"Harvard has taken a leading part in the modern revival of Attic drama,"[40] said classical historian John Edwin Sandys. He found that a performance there in 1881 in the original Greek was admirably acted. "Art and archeology, as well as scholarship, united in making the presentation perfect in every detail,"[41] Sandys felt.

Bronson Howard, a successful playwright, often wrote about how he revised his plays to give them more universal appeal. Montrose J. Moses, who called Howard the Dean of American

Drama, said that Howard was a pioneer in the drama of contemporary manners. In "The Autobiography of a Play," Howard describes how he revised *Lillian's Last Love* into *The Banker's Daughter*. The major revision was greater stress on the love story in order to provide more universal appeal. Howard's most successful play, *Shenandoah*, a Civil War love story, was also a revision of a play of Howard's that had failed many years previously.

The first American dramatist to make a fortune out of writing plays, Howard said that his plays were the combined effort of the theater manager, the literary attaché, and himself. Most large theaters had a literary attaché, who generally revised and sometimes rewrote all of the plays put on at his theater.

In 1886 Howard lectured at Harvard on "the laws of the drama." Howard added to strictures on the "well made" play a number of suggestions concerning stage directions, sets, and other practical matters. In 1890 Howard founded the American Dramatists Club, a professional organization to help playwrights communicate with one another. Two things were especially harmful to the dramatists: the star system was warping plays around popular actors, and traveling companies were growing monopolistic, giving a few Americans control over most theaters in the larger cities. A few years later, when the syndicate was broken, actors and playwrights once again had greater control over their own destinies.

Other American playwrights also voiced their views on drama. Augustin Daly constantly deplored the poverty of American plays, but just as regularly went abroad for his choice of plays to stage in his theater. James A. Herne argued for greater realism in character portrayal, and Augustus Thomas often prefixed discussions of dramatic technique to his plays.

Dion Boucicault took particular aim at the drama critic. In an article in the *North American Review* in 1877 called "The Decline of the Drama" Boucicault made his complaints against critics specific. They were: first, by giving readers ready-made opinions, critics deprived the public of their responsibility for making their own judgments; second, newspaper critics stressed what was racy and readable rather than what was exact; and finally, critics tended to kowtow to an editorial line, thus providing incomplete and sometimes false appraisals of the plays reviewed. Surprisingly some of the New York newspapers, such as *The Mirror*, acknowledged the accuracy of Boucicault's charges.

Several novelists who were also interested in drama wrote

occasional dramatic criticism. In a review of Boucicault's *The Shaughraun* in *The Nation* in 1875, Henry James decided that the perennial American interest in Irish plays was due to the fact that "an Irish drama is always agreeably exciting."[42] Declaring Boucicault's acting to be "simply exquisite," James felt that this play could well deserve a run of four or five months.

William Dean Howells congratulated the comic playwright-actor-director Edward Harrigan on his versatility and his truthfulness. "Consciously or unconsciously," Howells said, "he is part of the great tendency toward the faithful representation of life which is now animating fiction."[43]

Several other now-forgotten names were influential a century ago. Henry Austin Clapp served as drama critic of the *Boston Daily Advertiser* from 1868 to 1902. Known through the country, Clapp was a sturdy defender of Genteel manners and morals. So was John Ranken Towse, the drama critic of the *New York Evening Post* from 1874 to 1926. Towse believed that the theater could not evade its responsibility as "an elevator of public mind and morals," and thus should "illustrate and enforce the soundest principles of art, morality, and social law under the seductive guise of entertainment."[44]

Towse and other critics had high praise for the acting ability of John Gilbert (1810–1889). Towse believed that Gilbert's role as Sir Anthony Absolute in Sheridan's *The Rivals* "has never been equalled anywhere in the last half century."[45] In the view of William Winter, Gilbert gave "the best performance of Caliban that ever was seen in America."[46] Brander Matthews said, "I have never seen, nor has anyone else in the past half-century, any rendering of Sir Peter Teazle in Sheridan's *The School for Scandal* comparable with John Gilbert's."[47]

Laurence Hutton wrote many books on the theater in an informal, impressionistic style. He edited five volumes of the *American Actor Series*, and gave some good advice on how to build a native American drama in *Curiosities of the American Theatre*, published in 1891.

The rapid growth of newspapers in America made the role of newspaper critic a very influential one. In 1880 the United States had 7000 daily newspapers. The *New York World* under Joseph Pulitzer achieved a daily circulation of 189,000 by 1887, and shortly thereafter William Randolph Hearst's *New York Journal* surpassed the *World*. In 1900 there were twenty-five regular newspaper drama critics in New York City alone.

The newspaper drama critic in larger cities became a well-known personality. Frequently he was asked to write prefaces to books, and his picture appeared on billboards. His role was a broad one. He not only informed the public concerning plays and actors, but he provided a public forum for debating vital esthetic issues, and he reflected his society's concern for art, morality, and their interconnections.

Their limitations were readily apparent. They were forced to write hurried reviews. Often they were reporters with little background in the theater. They generally followed the editor's (or publisher's) whims. Sometimes they reviewed only those plays that purchased advertising. But they unquestionably developed a wider market for drama, preparing for the age of cinema. And they occasionally discovered critical insights of importance in the understanding of dramatic art.

In the forefront of academic critics in the early years of the twentieth century were Brander Matthews, George Pierce Baker, and Joel E. Spingarn. Brander Matthews, the first professor of dramatic literature in America (at Columbia from 1900 to 1924), wrote many works on drama that helped gain a wider audience for plays. Since he himself wrote plays, his criticism tends to follow theatrical requirements quite closely. Matthews edited old plays and founded several dramatic societies. He also wrote widely on behalf of a number of American dramatists and their plays.

George Pierce Baker, long an influential teacher at Harvard and at Yale, believed that the essentials of drama were action and emotion. His students included, among others, Eugene O'Neill, Philip Barry, Sidney Howard, Robert Edmond Jones, and John Mason Brown. Baker felt that even cultivated audiences were more interested in plot action than in subtle characterization or witty dialogue.

Joel E. Spingarn, another Columbia professor, objected to the current talk about "dramatic technique," *scènes à faire*, and audience influence — the sort of thing that concerned William T. Price in his American School of Playwriting founded in 1900. "What the unities, decorum, *liaison des scènes*, and kindred petty limitations and restrictions were to dramatic theory in the seventeenth and eighteenth centuries," said Spingarn, "these things are to criticism in the nineteenth and twentieth. They constitute the new pedantry, against which all criticism, as well as all creative literature, must wage a battle for life."[48] Studying "laws of the drama" rather than plays would be like a lover studying "laws of love" rather than his lady's beauty,

Spingarn said. So he asked for "creative criticism," that would put aside moralizing in favor of an esthetic evaluation resulting from a sensitive critic's creative identification with the drama. Ludwig Lewisohn, meanwhile, also took American critics and playwrights to task for being unimaginative and overly conventional.

Since 1900 America has suffered no dearth of critics, many of them talented and stimulating writers. Some of these would be James Huneker, Percy Hammond, Walter Pritchard Eaton, and Norman Hapgood. Huneker was an iconoclast whose eclectic taste in music and drama helped introduce many European masterpieces to American theatergoers. Discussing Ibsen, Huneker said, "Life is a huge misunderstanding, and the Ibsen dramas hinge on misunderstandings. If his characters are sick, so is latter-day life. In Ibsen there rage the thinker, the artist, the critic. These sometimes fail to amalgamate, and so the artistic precipitation is cloudy."[49] Percy Hammond, also an individualist, thought that critics could never satisfy actors. Actors covet praise, said Hammond, but the critic who gives it must beware because "the more you praise an actor, the more he despises you."

Dramatizations of novels have always been popular in America. Usually the stage adaptation is made by someone other than the novelist, someone who knows more about the theater. During this period the leading novelists, such as Henry James, Howells, and Twain, all tried their hand at drama and failed. Sometimes their novels became successful plays in the hands of an adroit adapter.

An interesting reversal of this process occurred in the early years of this century. A number of popular plays were turned into successful novels, generally written by someone other than the playwright. Many of the plays of David Belasco, for example, were first read by the public in novel form. Critics sometimes sharpened their acumen by comparing the stage version to its derivative novel.

The leading American playwright was now Clyde Fitch, who, in an essay, "The Play and the Public," described his credo. "Be truthful," he said. "Reflect the real thing with true observation and sincere feeling, that is art in a modern play."[50] Walter Pritchard Eaton gave Fitch credit for the fact that now the majority of plays being staged in America were of American origin. "Mr. Fitch's plays," said Eaton, "will afford twenty, fifty, a hundred years hence a more authentic and vivid record of American life from 1890 to 1910 than any other documents."[51]

Brander Matthews predicted that historians of American drama would find that the maturation of the American theater at this time was retarded by these events: the premature deaths of Clyde Fitch and William Vaughn Moody, and the premature birth of Bronson Howard. Although he had enjoyed commercial success, Fitch died just as he was developing the sort of skill shown in the third act of *The Girl with the Green Eyes*, "a masterpiece of dramaturgic skill and of psychologic veracity."[52] Matthews described Moody as "a poet who was conscientiously acquiring the art of the playwright when his career was cut short."[53] Bronson Howard, said Matthews, had theatrical instinct and a keen sense of character. But unfortunately in his day there was more stress on speed and cleverness than on careful construction and long-lasting appeal, and so already his plays seem shallow and dated.

During this period, not a fruitful one for American drama, American theater thrived prodigiously. The influence of such seminal modern playwrights as Ibsen, Strindberg, and Chekhov paved the way for a renewed interest in the art of the theater. The Little Theater movement tended to bring spontaneous drama into nearly every village in the country. Public reading of plays became popular. Books on the history of the theater and of drama appeared. Colleges introduced courses in drama, and also instituted their own theatrical groups. Even adult educational programs like Chautauqua began to stress plays. The country was preparing for the dramatic renaissance of the 1920's.

One playwright, Percy MacKaye, tried to instigate a "people's drama" through civic pageants. Although his idea seemed a good one, his own masques and pageants seemed to be too scholarly for mass appeal, as did his poetic dramas. But he reminded Americans of the fundamental appeal of the mimetic urge.

In contrast to the Revolutionary War, the federal government in World War I encouraged drama. Each army camp had a Liberty Theater, to which amateur and professional acting groups were sent. Also, soldiers wrote, acted, and directed their own plays. Community theaters were established near army camps. Now the government found such amusement as drama to be a wartime necessity, and also resolved to install permanent theaters on every peacetime army base. Some credit for the tremendous change in attitude by the American public toward drama would have to go to the newspaper critics whose standards may have been suspect but whose constant output educated their readers into a changed posture.

12. Russian Criticism

Like most drama, Russian plays had their origin in the church. After witnessing the mystery plays he saw at a synod in Florence in 1439, Avraamy, Bishop of Suzdal, described his reaction enthusiastically. He gives a full account of the plots, which dealt with the Annunciation and the Ascension, but he seemed particularly impressed by the pulley system used to raise and lower angels.

The Russian Orthodox Church rites lend themselves to drama less than their Greek and Roman counterparts. There was thus no well developed medieval church drama in Russia, as there was in western Europe.

By 1600 schools in western Russia were staging Latin or Polish plays from western Europe. These plays, which went first to the Kiev Academy and then on to Moscow, resembled medieval miracle and mystery plays. By 1650 they were a standard part of the school system in western Russia. Shortly thereafter the Kiev Academy taught principles of neoclassical dramatic criticism, as they had evolved in Italy and France. There seemed to be little reaction between the critical principles and the school drama. A puppet theater also flourished in the Ukraine at this time.

In 1672 Czar Alexis asked Dr. Gregori, Lutheran pastor of the German Liberty in Moscow, to form a troupe of amateur actors. The German repertoire was translated into stilted Church Slavonic.

The first significant Russian drama, according to Prince D.S. Mirsky, occurred around the year 1700. Demetrius of Rostov wrote some excellent, if baroque, religious verse drama, at times even mixing humor and realistic dialogue into his sacred plots. In 1705 Theophan Prokopovich wrote a tragicomedy *Saint Vladimir* modeled after Italian Renaissance drama. Though the play tells the story of Vladimir's acceptance of Christianity in 989, there are political overtones—Vladimir resembles Peter the Great in using his power to choose Christianity over the opposition of heathen priests who bear a striking similarity to Roman Catholic and ultra-Conservative priests opposing Peter.

Under Peter the Great, the German influence continued. Public theaters opened with chiefly German plays, and the school drama continued in the seminaries and academies.

Russian dramatic criticism was still virtually non-existent. There were folk plays, which were considered to be beneath criticism, church plays, which were considered to be above criticism, and court spectacles, which in Russia were beyond criticism.

The first regular Russian tragedy was *Khorev*, written by Alexander Sumarokov in 1749. The play, which followed classical French standards, was acted before Empress Elizabeth by players from the Cadet School. Sumarokov also wrote the first serious dramatic criticism, an "Epistle on the Art of Poetry" which closely follows Boileau's *Art of Poetry*. Admitting that he had also learned much from Racine, Sumarokov said that he had to be his own guide as far as the Russian language was concerned, since there was no other work on the topic that he could consult.

Russia's first regular acting troupe was formed at this time at Yaroslavl by Feodor Volkov. Hearing of them, Elizabeth called them to St. Petersburg where in 1756 they established the first permanent Russian theater. Sumarokov became its director and Volkov its leading actor. For stage fare Sumarokov wrote adaptations of French plays. The acting continued to be better than the plays, according to Mirsky, especially during the time of the great tragic actor Dmitrevsky.

In 1762 Catherine the Great released the nobility from many of their governmental responsibilities. With new time on their hands, many of them turned their attention to the arts, including drama. Russia's first great play, *The Minor* by Denis Fonvizin, appeared in 1782. Like all classical Russian comedies, it has a pair of virtuous but dull lovers. Its fame derives from its trenchant satire on the crudeness and barbarity of uneducated country gentry trying to rear their son and failing miserably.

As a sign of the paucity of Russian criticism is the fact that the first Russian periodical devoted exclusively to the theater was published in German in 1789 as *Russische Theatralien*.

As one might expect, Russophiles clamored for a native Russian drama, free from French and German influence. The actor and playwright P.A. Plavilshchikov wrote an appeal for native drama in the periodical *Spectator* in 1792. "What boots it to a Russian," he asked, "to know that some Tatar Genghis Khan conquered China and performed many noble exploits there? We have our own manners, our own nature, and consequently we ought to have our own tastes."[1]

Despite the fact that it was considered unpatriotic to support French plays during the Napoleonic wars, French and German plays predominated on the Russian stage. The sentimental plays of the German August von Kotzebue were especially popular in the early 1800's. When Kotzebue was appointed director of the German theater in St. Petersburg, his influence spread even more widely. Other dramatic forms that were popular were melodrama and musical comedy. Since many Russians were illiterate, the stage provided the only literary technique by which they might be reached. Theater as education became a longstanding Russian tradition.

Vasily Zhukovsky, forerunner of the romantic movement in Russia, analyzed the acting of French actress Mlle. George in a series of reviews in *The Messenger of Europe* in 1809. His conclusion was that her "inner coldness" ruined her effort to arouse the appropriate emotional response in the spectator. This started a conflict which raged for a century between supporters of the correct but cold Petersburg acting tradition and the rough but impassioned Moscow school of acting.

Governmental censorship deterred the growth of Russian criticism. Since actors at state theaters were considered to be official government representatives, they were beyond criticism by the public. Ironically, as personal chattels of the emperor they could suffer even corporal punishment within the establishment! In 1815 a governmental directive stated: "Opinions concerning the imperial theater and the actors in His Majesty's service are taken to be inappropriate in any periodical."[2]

In 1825, the year of the Decembrist uprising, appeared one of Russia's great plays, the comedy *Woe from Wit* by Alexander Griboyedov. Following Molière, Griboyedov wrote a brilliant satire on the impossibility of idealism transforming the world. The hero, Chatsky, becomes the first in a long line of "superfluous characters" or ineffectual idealists in Russian literature. In dialogue Griboyedov achieves the impossible, Mirsky said. He uses unexpected but appropriate punning rhymes. "For epigram, repartee, terse and concise wit, Griboyedov has no rivals in Russian,"[3] according to Mirsky.

As a successful young diplomat Griboyedov was appointed Russian minister to Persia. While negotiating a treaty in Teheran in 1829, he was killed by a mob which attacked the legation and murdered all but one of the Russians.

Following the Decembrist rebellion Czar Nicholas I tightened all literary and dramatic censorship. One exception concerned the newspaper *Northern Bee*, whose editor Faddy Bulgarin persuaded Nicholas that good actors needed the recognition that only periodicals could give, and that a true critic would refrain from "offensive dealing in personalities." His paper was thus given permission to review plays, and soon other periodicals were also reviewing plays. Bulgarin played it safe by adjusting his critical remarks according to what he thought would be politically acceptable. Most Russian critics have followed this practice to the current day.

While restricted to his estate in 1825, Alexander Pushkin began to write his play *Boris Godunov*. At the same time he did a lot of thinking about tragedy and popular drama. His critical writing remained unpublished in his lifetime. Only his friends thus read his criticism until it was published, some in 1841 and the rest in 1895.

Pushkin was greatly influenced by Shakespeare. He regretted not knowing English better, because he felt that Shakespeare would be a far better model for Russian dramatists than Racine, who had greater influence at the time. Like A.W. Schlegel, whom he quoted, Pushkin felt that Shakespeare had no match in creating characters who were dynamic, living organisms rather than bundles of logical consistencies.

Pushkin also quoted Schlegel on how a nation's idiosyncracies would shape its drama. Pushkin said: "Climate, type of government, religion lend each people a particular physiognomy. There is a pattern of ideas and feelings, a myriad of habits, beliefs and customs appertaining exclusively to a given people."[4]

Pushkin felt that Russia could not have an important theater until there existed a receptive, discerning audience. He was shocked at Russian theatrical manners. People talk, blow their noses, and do everything to disrupt the play. The public will need education before the theater can be a serious factor in national life, he said.

According to Pushkin, what does a playwright require? Above

all, freedom. Other requisites are some background in philosophy, objectivity, intuition, vivid imagination, and a historian's political ideas.

Pushkin wondered why his contemporaries still followed the precepts of "that ponderous pedant Gottsched," when esthetic theory had evolved far beyond the German critic. Verisimilitude, praised by neoclassic critics like Gottsched, found little function in Pushkin's canon. If one means by the term the strictest observance of costume, local manners, and other historical niceties, the greatest playwrights—by which Pushkin meant Shakespeare, Calderón, and Racine—had sinned. Yet critical consensus placed their drama at the summit. The only verisimilitude Pushkin accepted was "authenticity of passions" and verisimilitude of emotions proper to the given situation.

Pushkin disliked Sumarokov. He gave us "imitations of Parisian diversions" in a "barbarously effete language,"[5] Pushkin felt. This kept the Russian theater alien to the Russian people. Vladislav Ozerov tried to remedy this by writing on Russian subjects. But this is not the answer, said Pushkin. Shakespeare wrote of Venice and Rome, Racine of Greece and Rome. The answer lies in artistic integrity, dealing with the essentials of human nature.

Pushkin gave as an example in the right direction the anonymous play *Martha the Seneschal's Wife*, which told of the heroic struggle of a widow to prevent the fall of Novgorod to Ivan, Grand Duke of Moscow. The author is praised for historical accuracy and remarkable restraint in not taking sides in the battle. Such honesty can lead Russia to a great national drama, Pushkin said.

"Gogol began the history of Russian criticism,"[6] Pushkin wrote in his diary in 1835. At the time, having secured his plot from Pushkin, Nikolai Gogol was writing Russia's greatest comedy, *The Inspector General*. Mirsky said it was "one of the few Russian plays constructed with unerring art from beginning to end."[7] Although Gogol intended it as a personal satire against corrupt officials, the public insisted on regarding it as a social satire against a corrupt system.

To show his dissatisfaction with what he considered to be the misinterpretation of his play by both the critics and the public, Gogol wrote a one-act play called *A Theater Lets Out after the Performance of a New Comedy*. Gogol, like Pushkin, felt that the theater had a crucially important educational function, but that ignorance, censorship, and critical hostility were keeping the theater from its proper role. Censorship forbade the staging of Gogol's one-act play until 1902.

In "Petersburg Notes for 1836" Gogol said that nothing was more ridiculous than Russian actors trying to play French counts. Gogol deplored the widespread popularity of melodrama and vaudeville. The great Molière and the noble Schiller must be ashamed of us, he said.

Our stress upon the bizarre, upon murder, arson, and savage passion, makes us look like decadent bloodthirsty Rome, he felt. "I can envisage the strange bewilderment of our posterity, thinking to discover our society in our melodrama,"[8] he mused.

In *Selected Excerpts from Correspondence with Friends*, published in 1847, Gogol saw satiric comedy as a social corrective device. He praised *The Minor* and *Woe from Wit* as "true social comedies," based not on individual revenge but on protest against social abuses. His criticism fits well into his own best comedies. Later critics built upon Gogol's concept of comedy as an instrument for public correction.

To maintain the artistic unity of the play, Gogol calls for a strong lead actor, which presages, in Laurence Senelik's opinion, "Evreinov's argument for a single point of view in monodrama, Sologub's insistence on the dramatist as be-all and end-all, and Meyerhold's advancement of the director as ultimate 'author of the spectacle'."[9]

Vissarion Belinsky was an early champion of Gogol on humanitarian grounds. Later, when Gogol seemed to kowtow to the czar and his regime, Belinsky attacked Gogol in a letter which was a clarion call to Russian reformers for many decades. Belinsky felt that Pushkin was Russia's only great tragedian, not only for *Boris Godunov* but for his short plays (*Salieri and Mozart*, *The Covetous Knight*, *The Nixie*, *The Stone Guest*) which he felt were incomparable in originality, spontaneity, profundity of concept, and artistic form.

No other form of literature so moved us a tragedy did, said Belinsky. Why is this so? Because when fate chooses to crush one of humanity's noblest vessels, the struggle so enhances human dignity that all fellow members of the human race are elevated.

"There is something imperfect and fatal in the conditions of life," said Belinsky. "Life is formed out of mobs and heroes, and these two facets are in eternal enmity."[10] To illustrate his point, Belinsky described how we first dislike the boorish Richard II, but after he is deposed by his cousin, he acts with regal dignity. Now we respect him, and regret his loss of power. "But to bring out all the forces of his spirit, to become a hero, he had to drain to the dregs the cup of calamity, and perish,"[11] Belinsky stated.

Comedy, for Belinsky, is tragedy's obverse, showing by its exposure of foibles a "negative reality" of the world as it should be. Spectators should not complain about "open-ended" Russian plays as indeterminate, he said, because the resolution of the plot occurs in the mind of the sensitive viewer.

To Belinsky, the function of criticism is to act as a corrective against literary, social, or political evils. Like his followers, Nikolai Chernyshevsky and Nikolai Dobrolyubov, Belinsky felt that drama and its criticism needed to give highest priority to the improvement of society. They stood in direct opposition to the pietism, mysticism, and nationalism of Slavophile dramatists and critics.

Belinsky says that French dramatists do not write great plays but they are nonetheless important in the development of French culture. "Not one comedy of Molière can bear aesthetic criticism," he stated, "but Molière had an enormous influence on contemporary society and raised French theater high, a thing that required genius."[12]

Eugène Scribe was another example of this condition, Belinsky believed. Although not one of Scribe's plays is great, he said, Scribe's theater will always be important, because he speaks to the modern Frenchman in his present condition of bewilderment and hope.

By 1850 the role of the Russian drama as a societal corrective was widely understood. Some people even referred to the Moscow Maly Theater as "the other Moscow University." One rebel against this view was Vasily Sleptsov, who was not willing to sacrifice art to tendentiousness. He attacked Nikolay Leskov's play, *The Profligate*, for its crudity in preaching a message. To Sleptsov, writers of problem plays worked backwards. Instead of using the play as a problem solver for himself, the dramatist should be so thoroughly familiar with his material that he can let the play write itself, following its own inner needs for shaping, structure, and unity. Never mind the moral—that will be implicit in the play's material. Too many problem plays have long speeches of undigested data. This is not drama, said Sleptsov. This is an essay, and should not be disguised as a play.

The Russian theater in the time of Gogol had been dominated by the great actor Michael Schepkin. A pioneer of realistic acting,

Schepkin used natural gestures and voice tones to penetrate beneath the surface of the characters he represented so as to achieve universal portraits of human nature.

During the latter half of the nineteenth century Russian drama was dominated by the plays of Alexander Ostrovsky and his school. Ostrovsky was a government clerk who had left Moscow University after a quarrel with the university officials. From 1847 until 1886 he wrote about fifty plays. His output raised Russian drama to the point where it could merit comparison with the West, in Mirsky's opinion.

The critic Apollon Grigoriev was Ostrovsky's herald. Grigoriev believed in "organic criticism," a position stating that in order to succeed, an art form (such as drama) must be an organic growth from the nation's soil, or soul. Transplants from abroad are acceptable only if they coalesce with the native stem, he said. To Grigoriev, the characteristic Russian trait was meekness, in opposition to the predatory quality of man in western Europe. This view found favor with the Slavophiles, those Russians who asserted that their country had a mystical, spiritual purity that should never be sacrificed in any modernization program.

Ostrovsky, too, pleased the Slavophiles. He built his plays upon the realism of "*byt*," life considered in its local and temporal aspects. Ostrovsky's plays are slices of life. He omits himself from his characters. In his tragicomedies, "the breadth, the grasp, the variety of Ostrovsky's vision of Russian life are almost infinite,"[13] Mirsky judged. Although Ostrovsky lacks the psychological profundity of a Dostoevsky, he creates effective plays through the interactions of his many sharply defined characters.

The plays of Ostrovsky became a focal point of mid-century Russian criticism. When the Slavophiles praised Ostrovsky for his use of folk materials, the Westernizers responded by calling his plays formless. The young critic Nikolai Dobrolyubov attacked Ostrovsky's best play, *The Thunderstorm*, as a surrender to the forces of conservatism and tradition. Ostrovsky, said Dobrolyubov, had only two kinds of characters: aggressive dolts who dominated "the kingdom of darkness" by their cruelty, selfishness, and ignorance; and those who protested futilely against the aggressors.

Grigoriev came to Ostrovsky's defense, finding in the play a deep expression of the playwright's love of the undefiled Russian middle class. In addition, Grigoriev pointed to many examples in Ostrovsky's plays of characters that did not fit into Dobrolyubov's categories.

Dobrolyubov now found what he called "a ray of light in the kingdom of darkness." The adultress Katerina in the play rebels against the aggressors, so perhaps there is hope after all. Several years later Dmitry Pisarev attacked Katerina for being immoral and a fool. "In reality," said Mirsky years later, "it is a great poem of love and death, of freedom and thralldom. It is intensely local and Russian."[14] In fact, Mirsky thought it was so full of Russian "*byt*" as to make it scarcely intelligible to a non-Russian.

In his later plays, Ostrovsky often chose historical themes. He tended to insert more intrigue and action than in his early work, although his resistance to the "well made" play of Scribe and Sardou probably helped keep Russia free from that genre. In the 1880's Ostrovsky became artistic director of the Moscow Imperial Dramatic Theater. He died in 1886.

Another writer of realistic drama was Alexey Pisemsky. His play, *A Hard Lot*, tells of a serf whose wife has been seduced by the master while the serf was absent. Grief stricken, the serf kills the illicit child and then surrenders to the police for punishment. Many critics praised Pisemsky for achieving a judicious ending to a difficult plot.

Eager to educate the peasants, S.A. Yurev established a Peasant Theatre on his estate in 1862. Here he drilled the peasants in their productions of plays by Ostrovsky and Pisemsky, as well as his own dramatic versions of fairy tales. He succeeded Ostrovsky as president of the Society of Russian Dramatic Writers.

Yurev found that the Meiningen Players' stress on ensemble effect struck a native chord in Russia. In an article in *Russian Thought* in 1890 Yurev said, "Our stage is instinctively inclined to produce drama in which the hero is not one character but a collective personality composed of a multitude of personalities standing on an equal artistic footing, or the collective personality of the nation."[15] Here Yurev was sowing seeds for the Moscow Art Theater as well as for the Soviet doctrine of socialist realism.

Self-sacrifice for the group became a moral principle to Yurev. The dramatist too must be willing to direct his energies toward group goals. "This legitimate demand of his ego the artist must restrain within himself," sacrificing his ego "to his divinity, the art, the whole, the drama in which he takes part. This spirit of self-sacrifice in the name of art, being an elevated artistic power, is at the same time a moral power which ennobles the artistic milieu."[16]

Alexey Tolstoy surpassed Ostrovsky as a writer of historical plays. The hero of his *Czar Theodore*, published in 1868, is the good but weak sovereign with an excellent set of values but a complete inability to enact them because of crafty councillors. In their reviews Russian critics would point out how modern Russia could learn from its past history.

Dmitry Averkiev wrote *On Drama*, the first Russian work devoted exclusively to dramatic theory. It appeared in installments in *Russian Messenger* in 1877-78, and was reprinted in 1893 with supplementary material. A journalist and playwright, Averkiev showed a preference for Aristotle and Lessing. Averkiev felt that comedy and tragedy should not be mixed. He said that the only true plot for drama is man's struggle against his fate. Averkiev thereby ruled out plays involving conflict of person against person.

Laurence Senelik feels that Averkiev's best contribution lay in his understanding of comedy. Averkiev said that the high point of a comedy comes in the suffering of the protagonist. Since the protagonist is the only person who believes he is suffering, the principal effect comes as the audience realizes his misconception. Molière's comedy can well be explained in this manner, Senelik feels.

In his shocking treatise, "What Is Art?" Leo Tolstoy built an esthetic upon a purely moral base. If a work does not inculcate a moral truth, and if it is not immediately intelligible to even an uneducated person, the work is not art. The test of an art work to Tolstoy is "does the work of art communicate feelings deriving from love of God and one's neighbor? Only if it does so is it healthy art."[17] Tolstoy said that after reading Shakespeare for over fifty years the result was always the same—perplexity, disgust, and boredom. Shakespeare not only lacked art, said Tolstoy, but his world view was "the most vile and vulgar." Drama in its highest form requires a religious content, Tolstoy said. "The only man who can write drama," he believed, "is the one who has something to tell people, something of the greatest importance: the relationship of man to God, to the world, to all that is eternal and infinite."[18]

Tolstoy found little drama in Anton Chekhov's plays. Interestingly, in chiding Chekhov about the lack of action in his plays he frequently used Shakespeare as a model of great drama.

Trained as a doctor, Chekhov first wrote short stories to help pay his university expenses. But he had loved the theater even as a child, and ultimately he wrote broad farces for the theater, in preparation for a series of plays that at first confused and then often charmed playgoers. The lack of outward action in his serious plays is compensated for by the evocation of the atmosphere of group emotions as persons' psyches interact. But most of his comments about the theater are hardbitten realism.

In a letter to Vladimir Nemirovich-Danchenko, co-founder with Konstantin Stanislavsky of the Moscow Art Theater, Chekhov said that talk about a "theater for the people" was nonsense. "We mustn't bring Gogol down to the people," he said, "but raise the people up to Gogol."[19]

"I implore you," wrote Chekhov to the dramatist Ivan Shcheglov, "please fall out of love with the stage."[20] He went on to say that the theater's good is overstated. Moreover, it does not educate the public but panders to it. "Until the literary man in you triumphs over the dramatist," Chekhov warned, "I will give you hell."[21]

Chekhov liked Eleonora Duse's simplicity and honesty, but had no use for Sarah Bernhardt's pomposity, which he parodied in his character Arkadina in *The Seagull*. On the whole he had little use for actors — although he married a star of the Moscow Art Theater, Olga Knipper.

Most of Chekhov's advice to fellow dramatists consists of hints about stagecraft — avoid cliches, be compact, use realistic dialogue. His credo as summarized by Laurence Senelik was to show the commonplace surface of life and let the deep hidden meaning rise to be seen by itself.

Chekhov's plays as performed by the Moscow Art Theater under Stanislavsky's direction provided an instant theatrical renaissance in Russia. Soon everyone was admiring the ensemble effect that Stanislavsky achieved, and trying to analyze Chekhov's plays to see how they contributed to that effect.

In 1900 Sergey Sergeyev attributed Chekhov's unique success to the creation of mood or atmosphere, which grips us even when we lose interest in the plot. Yuly Aikhenvald, drama critic for *Russian Thought*, said that what was really happening during the silences of Chekhov's plays was that the characters' souls were communicating with each other. Aikhenvald preferred closet drama to stage fare, and stirred up such a fuss over his preference that a group of stage people responded in 1912 with a book, *Debating A Theater*, in which it was pointed out that staging and acting provided qualities lost in the mere reading of a play.

A group of dramatists interested in symbolism also found in Chekhov a kindred spirit. Chekhov, like many of his contemporaries, found the symbolism of the Belgian dramatist Maurice Maeterlinck very intriguing. The Russian symbolists found that Chekhov often used symbols in his plays, and that Treplev's play in Act I of *The Seagull* contained many symbolic and futuristic elements. In the dramatic fervor as the new century began, the Russian symbolists theorized imaginatively about the nature of drama and its effects.

Chief spokesman for the Russian symbolists was Valery Bryusov. Although he respected Stanislavsky, Bryusov attacked theatrical naturalism as "unnecessary truth." Bryusov said the Moscow Art Theater was too concerned with matters of outward form; it needed to be more concerned with the play's content, which relates to the inner life of the play.

Bryusov saw the danger of symbolist plays overstressing the set at the expense of the text, so he recommended a return to the simple sets of Shakespeare and the Greeks. He felt that no matter how beautiful or how ingenious, sets were improper when they focused on themselves rather than on the play's central purpose. The harder we try by realistic staging to disguise the distinction between life and the stage, the more we become aware of the distinction.

Bryusov felt that since Aristotle had defined a drama as a representation of an action, mood plays (such as those of Chekhov and Maeterlinck) were of limited value, since they tended to have little outward action. Actors, however, become very important, because they are the ones portraying the action.

Andrey Bely (the pen name of Boris Bugaev) felt that much of Chekhov's appeal derived from symbolism. Bely felt that *The Cherry Orchard* by Chekhov presented life as a skein of lace through whose interstices the elusive meaning of life could be discerned. Thus the seeming irrelevancies, long pauses, and eruptions of meaningless action were really functional, because they exposed the terrifying reality of life as it is lived beneath the surface. It is interesting that Sigmund Freud was pioneering in medicine and psychology along a similar vein at this time.

In 1907 Bely compared Chekhov to Bryusov. Whereas Bryusov tended to see the world as composed of symbols, Chekhov takes everyday objects and transforms them into symbols, with a Bergsonian knack for interlacing individual moments into time's eternal loom. "The power of the instant," said Bely, "is a natural protest against the mechanical organization of life. The minutiae of life will appear ever more closely to be the guides to Eternity. Thus, realism imperceptibly crosses over into symbolism."[22]

For Bely, drama's job was to represent the phenomena of this world in the light of an ideal world order. "From the point of view of contemporary psychology," he said, "reality is the sum total of all possible experience (inward and outward). The visible world is but a small part of reality."[23]

To Bely, symbolism was the "Apocalypse without a Second Coming."[24] Possibly because of the failed revolution of 1905, Bely now saw drama as leading the vanguard in man's struggle against fate. "Perhaps the ultimate purpose of drama," said Bely, "is to contribute to man's transfiguration in such wise that he will begin to create his life on his own. Fate is not fatal!"[25]

Bely believed that the loss of faith in God meant that drama could never again return to being religious ritual. The new esthetic took on the fervor of a religion. In Bely's words, "the symbolist bond is the religion of a confederated path to happiness. There everyone is a participant, everyone a creator, everyone a symbol. There are no actors or spectators there. There drama is a creative relationship with life, and consequently no one seriously needs symbolist theater."[26]

Alexander Blok, like Bely, liked Ibsen. Blok felt that Russia lacked a great dramatic tradition, and that geniuses like Griboyedov and Chekhov were accidental occurrences who left no trail in their wake. Maxim Gorky was no playwright at all, in Blok's eyes, because his plays lack conflict and are tedious and depressing. He makes his workers angels and his bosses devils, and he calls that realism, Blok complained.

Blok found the theater a necessary escape from the loneliness of lyric poetry. In a long article "On the Theatre" in 1908 Blok speaks of the dramatist gratifying the spiritual hunger of the audience. Through the theater, Blok said, the wholeness of life can be restored.

Blok said Maeterlinck condemned his own plays when he admitted they were afflicted with a "paralysis of external action." In Maeterlinck, said Blok, there is such a deep penetration into the depths of human consciousness that finally one arrives at the spot where "everything is at one." Now this might be good mental hygiene, said Blok, but it is scarcely drama—where is the conflict, contradiction, and inconsistency of life?

The two best modern Russian plays, in Blok's opinion, were by Mikhail Kuzmin and Leonid Andreev. Kuzmin's *The Converted Courtesan* Blok called a "a holy farce." It tells of a harlot who, upon being converted into entering a nunnery, convinces her lover to enter a monastery situated across the river, where they can admire each other in Platonic bliss. Blok liked Kuzmin's humor, irony, restraint, and playful prose. Andreev's *The Life of Man* was praised by Blok because it dramatized man's confrontation with fate in a dreadful, awesome scene. Minor characters are made puppet-like, to properly focus on the protagonist and his wife. The greatness of the play, Blok felt, stemmed from the dramatic realization that in shaping up to our fate, we are not puppets but have an importance represented by our human dignity.

An educator and playwright, Innokenty Annensky, disagreed with Blok's appraisal of Gorky. He found symbolic elements underlying Gorky's stark realism. The true protagonist of *The Lower Depths*, he said, was fate. The new hero, in Annensky's opinion, was not an individual but the whole community. By showing the basic humanity in even the most lowly persons, Gorky can achieve a sublimely esthetic effect even out of a story of cruelty in a brothel. Natasha, in *The Lower Depths*, keeps saying, "Something will happen soon." Of course it will not. We know it, but we too say it about ourselves. Luka, the skeptic, tells people agreeable things because he knows that even "on the dungheap, praise causes every soul to blossom forth and reveal itself the more. What would our life be like," asks Annensky, "this life of most placid philistinism, if every so often various Lukas had not lied to us about a land of righteousness?"[27]

Unlike Bely, Vyacheslav Ivanov felt that the theater should return to its origin as religious rite. Having carefully studied early Greek religion, Ivanov was convinced that only with religious content could drama ever achieve its highest form. Ivanov followed the belief of Vladimir Solovyov that an artist-priest, who could be the dramatist, was needed to synthesize individual spirits with God's spirit. Religious myth, rather than politics, was man's best guide to God, he felt.

Ivanov made much of the feminine component of tragedy, going back to Dionysus as one especially attractive to women (or in some cases feared by them). Dionysian rites were chiefly concerned with women, revealing to them hidden depths and ineffable psychic mysteries. Women played an important part in Greek tragedy, Ivanov said, and Aeschylus even used a feminine chorus in *The Suppliant Women*. Ivanov believed that a return to the use of a Grecian-type chorus will help moderns become participants rather than spectators in the theater. In an introduction to a play written by his wife, Ivanov "proposed a new form of drama, restored to something approaching the religious function of Greek tragedy, whose task was to forge a link between the poet and the crowd."[28]

Fyodor Sologub (whose real name was Fyodor Teternikov) agreed with many of Ivanov's principles. A poet and novelist, Sologub consented to the use of spectators as chorus, and a return of drama to religious ritual. We need no drama of everyday life, he said. "The only thing that has to be performed is the eternal mystery. One eternal dialogue is held, and the questioner himself both answers and hungers for a reply. And what are to be the themes? Only Love, only Death."[29] When we get down to the real I, said Sologub, we have returned to the universal, which is drama's goal. In the tragic theater "the individual could be brought to assert his own will in harmony with that of his maker."[30]

Children love to play act, Sologub said, because only they understand the true nature of life — it is a game, fun when it is played, but frustrating if taken seriously. Future drama should incorporate dance, he felt, since dancing is a playful act appropriate to the game of drama.

In the continuing struggle as to who should dominate in the theater — dramatist, actor, director, or designer — Sologub clearly chose the dramatist, since the play is his creation and his only. To the charge that this would turn actors into puppets, he replied that we are all puppets, pulled by invisible strings for unknown purposes.

Perhaps partly as a result of the decadence of the Orthodox Church, it was now commonplace for the Russian theater to be imbued with a religious purpose. A.E. Redko said that "V. Kommissarzhevskaya's theatre turned itself into a kind of church, in which the producer and the actors celebrated exactly like priests in the traditional church, in the name of the infinite power guiding the world."[31]

Nikolay Evreinov was at once a polar opposite to Aikhenvald and to Sologub. Whereas both Aikhenvald and Sologub enshrined the playwright, Evreinov felt that drama did best with a minimum of his input. Evreinov quoted Gordon Craig who, when driven frantic by the lack of stage experience of modern dramatists, said, "We shall do without them, since they fail to provide us with the most important thing — something that is beautiful in a stage sense."[32]

The theater has become too literary, said Evreinov. We would do better to go back to the days of Thespis, to monodrama. Gestures communicate better than words, he felt. In an effort to reduce the distance between actor and spectator, Evreinov said that background characters must remain in the background. He believed that the essence of drama lay in co-experiencing the feelings of the protagonist, and the spectator cannot deeply empathize with more than one other person. Some of Evreinov's plays have only one character, and some are supposed to take place in a fraction of a second!

Probably the best application of monodrama, which really never had a large following, was Gordon Craig's *Hamlet* at the Moscow Art Theater in 1912. As described by Laurence Senelik, "Craig envisaged the play as seen through Hamlet's mind's eye, the rest of the characters portrayed only as seen by the prince, who was accompanied by a phantasmal figure of Death."[33] Other near approaches to monodrama are plays representing a dream or hallucination, such as Gerhart Hauptmann's *Hannele*, Maeterlinck's *Blue Bird*, and Andreev's *Black Masks*.

The novelist Leonid Andreev wrote a series called *Letters on the Theater* from 1911 to 1914. In them he stated that the reason for the extraordinary success of Chekhov's plays when performed by the Moscow Art Theater was not only their artistic creation of mood but also what he called "panpsychism," meaning that every little facet of the play seemed animated with life. Chekhov had thus injected psychology into modern drama, and now the need was for more psychological plays.

"Chekhov," he said, "and the theater with him, created not only things, but *time* itself, not as a watchmaker does, but as a psychologist does."[34] Chekhov, he said, taught time to act—through thought-filled pauses and emotion-filled silences. "Germans who knew no Russian wept copiously," said Andreev, "when the *animation* of time in Chekhov's plays spoke to them from the Art Theater stage in the international language of pauses. The very fact that the theater knew so well how to render elusive time subservient to its great artistic power makes the theater forever glorious and immortal!"[35]

Andreev dealt with cinema's inroad upon the theater. We should welcome the competition, he said, because now we can leave spectacle and constant action to the cinema and concentrate upon the theater's strengths: language, psychology, and at its best, panpsychism. Symbolism, he felt, had served a useful purpose, reinfusing spirituality into the drama, but now it was deservedly declining, because it was only a means and had been mistaken for an end. Too concerned with technique, it made the error of assuming it was possible to embody on the stage all of the modern conceptions of a soul.

Having the advantage of flesh-and-blood actors in the theater, drama should outdo the cinema by reducing the psychic distance between actor and spectator. How might this be done? Perhaps, said Andreev, in new mystery plays. When an audience is truly gripped, as in Chekhov's plays, the panpsychism created by the interaction between actors and spectators turns the spectators into actors. "People are swayed this way," said Andreev, "only by prophets, warriors, and brilliant psychologists, who can bring the soul of each of us near to the soul of all humanity, all the world."[36]

Modern life has gone within, Andreev felt. "Life has become psychological," he said. "Along with the everlasting heroes of the drama, love and hunger, comes a new hero, the intellect."[37]

In a letter that Vsevolod Meyerhold sent to the English dramatist George Calderon, Meyerhold, who had been an actor under Stanislavsky and later became a famous director, summarized the history of Russian drama. The three big influences he found were those of Pushkin, Gogol, and Michael Lermontov. Meyerhold said that folk drama in Russia had been greatly influenced by a tour of Italian *commedia dell'arte* plays during the reign of Empress Anna Ivanovna. Serious drama benefited greatly from Pushkin's plays, Meyerhold said, but Pushkin could have benefited from the rules-free approach of Calderón de la Barca and Lope de Vega had he been more familiar with their work.

"Gogol," said Meyerhold, "forges a link with the French theater of the seventeenth century by instinctively injecting into Russian comedy an element of the humor and peculiar mysticism of Molière."[38] In the style of Lope de Vega, Lermontov developed a Theater of Action. Lermontov's play *Masquerade* was banned by the censors for its excessive passion.

Ostrovsky also learned much from Lope de Vega and Cervantes, Meyerhold felt. Turgenev's drama was too intimate, being apparently intended for the drawing-room rather than the stage. Moreover, his plays lack action, hoping to substitute mood for plot. Chekhov followed in Turgenev's style but added a new element: musicality. Since Chekhov's drama was not built upon the sturdy Russian foundation of Pushkin, Gogol, and Lermontov, it lasted only ten years and then died out, said Meyerhold.

Meyerhold acknowledged the value of the Russian symbolists in both their plays and their criticism but felt that most of their innovations, however commendable, failed for lack of theatricality. They too, he believed, should have read Lope de Vega's *The New Art of Writing Plays*, for its stress upon what brings people to the theater. Meyerhold himself became an innovative director, and as Stanislavsky's star inevitably waned his just as surely rose.

The Soviet revolution proved to be as big a blow to dramatic criticism as it was to Soviet drama and Soviet literature in general. It took some time, however, before the theater was reined into conformity with Communist Party ideology.

Georgi Plekhanov, Lenin's teacher, was the founder of Marxist literary criticism. Plekhanov pointed out that all criticism should be based upon the "scientific sociology" of Karl Marx. Criticism that was purely esthetic or subjective had to be opposed because of its lack of Marxist ideological content.

During the 1920's there was an amazing feeling for innovation and experimentation in Soviet literature, including drama. Futurism, which had developed along with Symbolism, became one of the forces in the new Soviet theater. Expressionism, thriving in post-war Germany, found its way into Soviet dramatic technique. Meyerhold, now the most prominent theatrical director, invented such techniques as constructivism and "biomechanics" to show how drama would help the new society find its way. In 1921 Meyerhold staged the poet Vladimir Mayakovsky's *Mystery-Bouffe*, an expressionistic verse drama of how the proletarians will crush the bourgeois elements. In 1929 Meyerhold staged two prose plays by Mayakovsky, *The Bedbug* and *The Bathhouse*, on similar themes.

Lenin confessed that he did not understand Mayakovsky's works, but he added that the party spirit in literature need not restrict freedom. He said that "literary work lends itself least of all to mechanical leveling, to standardization,"[39] and that for artistic creation "it is absolutely necessary to secure greater scope for personal initiative, for individual leanings, scope for thought and fantasy, form and content."[40] The record of twentieth-century Soviet dramatic criticism is to chart how far party critics have deviated from Lenin's theoretical position as stated here.

As a practical matter, Lenin was not about to permit freedom of literary thought. When his old rival, A.A. Bogdanov, founded the Proletcult for the purpose of training working-class writers to produce a specifically proletarian literature, Lenin smelled undesirable separatism and placed the Proletcult under the studied scrutiny of the Commissariat of Education.

The first Soviet Commissar of Education was Anatoly Lunacharsky, who, among other activities, had written some plays. A champion of Meyerhold, Lunacharsky managed to walk a tightrope between Lenin's theory and Lenin's practice. On the one hand he accepted the ideological struggle. "We are in a struggle of ideas," he said. "Not a single honest and conscientious Communist can deny the nature of this struggle in the question of present-day literature and its evaluation."[41] He added the basic criterion for evaluating a literary work: "Everything that aids the development and victory of the proletariat is good; everything that harms it is evil."[42] A Marxist critic, he felt, was "a fighter and a builder" who would educate not only the audience but the dramatist as well. When bourgeois drama was utterly hostile to the cause of the proletariat, said Lunacharsky, the proper treatment was not Marxist criticism but Marxist censorship.

On the other hand, Lunacharsky believed that Marxist critics should try to avoid class hatred and malice. They should praise not only works dealing with topical problems, because some plays which initially appear to be nontendential often have an important contribution to make in furthering the proletarian cause. In the best Marxist drama, he felt, there would be not naked propaganda but Marxist ideas artfully merged into the characters' thoughts and actions.

Tolstoy was right, Lunacharsky said, in condemning work full of sophisticated ornamentation — such plays must be rejected by Marxist critics. But even here a word of caution is given. Some Marxist works are written for the intelligentsia, and it is unreasonable to expect the writer to oversimplify their material. After all, said Lunacharsky, "we cannot bring all of our literature down to the level of the as yet uncultured peasant masses or even of the workers."[43]

When the first Five-Year Plan was instituted in 1928, the Russian Association of Proletarian Writers (known as RAPP) assumed a virtual dictatorship over all Russian literary production. When Valentin Katayev playfully spoofed Moscow's housing shortage in his 1929 farce called *Squaring the Circle*, RAPP promptly rapped his knuckles. Alexander Afinogenov likewise drew the criticism of the authorities for his play *Fear*, produced in Leningrad in 1931. Although the play's theme is that there was more fear under the czar than under the current regime, audiences vigorously applauded the part of the play realistically describing current fear of the Communist Party.

In 1932 the Central Committee of the Communist Party declared RAPP leaders to be Trotskyites and liquidated RAPP, replacing it with a single union of Soviet writers open to both party members and non-members. At a literary congress held in 1934 the need to improve literary performance was discussed. The doctrine of "socialist realism" was pronounced as dogma, replacing critical realism. Critical realism had advocated a merciless depiction of truth as seen in the light of Marxist ideology. Truthfully admitting Soviet shortcomings, whether of housing, fear, or whatever, was beginning to prove embarrassing, now that the Soviets had been in power for seventeen years and there still remained gigantic problems. So Gorky suggested a fusion of realism and romanticism into something called "socialist realism." Its realism speaks of capitalistic exploitation in a czarist past; its romanticism describes how wonderful the future socialist state will be. What is left out from a literary standpoint, of course, is the present.

At the conference Andrei Zhdanov said, "Soviet literature is tendentious, for in an epoch of class struggle there cannot be a literature which is not class literature, not tendentious."[44] Writers, he said, must learn to avoid objective reality and substitute for it revolutionary reality. "The truthfulness and historical concreteness of the artistic portrayal should be combined with the ideological remolding and education of the toiling people in the spirit of socialism. This method is what we call socialist realism."[45]

Another speaker at the conference, Nikolai Bukharin, further defined the term. He said, "Socialist realism is a distinct method in art, the counterpart of dialectical materialism, the translation of the latter into terms of art. Socialist realism, as a method, is the enemy of everything supernatural, mystic, all other-worldly idealism."[46] Bukharin pointed out that socialist realism was anti-individualistic, not in the sense of opposing the growth of human personality but in the sense of building a collective bond uniting peoples.

The assassination of a close friend of Stalin in 1934 triggered the beginning of a series of purges that ultimately involved millions of Russians, including dramatists, critics, generals, and former high Communist Party officials. The liberal magazine *Novy Mir* (*New World*) finally had to cease publication in 1938 because its editor and many of its contributors were either dead or in Siberian work camps.

The fate of Meyerhold was apocalyptic. He who had called upon actors to look upon themselves not as stars but as "instruments for social manifestoes" was suddenly suspect. In 1936 Meyerhold produced a non-ideological *Camille*; Pravda attacked him as being "foreign," and even worse, "the father of formalism." His theater was liquidated by the government, and the Committee on Arts ordered all Soviet theaters to hold meetings at which actors and directors would condemn Meyerhold and support the government's censure of him. Out of work, he was given a job by his rival, Stanislavsky.

When the Committee on Arts asked Meyerhold to speak at a national convention of theater directors in 1939, it seemed as if perhaps he was being forgiven his sins. Meyerhold's speech is a great classic.

I have been asked to tell you about my past errors, Meyerhold began. True, I probably should have discouraged "Meyerhold mania" when I saw it in young directors. True, I may have desecrated some classics in my particular method of staging them. But am I a formalist? "I was responsible for several productions in which I wanted to test some recent ideas in the field of dramatic form. They were experimental productions in which form occupied a dominant place."[47] But, he said, such productions were few. "Even so a master must have the right to experiment. He must have the moral right to test his creative ideas no matter how they turn out in the end. He must have the right to make mistakes, because all mortals have that right."[48]

Meyerhold went on to state that most of his creative work bore no trace of formalism. Instead he had devoted his efforts toward finding an organic style that suited the play's content.

Then Meyerhold's bravery rose to the fore. If what passes for drama in Moscow theaters today is considered to be an achievement of Soviet drama, "I prefer to be considered a formalist,"[49] he stated. He said he found the current dramatic fare to be pitiful and terrifying.

"This pitiful and sterile something that aspires to the title of socialist realism has nothing in common with art,"[50] he declared. Yet without art there can be no theater. If you go to Moscow theaters today all you find are colorless, boring productions that are all alike except as they differ in their degree of worthlessness.

"Was this your aim?" Meyerhold asked. "If so, you have committed a horrible deed. You have washed the child down the drain with the dirty water. In your effort to eradicate formalism you have destoyed art!"[51]

Meyerhold was arrested the next day and sent to Siberia, where he died in 1942. Several weeks after his speech his wife was found brutally stabbed to death. Their property was confiscated. In the official report of the convention there appears no record of his speech.

Nikolai Gorchakov, formerly Meyerhold's assistant, wrote a book in exile called *The Theatre in Soviet Russia*. Responding to the question of why it took twenty-one years after the revolution to subdue the Russian theater, he replied that he found two reasons: the Russians are a theatergoing people, and perhaps there would have been a public outcry against too early repression; the Russians are an artistically gifted people, and such creative perception and artistic interest can never be wholly disciplined away.

Prince Dmitry S. Mirsky, author of the authoritative *A History of Russian Literature*, disappeared from Soviet life and has never again been seen. The Central Committee of the Communist Party issued a resolution on literary criticism in 1940 in which critics were attacked for their feeble contribution to ideological education.

During World War II most dramatists responded by writing patriotic plays. Leonid Leonov and Konstantin Simonov were particularly lauded by Soviet critics for their nationalistic drama. Alexander Korneichuk's *The Front*, a play in 1942 which criticized older inefficient Red Army officers, was accepted as legitimate self-criticism.

In a speech in Moscow in 1946, A.M. Egolin, a member of the Soviet Academy of Sciences, decried the state of Soviet literary criticism. "Our critics," he said, "lack principles and political acumen. The analysis of works of art is often of a formal nature, detached from the political content. Literary criticism must become a means of ideological propaganda."[52]

Egolin then pointed out that such great writers as Pushkin and Gorky had been leading critics. "Is it not strange," he asked, "that our Soviet writers hardly ever come out with critical articles?"[53]

It is proper for modern Russia to produce foreign plays, Egolin stated. Which ones should they be? "Those, of course, which unmask the bourgeois reality,"[54] he replied. He then berated the critic P. Gromov for having praised two American movies that brought out American patriotism. How was it possible, Egolin asked, that a Soviet critic would fail to seize the opportunity to point out how superior Soviet love of fatherland is to the American version?

Also in 1946 the Central Committee publicly chastised two Leningrad literary reviews for publishing works "alien to Soviet literature." Written by Zhdanov, who was charged with carrying out its provisions, the decree deplored the Western influence upon Soviet culture and charged writers with a specific duty to inculcate Soviet patriotism.

The Ukrainian playwright Alexander Korneichuk said that this decree provided a clear outline for the further development of Soviet drama. He said that the aim of Soviet literature is to show the whole world "the moral beauty and might of victorious Soviet man." Now Soviet writers must expose bourgeois survivals in our minds, he said, "and portray truthfully and to condemn unfavorable aspects of our life, and to show the best sides of the Soviet man's character in his struggle with negative forces."[55]

The death of Stalin in March, 1953, raised hopes that perhaps Soviet playwrights would be given more freedom. Actor Ruben Simonov immediately called for more boldness in Russian dramatists, saying that the theater was dull and cold due to poor plays. At a conference of critics in September, 1953, the critic A. Tarasenkov called for a return to controversy: "We have lost our taste for controversies; many of us forget that the truth is born in controversy, in the clash of opinions."[56] At that conference the cinema producer M. Papava complained of the emotional poverty of Soviet films: "They don't make you laugh or cry."[57]

The poet Alexander Tvardovsky, who edited *Novy Mir*, thought the time had arrived for venting the pent-up frustration, so he printed an article by the critic Vladimir Pomerantsev which candidly described Soviet literature as sick. Asking for an end to Communist Party didacticism, the article requested that both writers and critics approach their work, at long last, with intellectual and emotional honesty and independence. Tvardovsky was immediately replaced as editor by the seemingly more conservative Konstantin Simonov.

Ilya Ehrenburg's novelette *The Thaw* gave the name to this period in Soviet cultural history. For a time it seemed as if even Simonov encouraged dissent. He called for a broadening of socialist realism, and asked for publication of the banned works of the satirists Ilya Ilf and Evgeny Petrov.

Leonid Zorin's play, *The Guests*, was staged in Moscow and Leningrad in 1954. A direct attack upon Soviet bureaucracy, the play tells of the revolt of the son of a tyrannical high Soviet official.

Along with de-emphasis of Stalin came a shift in cultural ideology. Whereas it had formerly been ruled that Soviet drama should show no conflict between Russians, since in a socialist state all persons are supposed to live together in harmony, now conflict was once again permitted in drama. Alexander Korneichuk stated that although conflict was needed in a play, it was not the chief purpose of Soviet drama, which was to depict the new way of life and how to get there. Korneichuk cited as examples Konstantin Simonov's play *Alien Shadow* and A. Arbuzov's *Years of Wandering*.

In an article in the journal *Theater* in 1955 A. Anastasyev boldly attacked the no-conflict theory. For years, he said, directors had given up creative experimentation, fearing they might be penalized for something unacceptable. Out of fear of being called "formalists" they were surrendering their very individuality, he argued. The whole field of dramatic criticism had been distorted by the formalism bogy, he felt. "What is needed," he concluded, "is a complete break with the absurd theory that a detailed professional analysis of the form of a drama, its dialogue, plot, and dénouement, is something akin to formalism."[58]

Probably the high point of the thaw was reached at the Twentieth Congress of the Communist Party in February, 1956, when the novelist Mikhail Sholokhov gave a speech making fun of literary commissars and of Soviet writers who tried to kowtow to them.

The Hungarian uprising of October, 1956, ended the thaw, particularly when it was pointed out that writers had helped fan the rebellious fire. In a speech in 1957 the general secretary of the Communist Party, Nikita Khrushchev, said, "The lesson of the Hungarian events, when the counterrevolution used certain writers for its dirty ends, reminds us what political complacency and weakness of will with regard to the machinations of the forces hostile to socialism may lead to."[59] We would not be Marxist-Leninists, Khrushchev added, if we did not resist the efforts of bourgeois art and literature to penetrate the spirit of the Soviet people. Khrushchev went on to lament how rarely Soviet writers succeeded in giving a true picture of the common people. Writers need to live close to the people in order to portray them better in literature, he said.

By 1958, however, a second thaw was under way. Meyerhold's influence was once again spoken of with reverence. His pupil, Nikolai Okhlopov, returned from exile, and was made senior director at the Mayakovsky Theater. Valentin Pluchek at the Moscow Satire Theater revived Mayakovsky's plays *The Bedbug* and *The Bathhouse*, complete with the use of such "formalistic" tricks as the use of a color cartoon film, and actors rushing through the auditorium stirring up the audience. Another repatriate from exile, Yuri Zavadsky, revived Lermontov's romantic study of jealousy, *Masquerade*.

Many Western plays now appeared on the Moscow stage. Not only Shakespeare, Ibsen, and Wilde, but even Jean Girardoux, Lillian Hellman, John Osborne, and Arthur Miller were now on the boards. Nikolai Pogodin, who had never before veered from the party line, published a play of Platonic love entitled *Petrarca's Sonnet*, in which Pogodin castigated philistine conformism within the party and defended the rights of the individual conscience. The journal *Novy Mir*, now again under Tvardovsky's editorship, printed a number of satires against government bureaucracy, although it could never quite bring itself to publish Boris Pasternak's *Dr. Zhivago* when he submitted it to the journal.

The second thaw ended when Francis Gary Powers, pilot of an American U-2 reconnaissance plane, was shot down over Russia in 1960. The Cuban missile crisis of 1962 further widened the breach between the Soviet Union and the West. In 1964 Khrushchev was removed from his leadership role, and there have been no further thaws, although détente became a goal of Soviet-American relations for several decades.

Alexander Solzhenitsyn's first love was the theater. He studied acting under Moscow director Yuri Zavadsky. In 1954 he wrote a play, *The Stag and the Camp Prostitute*, which has never been produced in the Soviet Union, even though *Novy Mir* saw fit to publish his story of life in a work camp, *One Day in the Life of Ivan Denisovich*. Several other plays and novels by Solzhenitsyn have also not been published by the Soviet Union.

With the death of Nikolai Okhlopov in 1966 the direct influence of Meyerhold in the Soviet theater came to an end. One of Okhlopov's experiments had been to use large civilian choruses as part of a people's theater.

Valentin Pluchek, director of the exciting Moscow Satire Theater, admitted in 1967 that there was no Theater of the Absurd in Russia. He confessed, however, that many avant-garde theater people in Russia knew of the absurdist drama and admired it. They also had a fondness for the plays of "angry man" John Osborne, Pluchek said. Pluchek's personal preference was Peter Weiss's play *Marat/Sade*. Would he stage it? He laughed. "I don't think that in the jubilee year of the revolution," he replied, "we can put on a play in which revolution occurs in a madhouse."[60]

More recently a play of controversial subject matter was well received in Moscow. In 1973 *The Ascent of Mt. Fuji*, by Chingiz Aimatov and Kaltai Mukhamedzhanov, was staged. A well known novelist, Aimatov is also a member of the Communist Party. The play tells of a reunion of four friends, at which they discuss their missing colleague, a poet who had been imprisoned during the war for writing a pacifistic poem. None but the friends had seen the poem, so one of them had informed the party, and none of them had come to his defense. The play consists of a series of discussions of responsibility and guilt. Freely discussed are such concepts as God, morality, loyalty, and truth. Russian society will no doubt continue to seek for drama dealing with such values as long as Soviet cultural repression continues.

In summary, Russian dramatic criticism has added little original thought to the international canon. Early Russian drama tended to be evaluated for its religious worth. As the Renaissance belatedly hit Russia, neoclassical principles of dramatic excellence prevailed. From the time of Pushkin, drama was assumed to have a didactic function in Russia. It is thus unhistoric to assume that the push for tendential drama is a purely Soviet phenomenon.

Realism became the prevailing style in the drama of Gogol, Ostrovsky, and Chekhov. Chekhov, however, added subtle dramatic devices which gave him a worldwide influence as an innovator in the theater. Particularly as staged by the Moscow Art Theater under Stanislavsky's careful direction, Chekhov's plays proved to be a highlight of recent world drama.

During the first two decades of this century Russia produced a large number of dramatic pioneers. Generally classified as symbolists, these writers showed great originality and bravery in suggesting departure from traditional dramatic modes. Whether their work would have borne more permanent fruit had it not been diverted by World War I and the Communist revolution remains a question.

So busy fighting the White armies, staving off famine, and establishing itself in the European family of nations, the new Union of Soviet and Socialist Republics found little time to police its internal cultural development in the 1920's. As a result all types of Soviet literature, including drama, showed great originality and promise. The dramatic innovations of Meyerhold were particularly noteworthy.

As the Communist Party seized firmer control of internal affairs, however, restrictions were increasingly imposed upon all cultural life. Both the drama and dramatic criticism entered a period of stagnation from which they have never recovered. The concept of socialist realism, proffered supposedly as a useful guideline to Soviet writers and critics, has instead been a handy club to threaten anyone who might show independent thought or artistic creativity. Political repression in a police state can be accomplished quite easily by labeling a non-conformist as "bourgeois," "formalist," or "alien to the spirit of the Soviet people." As long as the definition of the terms, and their applications, reside solely within the party apparatus it is futile to expect the nation to live up to its great promise both in drama and in criticism.

13. 20th Century European Criticism

Probably nothing is more characteristic of twentieth-century art forms than their cosmopolitan quality. Despite emphasis upon folk elements, the drama of our century is as much at home in Buenos Aires or Moscow as it is in Paris or New York. The many dramatic innovations of our time—naturalism, expressionism, the grotesque, fantasy—find vigorous supporters and vehement detractors in almost every nation where plays are performed. And so it is reasonable to expect that the chief conditioning factor in a modern critic's outlook is less his country of origin than his specific sensibility and taste.

Eric Bentley has properly mentioned that the two antipodes of modern drama are realism and non-realism. The varying shades and precise combinations of these polar approaches define the wide limits within which modern drama operates. Moreover, the fluidity of dramatic form is scarcely less remarkable than the versatility of contemporary dramatic criticism.

The role played by "little theaters" and "art theaters" is well known. Beginning with the Meiningen Players (a result of the deep impression made upon the Duke of Saxe-Meiningen by Charles Kean's "ensemble" effect in a Shakespearian production in 1859), the concept of an intimate, serious audience for drama spread rapidly. The Théâtre Libre in Paris, the Independent Theatre in London, the Freie Bühne in Berlin, the Moscow Art Theater, and the Abbey Players of Dublin were all early pioneers in introducing plays that otherwise had no audience. Along with the plays came stirring defenses of the dramatic fare.

The Moscow Art Theater, organized by Stanislavsky and Nemirovich-Danchenko, was particularly influential. A confluence of native Russian "ensemble" techniques with elements of the Meiningen Players and the Théâtre Libre, the Moscow Art Theater came to be highly regarded for its unity of effect, with no star actors "stealing the show," but with each actor rendering his role out of a deep sense of identification with the character. A high point in modern drama was the performance, around 1900, of a Chekhov play by the Moscow Art Theater.

Chekhov's greatest critic in the West has been the relatively obscure English dramatist, George Calderon. In a preface to his translation of *The Sea Gull* and *The Cherry Orchard*, Calderon in 1912 defined the revolutionary contributions to dramatic art made by Chekhov. Chekhov's plots, said Calderon, are "centrifugal," that is, they focus not upon the events themselves but outward upon the larger process of the world which those events illuminate. Chekhov also captured atmospheric effects by rendering group emotions, noticing that people behave differently in groups than when alone. Another feature of Chekhov's style brought out by Calderon is his ironic contrast of moods, showing life's tragicomedy at work; not only is Lopakhin's joyous purchase of the cherry orchard the moment of Madame Ranevsky's demise, but more importantly Lopakhin himself says at the same time, through tears: "If only we could change this distorted, unhappy life somehow." Chekhov's use of so human a "villain" and a "fallen woman" as "heroine" also shows his daring desertion of character types. His dramatic art was immersed in such deep well-springs of human understanding that "to understand is to forgive, and it would be strange not to forgive." Calderon also showed Chekhov's great artistry in his use of disconnected dialogue, stage pictures, and subtle but lifelike methods of disclosing character traits. Although he is the leading interpreter of one of the greatest artists of modern drama, Calderon is somehow overlooked by most writers in the field.

While serving as director of the Court Theatre in London from 1904 to 1906, the playwright Harley Granville-Barker introduced many new dramatists to the English audience. The actor Maurice Evans says that the theater of ideas scarcely existed in England in 1900, but by the end of 1906, "ideas were the rage. In one leap, the English stage had grown up, and the Modern Theatre had arrived."[1]

Another influence that eventually proved to be profound was that of the Swedish dramatist August Strindberg. In 1888 he published the play *Miss Julie*, with a preface that represented a new departure from naturalism. In place of the "well made" play that was the outward form that Ibsen had built upon, Strindberg based his play upon characters who are "conglomerates," as he said, for he felt that the rapid transitions of modern life made people vacillating, out-of-joint, torn between the old and the new. "Since the persons in my play are modern characters, living in a transitional era more hurried and hysterical than the previous one at least, I have depicted them as more unstable, as torn and divided, a mixture of the old and the new,"[2] he said. Dialogue and sets were also to be jagged and dissonant; monologue, pantomime, and the dance are revived. The point of the play is moral relativism, with the same pluralistic standards that Pirandello used later. Strindberg also antedated Chekhov in such things as "hero-less" drama, jagged dialogue, and use of monologue.

Strindberg's second contribution lay in Chamber Drama, a form of fantasy suggested to him by Maeterlinck's technique. These plays, such as *The Dream Play*, *The Road to Damascus*, and *The Ghost Sonata*, are based upon the illogic and free association of a dream. In his preface to *A Dream Play* in 1902 Strindberg explained: "Anything may happen: everything is possible and probable. Time and space do not exist."[3] As for characters, they are "split, doubled, and multiplied: they evaporate and are condensed, are diffused and concentrated."[4] In true twentieth century style, he states that modern drama needs fluid form — a theme should be allowed to find the form that suits it best.

Strindberg's deliberate departure from realism has come to be called expressionism. Besides O'Neill, who expressed great indebtedness to Strindberg, the chief expressionists were a group of German dramatists who wrote during the World War I period. An adverse critic of expressionism, Georg Simmel, called it an attempt to seize the essence of life while overlooking life's content. A more sympathetic critic, C.E. Dahlstrom, finds expressionism subjective, lyrical, spiritual, unconscious, and a search for the divine while asserting man's dignity. Leading playwrights of the movement include Reinhard Sorge, Paul Kornfeld, Georg Kaiser, Ernst Toller, and Karel Capek. Kornfeld's advice to actors in his play *The Seduction* is that microscopic naturalism is far less convincing than the stylization of expressionism, which uses exaggeration and distortion consciously to achieve a given purpose.

The Weimar Republic was the breeding ground for another

important movement, the Epic Theater. Years before, Romain Rolland had asked for a People's Theater, which would provide recreation as well as be a source of energy and a guiding light to the intelligentsia. Erwin Piscator, in his book *The Political Theater* (1929), lays claim to founding Epic Theater, which is intentionally didactic, using films as well as acting, and attempting a deliberate fusion of epic and drama forms.

Bertolt Brecht, the leading writer of Epic drama, even goes so far as to fuse the lyric in with the other forms. The intent, nevertheless, is objective realism, so that spectators can make dispassionate analyses of social problems, without emotional involvement that prevents clear thinking. Brecht's play *The Resistible Rise of Arturo Ui* in 1941 "materialises out of a comparison between Nazism and Chicago gangsterism,"[5] says Ronald Hayman. Brecht believed that human society, corrupt as it was, could be changed, Hayman felt, and that drama's technique needed to be modified in order for it to serve as social reform.

Instead of acting out sequences, this drama uses narration in order to awaken the observer into making sound decisions after arguments and pieces of knowledge have been presented. Brecht also uses music, but the singers are also narrators; pouring forth one's soul in music, he says, is a private matter. Acting in Epic drama is the converse of Stanislavsky's method; the actor must stay outside the character, lest undesirable subjectivity enter. The playwright's job is not to express himself, but to cancel out himself as he creates images informative of the external world.

Despite his theoretical aloofness from non-realistic elements, Brecht has shown in his plays a synthesis of such taboo techniques as stage illusion, suspense, and sympathy with the other realistic devices of Epic Theater. His best plays, such as *Beggar's Opera*, *Mother Courage*, *The Good Woman of Setzuan*, and *The Caucasian Chalk Circle*, use tableaux, charades, and chorus, as well as realistic elements. Though he avers that "the main thing is to teach the spectator to reach a verdict,"[6] Brecht works much art and entertainment into his peculiar sort of synthesis.

Jean-Paul Sartre lies at the opposite extreme from Brecht. Though both wish to synthesize the individual and society, Sartre begins with the individual and Brecht begins with society. But just as Sartre cannot be completely subjective, neither can Brecht be wholly objective. Sartre describes existentialist drama as violent and brief, centered around a few characters, and compressed in time and space.

In fact, he says, the Three Unities can almost be revived for this type of drama. The play should remain somewhat distant, not familiar, for it resembles a religious ritual in that it forges a myth for the audience, by giving them an enlarged image of their universal plight. H.A. Mason has charged that Sartre's philosophy is never worked into the grain of his plays, but Bentley agrees with John Russell that this "inner rhetoric" of the theater is drama, as well as philosophy.

The discovery of electric lighting for stage effects wrought a profound influence upon modern drama. The Swiss stage designer, Adolphe Appia, was the most important innovator in modern stagecraft. He studied the psychological effects of light changes, and he recommended that the director be the chief impresario of the organic unity of the play, acting, lighting, costuming, and other artistic effects. He found four plastic elements in staging: perpendicular scenery, horizontal floor, lighted space, and moving actor. Other directors who have stressed stage effects, sometimes at the expense of the written play, include Max Reinhardt, Gordon Craig, Stanislavsky, Theodore Komisarjevsky, and Jacques Copeau.

Son of the actress Ellen Terry, Gordon Craig was, like Appia, a pioneer in creating innovative settings for the modern stage. Craig's books, *The Art of the Theatre* (1905) and *Towards a New Theatre* (1913), aimed to create a Wagnerian synthesis of dramatic arts, in which neither the text, the actor, nor the set would dominate.

Copeau's Théâtre du Vieux Colombier deserves special mention. In 1903 Guillaume Apollinaire had protested against photographic copywork as stage illusion, and requested *un drame surréaliste* (thus coining a crucial term, surrealism). Apollinaire wished to employ fantasy, cubism, symbolism, and numerous other non-realistic techniques in an effort to bring a "new joy" and a "voluptuousness" into a theater which would be a synthesis of all the art forms. His ambitious effort is now largely forgotten, but he helped influence at least three important figures: Sergei Diaghilev, Copeau, and Jean Cocteau. Diaghilev worked largely with dance, music, and scenery. Copeau founded the Théâtre du Vieux Colombier in 1913 as an experiment at synthesizing many art fields. Copeau trained a group of persons to be proficient in every aspect of the theater, and he had the good fortune to be surrounded by persons of high talent. As Eric Bentley says, "Who would not like to have seen *Parade* in 1917 — text by Cocteau, décor by Picasso, music by Erik Satie, choreography by Leonide Massine?"[7] André Gide was sure that "in leaving reality behind, the theater is today weighing anchor."[8]

The leading playwright of this new theater is Jean Cocteau. In both theory and practice he has shown some of the possibilities of infusing poetry and fantasy into modern drama. His *Call to Order*, a collection of criticism that Francis Fergusson considers one of the works which lay the basis for a contemporary theory of drama, shows that Cocteau rejects Wagnerian "hypnosis" as well as pedestrian realism. He wishes to have something skeptical and French, a recovery of the rationalist sense of form that the great French dramatists had. Cocteau felt that *King Ubu* by Alfred Jarry and *The Breasts of Tiresias* by Apollinaire had been the first plays to synthesize the problem play with symbolist drama. To show his daring, in the preface to his play, *The Wedding on the Eiffel Tower*, Cocteau said, "A theatrical piece ought to be written, presented, costumed, furnished with musical accompaniment, played, and danced, by a single individual."[9] Realizing that no such "universal athlete" exists, Cocteau said the next best thing would be to create a friendly group of stage people who could operate as if one. Similarities between Evreinov's monodrama and Cocteau's views are obvious.

A dramatist working to restore poetry into the modern theater is André Obey. Obey differs from Cocteau in writing drama which demands much more imaginative acting. Here Obey is fortunate in working with the dramatic ensemble trained by Jacques Copeau. For the Vieux Colombier has what Fergusson has called "the idea of a theater" — a serious purpose combined with sufficient talent to know the best way to approach dramaturgy.

Another unique trend in modern drama is the Italian "theater of the grotesque." Its founder, Luigi Chiarelli, wrote his play *The Mask and the Face* in 1916 in revolt against traditional sentimental Italian melodrama. The outstanding figure in the movement was the professor and playwright Luigi Pirandello. Pirandello felt that the combined form of tragicomedy breaks down comic detachment. We laugh at a painful occurrence to someone else, unless we empathize closely with that person.

Since man has reason, says Pirandello, he can only tolerate the irrationality of existence by inventing artificial categories for his own purposes. We ludicrously cling to these false constructs even after they have been shown to be illusory. Thus, we wear masks for the convenience of ourselves and others, but after all, they are simply masks, not reality. A mere comic writer laughs at man's deception, including self-deception, but the humorist will see the serious and painful aspect of the masking process, Pirandello felt. Pirandello's approach is in some ways a modern version of Ben Jonson's theory of the comedy of humours.

Technically, Pirandello's plays are an effort to convert intellect into passion. By subordinating plot action, he wishes to go beyond sensational suspense into the realm of contemplation. Like Shaw, Pirandello turns his back on romanticism; like Chekhov, he shuns traditional plot suspense; like Cocteau, he objects to drama being considered a form of Wagnerian hypnosis. If it is objected that the result is too philosophical to stage, Pirandello can show that much nonrepresentational drama, his own as well as others, has continued to show stage vitality as the century nears its final years.

The French philosopher Henri Bergson developed a theory of humor based, like Pirandello's, on detachment. A comic figure, said Bergson, gives the same stereotyped response to diverse stimuli. Bergson defined the comic as "the mechanical encrusted on the living."[10] But if there is no detachment between the observer and the comic figure, humor does not result. The reason we do not laugh at a man with a mechanical limp is that we feel sorry for him, Bergson said. Comedy, he believed, requires "an anesthesia of the heart."

The English psychologist Edward Bullough expanded Bergson's principle into a general concept applying to all esthetics, including drama. In an essay called "Psychical Distance" in 1912, Bullough showed that proper reaction to all art forms requires a certain optimum distance between performer and spectator. For example, when an actor, as a person, speaks to the audience directly in the midst of a play, the distance is lost, and the dramatic illusion dissolves. An example of too much psychical distance might be an art work incorporating abstruse symbolism. Some modern drama, like Brecht's Epic Theater, dares to intentionally destroy the dramatic illusion in order to achieve what Brecht thought was a more important, a more political effect.

The Hungarian critic George Lukacs developed a sociology of modern drama cast in Marxian terms. Early playwrights had spontaneous communication with their audiences, he said, because they shared a common religious viewpoint. Capitalism and rationality, however, had destroyed this viewpoint by reorganizing society along its economically most productive lines. Isolated from the masses, bourgeois dramatists wrote intellectual plays for elite audiences. Cut off from serious drama, the public turned to vaudeville and melodrama. The Little Theater movement made a valiant attempt to restore serious drama to the common people, but it failed.

Bourgeois drama has new heroes, said Lukacs. They are passive, acted upon, defenders rather than attackers. For bourgeois drama, he said, the conflict is to show man as merely the intersection of great forces that he is powerless to control. Bourgeois drama is drama not of the individual but of individualism. Renaissance drama involved great individuals, who performed great deeds. Today, Lukacs said, "survival as an individual, the integrity of individuality, becomes the vital center of drama."[11] "Since so much of the inner man has fallen prey to destiny, the last battle is to be enacted within."[12]

Because modern bourgeois life lacks a mythology, Lukacs said, its dramatic themes are anchorless. In the absence of deep themes, the drama is thrown back onto character. But character study is uninteresting, he felt, unless based on abnormal conduct or pathology. "In pathology alone," he said, "lies the possibility of rendering undramatic man dramatic."[13] He believed that nothing but pathology gives the concentrated action and the sensual intensity that transforms the ordinary act into something symbolic and thus universal. Lukacs could well understand the violence and sexuality of modern motion pictures and television programs.

The Polish dramatist and painter Stanislaw Witkiewicz approached modern drama quite differently. To him, a play should transport the audience to experience metaphysical feelings. Influenced by Picasso, Witkiewicz sought for "Pure Form" in the theater. He too felt that realistic drama had reached a dead end. Fantasy, pursued along purely formal lines, could help the audience achieve an apprehension of the mysteries of existence, he said. Like Gordon Craig, he tried to achieve a creative synthesis of the arts within his dramatic unity.

The Belgian critic Henri Ghéon would have cautioned Witkiewicz that such an artistic synthesis is not easily attained. In his search for such a unity, Richard Wagner found that one of the arts, music, submerged the dramatic elements, Ghéon felt. Two English critics, however, would have agreed with the stress on inner action mentioned both by Lukacs and Witkiewicz. C.E. Vaughan in his *Types of Tragic Drama* stated that the whole history of drama is in the direction of depiction of inner states of feeling. Allardyce Nicoll in *The Theory of Drama* said that the outwardly static but inwardly alive plays of Chekhov and Maeterlinck constituted the most creative aspect of modern drama. "The modern age has found the world of the subconscious,"[14] Nicoll asserted.

A dominant theme of modern criticism is discussion of whether drama can regain its classical greatness until its dialogue returns to poetry. William Butler Yeats, the Irish poet and playwright, felt that only poetry can move spectators to the spiritual illumination and transformation of great drama. Yeats's criticism was important in helping rally the Irish nation to support its native drama. His *Advice to Playwrights* voiced the principles underlying the Irish dramatic renaissance: the play's theme was to be a criticism or a vision of life; the play's elements needed to contain "the logic of carefully wrought form"; and playwrights needed to be granted freedom from all traditional esthetic conventions.

Yeats saw the need for radical reform in the theater. Since great drama liberates the mind, the theater should be a place of intellectual excitement. He quoted Sainte-Beuve's dictum that there is nothing immortal in literature except style. The dramatist must not only give a character that language which is his and nobody else's, but have him speak it with so much emotional subtlety that the hearer will not know whether it was the thought or the word that moved him, or whether the two can be separated at all.

Acting and scenery Yeats felt should be simplified so as not to destroy the overall effect wrought by the mythic theme poetically executed. He said that tragedy constantly breaks down the dykes separating man from man, whereas comedy performs its scenes upon the dykes. Yeat's inherent affinity for lyric expression and symbolism kept his plays from a very broad following, but it also showed there was a place for poetry in modern drama.

Somerset Maugham, who wrote a number of successful prose plays, pronounced what he hoped would be the death knell on prose drama in *The Summing Up* (1938). It was a mistake for drama to abandon verse, he said. Poetry gives greater emotional effect, "but more than that," he felt, "verse delivers a play from sober reality. It puts it at a higher level, at one remove from life, and so makes it easier for the audience to attune themselves to that state of feeling in which they are most susceptible to the drama's specific appeal."[15]

T.S. Eliot both as dramatist and critic sought to return poetry to the theater. His theory was that literary works do not exist in isolation from the past members of their genre. Hence, one always asks of a new work whether it builds upon a tradition, and if so what its original contribution is to its genre. Since *Everyman*, Eliot felt, the theater has declined, because as it moved toward photographic realism it moved away from art. Great drama, Eliot said, requires a dramatic convention, a form which can "arrest the flow of spirit at any particular point before it expands and ends its course in the desert of exact likeness."[16]

Eliot's search for proper language in drama was for a modern rhythmic idiom which would have the emotional force of poetry without sounding artificial to a modern audience. Prose, said Eliot, is superficial and ephemeral compared to the permanence and universality of verse. He also believed in the three dramatic unities of theme, time, and place, because he thought that they, like verse, give concentration and intensity to a play.

Christopher Fry agreed with Eliot on two main points: modern drama should be in verse form, and drama will have to return to its role as religious liturgy if it is again to be a vital art form. Fry said that when he wrote a comedy, the characters first presented themselves as qualified for tragedy. "If the characters were not qualified for tragedy," he said, "there would be no comedy. In a century less flayed and quivering we might reach it more directly, but not now unless every word we write is going to mock us."[17]

Noting that three of Fry's plays were opening within one week on London stages in 1951, Harold Hobson, drama critic for the *London Times*, accounted for Fry's popularity. First of all, said Hobson, London playgoers, starved for rich language after years of dialogue by Shaw, John Galsworthy, and Terence Rattigan, find that Fry's rich vocabulary gives them "almost a pentecostal feeling that he is speaking a new and inexhaustible tongue."[18] Then too, Fry is a romantic, and the thwarted romanticism is a welcome relief after years of austere realism. Fry's wit appeals to the sophisticated Londoners, Hobson felt, and his sense of humor was directed against his own pretentiousness: "He is forever pricking the balloons of his own eloquence."[19] Fry's great weakness, to Hobson, was his plots. Not being a born story teller, he had not evolved moods or themes, as did Chekhov and Maeterlinck. If he were to encompass great stories or themes in his plays, he would rank among the century's finest dramatists, Hobson believed.

Shakespearian criticism has continued to be one of the important branches of modern dramatic criticism. The chief tendencies recently have been to uncover new textual evidence concerning the plays, to study imagery for the purpose of gaining new insight into the plays, and to study the relationship between the plays and Renaissance thought. The chief textual pioneers have been A.W. Pollard, R.B. McKerrow, W.W. Greg, and J. Dover Wilson.

Pollard, using bibliographic techniques, has asserted that, contrary to previous beliefs, the general Shakespearian text is relatively pure, if one differentiates between the pirated quartos and other texts. McKerrow has gathered evidence to show that at least some of the plays were printed from Shakespeare's own drafts, or from transcripts of the drafts. Greg has evolved principles of emendation that replace an editor's whimsy with a series of criteria for determining the conditions under which a particular text was published. Wilson concerned himself largely with new interpretations growing out of recent textual discoveries. J.M. Robertson, who rejects much of the Folio as spurious, agrees with Charles Lamb that many of the plays are not stageworthy.

Caroline Spurgeon did a masterful analysis of Shakespeare's imagery, showing how each tragedy has its dominating images, which heighten emotional effects in a way similar to Wagner's leitmotifs. A.C. Bradley specialized in a study of Shakespeare's characters, and Granville-Barker, with extensive theatrical background, defended the plays as acting vehicles against the attacks of Lamb and Robertson. Tolstoy drew Shaw's praises, however, for stating that Shakespeare's plays could not possibly be great art, for they failed to transmit the highest religious feeling, and they did not unite all readers in one common feeling. Sir Walter Raleigh wrote an admirable introduction to Shakespeare in the English Men of Letters Series. The Germans, William Creizenach and L.L. Schücking, discarded romantic eulogy in favor of studies of Elizabethan staging conditions; Schücking shows, for example, how the monologues may actually have been intended for the intimate theatergoers surrounding Shakespeare's stage. G.B. Harrison finds many topical allusions in the plays; T.S. Eliot sees in Shakespeare the growing Renaissance stress on individualism and self-dramatization, of which Hamlet is only one example.

The newness of modern drama has led many critics to assume that someone needs to write a new *Poetics* for the contemporary theater. Charles Morgan, drama critic for the *London Times*, attempted that task in 1933. The principle underlying Morgan's esthetics is what he called "illusion," by which he meant the feeling of being transported, ecstatic, as if seized by a mysterious power. He felt that this standard could be applied universally to all plays as a measure of their power, that it establishes a standard of judgment which can vary according to the type of play, and it can be used in both traditional and non-traditional drama. The basic criterion seems so impressionistic that Morgan's approach never gained wide use.

A roll call of prominent English critics of this century would have to include James Agate, W.L. Courtney, Desmond MacCarthy, Ashley Dukes, Gilbert Cannon and John Palmer. Agate specialized in criticizing acting; MacCarthy was a brilliant, if erratic, impressionist; Dukes directed his own theater for many years, and wrote a number of books on drama. Certain classical scholars have also opened up new understanding of Greek drama. Outstanding have been S.H. Butcher, H.D.F. Kitto, and the Cambridge cultural anthropologists. Gilbert Murray, for example, has shown how parts of Greek religious ritual correspond to the parts of the plot as described by Aristotle.

Ivor Brown was one of England's most distinguished contemporary critics. His outlook he phrased as follows: "The first business of criticism, in any art, is to assist and extend the enjoyment of that art by writing about it intelligently, agreeably, and with sensitive response to its beauties, and with a good-tempered and, if possible, witty dismissal of its follies."[20] The critic, he says, may censure, "but his damns must follow deliberation and his curses be tempered by courtesy."

W.A. Darlington believes that a criticism is an emotional reaction experienced subconsciously, and thus not amenable to logical argument. Eric Keown, who says that billboards play a more important role in a play's success than do dramatic critics, feels that readers must come to know the temperament of a critic before they can properly evaluate his comments. And T.C. Worsley insists that critics and theatrical people must ever be at war, for the critic can never afford to fully acknowledge Lope de Vega's dictum that "the box-office pays the bill, and thus should call the tune."

A controversy between two academic critics over Restoration comedy led to a further refinement in the theory of comedy. L.C. Knights asserted that Restoration comedy had no significant relationship to the best thought of its time. These comedies, Knights concluded, are not so much immoral as they are "trivial, gross, and dull."

F.W. Bateson retorted that Knights had misinterpreted these comedies, just as had such critics as Macauley, Lamb, and Hazlitt. In their best scenes, Bateson said, most of the grossness and all of the triviality disappears. Even the sexual banter had a serious social function, he argued. To defend his point Bateson defined comedy as drama containing "the agreeable reversal of an expectation that will itself be reversed."[21] The dramatist must assume two separated planes of reality in his audience. The ridiculous arises in the viewer's sudden transition from everyday objective reality to the subjective plane of dream fantasy or irrational dream-fulfillment. "The possibilities of serious social comment within the comic framework," said Bateson, "seem to depend upon the degree to which either or both of the opposed planes of meaning are conceptualized."[22]

Some critics interpreted John Osborne's play *Look Back in Anger* (1956) as a turning point in modern English drama. Osborne achieved a directness in attacking British social conventions that was relatively rare in the London theater. Osborne's thesis was that there was room at the top in English society only for those willing to pay the price of social climbing. John Rowdon mused that "the only part of English life that has been left untouched by the welfare state is its snobbery."[23]

Accepting the epithet, Osborne replied, "To be angry is to care. English playwrights like to indulge their audiences, and English audiences like to be indulged."[24] But, he added, I shall not play your silly game. I shall wake them up to their own smallness.

Osborne felt that American playwrights Arthur Miller and Tennessee Williams had prepared London theatergoers for his type of drama. "These men conditioned English audiences emotionally for the kind of plays I am writing," he said, plays which describe the "real despairs, frustrations, and sufferings of the age we are living in."[25]

Anger is also a key emotion for Friedrich Duerrenmatt, Swiss dramatist whose play, *The Visit* (1956), uses elements of expressionism and the grotesque to show the prostitution of integrity in the modern world. In *Problems of the Theatre*, written in 1961, Duerrenmatt stated that tragedy, which presupposes a formed, logical world, is inappropriate today. Comedy is the proper medium for an unformed, chaotic world, "a world turned upside down, a world about to fold like ours,"[26] he said.

Tragedy implies guilt, but we moderns feel no guilt, Duerrenmatt said. Instead we all feel we are victims. "Our world has led to the grotesque as well as to the atom bomb. It is a world like that of Hieronymous Bosch whose apocalyptic paintings are also grotesque,"[27] he added.

Duerrenmatt describes modern man as a reckless driver going ever faster down life's highway. Questions could be asked about the driver's qualifications, about whose car it is, and what is the driver's destination. But "the driver would much prefer the passengers to praise the beauty of the countryside."[28] The ethical dramatist today cannot simply praise the landscape. But alas—he too cannot get out of the car heading for catastrophe. His response—"fear, worry, and above all anger open his mouth wide."[29]

But drama, Duerrenmatt feels, can still show modern man's courage. We must accept a world we did not choose, and do not feel at home in, but we must never capitulate before it. Like Schill, in *The Visit*, we can set a pattern of dignity and courage for others to follow.

The Polish director Jerzy Grotowski influenced the serious theater in Europe and America for the past several decades. He founded what he called "a Poor Theater," one in which actors wholly surrender themselves in their acting. Such actors must free themselves from all self-conceit and pretense, from all impulse and compulsion. There needs to be a thorough control of every aspect of the body, as well as the discovery of the innermost core of one's personality. The purpose of such Spartan discipline is to get the viewer to do likewise. The theater thus acts as a psychoanalytical purge agent.

Grotowski says that since cinema does certain things better than the stage, drama should confine itself to its strength—the live actor and his closeness to the viewer. Grotowski says that the audience he seeks is not the tavern habitué, but the person seeking "the truth about himself and his mission in life." The themes of this kind of drama, Grotowski believes, will be universal myths: "for instance, religious myths: the myth of Christ and Mary; biological myths: birth and death, love symbolism or, in a broader sense, Eros and Thanatos; national myths which it would be difficult to break down into formulas, yet whose very presence we feel in our blood."[30]

"I do not feel that the crisis in the theatre can be separated from certain other crisis processes in contemporary culture,"[31] Grotowski said. The decline of religion has led to the disappearance of the theater as sacred ritual. Now, he believes, it is necessary to create a secular sacrum in the theater. To save society, "a secular consciousness in place of the religious one seems to be a psycho-social necessity for society."[32] Although the commercial theater hardly seems to be the place to look for such high purpose, concludes Grotowski, there are always "secular saints" like Stanislavsky who can spark theater lovers to rediscover the power of the theater to spiritualize everyday life.

Sometimes a critic pays homage to a predecessor in language that gets at the heart of criticism. For example, in extolling his predecessor Kenneth Tynan as theater critic of *The London Observer*, Robert Cushman in 1980 summarized the attributes of a good drama critic. Tynan, says Cushman, was the best modern critic because he was observant, sensitive, witty, a good judge of acting, with wide sympathies ranging from high tragedy to slapstick farce. "Criticism is a peculiar activity," Cushman said, "since it is only as valuable as the sensibility of the person doing it. It requires a self—and yet that self must never become explicit."[33]

Tynan could applaud works with which he disagreed, provided they moved him, Cushman believed. "The worst you can say of him," Cushman felt, "is that he was inclined to build flimsy theoretical edifices on his purely instinctive enthusiasms."[34] If we want to know how our theater looked and felt, we read Tynan. Cushman concluded, "I never saw Olivier's Coriolanus or the first visit to London of the Moscow Art Theater but reading his accounts of them I can sense their quality exactly."[35]

The theater critic for *The New Statesman*, Benedict Nightingale, recently tried to account for the fact that modern dramatists seem to flourish more abundantly in England than in the United States. He felt that the long British stage tradition, plus British pride in their language and culture, were unique assets. British playwright David Rudkin says, "When the cultural order is breaking down, and the myths are not standing up to the reality of experience, people seem to need to ritualize their doubt and anxiety in a public way."[36] Americans may go to church, a football game, or the movies—the Englishman attends the theater.

Nightingale also referred to government support to British drama. In 1976 a total of 360 dramatists received some type of governmental stipend. Also, the many repertory companies employ a resident dramatist and pay him for his work.

England's size impresses Nightingale as an asset, for if there is a promising British playwright, London theater managers know about him. Also, Broadway production costs are prohibitively high, sometimes ten times as great as in London, which "has become a tryout town for New York,"[37] according to Nightingale.

In the United States, Nightingale says, drama critics are too demanding and too influential. British audiences are more likely to overrule a critical panning than American ones. Then too, British playwrights are not so readily wooed away by Hollywood or television studios. In fact, British television stations must present several hours of original drama each week in order to keep licensed. Nightingale feels that the attitude of British playwrights toward the public is more respectful, and in return they earn greater respect.

In conclusion, it can be said of European dramatic criticism in the twentieth century that, like European drama, there is a wide range of outlook, ranging from traditional concern with plot, character, acting, and sets to revolutionary ideas for wholesale change in the approach to the theater. In some ways the criticism is an even more lucid mirror of these troubled times than the plays themselves. For the plays at best capture the terror, anguish, and dissatisfaction of a world that can harbor a holocaust and then prepare for worse things. But the criticism has to be more explicit in its evaluative judgments, not only explaining radical theatrical innovation but also assessing whether morally and esthetically the new departure is something to be encouraged. No doubt the critics have shown little of the spontaneity, creativity, and literary excellence of the dramatists. But they at least have provided theatergoers with an understanding and an awareness of widely disparate dramatic forms. To that extent they can certainly be said to have fulfilled their function.

14. The Theater of the Absurd

Perhaps the most distinctive school of drama in the twentieth century has been the Theater of the Absurd. A movement that has in turn bewildered, shocked, and enlightened modern playgoers deserves special treatment because of its origins, aims, techniques, and influences.

In their excellent anthology *Masters of Modern Drama*, Haskell Block and Robert Shedd describe how the anarchy and nightmare of contemporary politics has resulted in "a distrust of ready-made ideologies, in the theatre as well as in politics."[1] Bizarre and grotesque theatrical techniques indicate to Block and Shedd "the dissolution of moral and spiritual absolutes in our time."[2]

George Wellwarth finds the modern theater to be one of protest and paradox: its common theme is protest and its common technique is paradox. The protest is against the social order in English and German drama, Wellwarth believes, and against the general human condition in French drama. Modern dramatists, he feels, voice the bitter cynicism of persons lacking both faith and hope. They find it hard to speak because they find so few listeners. So they have been driven to the use of paradox in order to attract attention.

The opening gun of the revolution was fired by French dramatist Alfred Jarry, whose play *King Ubu* made a sensation at its première in Paris on December 10, 1896. The play was originally a schoolboy prank aimed at a dictatorial teacher Jarry had suffered. Jarry used what he called pataphysics, strict logic employed to arrive at patently absurd conclusions. Since reason cannot explain the mystery of death, Jarry finds it worthless and therefore satirizes it.

Among those present at Lugné-Poë's Theatre de l'Oeuvre on that historic occasion were Yeats, Copeau, and the symbolist poet Stéphane Mallarmé. Yeats was shocked, rightly sensing that he was witnessing the end of a dramatic epoch. Mallarmé found King Ubu to be "a prodigious personage. He enters into the repertoire of high taste and haunts me,"[3] Mallarmé confessed. Jacques Copeau rejoiced. "*King Ubu* is hundred per cent theatre," he said, "pure theatre, synthetic and creating on the margin of reality a reality based on symbols."[4]

One can easily understand how the audience could be shocked at Ubu. Cruel and ruthless, he makes himself King of Poland and then tortures and kills many people. As if with prophetic insight, Jarry prefigured in Ubu the reality of Hitler, Stalin, and Mao-Zdedung. Far-out poetic fantasy foreshadowed grim realistic tragedy.

The Theater of the Absurd grew out of the same soil as did the philosophy of existentialism. Clyde Smallwood found four existentialist concepts in Absurdist drama: "Man is nothing else but what he makes of himself"[5] (Sartre); man's perennial instability leads him to anguish; reason cannot make sense out of the human condition; man has within himself the power to be, but it takes a supreme effort, a "bounding leap."

Whereas existentialist drama might argue about the meaninglessness of modern life, Absurdist drama merely presents it. "It is this striving for an integration between the subject matter and the form in which it is expressed," says leading Absurdist critic Martin Esslin, "that separates the Theatre of the Absurd from the Existentialist theatre."[6]

Nonetheless it was the existentialist Albert Camus who gave the first extensive literary treatment to the feeling of the absurd. In *The Myth of Sisyphus* Camus described modern man's position as absurd because his innate desire for order is irrational in a universe that itself lacks purpose. A frantic search reveals that the only thing one can be certain of is that one can be certain of nothing. This, then, becomes the byword of the Absurdist playwright: Why does modern man insist upon trying to make sense out of a senseless universe? This is absurd.

The Rumanian playwright Eugène Ionesco, in an essay on Franz Kafka, defined the absurd as "that which is devoid of purpose.

Cut off from his religious, metaphysical, and transcendental roots, man is lost; all his actions become senseless, absurd, useless."[7]

The Absurdist dramatist Arthur Adamov says in *The Confession*, his autobiography: "I am separated. What I am separated from I cannot name. Formerly it was called God. Today it no longer has any name."[8] Analyzing himself, Adamov found that alienation and passivity are the symptoms of his spiritual sickness.

"The crisis of our time is essentially a religious crisis," Adamov said. "It is a matter of life and death. From whatever point he starts, modern man comes to the same conclusion: behind its visible appearances, life hides a meaning that is eternally inaccessible."[9] Man's dilemma, Adamov concludes, is that man knows it is impossible to discern life's meaning, and yet it is also impossible to give up the important quest.

It is not only that for many moderns God is dead. In addition, as Esslin says, "mankind has learned the bitter lesson of the falseness and evil nature of some of the cheap and vulgar substitutes that have been set up to take His place."[10] Having seen wars, stalags, and genocide, faithless people are "searching for a way in which they can, with dignity, confront a universe deprived of what was once its center and its living purpose, a world which has become disjointed, purposeless, absurd,"[11] in Esslin's view. Conventional dramatic techniques will not suffice to depict these shockingly new conditions, Esslin feels.

According to Esslin, Absurdist drama asks spectators to focus on this disorganized world, assuming that sensitive members of the audience will naturally want to re-orient it. "The madness of the times," he says, "lies precisely in the existence, side by side, of a large number of unreconciled beliefs and attitudes."[12] Some of those he mentions are conventional morality versus advertising ballyhoo; conflicts of science and religion; and loud clamor supposedly in the public interest that is really selfish at heart. No, it is not the dramatist who is mad, Esslin concludes, but rather the society that his plays so artfully portray.

Ionesco calls his play, *The Bald Soprano*, a tragicomic picture of life at a time "when we can no longer avoid asking ourselves what we are doing here on earth and how, having no deep sense of our destiny, we can endure the crushing weight of the material world."[13] Even the rebel Antonin Artaud agrees that "the highest possible idea of the theater is one that reconciles us philosophically with Being. It was with just such an intention that the theater was created, to include man and his appetites only to the degree that he is magnetically confronted with his destiny, not to submit to it, but to measure himself against it."[14]

Paradoxically, though it is based upon absence of faith in God, Absurdist drama, in Esslin's words, "comes nearest to being a genuine religious quest in our age: an effort, however timid and tentative, in search of a dimension of the Ineffable; an effort to instill in man again the lost sense of cosmic wonder, to shock him out of an existence that has become trite, mechanical, complacent, and deprived of the dignity that comes of awareness."[15] Absurdist drama thus attempts to give "the cosmic connection" to the masses of people for whom God seems to be dead.

Esslin sees, therefore, in Absurdist drama a return of drama to its original religious purpose. "Like ancient Greek tragedy and the medieval mystery plays," he says, "the Theatre of the Absurd is intent on making its audience aware of man's precarious and mysterious postion in the universe."[16] It is precisely this experience of the ineffability, the emptiness, the nothingness at the basis of the universe that forms the content of Eastern as well as Christian mystical experience."[17] Esslin goes on to show similarities between Absurdist drama and Zen Buddhism. Asked about the nature of enlightenment, Zen masters respond with kicks, blows, and a series of nonsense problems.

Ionesco, for one, is far from pessimistic about man's future. Confronting man with the harsh realities of his existence, he feels, can be the first step on the road to liberation. "To attack the absurdity of the human condition," he said, "is a way of stating the possibility of non-absurdity. I feel that every message of despair is the statement of a situation from which everybody must freely try to find a way out."[18]

J.L. Styan, noting that Absurdist drama is didactic, trying harder to enlighten than to amuse, says that this drama is "dark comedy," mixing tears and laughter. "Where in life their reconciliation is necessary if we are to make peace with ourselves," Styan says, "in drama their conflict is serviceable if that peace is to be disturbed."[19] Styan even adds a fourth unity to drama's three traditional ones, "a final tone and climate in which opposites may flourish together in the audience's mind."[20]

An interesting influence upon Absurdist drama has been early motion picture comedy. "Chaplin and Buster Keaton are the perfect embodiments of the stoicism of men when faced with a world of mechanical devices that have gone out of hand,"[21] says Esslin. Other comic film artists that have influenced this drama are Laurel and Hardy, W.C. Fields, and the Marx Brothers. Ionesco has the old man in *The Chairs* impersonate the month of February by "scratching his head like Stan Laurel." At the American première of *The Shepherd's Chameleon*, Ionesco was asked who had influenced his work the most. He replied that he had been nourished by the French Surrealistes but that the three biggest influences on his work had been Groucho, Chico, and Harpo Marx!

It took drama critics a long time to understand the purpose behind the seemingly trite language used in Absurdist drama. In totalitarian countries, however, citizens learn to decipher the bureaucratic double-talk, just as in democratic countries people learn to decode advertising slogans, euphemisms, and circumlocutions. Absurdist playwrights thus show a precarious state of communication among their characters. "It is merely a satirical magnification of the existing state of affairs," says Esslin. "Language has run riot in an age of mass communication. It must be reduced to its proper function—the expression of authentic content, rather than its concealment."[22]

By tying together the realistic with the improbable or the nonsensical, says Seymour Reiter, Absurdist playwrights show the absurd premises of modern life. Time and space categories can be violated, as in dreams. Henri Bergson had shown that comic absurdity used the same principle used in dreams, that is, violating our traditional categories of association. Also, Absurdist drama uses trivia in a repetitious and rhythmic way, so that the repetitive pattern makes the trivia formally and thematically significant—it shows the triviality of most modern-day concerns.

In 1961 Tom Driver interviewed Samuel Beckett, the Irish dramatist whose plays written in French have formed the core of the Absurdist drama. Driver reported that Beckett finds the modern world to be "a buzzing confusion." "The confusion is not by invention," said Beckett. "It is all around us and our only chance now is to let it in. The only chance of renovation is to open our eyes and see the mess. It is not a mess you can make sense of."[23] Although in previous eras drama turned its back on life's chaos, fearful it might grow formless if depicting the mess, in the modern world the mess is so all-compassing that the dramatist has no choice but to let it into his plays. The new drama would have a new form, Beckett believed. "To find a form that accommodates the mess, that is the task of the artist now,"[24] he said.

Driver asked Beckett whether life, death, and religion are his key themes. The inscrutability over life and death certainly fascinated him, Beckett replied. If we believed in either total salvation or total damnation, modern drama would have no theme, he said. We are hung up on the inexplicable, he continued, and "the key word in my plays is 'perhaps'."[25]

Beckett disavowed a religious purpose in his plays, but agreed that they deal with what religion deals with—distress. The world has not only chaos but compassion, Beckett said.

Harold Clurman had said that Beckett's *Waiting for Godot* was a reflection "of the impasse and disarray of Europe's present politics, ethic, and common way of life."[26] Driver pointed out that not only Europe but America and all "mature" societies arrive at a point where their economic and technological success leads them to examine the ultimate goals of their culture. "At present," said Driver, "no political party in Western Europe or America seems possessed of a philosophy of social change adequate to the pressures of current history."[27]

In Beckett's plays, Driver feels, time stands still because we have no future that we can clearly discern. Driver believes that these plays are a partial way out of the mess, "the murmuring of a man refusing merely to exist."[28] Critics who condemn Beckett for no clear-cut solution to the mess miss a crucial point, Driver said. His honesty is his dogma. Seeing no way out, he honestly says so. Perhaps an accurate picture of modern man's dilemma is the first step toward a solution. This may even be, concluded Driver, a dramatic example of Paul Tillich's "the courage to be."

Niklaus Gessner made a careful study of the dramatic devices employed by Beckett in creating his unique style. Gessner found that in *Waiting for Godot* Beckett employed at least forty-five stage directions indicating that a character was leaving the upright position, in other words, deserting the dignity of man. Gessner also found ten varying types of disintegration of language in the play ranging from clichés, simple misunderstandings, double entendres, and repetitions of synonyms to monologues (as a sign of dialogue breakdown) and one character's outpour of chaotic nonsense.

In the play Estragon constantly complains about boots that pinch his feet. When he finally takes the boots off and finds nothing in them, Vladimir says, "There's man all over for you, blaming on his boots the faults of his feet."

Vladimir, meanwhile, constantly fiddles with his hat. He says that he cannot think unless he wears it. Then he, Estragon, and Lucky start switching hats in a three-way comic routine reminiscent of the Marx Brothers in *Duck Soup*. As Seymour Reiter observed, it is as if everyone is looking for a "quick-fix" philosophy that fits his situation. Of course the search is futile, which is comic to witness but tragic to ponder.

Estragon asks his friend, "Shall we go?" Vladimir replies, "Yes, let's go." Stage direction: "They do not move." This sounds precisely like a United Nations resolution on Afghanistan or the Middle East. Is the bigger absurdity on the stage or in life?

Critics bemoaning the absence of plot in the play refuse to realize that this is a drama of situation rather than of events in sequence, Esslin believes. The subject matter of Absurdist drama is the playwright's personal intuition of the human situation, he adds. The events in *Waiting for Godot* are not a plot, Esslin explains, but "an image of Beckett's intuition that *nothing really ever happens* in man's existence."[29] In place of a clash of opposing temperaments as found in traditional drama, Beckett's theater concerns itself with posing metaphysical questions about man's place in the universe.

At one point in the play Vladimir says, "We'll hang ourselves tomorrow. Unless Godot comes." Estragon asks, "And if he comes?" Vladimir replies, "We'll be saved."

Mankind can end civilization through suicidal atomic war. But if God comes, man will be saved. In place of God one might substitute "universal disarmament" or "world community" or whatever universal salvation plan one might believe in. It is impossible, however, for a sensitive person not to respond in some fashion, which of course is Beckett's intent.

Beckett, speaking to Alden Whitman of the *New York Times* in 1967, said, "*Godot* is not despair, but hope. *Godot* is life — aimless, but always with an element of hope."[30]

Mel Gussow appraised Beckett's achievement upon his seventy-fifth birthday in 1981. "He has refined the nature of playwriting," said Gussow, "freeing it from traditional bonds of length, plot, character development, and stage movement. In his hands, stasis has become a dramatic art."[31] Gussow found Beckett's influence to be a profound one, influencing, among others, such dramatists as Edward Albee, Fernando Arrabal, David Mamet, Harold Pinter, Sam Shepard, and Tom Stoppard.

Gussow said that although most critics panned *Waiting for Godot* for lack of action, by now one paperback version alone has sold over 1.3 million copies. Recently a South African production was perceived as timely — many there are waiting for emancipation.

Asked why his most recent plays seem to get shorter and shorter, Beckett whimsically replied, "Joyce was a synthesizer, trying to bring in as much as he could. I am an analyzer, trying to leave out as much as I can."[32]

Although he was born in Rumania, Eugène Ionesco spent his boyhood in France, and so his plays are written in French. Later, upon his return to Rumania, some of his teachers were Nazis. Much of his drama can be understood as a protest against the tyranny of dictatorship. In *The Rhinoceros*, for example, he shows that people are so sheep-like that they will even turn themselves into animals, if necessary, in order to conform to peer-group pressure.

Though he writes with a serious purpose, Ionesco prefers to use comedy as his satiric medium. The comic, which he defines as the intuitive perception of the absurd, seems to him more conducive to despair than is tragedy. "The comic offers no way out," he explains. "The comic alone is capable of giving us the strength to bear the tragedy of existence."[33]

Ionesco plans to wake up lazy twentieth century man from his complacency and conformity. "We need to be virtually bludgeoned into detachment from our daily lives, our habits and mental laziness," he said. "Without a fresh virginity of mind, there can be no theatre. The real must be in a way dislocated, before it can be reintegrated."[34]

To achieve this effect, Ionesco admits, he sometimes uses tricks, such as grafting a serious interpretation on to a text that is absurd, wild, or comic. In his first play, *The Bald Soprano*, for example, Ionesco says that "it was by plunging into banality, by draining the sense from the hollowest clichés of everyday language that I tried to render the strangeness that seems to pervade our whole existence."[35] He says that since drama requires conflict, perhaps the intermingling of tragedy and farce, realism and fantasy, will serve as the basis for a new dramatic structure.

Alain Bosquet has identified at least thirty-six comic techniques used in *The Bald Soprano*, ranging from negation of action (scenes in which nothing happens), loss of characters' identity, misleading title, opposing explanations of the same thing, disconnected dialogue, and the raising of false expectations, to such linguistic devices as cliché, misuse of foreign language, and even complete loss of meaning, with language degenerating into pure sound patterns.

Rather than write about such "secondary problems" as politics or sex, Ionesco says he prefers to write plays about nothing. He agrees that *The Bald Soprano* has no action, "simply theatrical machinery functioning in a void. It illustrates 'comically' the emptiness of a world without metaphysics,"[36] he said.

He feels that he addressed his topic even more directly in *The Chairs*, a play in which a large crowd of guests are never seen, an orator cannot speak, and the two honored old people commit suicide. His subject here, he says, was not the orator's eulogy, nor the failures of life, "but the chairs themselves, that is to say, the absence of people, the absence of God, the unreality of the world, metaphysical emptiness."[37] His characters, he agrees, "are not fully conscious of their spiritual rootlessness, but they feel it instinctively and emotionally. They feel 'lost' in the world, something is missing which they cannot, to their grief, supply."[38]

Ionesco repudiates the "well made" play that is built around suspenseful action. He insists that his function as a dramatist is not to tell a story: "a play is a structure that consists of a series of states of consciousness which become intensified, get entangled, either to be disentangled again or to end in unbearable inextricability."[39]

Most plots are trite, Ionesco feels. The plays end only because the audience is tired and needs to go home to sleep. So Ionesco sometimes tells directors to cut his plays wherever they wish, or to supply other endings to his plays. Brecht too, at the conclusion of *The Good Woman of Setzuan*, says he does not like the ending, and invites the audience to write a better one. Ionesco asks how, in a meaningless world, can a dramatic plot be true to life and still have meaning? "It was not for me," he said, "to conceal the devices of the theatre, but rather make them still more evident, deliberately obvious, go all-out for caricature and the grotesque, way beyond the pale irony of witty drawing-room comedies."[40] Here he felt he could use farce, parody, and even burlesque.

A spirited critical war between Kenneth Tynan and Ionesco helped elucidate the playwright's goals and methods, as well as review the role of the drama critic. In 1958, writing in *The London Observer*, Tynan called Ionesco's world one of isolated robots. "It is not mine," Tynan said, "but I recognize it to be a valid personal vision, presented with great imaginative aplomb and verbal audacity."[41] But could this be, as some asserted, the gateway to the theater of the future. Hardly, Tynan thought, unless one sought a blind alley or a self-imposed vacuum.

The following week *The London Observer* carried Ionesco's response, in which he defined the playwright's role. "A work of art has nothing to do with doctrine,"[42] he declared. Politics separates man from man and creates great misunderstanding, he said. "The true society is extra-social," he stated, "that which is revealed by our common anxieties, our desires, our secret nostalgias."[43] We are governed more truly by these things than by our rulers. The "robot characters" that Tynan objected to are those who are slave to custom or to their ideology, and I intentionally showed their emptiness, said Ionesco. "If anything needs demystifying," he declared, "it is our ideologies, which offer ready-made solutions in a language that congeals as soon as it is formulated."[44] We must re-examine these ideologies in the light of our anxieties and our dreams, he said, and "their congealed language must be relentlessly split apart in order to find the living sap beneath."[45]

What is the critic's job, asked Ionesco, and where should he look for his criteria? "Inside the work itself," he answered, "in its universe and its mythology. The best judgment is a careful exposition of the work itself."[46]

A week later Tynan's final rejoinder appeared. I regret, said Tynan, that a man with such a positive attitude towards art as Ionesco has should have such a negative attitude towards life, and in fact should deny the umbilical relationship between the two. I fear, he continued, that Ionesco builds his ivory tower of art in order to escape criticism. Tynan recalled that Cyril Connolly once said that it was closing time in the gardens of the West, and that "from now on an artist will be judged only by the resonance of his solitude or the quality of his despair."[47] "Not by me he won't," Tynan responded abruptly. "I shall respond to the honesty of such testimonies, but I shall be looking for something more—for the artist who concerns himself, from time to time, with such things as healing."[48]

An even more revolutionary approach to drama than Ionesco's was that of the surrealist poet and dramatist Antonin Artaud. Martin Esslin feels that Artaud's chief contribution to the Theater of the Absurd was not so much his plays as his critical essays and his stage experiments as a producer. Like Ionesco disgusted with language as a medium, Artaud sought to express what language could not, through gesture, shapes, light, and movement. Influenced by the Marx Brothers, the music hall, and the Balinese theater, Artaud turned his back on drama as literature. Instead, he said, the theater should express dreams, in which our unconscious longing for crime, erotic sex, savagery, and even cannibalism is expressed. Perhaps he felt that the release at the unconscious level will clean out this detritus at the conscious level.

Artaud's approach to religion was unique. "Far from believing that man invented the supernatural and the divine," he said, "I think it is man's ages-old intervention which has ultimately corrupted the divine within him."[49]

Artaud was fascinated by the comparison made by St. Augustine between the plague, which killed without destroying internal organs, and the theater which, without killing, provoked mysterious changes in theatergoers. To Artaud the contemporary world was in such a total crisis that its only possible future was either purification or death.

"The theater, like a plague," he said, "is a delirium and is communicative."[50] He found in both the theater and the plague something at once victorious and vengeful. "We are aware," he said, "that the spontaneous conflagration which the plague lights wherever it passes is nothing else than an immense liquidation."[51] Similarly the theater at its best acts as a social purgative, he believed.

Like the plague, the theater returns man to his dark primitive myths, he said. "It releases conflicts, disengages powers, liberates possibilities, and if these possibilities and powers are dark, it is the fault not of the plague nor of the theater but of life."[52]

If the theater, or the plague, in the process of draining moral and social abscesses happens to be destructive, in either case what is really at work, he said, was the avenging finger of God. Thus either force is ultimately beneficial, for "impelling men to see themselves as they are, it causes the mask to fall, reveals the lie, the slackness, baseness, and hypocrisy of our world; and in revealing to men their dark power, their hidden force, it invites them to take, in the face of destiny, a superior and heroic attitude they would never have assumed without it."[53]

The only remaining question, Artaud felt, was "whether, in this slippery world which is committing suicide without noticing it, there can be found a nucleus of men capable of imposing this superior notion of the theater, men who will restore to all of us the natural and magic equivalent of the dogmas in which we no longer believe."[54]

The new theater that Artaud envisioned would have an entirely new language. In place of traditional dialogue, Artaud saw an artistic blend of the panoply of theatrical powers: music, dance, plastic art, pantomime, gesture, chant, architecture, lighting, and scenery. He also recommended the use of symbols, particularly those from the Bible, such as the needle's eye through which the camel cannot pass.

Artaud found this synthesis of the arts in Balinese drama. Whereas Western theater deals with superficial things like how to make love or make money, the Balinese theater is applied metaphysics. The Balinese have not lost, he said, "the sense of that mysterious fear which is one of the most stirring and essential elements of the theater."[55] Rather than display psychological complexes, the Balinese show us how to recover "the religious and mystic preference of which our theater has completely lost the sense."[56]

Bearing profound spiritual values, the Balinese theater is nonetheless a people's theater, which gives us an appreciation of their extraordinary intellectual level, Artaud said. Their celebration of joy and grief is in rites seemingly dictated by supernatural intelligence. For example, he describes the exquisite beauty of the women's headdress: "feathers and pearls of so beautiful a coloration that their combination has a quality of *revelation*, and the crests of which tremble rhythmically, responding *consciously*, or so it seems, to the tremblings of the body."[57] Here matter itself is used as spiritual revelation, he felt, achieved by a marvelous synthesis of form and content, message and vehicle. For Artaud, drama had never achieved a more organic unity than that of the Balinese theater.

Not to solve social or psychological conflicts but to express certain long buried truths by significant stage techniques would be to restore the theater to its lost greatness, said Artaud. "To link the theater to the expressive possibilities of forms, to everything in the domain of gestures, noises, colors, movements, and so on, is to restore it to its original direction, to reinstate it in its religious and metaphysical aspect, is to reconcile it with the universe."[58]

Since the Renaissance the Western theater has progressively degenerated into a type of storytelling popular psychology, Artaud believed. In his view, "stories about money, social careerism, the pangs of love unspoiled by altruism, sexuality sugar-coated with an eroticism that has lost its mystery have nothing to do with the theater. These torments, seductions, and lusts," he said, "before which we are nothing but Peeping Toms gratifying our cravings, tend to go bad, and their rot turns to revolution."[59]

We need to clarify our objectives, Artaud said. "If we are prepared for war, plague, famine, and slaughter, we have only to continue as we are, continue behaving like snobs."⁶⁰ The anarchy of modern drama and modern art merely reflects the anarchy in people's minds. "This empiricism, randomness, individualism, and anarchy must cease,"⁶¹ he declared. Enough of personal poems that benefit only the poet. Enough of "closed, egoistic, and personal art. Our spiritual anarchy and intellectual disorder," he stated, "is a function of the anarchy of everything else."⁶² It helps not a bit, he added, for modern drama to merely mirror society's anarchy.

Either we will return to drama's original function as religious rite, capable of recovering within ourselves those energies which ultimately create order and increase the value of life, he said, or else we might as well abandon ourselves now, and recognize that we are no longer good for anything but disorder, famine, blood, war, and epidemics. The theater, said Artaud, was man's last hope to overcome the sensuality and anarchy that were destroying modern civilization.

To the theater charged with the job of salvaging contemporary society Artaud assigned the bizarre title to Theater of Cruelty. I do not mean the cruelty of hacking one another's bodies, he said, "but on the contrary, a pure and detached feeling. Life cannot help exercising some blind rigor; this pure implacable feeling is what cruelty is. I have therefore said 'cruelty' as I might have said 'life' or 'necessity', because I want to indicate especially that for me the theater is act and perpetual emanation."⁶³

For Artaud creation was cruelty, existence and death were cruelty. Cruelty, he said, was our appetite for life, that pain apart from which life could not continue. Cruelty cements matter together, and molds the features of the created world. "Good is always upon the outer face," he stated, "but the face within is evil—evil which will eventually be reduced, but at the supreme instant when everything that was form will be on the point of returning to chaos."⁶⁴

The cruelty Artaud intends is "a kind of moral purity which is not afraid to pay life the price it must be paid."⁶⁵ This theater, he says, will choose subjects and themes "corresponding to the agitation and unrest characteristic of our epoch. These themes will be cosmic, universal, and interpreted according to the most ancient texts drawn from old Mexican, Hindu, Judaic, and Iranian cosmogonies."⁶⁶ For example, Artaud conceived of a spectacle called *The Conquest of Mexico*, in which the tyrannical anarchy of the colonizers would be contrasted with the profound moral harmony of the conquered.

Artaud saw the new theater grounded in a metaphysics dealing with Chaos, Creation, and Becoming, cosmic ideas which furnish "a primary notion of a domain from which the theater is now entirely alien. They are able to create a kind of passionate equation between man, society, nature, and objects,"[67] he said.

A number of specific changes in theater were recommended by Artaud. There would be no written script or scenario. Chant and intonation are to be used, and the kind of language found in dreams. The chief effect would be of spectacle, achieved through cries, groans, apparitions, beautiful costumes, fetching music, and ravishing colors. Age-old costumes would supplant modern dress, and antique musical instruments, when not being played, would be a part of the set. Large masks and manikins would be employed, and lighting would be used symbolically to evoke basic emotions.

In place of a normal theater, a large barn would be used, reconstructed to resemble a church or temple. The staging would be like theater-in-the-round, with no barrier between actor and spectator. Each work must contain an element of cruelty, without which Artaud thought that modern drama was impossible. "In our present state of degeneration," he said, "it is through the skin that metaphysics must be made to re-enter our minds."[68]

Thus the theater to Artaud was a type of spiritual therapeutics. By no means did he advocate violence for its own sake. Rather the violent stage scenes purge the spectator from any admiration of such behavior. "I defy any spectator to whom such violent scenes will have transferred their blood to give himself up once outside the theater, to ideas of war, riot, and blatant murder,"[69] he stated.

England's leading Absurdist playwright has been Harold Pinter. The shallowness of realistic drama such as problem plays is that they water down reality by presupposing a solution, or that a solution exists, or that it is possible to know a character's total motivation, in Pinter's opinion. "If life in our time is basically absurd," said Martin Esslin while discussing Pinter's plays, "then any dramatic representation of it that comes up with neat solutions is bound to contain oversimplification, to suppress essential factors, and reality expurgated and oversimplified becomes make-believe."[70]

Perhaps Pinter's best play was *The Homecoming*, in which an American professor takes his wife to his London birthplace in order to introduce her to his father and his brothers, who not only steal her from him but turn her into a professional prostitute—with her enthusiastic consent. So it is an ironic homecoming: the wife finds her emotional home in this immoral family, the place where she belonged. Some critics saw her as a symbol of the United States joining England as a country which has lost its integrity.

Reviewing Pinter's *No Man's Land* in 1976, Walter Kerr found it to be a "genial, hypnotic, wryly rewarding play,"[71] one that depicts how much of our time is spent fencing with people in persiflage, where the underlying content is to try to find out who the other person really is, as he endeavors to find out who you really are.

Martin Esslin feels that Pinter's dramatic achievements are economy, accurate observation, emotional depth, fertile invention, masterful dialogue, and "above all, his ability to turn commonplace lower-class people and events into a profoundly poetical vision of universal validity."[72]

America's major Absurdist dramatist, Edward Albee, expresses a sardonic satire in the symbolism of his plays. *The American Dream* (1960) tells of a "gorgeous young man" whose twin brother (the American dream) died at birth. Further proof that America has never lived up to its ideals is seen in the gorgeous brother, who has no feelings and is merely a plastic imitation of what his brother would have been. In *Who's Afraid of Virginia Woolf?* (1961), Albee depicts a history professor and his wife, George and Martha, who cannot have children but pretend to have an outstanding son. Once again the vaunted progeny of George and Martha proves to be a dream, an illusion. The American myth has never materialized, Albee seems to be saying.

Asked to define the Theater of the Absurd, Albee called it "an absorption-in-art of certain existential and post-existential philosophical concepts having to do, in the main, with man's attempts to make sense for himself out of a senseless position in a world which makes no sense, because the moral, religious, political, and social structures man has erected to 'illusion' himself have collapsed."[73] Albee then quoted with approval Esslin's affirmation that Absurdist drama "does not reflect despair or a return to dark irrational forces but expresses modern man's endeavor to come to terms with the world in which he lives, to free him from illusions that are bound to cause constant maladjustment and disappointment. For the dignity of man lies in his ability to face reality in all its senselessness; to accept it freely, without fear, without illusions — and to laugh at it."[74]

The academic critic Robert Brustein describes Christopher Durang as "an outrageously funny Absurdist, suspended somewhere between Ionesco and Lenny Bruce."[75] Durang's play, *The Vietnam-*

ization of New Jersey Brustein understands to be a satire on the presentation of the guilt complex as seen in David Rabe's play *Sticks and Bones*. Brustein feels that Durang has put an end to the Vietnam War, dramatically speaking. Durang, says Brustein, satirizes "the heavyhanded symbolism, the fake piety, the ponderous confrontations and the cut-rate merchandising of guilt and indignation"[76] of modern American drama. Durang's trenchant axe cuts both Right and Left positions regarding the Vietnam War. Satire is thus far Durang's major achievement, Brustein believes.

The Spanish Absurdist playwright Fernando Arrabal has lived in Paris since leaving Spain over thirty years ago. His father, an officer in the Spanish Republican army, had been jailed by Franco. One day he escaped from jail and disappeared. "The image of this invisible father," says Richard Eder, "is the goad for the son's lifelong tragicomic literary assault upon anything that resembles a prison bar — manners, morals, or whatever."[77]

Although he calls himself an anarchist, Arrabal lives an unthreatening life with his wife and children. His play *The Automobile Cemetery* is a depiction of Christ as an itinerant rock star after the destruction of the world by nuclear bombs. In a recent play, *The Extravagant Triumph*, he satirizes Castro's totalitarian control of Cuba. Arrabal says, "I think this is the best moment for the theater, simply because it is in a desperate situation. It has to go somewhere. We must look again for words, after so much wordless theater. The wordless theater was a theater for rich times. Now we need a different kind of theater."[78] Maybe, he says, we need a return to light comedies, because "they are very moralizing; people are sick of going to the theater and being terrified."[79]

In summary, it can be said that a number of drama critics, especially Martin Esslin, have given readers an understanding of the origin, aims, techniques, and achievements of the Theater of the Absurd. Some critics have also pointed out its limitations and shortcomings. David Grossvogel says that "the difficulties experienced by Ionesco and Beckett do not concern the stage."[80] Nauseated by existence, Beckett creates drama which is "merely another deception, another means of killing time (which, like all other things in his world, will not die)."[81] Ionesco, says Grossvogel, finds living difficult, so he plays practical jokes on the stage in order to endure life. But when he sheds the clown image and seriously tries to convert us to his philosophy, Grossvogel feels, he loses his art and forfeits any consideration as a major dramatist.

Another critic hostile to Absurdist drama is Frederick Lumley. Beckett's plays are anti-theater, in Lumley's opinion. Their static plots will always limit their appeal, he feels. He quotes V.S. Pritchett approvingly: "Does language become a gabble-gabble ritual to make tolerable the meaninglessness of life?"[82] No, says Lumley, the wordlessness of this anti-theater is nowhere near being sufficient to give expression to our complicated times.

The Polish critic Jan Kott, however, feels that Absurdist drama captures the feeling of modern life. He finds it to be more in the tradition of Shakespeare and medieval morality plays than of the traditional nineteenth century drama. Absurdist plays employ the grotesque, which differs from tragedy in that whereas the tragic hero fights fate nobly, the grotesque protagonist fights quite feebly. The reason for the difference is that one of the tragic hero's choices was desirable, but both of the grotesque hero's choices are undesirable—this is absurd! The downfall of the tragic hero thus affirms the recognition of the absolute, Kott says, but in his downfall the grotesque hero mocks the absolute for leaving him no fair choice. After defining tragedy as the theater of priests and comedy as the theater of clowns, Kott concludes, "When established values have been overthrown, and there is no appeal, to God, Nature, or History, from the tortures inflicted by the cruel world, the clown becomes the central figure in the theatre."[83]

Martin Esslin points out that since Absurdist drama is basically subjective, critics who approach it on purely rational grounds are in difficulty. The right way to criticize any drama, he feels, is to search out its purpose, and see how well that purpose is achieved. Since Absurdist plays are basically poetic (if not in form at least in concept), the proper criteria for their criticism are poetic, Esslin says: "suggestive power, originality of invention, psychological truth of the images concerned, depth, universality, and the degree of skill with which they are translated into stage terms."[84]

The theatergoer will know when he is in the presence of high dramatic art, Esslin believes, when the play's invention springs from deep layers of profoundly experienced emotion so that it expresses "real obsessions, dreams, and valid images in the sub-conscious mind of its author. This quality of depth and unity of vision is instantly recognizable and beyond trickery,"[85] Esslin avers.

He also has an answer to those who feel that Absurdist wordlessness or linguistic breakdown cannot communicate on the stage. "The dethronement of language and logic," he says, "forms part of an essentially mystical attitude toward the basis of reality as being too complex and at the same time too unified to be validly expressed by the analytical means of orderly syntax and conceptual thought."[86] By protesting against man's inhumanity toward his fellow man, Esslin believes, this innovative drama of our century is making a giant stride toward helping modern man recover his dignity.

15. American Criticism Since 1920

Just as World War I marked a drastic change in American culture generally, so did it in the areas of drama and dramatic criticism. In less than a decade after the war ended, the American theater witnessed a revolutionary alteration in the number of plays produced, the dramatic themes and plots, and the changing attitude of the public towards drama.

Experimentation was in the air, not only in dramatic technique but also in stagecraft. Robert Edmond Jones was designing creative new sets, often in plays produced by Arthur Hopkins. Writing in *Theatre Arts Magazine* in April, 1921, Kenneth Macgowan praised their production of *Macbeth*. Jones, he said, "has attempted through significant form to create an abstract background expressing the spiritual relationships of the play."[1] This "epoch-making production is the beginning of something new," Macgowan continued. "It cuts off the past and locks the future just as surely as did *Hernani*, that great first romantic drama of France."[2] This wave of the future, he felt, would consist of the artistic synthesis of playwright, play, and actor. Unfortunately the synthesis was not quite achieved here, in his opinion, because of the "dull and tedious performance of Lionel Barrymore."[3]

John Ranken Towse attacked another Barrymore in a review of *Macbeth* in the *New York Evening Post* in November, 1922. Towse accused Hopkins of being "infected with some of the pernicious theories of Gordon Craig,"[4] thus attempting to disguise a faulty production by a luxurious set. John Barrymore's "lack of true passion" doomed the performance, in Towse's opinion, who felt that Barrymore, "an attractive, earnest, and intelligent comedian laboring under a burden much too heavy for him, was sadly ineffective."[5]

Expressionism was by now being seen on Broadway. In a review in *The Nation* in 1923 of Elmer Rice's *The Adding Machine*, Ludwig Lewisohn defined this innovation: "Expressionism has two chief aims: to fling the inner life of the dramatic figures immediately upon the stage; to synthesize, instead of describing, their world into symbolic visions that shall sum up whole cosmogonies in a brief scene."[6] This play, Lewisohn felt, gave dramatic expression to how machines brutalize human values: "This particular world of ours deliberately chokes the very sources of human life. It has made fetishes of ugliness and monotony and intolerance. From the intolerable repressions of Mr. Zero's life flames one explosion of the nerves."[7]

Looking back on a lifetime in service to the American theater as a director and a critic, Harold Clurman judged that in his opinion Broadway's best season was the one of 1924–25. Clurman pointed out that among the 228 productions staged that year were Eugene O'Neill's *Desire Under the Elms* and *S.S. Glencairn*, Sidney Howard's *They Knew What They Wanted*, Philip Barry's *The Youngest*, John Howard Lawson's *Processional*, *What Price Glory?* by Maxwell Anderson and Laurence Stallings, and *Beggar on Horseback* by George S. Kaufman and Marc Connelly. Musicals included *Lady, Be Good* by George and Ira Gershwin, as well as others by Cole Porter and by Richard Rodgers and Moss Hart. Plays from abroad were represented, among others, by Ferenc Molnar's *The Guardsman*, Shaw's *Candida*, and Maugham's *Rain*.

Actors that season included some of America's finest: Ethel, John, and Lionel Barrymore, James Cagney, Eddie Cantor, Katharine Cornell, Jeanne Eagles, W.C. Fields, Lynn Fontanne, Clark Gable, Bob Hope, Walter Huston, Eva Le Gallienne, Alfred Lunt, the Marx Brothers, Marilyn Miller, Paul Muni, Edward G. Robinson, Will Rogers, Barbara Stanwyck, Laurette Taylor, and Spencer Tracy.

A few years previously such a rich theatrical fare would have been unthinkable. The Little Theater movement, increased emphasis on drama in American colleges, the émigré exodus to Paris, the Jazz Age protest against the world that produced World War I, the enormous impact upon America of Continental theater – these are among the reasons for the sudden dramatic renaissance.

It is doubtful whether American dramatic criticism has ever equalled the caliber of American drama. Certainly in the 1920's there was a paucity of critics to match the playwrights.

No doubt the chief drama critic of the period was George Jean Nathan. Educated at Cornell University and the University of Bologna, Nathan was a romantic impressionist whose views could never be wholly trusted nor wholly ignored. His position well shows the strengths and weaknesses of impressionism as a critical approach.

The splendid iconclasm of Huneker shows its influence in Nathan's attitude. Nathan quoted approvingly Nietzsche's dictum that "convictions are prisons." Ever since Aristotle, Nathan said, critics have fettered the soaring art of the drama with rules that would banish all experimentation and growth. He liked Samuel Johnson's summary: "Every new genius produces some innovation which subverts the rules which the practice of foregoing authors had established."[8] "Dramatic criticism," said Nathan, "is an attempt to formulate rules of conduct for the lovable, wayward, charming vagabond that is the drama. For the drama is an art with a feather in its cap and an ironic smile upon its lips, sauntering impudently over forbidden lawns and through closed lanes into the hearts of those of us children of the world who have never grown up."[9]

Nathan was such a thoroughgoing impressionist that even his critical strictures are impressionistic: "Criticism is simply a sensitive, experienced and thoroughbred artist's effort to interpret, in terms of esthetic doctrine and his own peculiar soul, the work of another artist."[10] His eclectic taste and wide familiarity with Continental drama enabled Nathan to help introduce American theatergoers to such European dramatists as Gerhart Hauptmann, Ibsen, O'Casey, Shaw, and Strindberg, as well as such Americans as O'Neill and William Saroyan. In an article praising Oscar Wilde for perfecting epigrammatic style, Nathan favored Wilde for structural technique he himself used: shocking overstatement, humorous incongruity, and paradox with its bedfellow, anti-climax.

Impressionism in criticism hinges upon taste, and fortunately Nathan's taste made him a fairly reliable guide as a drama critic. The danger sets in when the brilliant epigrams are superficial rather than integral because then the brilliance can be mistaken for good taste and penetrating judgment. Nathan's personal tragedy as a critic was that he developed his technique when American drama was vastly inferior to Continental, so that when conditions were somewhat reversed, his techniques frequently backfired or fell flat.

In the post-war period a number of theater historians, who often included criticism in their works, added to the public's growing interest in drama. Chief among this group were Barrett Clark, Thomas H. Dickinson, Burns Mantle, Montrose J. Moses, George O'Dell, and Arthur Hobson Quinn. Barrett Clark edited the standard anthology of dramatic criticism, *European Theories of the Drama*, which first appeared in 1918. Besides editing many volumes of plays, Clark also wrote a number of volumes on modern drama. Burns Mantle was not only an active newspaper drama critic but he also edited yearbooks on the drama which are useful records of the period. Arthur Hobson Quinn wrote the most comprehensive history of American drama up to this period.

Besides teaching drama at several colleges, Clayton Hamilton served as drama critic for *Forum*, *The Bookman*, and *Vogue*. He also wrote several works on dramatic theory. Usually Hamilton's views are those that would be of value chiefly to budding playwrights.

Another academic critic, one who wrote widely on Elizabethan drama, was Ashley Thorndike. In his book *English Comedy*, published in 1929, Thorndike summarized theories of comedy and then added his own emphasis. Aristotle was the source of two of the theories—the ludicrous, as mentioned in the *Poetics*, and incongruity, as described in the *Rhetoric*. Bergson's theory, as practiced by Ben Jonson and Molière, was that the comic intent was invidious, finding something imperfect and seeking to purge it.

Thorndike pointed to excellent comedies, such as *A Midsummer Night's Dream* and *As You Like It*, which seemed to contain mirth that was not invidious. Even satiric Voltaire, said Thorndike, found that "laughter arises from a gaiety of disposition, absolutely incompatible with contempt and indignation." And so Thorndike concluded that some comedy is amusing because it is joyous and merry, filled with the good feeling expressed by Emily Dickinson's self-description of being an "inebriate of air and debauchee of dew." Such comedy, said Thorndike, amuses us by building upon the joy of life rather than upon ridiculing inferiority.

Max Eastman turned aside from his political criticism long enough to write two works on comedy, *The Sense of Humor*, which gives a thorough history of various theories of humor, and *The Enjoyment of Laughter*, which studies humor from a psychological viewpoint.

An academic critic who wrote widely on dramatic history, especially during the Elizabethan period, was Gerald Eades Bentley, who evolved a theory of farce. Farce, said Bentley, has a lengthy history, since such writers of comedy as Aristophanes, Plautus, and Shakespeare have used it. It is a degenerate (but popular) form of comedy, Bentley said, in which characters are so shallow and so exaggerated as to become caricatures. Chief effects of farce are achieved by plot situations, improbabilities, and physical discomfort. There can, however, be farce that is sophisticated and non-physical, such as Wilde's *The Importance of Being Earnest*. Even here, however, improbability, comic situation, and gross exaggeration remain the basis of the humor.

Stark Young was for years one of America's leading critics. In his book *The Flower in Drama*, Young described the acting genius of Eleanora Duse: "You force into everything the soul of its reality. Whatever part you take, romantic, rollicking comic, poetic, or highly naturalistic, you give the same truth to it by living out and bringing to completion its characteristic quality. You have no false purposes, you never conclude, you never solve, you only create and reveal. Our young actors need you."[11]

A playwright himself as well as a translator of Chekhov's plays, Young taught at several universities and served as drama critic for *The New Republic* and *Theatre Arts*. One of Young's contributions was to help introduce Americans to Japanese theater. Following up on this, Faubion Bowers wrote a detailed treatise on the esthetics of the Kabuki theater in Japan.

The death of the actor John Drew in 1927 brought from critic Burns Mantle the observation that Drew was now chiefly known for "a typical John Drew part," meaning one in which the male lead was a clothes horse. This was very unfair, Mantle felt, to a great actor who had demonstrated the versatility to play a wide variety of roles.

That same year Percy Hammond, in the *New York Herald-Tribune*, praised *Porgy and Bess* as a rare example of the successful adaptation of a novel to the stage. Hammond credited director Rouben Mamoulian, showman and esthete, for the success. As an example he cited a scene: "When among the details of the eerie obsequies over the corpse of the murdered Robbins he causes theatrical shadows to dance upon the walls, he is that most successful of combinations—artist and mountebank."[12]

Longtime critic for *The Nation*, Joseph Wood Krutch deplored the loss of the tragic vision in *The Modern Temper*, a book published in 1929. We cannot even appreciate classical tragedy any more, Krutch averred, because the vision of life in which man is a noble creature has vanished along with faith in God. We feel depressed upon seeing a great play by Sophocles or Shakespeare because we now see man's soul as commonplace and human emotions as mean, he said.

The function of art, in Krutch's paraphrase of Milton, is to justify the ways of God to man. Tragic catharsis helps the viewer find life more satisfactory, because of its exaltation of human dignity. Thus, for classical playgoers tragedy was not an expression of despair but a means whereby they were saved from despair. A too sophisticated society like ours, "distrusting its thought, despising its passions, realizing its impotent unimportance in the universe,"[13] can tell itself no stories except those which remind it of its manifold miseries. Yet our need for the historic consolations of tragedy does not diminish but rather increases under the dissonance of modern life. The loss of tragic vision robs us of the dignity that transforms our despair into triumphant joy. "The death of tragedy is, like the death of love," said Krutch, "one of those emotional fatalities as a result of which the human world grows more and more a desert."[14]

Krutch believed that Eugene O'Neill alone among modern dramatists was striving to regain the vision of classical tragedy. Ibsen wrote domestic tragedy, Krutch said, assuming that reason could solve life's problems. Shaw, in Krutch's view, "pursued rational optimism until it reached a *reductio ad absurdum* in which human beings become mere talking and arguing machines."[15] Despite his weaknesses, O'Neill had won for the American dramatist, said Krutch, "the right to be as serious as he wants to be and to aim as high as he can."[16] Krutch approved of the ideas O'Neill had written to George Jean Nathan: "The playwright today must dig at the roots of the sickness of today as he feels it — the death of the old God and the failure of science and materialism to give any satisfying new one for the surviving primitive religious instinct to find a meaning for life in. Anyone trying to do big work nowadays must have this big subject behind all the little subjects of his plays, or he is simply scribbling around the surface of things and has no more real status than a parlor entertainer."[17]

The dramatist considered by most critics of the period as second only to O'Neill in American drama was Maxwell Anderson, of whom John Gassner could say, "He brought a magnificence of speech and feeling into the theater, and he did so without neglecting the realities of modern life."[18]

Having achieved success with such plays as *Elizabeth the*

Queen, Winterset, and *High Tor,* Anderson tried to summarize what it took for a play to succeed. The successful play, he felt, had to deal with the inner life of a protagonist who, though imperfect, improves during the play's course, and who must represent the forces of good in some exceptional way. Excellence on the stage means moral excellence, he felt, and theatergoers admire strong conviction in the male characters and passionate faith in the female.

Anderson then discussed the theater's function—to hold up what is admirable in the human race. "Theatre is essentially a cathedral of the spirit, devoted to the apostolic succession of inspired high priests which extend further into the past than the Christian line founded by St. Peter."[19] "It is," he continued, "a church without a creed. Our theater, instead of being as the evangelical ministers used to believe, the gateway to hell, is as much a worship as the theater of the Greeks, and has exactly the same meaning in our lives."[20]

Anderson found the identical message in the *Oresteia* of Aeschylus and *The Green Pastures* by Marc Connelly—the Divine Himself must grow and change if He is to avoid injustice. Great plays like *Oedipus Rex, Macbeth, Little Eyolf,* and *The Little Foxes* taught a common theme—an evil action revenges itself upon the doer. "*Antigone* and *Hamlet* and ten thousand modern plays," said Anderson, "argue that injustice is a corrosive"[21] that eats the heart out of him who practices it.

"In brief," Anderson confessed, "I have found my religion in the theatre, where I least expected to find it, and where few will credit that it exists."[22] The stage attacks evil, that which takes humans back towards the animal, and affirms good, that which urges humans up toward God. Ultimately the theater is democratic, he believed, for it is the audience who make the very rules defining good and evil. "There is no comparable test that I know of," Anderson concluded, "for what is good in the human soul, what is most likely to lead to that distant and secret destination which the race has chosen for itself and will somehow find."[23]

Allan Halline, in a study of which plays by Anderson seemed to most nearly live up to his critical theory, found them to be *Mary of Scotland, Winterset,* and *Key Largo.* Said Halline: "To have evolved a profound and noble theory of drama, rooted in the classic age and transcending the present, is a significant achievement in criticism; to have created and impressed upon the consciousness of an age a body of drama measuring up to this ideal should prove to be a lasting contribution to art."[24]

Writing in *The North American Review* in 1931, Montrose J. Moses felt that what the American theater needed was the development of a native folk drama. Folk drama provided, he said, the universal glamor of folklore, dialogue that gave great scope to the actor, and a universal appeal that "somehow lifts the play out of its definite locale and makes it available to all countries."[25]

Alexander Woollcott in *The New Yorker* in 1932 wondered whether Lillian Gish, with the naïveté of a small town high-school girl, could make the role of Camille credible. Though seemingly miscast, she at times seemed able to capture the loveliness and the sorcery of "this fond and foolish old play."[26]

A string of successful plays, including *Reunion in Vienna*, *The Petrified Forest*, *Idiot's Delight*, *Abe Lincoln in Illinois*, and *There Shall Be No Night*, established their author, Robert Sherwood, as a leading spokesman for the theater of the 1930's. Even in his comedies, said Brooks Atkinson in the *New York Times*, Sherwood showed a serious purpose. The preface of "that worldly, iniquitous comedy *Reunion in Vienna* is black with despair about the moral collapse of the world," Atkinson wrote, and "in *The Petrified Forest* he portrayed the modern intellectual as an obsolete, futile member of society. The jester's mask," Atkinson continued, "fell of its own weight when, as it seemed to him at the time, Western civilization was beginning to break up."[27]

Then came a new sense of affirmation as Sherwood wrote several plays more nearly in accord with his own character. The reason *Abe Lincoln in Illinois* succeeded, said Atkinson, is that Sherwood possessed Lincoln's mind and spirit—a person with no pretense but a sincere concern for people and their welfare. *There Shall Be No Night*, a protest against the Soviet Union's invasion of Finland, has a preface voicing a new optimism, a faith in "man's unconquerable aspiration to dignity and freedom and purity in the sight of God."[28] Thus, said Atkinson, although Sherwood's judgments had changed, his ideals had remained steadfast. "In the theatre," Atkinson stated, "we have never had a man of Sherwood's stature, probity, and good will."[29]

A recent biographer of Clifford Odets feels that probably Odets was the most significant playwright of the Depression era. Margaret Brenman-Gibson finds in Odets the perfect voice of frustrated labor in the 1930's. Harold Clurman called the first night of *Waiting for Lefty* "the birth cry of the thirties."[30] Soon this play, said Clurman, would be "more frequently produced and more frequently banned all over the world—from Union Square to Moscow, from Tokyo to Johannesburg—than any other play in all of theatre history."³¹

Brooks Atkinson found that in *Golden Boy* Odets used a contrapuntal style of playing one theme against another. Dialogue was both the best and the worst part of the talent of Odets, said Atkinson. Its strength was in being vigorous, crisp, and salty, all the while revealing character by indirection. On the other hand, Atkinson wrote, Odets used language that was so cheap and trite that it sounded counterfeit.

Some critics likened the style of Odets to that of Chekhov, particularly as Odets used disconnected dialogue, subtle characterization, and evocation of atmosphere in such a play as *Awake and Sing*. By 1938, when Odets wrote *Rocket to the Moon*, an era was ending, Brenman-Gibson felt—the shift not only in Odets but in all American drama was away from politics and towards psychology. "The Depression was lifting," she wrote, "and the moral simplicities of that time were ended, and the individual soul's unshackling in the liberation of the working class was no longer a tenable faith."³²

A playwright and novelist who liked to innovate in his plays, Thornton Wilder wrote "Some Thoughts on Playwriting" in 1941. Wilder found four conditions separating drama from the other arts. First, it involves many collaborators. The gifted dramatist will wisely draw upon his compeers in the theater, actors, director, and set designer. Second, drama addresses itself to a group-mind, the audience, and to succeed it must therefore have a broad appeal. Other arts might presuppose an audience of connoisseurs, but drama must remain simple enough to attract the throng whose electric response is part of drama's unique power. Third, since theater involves pretense it must be accorded certain conventions. These conventions serve useful functions: they get the audience to use their imagination, and they raise the action from the specific, such as Juliet, to the universal, that is, any woman in love. Fourth, stage action occurs in a perpetual present tense. "A novel is what took place; a play is what takes place,"³³ said Wilder. And since there is no narrator to assist with the exposition (even though Wilder several times used one in his plays), the drama requires a higher degree of concentrated imagination than does the novel, he believed. Some of this concentration must have been latent in his play *The Matchmaker*, since its musical version, called *Hello, Dolly!*, has been a Broadway favorite for many years.

World War II proved to be the incubation period for two of America's best contemporary dramatists, Tennessee Williams and Arthur Miller. Williams, not afraid to fail, at his best can fuse lyricism, special stage effects, and poignant characterization into such excellent plays as *The Glass Menagerie* and *A Streetcar Named Desire*. In 1944 Chicago drama critics were able to muster up enough public support for *The Glass Menagerie* so that it ran for three months there, before tough-minded New York producers were willing to take a chance on the fragile masterpiece. One must add, however, that it won the New York Critics Circle award in 1945, and has become a fixture in contemporary American drama.

Williams has shown rare modesty as a playwright. He takes advice on his plays from other theater people, and revises his work constantly. By the fifth revision he feels his play is finally taking shape. He also feels that he does some of his best writing when a play is in production.

Chekhov, he says, was a great influence upon him. "I began to read Chekhov in depth when I was twenty-four," he said, "and I had never before come in contact with anything so penetrating, so beautiful."[34] He recalls that his decision to become a dramatist went back to seeing Alla Nazimova in a production of *Ghosts*. "She was so shatteringly powerful that I couldn't stay in my seat,"[35] he remembers.

Williams has stated that writing for him has been an escape from the uncomfortable world of reality. Life's ambiguity has always fascinated him. "It is not the essential dignity but the essential ambiguity of man that needs to be stated,"[36] he has said. Nevertheless he does accept the semi-Aristotelian idea of catharsis as a purgation of violence by its stage representation. "I have always felt a release from the sense of meaninglessness and death when a work of tragic intention has seemed to me to have achieved that intention,"[37] he said. "I would say that there is something much bigger in life and death than we have become aware of," he stated. "Further, I would say that our serious theatre is a search for that something that is not yet successful but is still going on."[38]

In 1961 Brooks Atkinson called Williams America's most gifted dramatist. "By the incantation of words, which combine lyricism and naturalism," said Atkinson, "he creates images of life that actors can express with great force. Writing from the inside out, like Chekhov, he can make something tangible out of moods and dreams."[39] Seemingly in an unwilling mood, Atkinson had to admit that perhaps Williams was right after all—life corrupts all of us; there is no escape from loneliness; and human relationships are cannibalistic in the sense that "we all use each other."⁴⁰

Walter Kerr felt that since Williams was "the finest playwright now working in the American theater,"⁴¹ even his failures were worth discussing, for "every failure he has represents a real loss not only to himself but to all of us."⁴² Some of these failures Kerr listed as poor plot resolution, flight from the concrete to the symbolic, and at times exalting method above substance.

"I think," said Williams in 1972, "I'm a minor artist who has somehow managed to create two or three major works. I'm not sure which they are."⁴³

In 1947, a year in which there was no Pulitzer Prize for drama, Arthur Miller's *All My Sons* won the Circle Critics Award over O'Neill's *The Iceman Cometh*. Two years later *Death of a Salesman* marked Miller as one of America's top dramatists. Yet he reacted vigorously to the charge that the play evoked merely pathos rather than tragic emotions, since Willy Loman lacked the stature necessary for a tragic hero. Common people are fit subjects for tragedy, Miller averred. As proof he pointed out that modern psychiatry takes Oedipus and Electra complexes from royalty and applies them universally to all people. Kings have no better brains than commoners, Miller argued. If tragedy applied only to the well bred, why does the mass of mankind cherish it above all other dramatic forms?

Tragedy to Miller was the outcome of any person's determined compulsion to evaluate himself justly. The tragic flaw is not in the hero but in the environment, he said. In a decent world the fair person would not suffer. Nevertheless, he said, tragedy exalts us because "it automatically demonstrates the indestructible will of man to achieve his humanity."⁴⁴

Miller recalled that at the initial rehearsal of *Death of a Salesman* he first saw the play as others see it, a group of terribly lonely people, cut off from one another, trying to save themselves separately. This alienation, said Miller, is immoral, a corrosive that might destroy us. "We ought to be struggling," he said, "for a world in which it will be possible to lay blame. Only then will the great tragedies be written, for where no order is believed in, no order can be breached, and thus all disasters of man will strive vainly for moral meaning."⁴⁵

In 1980 James Atlas defended Miller from charges of critics

such as Philip Rahv, Richard Gilman, and Robert Brustein that in his later plays Miller had run out of things to say. These critics, said Atlas, believe that only such themes as alienation, angst, and anomie contain high seriousness. Moreover, he added, to them popularity is philistinism. But Miller's ideas, if simple, are universal: guilt and betrayal in the family; responsibility for the consequences of one's actions; dread of failure in a society that has no place for it.

"The poetry in Miller's plays," said Harold Clurman, "is that of the impassioned moralist who, as in a parable, seeks to convey not so much a thought as an emotion which goes beyond the factual material."[46] Miller himself defines a play as a dramatic consideration of how people ought to live. "I don't regret my career," he states. "I feel I've been very lucky. But there is no question in my mind that I would have had at least again as many plays written and produced if there had been a live, high-grade professional theater in New York."[47]

American criticism of Soviet drama reflected the changing political ideology surrounding World War II. In 1942, shortly after having been killed by German bombs, Russian dramatist Alexander Afinogenov was lauded by H.W.L. Dana in an article in *Theatre Arts*. Afinogenov, said Dana, began his career by writing of class conflict outside the Soviet Union. Increasingly, however, he dared to deal with domestic political problems—trials, secret police, non-party intellectuals. His play *Fear* had nearly launched a drama of ideas within Russia. In *Distant Point*, a play written in 1935, Afinogenov used a small town in Siberia as a symbol of the Shangri-La that all people seek: "a world in which men shall live their lives in freedom and happiness. We all think of that, live for that,"[48] said Afinogenov.

By 1949 Harry Schwartz in the *New York Times* described how the Soviets used drama as a vehicle of the cold war against the United States. For example, Konstantin Simonov's play *The Russian Question* in 1947 had exposed the American press as "the prostituted instrument of evil capitalists."[49] In Boris Lavrenev's *Voice of America*, when an American army captain refuses to make an anti-Soviet radio speech, the Un-American Activities Committee hires a killer to murder him, but the captain safely escapes to the Soviet Union.

In 1952 Paul Barnett described in the *New York Times* how Communists in Vienna used American plays for propaganda purposes. Stereotypes drawn out of American plays were that in the United States the small person is destroyed in a capitalist-controlled jungle; judges conspire with gangsters to oppress the poor; and workers are robots manipulated by their bosses. The plays being produced were *All My Sons* and *Death of a Salesman* by Arthur Miller, Irwin Shaw's *The Gentle People*, Elmer Rice's *The Adding Machine*, and the early social protest plays by Clifford Odets.

Barnett felt that what was not being shown to Austrian audiences was the positive side of American life. He saw censorship as no answer but issued a plea for American dramatists to include positive features in their plays, and perhaps follow the example of Irwin Shaw, who withdrew production rights of his play *Bury the Dead* in areas where it might be used by America's enemies for propaganda purposes.

Two of America's most dependable journalistic critics at mid-century were Brooks Atkinson of the *New York Times* and John Mason Brown of the *Saturday Review*. Aside from a wartime stint as a foreign correspondent, Atkinson was the chief drama critic for the *Times* from 1925 until 1960. Readers of his column not only learned what the play was about but also received an informed critique based upon clearly stated grounds. He kept an open mind for experimentation but never believed that something was good simply because it was new. His cultivated taste educated a generation of theatergoers into experiencing theater as a high cultural event.

An example of his style is his article celebrating the twenty-fifth anniversary of the acting career of Alfred Lunt and Lynn Fontanne. He recalled how Alexander Woollcott had correctly predicted in 1924 that "we were seeing the first chapter in a partnership destined to be as distinguished as that of Henry Irving and Ellen Terry."[50] What accounted for the success of the Lunts in high comedy? Atkinson replied, "Although the manners of the Lunts are impeccable and worldly, the relationship of the characters they play is only one step removed from primitive nature—that is the essential part of the joke. Their talents are thoroughly individual, but they perfectly blend. Miss Fontanne's voice is low and sultry, Mr. Lunt's high and querulous."[51]

Atkinson was always able to place drama in its broader cultural milieu. In 1953 he regretted the tininess of modern drama compared to the magnitude of modern life. But, in historic perspective, he saw that there was always a long time lag between great events and their literary protrayal. Shakespeare wrote a hundred years after the Wars of the Roses, and Tolstoy fifty years after the Napoleonic compaigns. In this atomic age, Atkinson said, we are waiting for the other shoe to drop. "If any civilization remains when it is over," he predicted, "it will be the grand theme for artists in every medium."[52] Meanwhile, "the whole perspective of life is violently wrenched out of shape" and "plays of average stature are bound to seem trifling."[53] We are simply going to have to wait for the great plays "on the classical subject of a divided world struggling for salvation. The subject is too tremendous. The denouement is in doubt. Wait another hundred years."[54]

In addition to his regular columns, John Mason Brown wrote many books on the modern drama. He also edited, along with Montrose J. Moses, *The American Theater As Seen By Its Critics* in 1934. Before joining the *Saturday Review* Brown had taught at several universities and had been drama critic for *Theatre Arts Monthly* and the *New York Evening Post*. Like Atkinson, Brown delivered level-headed and occasionally inspired reactions to plays for several decades.

Upon the death of Philip Barry in 1949, Brown summarized Barry's career. Barry, he said, never stooped to Broadway's values, never surrendered to its limitations even in his success. He stood above "the brassy competence and the spiritual emptiness of the commercial theatre."[55] His most successful plays, such as *Paris Bound*, *Holiday*, and *Philadelphia Story*, had "sparkle, finish, bounce. Their charm was real, their originality unmistakable, and their tenderness a quality which neither their laughter nor their sophistication could obscure."[56] With an Irish gift for both anger and sweetness, he saw through the shallowness of the world of fashion in which he moved. "He refused to be atrophied by success,"[57] declared Brown.

When the plays of Christopher Fry reached New York in 1952, Brown quickly assessed their strong points and failings. Fry, said Brown, had Elizabethan vigor, dash, exuberance, the "fine madness," the worship of the metaphor, the indulgence in verbal beauty for its own sake. But lack of clarity and lack of movement kept the plays from being successful stage vehicles. *Venus Observed*, Brown said, charms our ears but also tires them. Fry, he felt, "gives us more than we can take and yet less than we want." The play's "brightness cannot hide its emptiness,"[58] Brown judged.

Monroe Spears agreed with Brown that Fry's inability to ever take commonsense reality seriously, even if to rise above it, kept his plays fantasy rather than comedy. "His plays are thematically superficial," said Spears, "in that the triumph is asserted, not earned, and structurally deficient in that there is no adequate sense of conflict."[59] Fry in Spear's opinion had not so much redeemed joy as merely affirmed it.

Perhaps the two leading academic critics in 1950 were Eric Bentley and Francis Fergusson. A native of England, Bentley received two degrees at Oxford and the doctorate at Yale. An actor, director, and translator, Bentley brought a rich background into his critical opinions. He bravely debunked O'Neill as a great playwright, saying "his sense of theatrical form is frustrated by an eloquence that decays into mere garrulousness."[60]

A fervent admirer of the Epic drama of Bertolt Brecht, Bentley sees Brecht's plays as a fusion of epic and dramatic, of realism and experimental stagecraft. But Bentley feels that much of the experimentation during the 1920's and 1930's has proved barren, for it focused attention on stagecraft rather than on plays. He recommends that drama keep close to its fundamental elements of poetry and acting. "The dramatist," he says, "is a poet who transmits his work through gesturing elocutionists."[61] Bentley feels that Strindberg was the most important figure in anti-realism, for his stress on drama for an intimate, selective audience: "His preface to *Miss Julie*, a document as rewarding to the student of modern theater as Aristotle's *Poetics*, and his *Dramaturgy* lay down the principles of the new art."[62] Bentley sees Shaw as a pioneer in discarding the "well made" play for a comedy depicting the relations between idealism and realism. "Tragedy," says Bentley, "cannot entail extreme optimism, for that would be to underestimate the problem; it cannot entail extreme pessimism, for that would be to lose faith in man."[63] His chief objection to most modern criticism is that it has accepted a compromise with the superficial techniques of show business, rather than to search for the important ideas underlying drama.

Francis Fergusson believes that, despite such excellent modern playwrights as Lorca, Eliot, Chekhov, and Cocteau, contemporary culture has lost the requisite notion of drama as a focal point in a society, the mirror of its actions and values. Sophocles and Shakespeare could both presuppose "the idea of a theater" all about them, so that their works could be broadly pleasurable, deeply artistic, and even meaningful in a larger philosophic and religious sense. Our reaction to modern dramatists, Fergusson says, leads us inevitably beyond drama to a search for this broader cultural integrity. Grateful for the insights provided by Kenneth Burke, modern poetry critics, and even recent cultural anthropologists, Fergusson returns to

Aristotle's basic formulation of a play as an imitation of an action, with plot the formal shaping factor. He restores the scholastic distinction between two Aristotelian causes: the formal and the final. The final cause of tragedy, to produce a given effect upon an audience, has been the aspect of plot-making most dwelled upon by Sarcey and most dramatists through history. But the consideration of the plot as the formal cause — as the "soul" of tragedy giving the play its form — he feels has generally been avoided since Aristotle's day. And partly this is true, he feels, because we do not have a theater which focuses, at the center of the life of the society, the complementary insights of our whole culture. Fergusson sympathizes with Eliot's reversion from mechanical realism, but wants to find more than the "convention" which Eliot seeks as a form in which to arrest life's flow. He feels that Cocteau has found a univocal sense of form, as well as a reaffirmation of the myth underlying life, in his un-Wagnerian everyday poesy. The whole problem, then, takes on a sense of urgency. "When the idea of a theater is inadequate or lacking, we are reduced to speculating about the plight of the whole culture,"[64] he says. Fortunately, the "histrionic sensibility" can be trained, even as can our ear for music — and therein lies our hope.

Other academic critics have provided useful insights. Alan Reynolds Thompson in *The Anatomy of Drama* gave an extended study of melodrama, and in *The Dry Mock* an account of how irony functions in drama. Thomas H. Fujimura analyzed the esthetics of the comedy of wit, particularly as seen in Restoration comedy. Fujimura found that the witty apprehension of life places discordant daily life bits into an integrated pattern, with the witty person believing in the free play of human intelligence. Fujimura quoted Freud's position of wit as a therapeutic safety-valve for the vicarious gratification of repressed sexual and malicious drives.

An Aristotelian from the University of Chicago, Ronald Salmon Crane complained that most dramatic criticism has been irrelevant, since it was directed at drama in general rather than at a specific genre or type. Each genre has its own criteria of excellence, Crane felt. He believed that dramatic criticism has been a long time recovering from the shock administered by William Archer in *The Old Drama and the New*, where Archer argued that drama flourished best when divorced from poetry. T.S. Eliot's plays demonstrated to Crane that poetry gives us a perception of order in an otherwise formless life, and that Eliot's plays thus provided the serenity and reconciliation which it was the function of an art form to provide.

In *Tragedy and the Theory of Drama*, Elder Olson stated that there were three viewpoints from which a play can be criticized: the average playgoer can simply say, "I like it" or "I dislike it"; the average drama critic explains how a play achieves its given effect through the use of various structures and devices; the higher critic analyzes the play's effect as an effect, taking into consideration whether the play's goal was a lofty one or a mean one.

Susanne Langer insisted that drama is neither ritual nor show business, neither church nor circus. Instead, she said, it is poetry, by which she meant creativity. Each play is an illusion, she pointed out, in which the script provides the form and the stage delimits the play's "world." Music, dance, and chorus are used to keep the play illusory, away from reality, in order that the play may achieve its poetic effect.

Ellen Douglass Leyburn has demonstrated the extent to which modern tragedy and comedy have interpenetrated each other. Tragedy now uses weak protagonists such as formerly were used in comedy, she feels, and modern comedy often has the serious purpose once ascribed to tragedy. "The shifts in the nature of both tragedy and comedy reflect the convulsion of society and of man's sense of himself,"[65] she says.

In *Elements of Tragedy* Dorothea Krook defined those elements as the act of shame, the suffering, knowledge, and affirmation. Whereas classical tragedy affirmed "an objective moral order which at once incorporates the human and transcends it,"[66] drama since Ibsen has tried unsuccessfully to affirm such an order, she stated. But she saw tragedy's lofty goal to be unchanged: "What a piece of work is man that weak as he is he should yet possess the power by his suffering perpetually to reaffirm and restore the eternal moral order itself, as it is violated by the acts of shame that he is perpetually liable to commit."[67]

In 1951 Richard Gehman wrote an article in *Theatre Arts* assessing the great power wielded by the eight critics of New York City's large daily papers. "They are on the border-line between being in and out of the theater,"[68] he said. He questioned whether it was good for drama to centralize so much power in a few persons. "Theatrical folk mainly fear them,"[69] he stated. "Few other specialized groups of writers receive such flattering, undivided attention."[70] Gehman said that the producer Jed Harris once barred Alexander Woollcott from all of his productions and said that Brooks Atkinson knew less about the theater than did his uncle, a tailor!

In a preface to his unsuccessful play *The Assassin*, Irwin Shaw said that critics had succeeded where the German army had failed: "The Germans tried to kill me but they at least had missed. The critics had not missed."[71] Ironically, Shaw later spent some time as a critic for *The New Republic*.

Walter Kerr, speaking of new horizons in the theater, stated in 1954 that the Ibsen-Chekhov cycle was now quite dead, and the theater was looking for but had not yet found a new cycle. With the whole world in a period of transition, Kerr said, everyone seems to want the theater to play the role of the church, politics, or sociology. But the theater needed to be reminded that its function as a critic of society is different than those disciplines. It will only succeed if it remains true to its role as an independent art form.

Kerr conceded that a drama critic should "soak up" previous writings about what constitutes dramatic excellence. "Once it has been soaked up, however, it should be expected to disappear into the general taste of the man."[72] Asking a critic to declare his standards would be as futile as asking Grandma for a mathematical description of how she bakes a four-layer caramel cake, Kerr opined. Kerr did not believe that writing for mass audiences should deter a dramatist from writing great plays, since in the past the best playwrights always wrote for mass audiences.

The critic Louis Kronenberger specialized in analyzing comedy, which he called "a kind of thermostat that regulates and corrects the emotional, ethical, intellectual temperatures at which we live. It is rooted in what is human — all too sadly human — about us."[73] To help the modern theater develop inner discipline and higher standards, he recommended the establishment of a repertory theater which would produce time-tested plays of excellence, so as to constitute a gradual education in good drama instead of "an occasional flirtation with a good play."

John Gassner has been this century's leading anthologizer of drama. In addition to writing sound criticism, he did a yeoman job of keeping up with new playwrights and their techniques. Like George Pierce Baker, Gassner has served as a catalyzer for dramatists, chief of whom has been Tennessee Williams. In dramatic theory, Gassner recommended adding the concept of "enlightenment" or understanding to Aristotle's pity and fear as time-honored elements of catharsis in tragedy.

S.N. Behrman, a writer of high comedy, defined the type as being based upon the articulateness of the characters. The essence of comedy is awareness, said Behrman. "The comic intuition gets to the heart of a human situation with a precision and a velocity unattainable in any other way,"[74] he believed.

One function of contemporary American critics is to assess the plays of foreign dramatists. Anne O'Neill-Barna, for example, writing of Sean O'Casey, found that his two great strengths were typically Irish traits: affirming the worth of the ordinary man, and using language with a pungent sense of humor. She attacked Yeats for not befriending O'Casey when he was under attack. She felt that Yeats had perhaps been too conceited to acknowledge the greatness of his Irish compeer.

James W. Flannery, on the other hand, felt that Yeats had depicted a role for Ireland to play in reviving and sustaining a spiritual culture that could survive when modern materialistic societies collapse. Flannery believed that the variety of style in the plays of Yeats was unprecedented. "Taken as a whole, his twenty-six plays represent the widest range of styles employed by any dramatist in the entire history of the theater,"[75] said Flannery. What is more, he added, Yeats had the key to the solution of modern Ireland's problems, for he "understood that personal freedom without social order, radical change without conservation of the best of the past, feeling without intellect, respect for self without respect for the rights and dignity of others, and violence without redeeming moral purpose, are only partial realities."[76]

Robert W. Corrigan is one of the best recent American critics of Chekhov. Many dramatists have sought to reveal inner character, said Corrigan, but Chekhov did what "Beckett and Ionesco would do well to learn"[77]—enclose the characters' subjective "actions" in an objective frame of specific details. Despite the fact that he cared deeply for fellow humans, Chekhov's artistic conscience disciplined him from direct statements that might lead to sentimentality. The total artistic objectivity, founded ultimately in deeply humane feelings, produced some of the masterworks of the modern theater, Corrigan said.

Elena Levin in the *Saturday Review* in 1972 recalled how Soviet dramatist Mikhail Bulgakov had bravely attacked the Central Repertory Committee of the Communist Party as "killing creative thought; it will end by destroying Soviet dramaturgy."[78] Bulgakov described himself as a satirist in the tradition of Saltykov-Shchedrin, a writer revered by Lenin. When Bulgakov asked Stalin for permission to leave Russia, Stalin responded by giving him a position with the Moscow Art Theater adapting classical Russian novels for the stage. Richard Eder in the *New York Times* had less praise for Bulgakov, criticizing him for the revisions he made to his play *The White Guard*. By featuring the moral bankruptcy of the White Army, Eder said, Bulgakov had destroyed the core of his play. "It is as if instead of saying farewell to her cherry orchard, Mme. Ranevskaya had begun peddling half-acre lots to replace it,"[79] he said.

Henry Popkin meanwhile pointed out that having begun to observe the International Copyright Convention in 1973, the Soviet Union was now more interested in the attention that foreigners paid to current Russian plays. Popkin said that Western drama has always been popular in the Soviet Union, but sometimes the plays are given different endings. A performance of *A Streetcar Named Desire* in 1976, for example, had Mitch killing Stanley Kowalski in a knife battle and then carrying off Blanche, ostensibly for a fresh start in life. Initial interest in David Rabe's *Streamers* was dropped when officials heard that the play dealt with homosexuality. "After all," said one of them, "we have only one lesbian in Leningrad."[80]

David Andelman described the exiled Czech playwright Pavel Kohout as having a political mission. Working now as dramaturg at the Burgtheater, Vienna's state theater, Kohout uses fantasy, imagination, and the absurd to preach the gospel of liberty, said Andelman. Kohout feels that his attack upon totalitarianism should give his plays universal appeal, Andelman explained, because virtually every country experiences totalitarianism at some point.

In an article in the *New York Times*, Nina Darnton showed that good plays in Poland are rare, due to both governmental censorship and lack of compensation to dramatists. Drama critics have little to do with a play's success here, she reported. The public makes its own choice. A popular Polish dramatist, Janusz Glowacki, said, "Actually, reviews here are like everything else in the newspapers; no one believes them. Sometimes a bad review can help."[81] Zygmunt Hubner, artistic director of one of Warsaw's largest theaters, says he cannot stage most American plays because of their profanity. The Polish theater has an educational function of providing models for theatergoers, so profanity is discouraged. A Polish play that recently avoided censorship at its staging in Cracow was *The Brother of Our Lord* by Karol Wojtyla (Pope John Paul II). Hubner feels that great as has been the influence of Jerzy Grotowski in the West, a much more influential modern dramatist in Poland is Tadeusz Kantor.

Margaret Croyden has recently reviewed Kantor's work in the theater. He began as a painter and set designer influenced by

Dadaists, Surrealists, and especially Wassily Kandinsky, who had been an early advocate of "total theater." In the 1930's Kantor formed an avant-garde group called Cricot (an anagram of the Polish word for circus). During World War II the group was driven underground and forced to play secretly in private homes. Kantor's present group, called Cricot 2, consists of sixteen non-professional actors who make their living as painters, poets, and dramatists. The group has received international acclaim for their surrealistic productions. "Actors use odd, exaggerated gestures, or distort their faces with a ghastly gray paint, reminiscent of German Expressionism,"[82] Croyden states. Large dummies are used, not as a substitute for actors, Kantor explains, but as a reminder of the reality of death. "Scenes are presented disjointedly, as in a dream or nightmare," reports Croyden, "so that the reality is shattered."[83] In this theater plot is secondary to painting—line, space, and texture. "The effect," Croyden concludes, "is to dramatize the grotesquery of the human condition through a highly developed art."[84]

In 1979 Mel Gussow declared Tom Stoppard to have joined Harold Pintner as one of Britain's most successful playwrights. At the time four of Stoppard's plays were being staged in London. His *Night and Day* describes the frustration of a union-loving reporter whose scoop interview with an African leader is kept from being printed by a union-imposed strike. Stoppard defines himself as a conservative in life and in drama. "My plays don't break rules,"[85] he says. Not particularly interested in psychological portrayal of characters, Stoppard says his role as a playwright is to tell a story. "Plays are events rather than texts," he declares. "They're written to happen, not to be read."[86]

South African dramatist Athol Fugard has received considerable recent acclaim. Steve Lawson says Fugard describes himself as a miniaturist, since most of his plays have few characters. *Master Harold...and the boys* tells of a white teenager who assumes he treats black people fairly. But a crisis develops—he hears that his alcoholic father is coming home from the hospital. "Tormented by a blend of love and resentment, he takes it out on the black men,"[87] Lawson says. Fugard acknowledges indebtedness to Beckett, as well as to "American playwrights who, at their best, had real craft—O'Neill, Williams, Miller, Odets. Young writers tend to forget that a play occupies three dimensions at once. One: space. Two: silence. And three: time. One of the first things I learned was how to occupy time on the stage."[88]

The academic critic Robert Brustein recently pointed out that modern drama, following Einstein, uses a relativistic approach to characters' motivations, no longer trying to explain each action. This, says Brustein, is similar to the Greeks and Shakespeare, who also do not try to give full explanations but rather hint darkly through intuition. As an example Brustein cites the combined dance-opera-drama called *Einstein on the Beach* by Robert Wilson in collaboration with the composer Philip Glass. The work subtly changes from causal, linear relationships to acausal, space-time relationships. The drama moves from paper airplanes to space travel, from trains to rockets, from firecrackers to Hiroshima. In the last interlude a bus driver monotonously croons a popular love lyric—our love language has not changed while everything else in the environment has. Brustein feels that this kind of imaginative art helps give us what John Keats called "a negative capability," the capacity to function despite fears, uncertainties, and widespread change.

In his book *The Theatre of Revolt* Brustein showed how revolt in modern drama is basically an extension of the revolt of the Romantic poets, including Keats. Tom Driver has agreed with Brustein on the Romantic influence upon current playwrights, adding that the emphasis has switched from a quest for reality to a quest about reality—after all, can anything really be termed "real," in the modern perspective? Driver, who for years has been on the faculty of Union Theological Seminary and thus handles philosophical and religious topics capably, also has found a number of interesting parallels in the plays of Beckett and of Chekhov.

In 1976 Lehman Engel published *The Critics*, a summary of the work of recent newspaper drama critics. He found George Jean Nathan to be simply "a sophomoric harlequin who used barbs that today are a pathetic waste of newsprint."[89] He felt otherwise about Walter Kerr's reviews. "They spy into hidden but significant corners," Engel said, "criticizing on the one hand, imparting a feeling of hopefulness on the other. They are written by a man of background and taste who loves the theater as though it were his favorite, if sometimes backward, child."[90] Most of Engel's other books on the theater deal with the musical drama.

John Corry in 1981 pointed out that in the previous two decades Neil Simon had written nineteen plays and sixteen movie scripts, many of them among the most successful of the period. Corry ascribes Simon's success to his attitude about life. "I'm so happy. It drives people crazy,"[91] Simon confessed. Told it was no small thing to have four plays running simultaneously on Broadway, Simon responded, "Clyde Fitch did that too. Now who remembers Clyde Fitch?"[92] Asked which of his plays would last, Simon replied, "The only sure one is *The Odd Couple*, although *The Sunshine Boys* is the best constructed play I've ever done."[93]

The death of Lee Strasberg in 1982 called forth summaries of his contributions to the acting profession. A follower of the Stanislavsky method as interpreted by Stanislavsky's pupil, Richard Boleslavsky, Strasberg was considered to be America's leading dramatic coach. He had been a cofounder of the Group Theater in 1930 and was best known for his direction of the Actors Studio. His "method" school stressed that actors should identify so deeply with the characters they portray that they feel that in a sense they "become" the characters. Among his Oscar-winning students were Marlon Brando, Sally Field, Jane Fonda, Rod Steiger, and Joanne Woodward. His other students included John Garfield, Ben Gazarra, Julie Harris, Marilyn Monroe, Paul Newman, Maureen Stapleton, Franchot Tone, and Shelley Winters.

Timothy Wiles, in a review of modern theories of acting, felt that Stanislavsky based his technique upon catharsis of character, Brecht upon catharsis of incident, and Artaud and Grotowski upon catharsis of actor and audience. Wiles believed that for acting to succeed there needed to be a creative interaction between text, actor, and audience.

Harold Clurman quoted O'Neill as saying that in his father's generation actors could act the great plays without understanding them, but nowadays actors understand them but can not act them as well. Nevertheless, Clurman felt, modern acting is reassuring. If we lack the great stars of previous eras, we have much better ensemble acting than they had. Improved acting instruction is paying realizable dividends.

Elenore Lester followed the careers of three playwrights who in 1960 had each won Vernon Rice Off-Broadway awards for their first plays: Edward Albee for *The Zoo Story*, Jack Gelber for *The Connection*, and Jack Richardson for *The Prodigal*. Except for several plays by Albee, their promise seemed never to have materialized. She felt that their work had perhaps been bypassed by the social protest movement of the late 1960's. With the visible element of that movement now dimmed, she thought that their stress upon the individual's struggle for self-definition might lead to a return to interest in their plays.

Drama of the "Me Decade," the 1970's, was largely concerned with such personal problems as neuroses, marital discord, and sibling rivalries, Roger Copeland wrote. Judging by our drama, he said, people are abandoning the effort to improve society in order to concentrate upon improving themselves. Although Copeland felt this could be a salutary beginning, its effect is to "Balkanize" the theater audience by appealing to a never-ending succession of subcultures and special interest groups. Great drama requires universal audiences, Copeland said, something more likely to be found today in Europe than in the United States.

Margaret Croyden believes that current drama stems from the rebellious spirit of experimentation found in the late 1960's. Dramatists like John Guare, Sam Shepard, David Rabe, and Arthur Kopit "dispensed with the well-made play, the conventional plot structure, in favor of nonlinear construction. They mixed real and dream worlds, the grotesque with the commonplace, obscenity with philosophy, and media images with comic strip characters,"[94] she said. Some of the playwrights returned to traditional public-pleasing forms, as did Lanford Wilson in *Talley's Folly* and *Fifth of July*.

"Sam Shepard *is* contemporary American drama,"[95] said Martin Esslin. Robert Coe agrees that Shepard, "writing for the American actor as surely as any dramatist, with a nearly absolute ear for the rhythms of the vernacular,"[96] has brought a sense of poetry into the current American theater. Shepard says he wrote *True West*, a play in which a moral brother and an evil brother reverse roles, because of his interest in "double nature." "I think we're split in a much more devastating way than psychology can ever reveal," Shepard said. "It's not some little thing we can get over. It's something we've got to live with."[97] Elenore Lester feels that Shepard's *Chicago*, written when he was twenty-one, is notable because it "welded existential angst to exuberantly comic adolescent fantasy and sharply revealed the psychic state of the tuned-in turned-out dropout of the early Sixties."[98]

Shepard's America, Richard Eder believes, is a land and a people engaged in civil war. Shepard's play *Curse*, which Eder calls absurdist realism, depicts American life as spiritual starvation, in Eder's opinion. In some ways a remarkable play, Eder says, still "the violent symbolic functions of its characters don't mesh with their incipient, recognizable humanity."[99] But Shepard sees only a bleak tomorrow, Eder feels, since he "treats this empty present as the barbarous forerunner of an inhuman future."[100]

A dislike of traditional structure joins modern dramatists like Albert Innaurato, David Mamet, and Christopher Durang. Margaret Croyden feels that their efforts to weld nonlinear structure onto smallscale realism have so far been unsuccessful. Richard Eder, however, believes that Mamet's use of dialogue is a distinct contribution. Eder finds a desperate energy behind apparent incoherences in Mamet's plays, "a passion for speaking that is so intense as to become lyrical." In fact, says Eder, Mamet might just possibly become our first true verse dramatist. Mamet tends to use few characters in his plays. Noting that only two persons appear in his *Life in the Theater*, John Simon slyly remarked that Mamet seems to be waiting for Sophocles to introduce the third character into drama! Eder judges that most of Mamet's plays have problems of clarity and structure, but in *Water Engine* he has finally begun to test his extraordinary command of mood, character, and language with the real changes and stresses of a plot and of external reality.

Christopher Durang seems to be venting a disillusionment over the failure of every ideology to improve the quality of modern life. In *Sister Mary Ignatius Explains It All for You*, for example, Durang has a group of former students return to embarrass Sister Mary with explanations for such things as rape and cancer. Her traditional answers do not satisfy them but neither do they humiliate her. For the students suddenly realize that no one else has better answers. Now their rage is directed not against the church but at what they feel is a silent God. Frank Rich finds Durang's anger to be born not so much out of liberal idealism as from a tragic sense of futility.

Nelvin Vos, on the other hand, feels that a Christian approach to modern comedy can help show the meaning of human existence. Vos analyzes the comic victor in Wilder's plays, the comic victim in Ionesco's plays, and the comic victim-victor in Fry's plays. Vos says that "the structure of dramatic comedy and the structure of Christ's passionate action bear an analogical relation to each other and that a study of these two may deepen our perception of the essential meaning of comedy and of the Christian account of human existence."[101]

Harold Clurman believes that modern playwrights are tentative in both theme and technique. "They stand on shifting ground," he says, and their "convictions, if they exist, are nearly always obliquely disclosed."[102] They have as much doubt about structure as about content, and their work betrays haste and lack of careful craftsmanship. "There is more lunging for novelty than penetration or substance,"[103] Clurman feels. But his final word is encouraging: "The theater dies from time to time, but never expires. The Theater's vitality springs not from trade but from nature; it lies deep in human need."[104] All that the modern theater needs, he concludes, is "generous nature, an unwavering attention — true love — to help it bloom."[105]

Margaret Croyden is somewhat less sanguine. She feels that the theater of the 1960's weakened theatrical language in favor of sound, movement, and image. This trend gave directors like Peter Brook and Jerzy Grotowski a special importance. True, they created exciting theater, she says, but "a whole generation of writers may have been lost in the process."[106] Most new dramatists have grown up watching television, and write as if one or two spectacular scenes can carry a play. "If serious drama is to survive," Croyden warns, "it must combine grand themes and emotional depth with new visual and aural techniques."[107]

16. Motion Picture Criticism

Until the advent of motion pictures, probably no more than twenty per cent of the American public had any firsthand acquaintance with theatrical entertainment. Theater admission prices were too high for the working classes. More affluent Americans often had religious compunctions or lived in areas where there was no thriving theater.

The motion picture democratized American culture. Anyone could afford the nickel or dime admission price. Millions of immigrants learned English reading the captions of silent films. Despite sophisticated opposition, in a short time the movies, as they were called, had almost universal participation. It is now estimated that before starting elementary school, the average American child has clocked 3,500 hours watching television, much of it in movie form, and that the average high-school graduate has already seen 500 movie films. Such a density of dramatic saturation has never before been achieved in any culture. It is thus fitting that attention be given to what criticism has had to say concerning the evolution of this art form cum entertainment.

The very economics of producing and distributing films means that cinema cannot exist without an immense number of patrons, and thus mass appeal is more crucial in cinema than in the other art forms. Early critics who made invidious comparisons between cinema and theater seemed not to appreciate this limiting nature of cinema.

As early as 1864 Louis Ducos du Hauron patented a complete motion-picture system in France, one with color film potential, but technical problems in film processing kept his system from becoming operative. In 1872 California railroad magnate Leland Stanford got English photographer Eadweard Muybridge to photograph a moving horse with twelve, and later twenty-four, separate cameras, thus establishing the effect of a horse in motion. The creation of a single camera capable of instantaneous high-speed photography came in 1882 when French physician Étienne Marey developed a photographic gun fired by a trigger.

Thomas A. Edison built the first movie studio, a tarpaper shack in West Orange, New Jersey, in 1892 called "Black Maria." In 1894 Edison offered the public his Kinetoscope, a coin-operated device that gave the peep-hole viewer about fifteen seconds of moving film.

In France in 1895 Louis and Auguste Lumière improved on Edison's Kinetoscope by developing their Cinematographe, which was a combination camera, projector, and printer. That same year the American, Thomas Armat, discovered a principle used in the modern projector, which gave each image a longer exposure as well as looped the film to ease the strain on it. This device, known as Vitascope, was used by Edison in 1896 at a New York music hall, initiating the movies as a popular entertainment medium. Before the year was over, many other machines appeared in music halls and vaudeville houses in many places in America and Europe.

The year 1896 saw two other important developments. The first traveling camera was used on a gondola in Venice by a cameraman attempting to give a feeling of his city. Also, *The Kiss*, a short film starring May Irwin and John Rice, scandalized audiences and brought the first of many demands for screen censorship on moral grounds.

An early effort to tell a story on film occurred in 1897, when R.G. Hollaman produced a three-reel Passion play in New York. At about this time Léon Gaumont in France produced a series of short sound films starring such well-known figures as Sarah Bernhardt and Constant Coquelin. The sound here was provided by synchronizing a phonograph record with the film.

By 1899 the Parisian magician and theater owner Georges Méliès was charming audiences with highly imaginative films which, in his opinion, "set the cinema along the path toward theatrical spectacle and introduced the extravagant costume film, imposing decor, and historical reconstructions."[1]

In the United States a theater actors' strike in 1900 gave a great boost to the young cinema. During the strike many vaudeville producers kept open by presenting solely Vitascope films. Because of the strike, masses of the American public became familiar with movies long before the large-scale European audiences followed suit.

The short-sighted vaudeville managers, as soon as the strike ended, relegated the Vitascope to the role of "chaser," designed to play between performances of live actors as the theater emptied and refilled. But a few enterprising young men, mostly from New York City's lower east side, saw the potential of motion pictures and staked their future on that vision. Men like Adolph Zukor, Marcus Loew, and William Fox, who had been leaders in the fur and garment industry, switched their talent to cinema and were soon the leaders in the new field.

The early years of the new century saw a marked contribution to cinematic art by a group of photographers in Brighton, England, led by G.A. Smith and James Williamson. Stressing facial expression, they used close-up shots a lot. Alternating between close-up and full shots, Smith anticipated the selective succession that later came to be known as montage. Williamson's film *Attack on a China Station* in 1901 anticipated both Edwin S. Porter and D.W Griffith. The Brighton school, said Hugh Gray, made popular the use of the chase, simultaneous action, exterior shooting, and subjects with social implications.

A landmark film was Edwin S. Porter's eight-minute *The Great Train Robbery* in 1903. On one hand it contained the seed of modern editing techniques, on another it inaugurated the popular era of the nickelodeon. Arthur Knight says that "in the truest sense, *The Great Train Robbery* marked the beginning of both the art and the industry of motion pictures."[2]

In 1905 John and Harry David remodeled a Pittsburgh storeroom into a nickelodeon, playing *The Great Train Robbery*. This started a national craze. Within four years there were at least 8,000 nickelodeons in the United States alone. There were opponents: The *Chicago Tribune* declared, "There is no voice to defend the five cent theater. Its influence is wholly vicious."[3] But there were also such defenders as social worker Jane Addams and poet Vachel Lindsay. Jane Addams said that movies "rightly conducted are a benefit and not a menace to the poorer classes."[4] Vachel Lindsay predicted that the movie theater would replace the saloon because escapism could be better achieved through the cinema—it was cheaper, worked more quickly and fully than alcohol, and had no anti-social after-effects.

Philosophers welcomed cinema's realism. Henri Bergson said it would be a priceless record of its times. Leo Tolstoy felt that "Russian life must be shown as it is," and that cinema could now do the job. Since he had always felt cramped by the few scenes possible on the theater's stage, Tolstoy looked forward to the many settings possible through cinema. Thomas Mann doubted whether its photographic likeness could ever qualify the cinema as art, but he did see it as having the breadth of epic in its narrative.

The ten producing companies, in an effort to create a monopoly, organized the Motion Picture Patents Company. They fixed rental and license fees to theater owners, and they restricted equipment used to that manufactured by them. Their monopoly was broken by the import of such European films as *Queen Elizabeth* starring Sarah Bernhardt, and the Italian *Quo Vadis?*, at which an admission price of $1.00 was charged. Adolph Zukor formed a rival company, called Famous Players in Famous Plays. By the time the monopoly was dissolved by court action in 1917, its stranglehold upon American cinema had already been broken.

By now an esthetic of the cinema was developing. The French critic Louis Delluc, who had initially opposed cinema, not only shifted to favor it but actually started producing his own films. André Bazin points out that the cinema picked up forms long abandoned by the theater, that underlying Mack Sennett comedies was sixteenth century farce. Also, says Bazin, the early filmmakers "effectively extracted what was of use to them from the art with which they were about to win their public, namely the circus, the provincial theater, and the music hall, which provided slapstick films with both technique and actors."[5]

Erwin Panofsky underscored the difference in acting between the theater and cinema. Eleanora Duse's only film *Cenere*, he said, is valuable only as a historical record of a great stage actress. He felt that the best early actors, such as Charlie Chaplin, Buster Keaton, Theda Bara, and Douglas Fairbanks, Senior, came not from the theater but from other performance media. Film acting differs from stage acting, Panofsky stated, in being more exaggerated but also richer, more subtle, and because of close-ups infinitely more precise.

Panofsky pointed out that the first films were not the filming of stage plays, but the process of giving motion to still pictures. When cinema started trying to film stage plays, it inevitably and understandably failed. The unique powers of cinema, in Panofsky's view, are dynamatization of space and spatialization of time. Although theater space is limited and thus static, cinema allows the viewer to travel with the camera, and thus space seems to advance, retard, grow larger, grow smaller—in short, come alive. Movie scripts, to be successful, need to keep both what is seen and what is heard in mind at the same time, and thus require what Panofsky called a good principle of coexpressibility.

In *The Art of the Moving Picture*, published in 1915, Vachel Lindsay produced the first important book-length critique of the cinema as an art form. Herbert Croly, editor of the *New Republic*, immediately invited Lindsay to be film critic for his journal. Gordon Craig and D.W. Griffith, among others, praised the book. Victor Freeburg used it at Columbia University in one of America's first college courses on the cinema.

Feeling that the cinema had great potential as art, Lindsay aimed to educate the public taste by appealing especially to art museums, academic institutions, and the world of literature and criticism. Lindsay saw cinema as fulfilling Walt Whitman's hope of art made available to every citizen. Sooner or later, Lindsay said, the movies would "bring the nobler side of the equality idea to the people who are so crassly equal. We Americans should look for the great photoplay of tomorrow that prophesies of the flags made one, the crowds in brotherhood."[6]

We who had thought in words since the days we worshipped Thor now suddenly are learning to think in pictures, Lindsay said. This new weapon of man will change the face of the whole earth, he predicted. "In after centuries its beginnings will be indeed remembered,"[7] he averred.

Using a poet's vocabulary, Lindsay found three main types of motion pictures. The action play, always popular in America because of the mania for speed, was for him sculpture-in-motion, a narrow form of the dramatic. The intimate play, which he called painting-in-motion, was an equivalent of the lyric. Finally, the splendor play, one form of which was fantasy, was architecture-in-motion, or for him the equivalent of the epic.

A strange paradox is at work in cinema, said Lindsay. Although the movies tend to turn actors into puppets, cinema at the same time tends to give puppets a human quality. Pursuing this idea, he found that "non-human tones, textures, lines, and spaces take on a vitality almost like that of flesh and blood."[8] The proper place to recruit capable film producers, he thus felt, would be not from the ranks of vaudeville managers but rather from painters, sculptors, and architects, that is, persons versed in producing impressive visual effects.

Lindsay cautioned against the use of music in cinema, fearing that since the script writer could not also write the music, disunity would probably result. Sound in film he also opposed, since it would be hard enough for the director to humanize the picture without having at the same time to try to humanize the sound.

In an effort to develop a poetics of the cinema and to identify its peculiar strengths, Lindsay pointed to thirty differences between cinema and the stage. Whereas stage exits and entrances are at side and back, cinema's are across the imaginary footlight line. In addition, an entrance or exit toward the camera magnifies the actor, thus heightening the audience's identification with him.

Another cinema trait is the ability to use action in place of words. A boy plucks a rose, and a girl accepts. "Moving objects, not moving lips," said Lindsay, "make the words of the photoplay."[9] A cinematic climax can never be words, but must be an action, thus strengthening the identification with the audience. Then too, seeing beauty is sufficient—no words are needed to explain a beautiful woman's face or figure.

A strength of theater is its unified audience, but then again the cinema, having no such stage spell, does not have the illusion so easily broken by a sneeze or a popcorn box, Lindsay felt. He believed that scenery was far more important in cinema because the audience lacked stage conventions concerning setting. He noted that film interiors tended (in his day) to be smaller than stages, but that stage exteriors were necessarily vastly smaller than cinema exteriors. The key terms in a stage play, which depends mainly on the actors, are passion and character, whereas cinema, which depends mainly on the director, has key criteria of splendor and speed.

The best films, Lindsay concluded, would come when cinema's peculiar forte would be used as the base. Because of the special requirements, plays would have to be written specifically for the cinema, he felt. On the whole, despite several poor prophecies, Lindsay's critique has stood up as a penetrating and creative analysis of the peculiar power of motion pictures.

The great director and producer at the time of Lindsay's book was D.W. Griffith. In contrast to the detailed screenplays used by Thomas Ince, Griffith generally used no script. Griffith took the camera away from the proscenium arch, where Méliès had placed it, and used it wherever it did the most good. Griffith also improved over the early montage efforts of Porter and others. According to Marvin Borowsky, Griffith "originated or improved upon the long shot, the close-ups, the pan shot, high-and-low-angle shots, the moving shot, the dissolve, soft focus, cross-cutting, the flashback, night photography and back lighting."[10] Borowsky also feels that he made remarkable contributions in editing, and in the use of tempo, scenery, and crowds. Dwight Macdonald agrees that Griffith was an instinctive genius, "creating a whole new art form *ex nihilo*."[11] He antedated the great Russian directors in both form (montage) and content (epic subjects). His only weakness, says Macdonald, was his failure to grow and develop.

Griffith adapted Thomas Dixon's Civil War novel, *The Clansman*, into a film in which cinema became of age, *The Birth of a Nation*. When critics accused Griffith of reinforcing racial prejudice, he responded in 1916 with *Intolerance*, an epic diatribe against dictatorship and injustice. In 1919 he joined with Charlie Chaplin, Douglas Fairbanks Senior, and Mary Pickford in forming the United Artists Corporation.

Recognized as the leading actor in the early days of cinema was the English comedian Charlie Chaplin. Parker Tyler, in *Chaplin: Last of the Clowns* analyzed Charlie's classic tramp as the outgrowth of a home in which his father died when Charlie was five and his mother was in and out of mental institutions. "Already burdened with an Oedipus complex," said Edward Murray in a review of Tyler's book, "Chaplin now felt constrained to take over the role vacated by his father; however, he was too small to provide the economic and emotional support required by his mother."[12] Generally the camera shots viewed the tramp from the low angle of a child. The tramp's clothes are too big, because his development was arrested — he is still a child at heart. His best communication is with children, and their world is the only one he is really at home in. "In brief," summarized Murray, "the tramp is 'really' a small boy in adult clothing, buffeted about by a hostile environment, and held back by his cumbersome, outsized shoes."[13]

World War I proved a deterrent to the movie industry, since the chemical then used as the base for film stock, cellulose nitrate, was an important ingredient in military explosives. But several technical developments were making a profound change in cinematics. Theaters were limited in size by the ability to project the sound of records used to accompany films. Just before the war Lee DeForest developed a selenium vacuum tube which vastly increased sound amplification. After the war DeForest discovered ways to transcribe the impulses of sound waves into electric impulses that could be photographed upon a strip of celluloid; then when the film was passed around a photoelectric cell in the movie projector, the images were transformed back to their original sound.

Facing bankruptcy, Warner Brothers used a record synchronized sound system called Vitaphone in 1926 for a program of talking and musical short films. The following year a dramatic breakthrough in sound films came with the movie *The Jazz Singer*, starring Al Jolson. Even though this was a silent film with four talking or singing interludes, the public's imagination was captivated by the concept of sound film, and by 1930 silent movies were virtually a thing of the past.

Another important technical innovation was the development of Technicolor in 1915 by a team of physicists headed by Herbert T. Kalmus. By splitting the light beam with a prism into the two ends of the color spectrum (red-orange and blue-green), the two films could be developed separately, passed through their appropriate dyes, and then laminated together to produce a reasonably accurate two-color process picture. Technicolor was used to tint the climactic sequences of such film classics of the 1920's as *Ben Hur*, *The Ten Commandments*, and *The Phantom of the Opera*.

It remained for Walt Disney to develop the full three-color process in his *Flowers and Trees* in 1932. Disney had already pioneered with the first sound cartoon in 1928, *Steamboat Willie*, the film that introduced Mickey Mouse. Still further Disney innovation came in 1940 with the use of directional or stereophonic sound in *Fantasia*. The first feature-length animated cartoon, Disney's *Snow White and the Seven Dwarfs*, took four years to make before it appeared in 1938 with approximately 477,000 photographed drawings.

Motion pictures played a crucial role in the transformation of values that occurred in the 1920's in the United States. Post-war disillusionment, prohibition, and a new openness towards sex were reflected in the films of the decade. Roadster cars, hip flasks, and flappers wearing short skirts made it seem fashionable to follow trends seen on film. Movie theaters used palatial architecture, and movie stars were adulated as if saints. Women like Clara Bow, Gloria Swanson, and Pola Negri, and men such as Douglas Fairbanks Senior, John Gilbert, and especially Rudolph Valentino, became the most important Americans to many of their fellow citizens.

Something of a counter-trend to popular cinema was the documentary film, a term coined by Scottish educator John Grierson in 1924. Sensing that the movies were swiftly replacing the home, the church, and the school as shapers of values, Grierson suggested that the movies should be deliberately used as tools in education for citizenship values. Ignored in the United States, Grierson received British government support in directing the attention of films to provide simple and dramatic presentations of the complex workings of an industrial society. The only film he personally directed, *Drifters* in 1929, showed that the herring found on an Englishman's breakfast plate got there only because of the daily toil and heroism of North Sea fishermen. Robert J. Flaherty's *Nanook of the North*, produced in 1922, depicted the rugged life of an Eskimo, and was used as a model by Grierson and other supporters of documentary films.

Probably the greatest director of this period was Sergei Eisenstein, son of a Russian shipbuilder, who was educated as a civil engineer and architect. Dissatisfied with the limitations of the theater, he turned to cinema and at the age of twenty-six he directed *Potemkin*, a realistic presentation of mutiny on a battleship in the abortive revolt of 1905. The film attracted worldwide attention for Eisenstein's use of non-professional actors (called "typage") and his technique of montage, meaning the crosscutting of images to represent complex ideas. Through additional films, as well as by his lectures and books on the cinema, Eisenstein became one of the most influential persons of the silent film era.

To Eisenstein, cinema was the first truly synthetic art, "an art of organic synthesis in its very essence, not a concert of contiguous but actually independent arts."[14] This being true, said Eisenstein, once we comprehend the laws of cinema we at the same time will have achieved an understanding of the fundamental laws governing all art.

At its best, Eisenstein said, film can achieve a symphony of color and sound denied to the theater. Film goes beyond theater, he felt, in that it could at once be epic in its reach of plot, dramatic in its treatment of theme, and lyrical in expressing emotional nuances. Typage appealed to him because it presented each new figure in the first glimpse of him so sharply and completely that from then on he was a known element in the film. Either amateur actors or those having "naturally expressive" faces were his choice, since the goal in realism is to avoid all sign of artificiality.

Eisenstein considered D.W. Griffith to be "the greatest master of the most graphic form in this field, parallel montage."[15] Eisenstein particularly liked the way Griffith used alternating shots of rich and poor people to achieve ironic contrast. He also enjoyed Griffith's montage as a device to heighten tempo.

Eisenstein felt that Griffith got much of his technique from the novels of Charles Dickens. Some of the influences were the use of inimitable bit characters, the use of a commonplace close-up of a familiar object as a lead-in to a serious topic, and flashbacks, montage, and city scenes. Eisenstein stated that "Dickens's nearness to the characteristics of cinema in method, style, and especially in viewpoint is indeed amazing."[16] Both techniques, he said, base their mass appeal upon sentiment, opposition to vice, finding the extraordinary in the ordinary, and bringing romance into dull prosaic reality.

Flaubert in *Madame Bovary* had also used montage, Eisenstein said. As Monsieur Derozerays gives a speech in the public square, Emma and Rudolphe grow increasingly intimate. The orator's comments cleverly reinforce the growing awareness of love. This cross-dialogue, said Eisenstein, is montage.

The term "montage" became a key one in Eisenstein's esthetic. André Bazin defined montage as "the creation of a sense or meaning not proper to the images themselves but derived exclusively from their juxtaposition."[17] André Malraux in *Psychology of the Cinema* said that "it was montage that gave birth to film as an art, setting it apart from mere animated photography, in short, creating a language."[18] Everyone seemed to agree that Griffith was the pioneer who first demonstrated the powerful effects made possible by montage.

Eisenstein's colleague, Lev Kuleshov, explained that "a succession of shots involves a complex set of relationships between them, relationships of idea, of duration, of physical movement, and of form, by the skillful manipulation of which an audience could be most powerfully affected."[19]

Since the basis of art is conflict, Eisenstein said, montage, which is a technical way of showing conflict, is a very useful artistic technique. "The dynamics of montage," he believed, "serve as impulses driving forward the total film."[20] Eisenstein even explained the structure of *Potemkin* as based upon the Hegelian dialectic of thesis, antithesis, and synthesis. Montage was the dynamic process that welded all of the film's diverse elements into an organic synthesis.

Eisenstein identified four types of montage. The first, which he called metric tonality, impels the spectator to imitate the perceived action, as for example, when the audience sways to the meter of rowers' beat. The second type, rhythmic montage, involves capturing the rhythm of moving objects, or of the spectator's eye moving along an object. Third, tonal montage, involves building an overall tone, as for instance the use of darker shots to evoke gloom, or of acutely angled shots to evoke a nervous effect. The final type, called overtonal montage, results from the counterplay between the film's dominant tone and its overtone. Just as in music there are overtones to the dominant, so there are in drama, he averred. As in the music of Scriabin and Debussy, to some extent the clash disturbs, to some extent it enhances the dominant theme, Eisenstein felt.

His fame brought Eisenstein to Hollywood, but his scenarios for *Sutter's Gold* and *An American Tragedy* were rejected by Paramount Studios. Eisenstein suggested a deterministic treatment for *An American Tragedy*, in which Clyde Griffiths is absolved of guilt for a crime occasioned by a materialistic society. Much to Theodore Dreiser's displeasure, Paramount chose Josef von Sternberg as director, since his emphasis lay upon Clyde's guilt of murder of his former girl friend.

After a brief stay in Mexico, Eisenstein returned to Russia. Three sound films he worked on were left unfinished, as governmental criticism attacked him for trying to work with capitalists. Although he received the Order of Lenin for *Alexander Nevsky* in 1938, the second part of a planned trilogy *Ivan the Terrible* was banned until after his death in 1948.

Like his friend Eisenstein, Soviet director Vsevolod Pudovkin had initial qualms about the effect of sound in cinema. Music and special effects could contribute to the overall effect, they felt, but heard dialogue might well be a distracting influence. In time both of them realized that dialogue could be synthesized into the artistic whole effect.

Imprisoned in a German POW camp for three years, Pudovkin escaped in 1918 and began studying chemistry. Seeing Griffith's *Intolerance* led him to enroll in the state institute of cinematography.

Ivor Montagu, who translated Pudovkin's books, *Film Technique* and *Film Acting*, believed that his main contribution lay neither in theory nor innovation, but in synthesizing the best elements from Griffith, Kuleshov, Eisenstein, and Stanislavsky, firing them with his own good taste and enthusiasm, so as to produce films that are often more influential than those of his forebears. His best silent films were *Mother*, *Storm over Asia*, and *The End of St. Petersburg*. Probably his greatest sound films were *Suvorov* and *Admiral Nakhimov*.

Cinema would achieve its fullness as an art form, Pudovkin said, only when it had freed itself from the dictates of an art form foreign to it—theater. Montage he saw as the core of the director's art. Writers ignorant of film technique are likely to have ninety per cent of their work altered by specialists, he warned. Beautiful sets seduce viewers from the central effect of the film, he said, and are only permissible if they "enter organically into its whole and become a part of its content. Every background *qua* background runs counter to the basic laws of films."[21]

Pudovkin believed that the Stanislavsky method of training actors was the best one. Stanislavsky had actors talk to each other in character but out of stage lines so as to give each actor a deep feeling of identity with the character portrayed. To Pudovkin this not only provided organic unity in the actor's role but also provided small details, lost in the theater, but picked up by the searching eye of the camera. The organic unity was especially important for cinema actors because of the disconnected sequence in which camera scenes are filmed.

Pudovkin thought that each actor should have his individual script, showing him the order to all of his shots, so that he can rehearse on specific effects appropriate to the part of the film. Nor is the actor finished when the camera stops. Pudovkin said that the actor should sit with the director in editing his part of the film. This not only helps the director make appropriate cuts but also assists the actor for his next appearance before a camera.

Just as in theater and dramatic criticism, the doctrine of socialist realism as enforced by the Soviet government pretty well destroyed creativity in cinema and film criticism. An art form which may have been the world's best in 1930 was insignificant within a decade or two.

In Germany expressionism was widespread after World War I. *The Cabinet of Dr. Caligari* in 1919 was an expressionist film that was the first important horror movie. It employed weird camera angles and bizarre sets to create a Gothic atmosphere of suspense and terror. E.A. Dupont's *Variety* in 1926, says Hugh Gray, was "a masterpiece of camera virtuosity that disturbed Hollywood by seeming to threaten its supremacy."[22] As in drama, as expressionism in cinema waned, so did the artistic results.

Rudolf Arnheim, one of Germany's leading film critics, moved to Italy in the 1930's and later became a professor at several American colleges. His book *Film as Art* creates a poetics of the cinema. Arnheim not only accepted the limitations of the silent film but felt they could be used as the basis for a high art form. Mechanical advancements, such as sound, color, and a wide screen, can permit greater realism but may interfere with the intended overall effect. Unless we limit technical developments, he said, "the film is on its way to the victory of wax museum ideals over creative art."[23]

Arnheim's chief contribution was to study the many possibilities of varied camera effects, and then correlate them with corresponding psychological effects in the viewer. For example, a camera lens can be focused to produce a blurred image, describing a drunken person, or someone confused, dazed, or coming out of anesthesia. Special lenses can produce functional distortion. Mirror images, from water or a highly polished surface, can create interesting psychological depth. Dissolving, or the gradual change from one shot to another, often highlights either similarity or contrast in montage, said Arnheim, "for the more easily one shot melts into another, the more striking it is if a connection of subject (similarity or contrast) between the two is suddenly noticed."[24]

Compared to the theater's three-dimensional stage, the cinema's two-dimensional screen may seem a limitation, but Arnheim saw ways to turn it into an asset. For one thing, striking camera angles can heighten the viewer's interest. Also, the film's margins provide a frame for which certain pictorial effects are possible. Then too photographic artistry can create emphasis, interpretation, symbolism, and beauty in itself.

The synthesis of picture and dialogue was a bigger problem in cinema than in theater, Arnheim felt. Whereas playgoers are tolerant of error, realizing that the performance is live and thus subject to human frailty, cinema fans expect perfection, realizing that retakes are possible to eliminate error. Since words are so crucial in theater, the director often subordinates setting to dialogue. The film director, however, less dependent on words for the overall effect, may be tempted to subordinate dialogue too much, and must take pains to acquire the proper synthesis with picture.

Despite the caveat concerning sound, Arnheim saw its powers. "No fairly complicated event or state of mind can be conveyed by pictures alone," he said. "Therefore, the addition of spoken dialogue has made storytelling easier."[25] Dialogue in sound, by saving time, space, and effort, has freed the director to use his frames for deeper effects, said Arnheim. On the whole, Arnheim has given the film profession a helpful guidebook for the evolution of cinema into an art form.

Called "the Aristotle of the cinema" by Hugh Gray, André Bazin has been one of France's leading film critics. Having a good background in literature, philosophy, and modern science, Bazin was able to write in a style understood by average persons. His main idea was that cinema is the most objective of all the arts (the French word for lens is "objectif"). He felt that a photographic image gave us the object itself, "freed from the conditions of time and space that govern it."[26] The cinema, he said, is objectivity in time. "Photography," he said, "does not create eternity, as art does; it embalms time, rescuing it simply from its proper corruption."[27] He thus saw photography as the most important event in art history. "Simultaneously a liberation and an accomplishment," he said, "it has freed Western painting from its obsession with realism and allowed it to recover its esthetic autonomy."[28]

Cinema reminds the theater to stay true to itself, Bazin believed, and not try to do things better done on film. He quoted Jean-Paul Sartre as saying that whereas in theater the drama proceeds from the actor, in cinema the drama proceeds from the décor. Having space limitations, theater should stress the human soul, said Bazin. Cinema, focusing on all of nature (since there are even microscopic and telescopic lenses), should choose as its scope the entire universe.

Bazin conceded that undoubtedly a stage play has an effect more uplifting, moral, and noble than that of a film. Where the film calms the viewer, the theater excites him, said Bazin. The theater also constantly legislates against creation of a mass mentality, he felt. "Theatergoers form a community; filmgoers are a crowd,"[29] he confessed. The audience in the cinema was simply a collection of solitary individuals.

The bright lights of the stage almost seem to act as a censor of the play's morals, he said, but cinema was, in the words of Jean Cocteau, "an event seen through a keyhole."[30] In a dark movie theater, said Bazin, we are all voyeurs, peeking as if through half-drawn blinds at the most private things happening to people.

Individual identification is stronger in the cinema, Bazin believed. For example, when the theater hero finally gets the pretty girl, we are jealous of him, but when the cinema hero gets her, we feel great, since we feel we are getting her.

The fact that cinema adapts plays from the theater Bazin interpreted not as a weakness but as a sign of maturity, since the adaptation was always a new work, tailored to cinema's requirements. Bazin also pointed out that cinema made it possible for Shakespeare and other classics to be enjoyed by millions of people who would otherwise never have that opportunity.

Bazin also formulated a law concerning montage: "When the essence of a scene demands the simultaneous presence of two or more factors in the action, montage is ruled out."[31] The example he cited was the seal hunt in *Nanook of the North*, where it was imperative to see hunter, seal, and hole all in the same shot, not alternately.

In Bazin's opinion, the sound film had already achieved maturity by 1940. In content it provided "major varieties with clearly defined rules capable of pleasing a worldwide public, as well as a cultured elite."[32] In form it had achieved "well defined styles of photography and editing perfectly adapted to their subject matter — a complete harmony of image and sound."[33]

The Absurdist playwright Antonin Artaud was one of many who acknowledged indebtedness to the Marx Brothers for artistic technique. *Monkey Business*, said Artaud, is "a hymn to anarchy and wholehearted revolt."[34] *Animal Crackers* he found to be extraordinary surrealism. It has, he said, "a powerful, total, absolute originality (I am not exaggerating, I am simply trying to define)."[35]

Citizen Kane by Orson Welles was praised by many critics. Bazin pointed out that Jean Renoir had pioneered in substituting depth focus for the technique of shot-reverse-shot, in which the camera focuses alternately on each speaker in a dialogue. But William Wyler and Orson Welles had perfected the depth shot, Bazin said. "*Citizen Kane* can never be too highly praised," he stated. "Thanks to the depth of field, whole scenes are covered in one take, the camera remaining motionless. Dramatic effects for which we had formerly relied on montage were created out of the movements of the actors within a fixed framework."[36]

Advantages of depth focus, said Bazin, were that the spectator was brought closer to the image than he is in reality, and thus he is more intimately involved in the action. Also, where montage had ruled out rich ambiguity, depth focus restored it as a possibility. This was one of the triumphs of *Citizen Kane*: "The uncertainty in which we find ourselves as to the spiritual key or the interpretation we should put on the film is built into the very design of the image,"[37] Bazin stated.

Andrew Sarris judged that *Citizen Kane* had a consistency of theme, structure, and technique. For example, the beginning and ending subtly suggest the theme, Sarris said. In the beginning of the film, "the intense material reality of the fence dissolves into the fantastic unreality of the castle and, in the end, the mystic pretension of the castle dissolves into the mundane substance of the fence. Matter has come full circle from its original quality to the grotesque baroque of its excess."[38]

The first American periodical film critic to gain a reputation was James Agee, who wrote criticism for *Time* and *The Nation* in the 1940's. No other critic has received higher praise from his colleagues. Among those who considered him America's best film critic were Arlene Croce, Bosley Crowther, Pauline Kael, Arthur Knight, and John Simon. Agee's approach was impressionistic, moral, and evaluative. He preferred original scripts to adaptations, since he felt that cinema had unique demands. Because Agee was a skilled writer, readers could visualize and comprehend the film he evaluated. To him a good film worked to awaken curiosity and intelligence. Although he felt that cinema was the greatest art medium of the century, he believed that the films of the 1940's failed to achieve their potential, for although there had been a growing sophistication in technique there had been but little corresponding growth in maturity of theme.

Unlike Germany and Russia, where dictatorships seem to have driven cinema into long-lasting doldrums, Italy after the death of Mussolini experienced a remarkable cinematic renaissance. Roberto Rossellini achieved moving effects in films like *Open City* and *Paisan*, partly through inspired acting by unprofessional actors. Rossellini's screenwriter in those films, Federico Fellini, began directing his own scripts, known for their unique combination of lyricism and irony. Films like *La Strada* and *La Dolce Vita* brought Fellini international recognition.

American critic Stanley Kauffmann believes that Michelangelo Antonioni is the greatest modern cinema director. Aristotle's precepts worked well in a world organized religiously, but modern individualism in a pluralistic society demands a new cinematic idiom, and Antonioni has created it, Kauffmann says. In place of classical unities Antonioni gives us mood, personality, and emphasis upon the physical world. He replaces character conflict with character immersion. Says Kauffmann: "He is reshaping time itself in his films, taking it out of its customary synoptic form, wringing intensity out of its distention."[39]

To show how Antonioni uses setting artistically, Kauffmann cites the beautiful color in the film *Red Desert*, where the tones presage a new world, making environment a leading character in the film, thereby providing a subliminal reinforcement of the film's values.

Japanese films have excelled in poetic fantasy, symbolism, and use of color. Arthur Knight says that *Gate of Hell*, a Japanese film produced in 1954, "revealed nuances in the psychological handling of color that made directors the world over increasingly aware of color as a dramatic, rather than purely a decorative, element in their pictures."[40]

The film classic *Rashomon* was created by Japanese director Akira Kurosawa in 1951. As a child Kurosawa had been influenced by Charlie Chaplin, William S. Hart, and other actors in silent films. He learned filmmaking under the veteran director Yamamoto.

Rashomon was adapted from two stories by Japanese author Ryunosuke Akutagawa. It tells of the rape of a medieval Japanese noblewoman and the murder of her and her husband, all as seen through the eyes of the victims, the murderer, and a bystander. Frank Gibney in the *New York Times* called it "a truly haunting story of man's infinite capacity for distorting reality through personal perspective."[41] Parker Tyler showed how when the camera shot the same incident four times, each from a different perspective, the result was four entirely different interpretations of the same event. Tyler compared the technique with the use of blurred images, used to show multiple aspects of a person or a situation at one point in time, or to blur the distinctions between past, present, and future.

Sweden's twin contribution to cinematic art has been actresses and directors. Actresses range from Asta Nielsen and Greta Garbo to Ingrid Bergman and Liv Ullman. Early directors who received acclaim were Victor Sjöström and Mauritz Stiller. Following World War II producer Alf Sjöberg and writer-director Ingmar Bergman collaborated in a series of realistic films, and Arne Sucksdorff used nature powerfully and symbolically in a number of films.

Ingmar Bergman's films reveal the type of metaphysical questioning found in the twentieth century theater. American critic Vernon Young finds a hostility towards older men in Bergman's early films, a direct outgrowth of his rebellion against authority figures, including his clergyman father and God. Edward Murray also finds Strindberg's influence upon Bergman: "Both artists rebelled against an oppressive Swedish Lutheranism; both reveal ambivalence toward

God and women in their work; and both these tempermental titans use their art as 'an instrument of the ego.' "[42]

Stanley Kauffmann finds the crux of Bergman's films to be the classic religious question: is the God-man relation still viable? Unfortunately, says Kauffmann, this constant spiritual wrestling of the author through his characters provides simply arena scenes, "rather than disciplined artistic experiences whose prime purpose is emotional involvement of the audience."[43]

On this point John Simon disagrees with Kauffmann. Although he seems to dislike most directors, Simon defends Bergman's technique. Simon likes it because of its "fullness, which is both a variety — the continuing elaboration of themes and elucidation of problems; and a unity — the blending of all Bergman films into a sustained questioning of the universe, a heroic struggle to come up with a clearer understanding of the questions at least, where answers seem to be increasingly unobtainable."[44]

Andrew Sarris stands closer to Kauffmann than to Simon in appraising Bergman's films. *The Seventh Seal*, says Sarris, is the first existential movie. Although set in medieval Sweden, the theme is ultra-modern: death is the crucial reality of human existence. What Bergman seems to be saying in this film, Sarris states, is the thought that "if modern man must live without the faith which makes death meaningful, he can at least endure life with the aid of certain necessary illusions."[45] Bergman's problem, in the opinion of Sarris, is that his cinematic work has declined because his technique was never a match for his sensibility.

Laslo Benedek, who directed a film version of *Death of a Salesman*, described the problem involved in adapting a stage play for the movies. This play was a natural for film, said Benedek, because of its many flashbacks in Willy Loman's mind between his present and his sinful past. Things like memory, fantasy, and daydream are excellent for cinema, Benedek said. "They have in common the vivid moment, the quick transitions, the 'dissolve', sometimes the vagueness of out-of-focus images, sometimes the precision of the close-up."[46] Since the flashbacks are very real in Willy's mind, they are filmed realistically. Willy's quick mental switches are exactly suited for the film's idiom, Benedek felt. Transitions work well on camera. When Willy talks to his wife, the camera follows him, right past his wife, to the woman recalled by Willy's conscience. His words are answered by the other woman. The transition, in Benedek's view, is smooth, organic, and artistic.

Stanley Kauffmann provided a useful rule-of-thumb concerning adaptations: "If we exclude trash, then the further down the scale from greatness toward competence that the original lies, the more likely it is to be successfully adapted for the screen; for it is less likely to be dependent on its original form for its effect."[47] When the original work is a famous one, Kauffmann believed, comparison of the film with the original is unavoidable, and hence disappointment is the likely result.

Mortimer Adler, editor of the series of books called *The Great Ideas*, took it upon himself to evolve criteria for excellence in movies. Comparing cinema to drama and to the novel, he began by listing cinema's limitations. First of all, pictures are vastly inferior to words in expressing thoughts, conveying complex information, and dealing with abstractions, Adler said. "The plot of the best cinema," he said, "is simpler, character is less definitely delineated, thought is less fully expressed, the constituent incidents are less fully represented than in a correspondingly excellent novel or play."[48] Restated, he said, this means that a film is less extensive than a novel and less intensive than a play. Thus, he added, a film can be made from a novel or a play, but not vice versa. Walter Kerr, incidentally, has recently confirmed the meager results that have come from the effort to turn successful movies into plays.

Adler then turned his attention to cinema's peculiar merits. Having a greater degree of narrative condensation than a novel or a play, he said, cinema is able to tell a story more effectively than those two forms can do. "If a more concentrated effect is more pleasurable," he said, "the motion picture is as superior to the drama as that, in turn, is to the novel."[49]

Adler stated that art, to achieve its optimum effect, needs to maximize both realism and fantasy in a unified art work. Cinema, he said, achieved this double maximization better than the play or the novel. "The motion picture," Adler said, "can be *at once* more realistic and more fantastic than other types of narration, even though it cannot be as realistic as the stage or as fantastic as a novel."[50] The best films, he felt, such as *Potemkin*, *The Informer*, Charlie Chaplin movies, and Mickey Mouse cartoons, realized this high potential of cinema.

Conceding that plays and novels can be more philosophical than films because of their greater reliance on words, Adler replied that it is not necessarily art's function to emulate philosophy. Art provides a purgation, he added, built upon its departure from reality, while its emotional force depends upon realism. The special excellence of cinema, he concluded, lay in maximizing the realistic and non-realistic factors that produced art's two chief effects. The good film thus is "extraordinarily effective in doing what art should do,"[51] Adler said.

Following World War II the rapid expansion of television made huge inroads upon movie attendance. Hollywood's response was to develop wide screens, too large for one's living room. In 1952 Fred Waller brought out Cinerama, with a wide, curved screen, three film strips, and seven-channel stereophonic sound all synchronized to provide an astonishly realistic effect. A somewhat similar system, CinemaScope, when used in *The Robe* proved so successful that within a few years most theaters around the world installed Cinema-Scope equipment.

Despite the benefits of wide-screen presentation, cinema still suffered drastically from the competition of television. Weekly attendance at movie theaters declined from about 90 million in 1947 to an average of about 42 million in the 1950's and 1960's. The number of movie houses decreased by nearly fifty per cent. Gross receipts also slumped, although increases in ticket prices kept revenues fairly constant.

Film executives finally stemmed the tide in 1959. They decided to make fewer pictures, put more money into each production, and count on longer runs. Sales of old movies to television, and rental of studio space to television companies, led to the elimination of red ink for most major film companies.

In 1954 the French director François Truffaut wrote an article in which he stated that the true author of a film is not the writer but the director, since it is he who must decide where and how to use words, camera shots, lighting, and all other cinematic effects. American directors deserved special praise, Truffaut said, because this "auteur policy" had been struggling against the pressures of so many special interest groups, such as studio bosses, stars, producers, writers, and others. In Europe the auteur policy had long ago been accepted, he felt, and thus creation of a European film was not so much of a tug-of-war.

Andrew Sarris as a film critic has long subscribed to the auteur theory. Edward Murray, in fact, feels that when the views of Sarris seem inadequate in evaluating a film, the trouble is generally traceable to his overdependence on the theory. Sarris, says Murray, is likely to stress the how more than the what. With little use for sociological criticism, Sarris tends to stress the personality of the director and what it contributes to the film's effect. In *The American Cinema* (1968), Sarris, seeking the "best in American sound movies between 1929 and 1966,"[52] ranked American directors according to criteria he developed.

Sarris says that the reason most film theory has evolved in Europe is that Europeans take cinema more seriously and are thus more concerned about film technique. Europe's two big contributions, Sarris felt, were montage as developed by Eisenstein, and *mise en scène*, or stage picture, as described by André Bazin, Alexander Astruc, and Robert Leenhardt. A long exposure on one scene can help the viewer become engulfed in the film, Sarris said. *Open City*, for example, showed "reality in all its ambiguity through Rossellini's unblinking camera."[53] Both effects can be carried too far, Sarris admitted: "Extreme uses of montage are too jazzy for the meanings they seek to express; extreme emphases on *mise en scène* result in sheer boredom."[54]

Erwin Panofsky said that a scenario or movie script had no literary existence apart from its film. Whereas most art forms depend for their existence upon ideas existing in the artist's mind, not so cinema. "It is only the movies," said Panofsky, "that do justice to that materialistic interpretation of the universe which, whether we like it or not, pervades contemporary civilization."[55] The reason for this he explained is due to the cinema being limited for its effects to purely physical objects like cameras, lenses, and screens.

When he stepped down as film critic for *Esquire* in 1966, Dwight Macdonald had completed forty years as a cinema critic. He defined the critic's job as to judge the film's quality, to give concrete examples of why it is excellent, mediocre, or poor, and to relate the film to others of its kind. Macdonald quoted Truffaut who said, "What is worthwhile, yet difficult, is analysis. What is interesting is not pronoucing a film good or bad, but explaining why."[56]

Macdonald felt that in *Shoot the Piano Player*, Truffaut had daringly mixed the genres of crime melodrama, romance, and slapstick comedy. "I thought the mixture didn't jell," said Macdonald, "but it was an interesting try."[57]

The three movie eras, according to Macdonald, were the classic silent film period, 1908–1929; the early sound era, 1930–1955; and the later sound era, 1955 to the present. Because of difficulties in learning to use sound, he felt that the second period produced the poorest films. The greatest period, to him, is the present, with great directors like Antonioni, Bergman, Luis Buñuel, Fellini, Kurosawa, and Truffaut, who are making the sound track "a structural element and not just an ornamental gimmick."[58] Ironically, he felt that the three countries that produced the best films in the silent era—Germany, Russia, and the United States—are now among those countries producing the poorest films. Governmental regulation had virtually killed cinema in the first two countries, and Hollywood was reeling under the combined attack of financial costs and television.

Evaluating the many films built around Bible spectacle, Macdonald evolved five "rules" for the genre: Unknown actors should be used. Only the Bible should provide the plot. The goal is to make the past come alive. Avoid spectacular sound effects, color, and sets. Tell the story reverently, and the story will carry the film. His preference in the genre was Pier Paolo Pasolini's *The Gospel According to St. Matthew*, because it was faithful to the Bible, made the past come alive, and made the people and the landscape seem authentic.

Vincent Canby feels that Luis Buñuel is the greatest living film maker. Buñuel's films function as a tonic, Canby believes. In his films "we have the unique opportunity of seeing the 20th century through the eyes of an artist who represents the highest order of 19th-century humanism. As a social critic Buñuel is merciless and as an artist he is civilized—a rare combination,"[59] Canby feels.

Kevin Thomas, on the other hand, casts his ballot for Akira Kurosawa, who made the name "Rashomon" come to stand for the relativity of truth. Kurosawa blends the dynamism of Occidental films with the pictorial quality of Oriental movies in a distinctive manner, says Thomas. A proof of Kurosawa's greatness is the large number of imitators he has spawned, Thomas feels. But none of his followers, in Thomas's opinion, capture "his humanism expressed in one of the most dynamic styles ever developed by a film director."[60]

Parker Tyler, who died in 1974, wrote nine books of film criticism. Traceable in Tyler's criticism are the background influences of such persons as Nietzsche, James Frazer, Gilbert Murray, Freud, Jung, Bronislaw Malinowsky, Ernst Cassirer, and Claude Levi-Strauss. To Tyler cinema is myth, not art. "The basic premise of the myth critic," says Edward Murray, "is that narrative art is an unconscious projection of the collective experience of men."[61] Thus, to explain a movie and its effects, Tyler drew upon such fields as anthropology, folklore, psychology, and religion. Although moviemakers produce a film with a "manifest content," what moviegoers see in that film is the "latent content," Tyler said. "The movie theater," he wrote, "is the psychoanalytic clinic of the average worker's daylight dream."[62]

In Tyler's view Hollywood stars embody mythological symbolism. "Adulation, often so shockingly naive, given to movie stars independently of their screen roles, provides a basis for thinking of them as semidivine, a vestigial form of the pagan divinities of classical Greece,"[63] Tyler stated. These glamorous persons fulfill "an ancient need, unsatisfied by popular religions of contemporary times,"[64] he said. "Somehow their wealth, fame, and beauty, their apparently unlimited field of worldly pleasure — these conditions tinge them with the supernatural."[65]

The movie palace for Tyler was more than a psychoanalytical clinic — it was a temple or church. Revive the star system, he advocated, because it gratifies so many latent needs. In ranking movies, Tyler's credo would search not for the artistic best but the mythological best.

A somewhat analogous condition is found in the criticism of Robert Warshow. Warshow tends to find art films pretentious, and in his own work the sociological perspective prevails. He thus sees gangster films as a reaction against the official "cheerful view of life" of bourgeois American society. The moral of the gangster film to him is that "there is really only one possibility — failure. The final meaning of the city is anonymity and death."[66]

"Americans pretend to be offended by violence but the screen refutes such hypocrisy,"[67] says Edward Murray. In interpreting Westerns, Warshow states that the function of the cowboy hero is to remind us that even in an age when style has no meaning, style is possible: "Even in killing or being killed we are not freed from the necessity of establishing satisfactory modes of behavior."[68] Murray grants that sociological criticism is useful in creating a background of meaning for a film, but to function at a higher level it must submit itself to the superior discipline of esthetic criticism.

If anything, John Simon, who has a doctoral degree from Harvard, would go beyond Murray in esthetic rigor. Simon is at home in many languages, many literatures, and many art forms. He finds few films to be truly art objects.

Esthetics to Simon is the morality of art. He feels that esthetics should be "a relevance to human life, an elegance of spirit, a generosity and adventuresomeness of outlook, and above all, a concept or intimation of what the ideal solution to an artistic problem would be."[69] The critic's job, he feels, is to hasten the coming of the day when there will be serious films for serious critics to review for serious people.

Some of his colleagues say that Simon is more of a literary critic than a film critic. Edward Murray questions whether Simon's criticism meets its own standard of being capable of raising the standards of motion pictures.

Just as Andrew Sarris concentrates chiefly upon the how of making movies, Pauline Kael focuses largely on the what, Murray states. Her vast knowledge, caustic wit, and brilliant writing style make her America's best film critic to many Americans, says Murray. Her first book, *I Lost It at the Movies* (1965), has been the best-selling book of American film criticism. Kael says that if modern audiences prefer structural incoherence in movies, perhaps it is because they feel that modern life does not make sense, and they want to see movies that reflect their own outlook on life.

Kael formulates these questions as those the film critic should ask: "Does the frame of meaning support the body of photographic, directorial, and acting styles; and conversely, do these styles define the frame of meaning?"[70] Form and content, in other words, need to be fused into an organic whole. Edward Murray's advice for Kael to follow in order to be America's best film critic is for her to discipline her thinking, do more careful research, show more love for art, and devote as much attention to form as to content.

Stephen Farber feels that Pauline Kael has fallen into her own trap. After attacking the auteur theory as being a simplistic devotion to preferred film makers, "she can outdo any auteurist in her unflagging loyalty to her favorite directors,"[71] said Farber. What is even more suspect is her taste, Farber declares, wondering how she can prefer the films of Brian DePalma, Irvin Kershner, and Sam Peckinpah to those of Alfred Hitchcock, Billy Wilder, and Federico Fellini.

Vernon Young was born in London, came to the United States in his youth, and in 1957 moved to Europe. His experience as actor and director gave him a good background for his criticism. Young tends to analyze films in terms of each country's ethos. In Italy, for example, where the family is paramount, leading films generally portray family values or the price of alienation. Since French people, in Young's opinion, do not separate intellect and intuition, wit is the keynote of French cinema. In Japan the most important factor is style. In a search for order to replace the tradition that vanished in

World War II, Japanese films have "an overanxious attention to surface clarity."[72]

British and American films are superficial, Young feels. Since empiricism is the British way of life, their films tend to be local rather than universal. The most authentic films to pragmatic Americans are documentaries, says Young. Hollywood's function is to escape reality: "Every shallow Hollywood film is shallow precisely because it travesties an existing cultural shallowness—the tacit belief that it's both desirable and possible to legislate passion and death from the scheme of things, and that social security alone can bring the good life into existence."[73]

Discussing pornography, Young quotes approvingly from George Steiner's *Language and Silence*, where Steiner says: "There may be deeper affinities than we yet understand between the 'total freedom' of the uncensored erotic imagination and the total freedom of the sadist. Both are exercised at the expense of someone else's humanity, of someone else's most precious right—the right to a private life of feeling."[74]

Like Young, Stanley Kauffmann had theater background as a basis for his critical credo. For ten years Kauffmann wrote plays, acted, and directed in a repertory theater. He has taught drama and film in universities, and in 1972 edited the anthology, *American Film Criticism*.

Since he feels there has been insufficient time to evolve an exhaustive poetics of cinema, Kauffmann has developed his own pluralistic standards of judgment. First, cinema is a popular art, designed for masses of people rather than for individuals. Next, Bazin was right in saying that the image, not reality, must predominate in film. "Life is as much a liar as art,"[75] Kauffmann says. Finally, style can transform material. *Macbeth* in lesser hands could well be melodrama, he feels.

Adapting terms from *The Mirror and the Lamp* by M.H. Abrams, Kauffmann says film criticism can focus on any of four points. The film can be evaluated as an art object, as an expression of the director, as something seen by a viewer, or as a representation of something in the world. Interesting enough, although he professes to scrap Aristotle, Kauffmann here reproduces Aristotle's four causes: the art object is the final cause, the director the efficient cause, the film the material cause, and the plot/theme is the formal cause.

Other Aristotelian concepts can be found in Kauffmann's description of tragedy's purification. Kauffmann says, "If a tragic climax, a purification through death and horrors, is to move us, two elements are essential in a work: its tonality must be consistently large, and there must be no sense of manipulation to distract us from a conviction of fate."[76] Implicit in Kauffmann's statement are such Aristotelian ideas as catharsis, climax, probability, necessity, magnitude, and the nature of the tragic hero.

There is even a trace of classicism in Kauffmann's objection to the mixture of genres or to changes of tone in the films of Truffaut and Jean-Luc Godard. In these instances Kauffmann appears to be far less flexible than, say, Pauline Kael.

"Language is, if not the enemy, at least the burden of the motion picture,"[77] Kauffmann believes. Because language is central to the theater, he believed it to be impossible to adapt a great play into a film script, for the play has used language so intrinsically that to reduce it to cinema's level is to undo the very form of the play.

Richard Grenier, film critic for *Commentary*, recently described how the Soviet director widely regarded as the best Russian director since Eisenstein has been reduced to begging in the streets, after being released from a five-year prison sentence. Sergei Paradjanov, whose *Shadows of Our Forgotten Ancestors* won sixteen international film prizes, was accused of anti-Soviet agitation and Ukrainian nationalism. Professor Herbert Marshall said of him that never since Eisenstein's triumph had a Soviet director enjoyed such international esteem. When the Soviet government tried to add an extra ten years on to his sentence, a petition signed by Antonioni, Fellini, Godard, Rossellini, Truffaut, and others helped get him free. But he is denied the right to every kind of work, and so has been reduced to begging. His films were noted for historical accuracy, folk customs, romantic love, and deep probing of the mysteries of the human soul.

The death of Rainer Werner Fassbinder in 1982 at the age of 36 occasioned a review of the German director's contributions to cinema. Calling Fassbinder cinema's first great satirist, Vincent Canby in the *New York Times* recalled that his films had won many awards. To Fassbinder, however, life seemed to be Catch-22, a series of dirty tricks, Canby said. Since all power is suspect, a society that puts its faith in property is doomed, Fassbinder believed. Even when we age, he said, "in the universe we remain children in a household that never acknowledges our presence."[78] Fassbinder's satire was so broad as to include not only materialism and bureaucracy but also democracy, fidelity, pity, and hope, said Canby.

Siegfried Kracauer believed that the modern world was "ideologically shelterless," and that it was cinema's function to "redeem the time."[79] Fassbinder's films, however technically proficient, can scarcely be said to serve that function, except to the extent that old debris needs to be cleared away from a site before a new structure is erected.

Michiko Kakutani recently discussed screenwriting in the *New York Times*. F. Scott Fitzgerald, who worked as a script writer, resented the affront to literary language required in a scenario; he said, "There was a rankling indignity in seeing the power of the written word subordinated to a more glittering, grosser power."[80] The critic Richard Corliss in his book *Talking Pictures* (1973) predicted that the director would have to yield some of his influence to the unsung screenwriter. John Brady in *The Craft of the Screenwriter* (1981) triumphantly declared that cinema's age of dominance by director and actor is ended, and "the era of the screenwriter as super-star is at hand."[81]

Thomas McGuane, who adapts his novels for the cinema, does not find the work demeaning. He says, "There's a feeling one's better off writing bad poetry than good screenplays, but I think it's a very interesting form that's viable in the twentieth century."[82]

Jerzy Kosinski, who recently adapted his novel *Being There* for cinema, accepts the role pragmatically. "To be blunt," he said, "you are not reviewed, and isn't it one of the original ambitions of a story-teller to open on every street corner?"[83]

William Faulkner, who needed his $1,000 per week from 20th Century-Fox to help support a huge family, resented what he called the "enormous intellectual and conventional limitations" necessary in order to aim at commercial success.

Kakutani describes how characters may have to be tailored to fit available stars. She cites how Joan Didion and John Gregory Dunne reworked a script six different times, each time structuring it for a different actress. "Which is how a picture about a social worker in Detroit and Cleveland," Dunne says, "evolved effortlessly into a script about a college professor's wife in Pomona whose life comes to a crisis at the Ojai Music Festival."[84]

As in classical Greek drama, film criticism evolved only after there were a number of noteworthy films that could be analyzed for excellence. In the early days of cinema, directors like Griffith and Eisenstein were light years ahead of most critics. Except for Vachel Lindsay's early contribution, most perceptive insights into cinema as an art form came from directors. By World War II, film criticism began to organize itself around key terms like montage and flashback. Throughout its history, film criticism sharpened its focus by constantly describing how cinema differed from theater. In general, the effort was to define cinema's nature—its powers and limitations—so that cinema would not attempt to do what another medium could do better.

Technical developments constantly presented new opportunities and new visions to moviemakers and their critics. Processing of film, use of sound and color, the wide screen—these and other mechanical matters influenced the direction in which cinema moved. Competition from television required drastic changes in cinema that are still under way.

Contrasting this chapter with its predecessors will show to what a small degree cinema operates at an intellectual level. With ideologies crumbling and a world poised on the brink of a possible atomic holocaust, Hollywood furnishes sex and violence as its contribution to the world's problems. Movies like *Star Wars* and *E. T.* suggest a combination of escapism and hope of cosmic aid that appeal to frightened viewers' delusions, fantasies, and aspirations.

Have film critics succeeded in their role? Certainly they have gone a long way toward helping us understand both the limitations and the powers of cinema. At their best, says Edward Murray speaking of such critics as James Agee, Stanley Kauffmann, Dwight Macdonald, and Vernon Young, they "see the art that is there, and also what that art means in the context of this picture, of other pictures by the same artist, and of the human condition. Film criticism can scarcely do more."[85]

17. The Achievements of Dramatic Criticism

Several kinds of conclusions can be drawn from this book. One is to show the historical additions to the criticism of plays, considering drama chiefly as a form of art. Another conclusion is to show the relationship between the history of dramatic criticism and the broader history of ideas, of which dramatic criticism is but a part. Finally, one might well ask what light does a study of dramatic criticism shed on the human plight in the nuclear age, as mankind desperately struggles to avoid an atomic holocaust? Each of these conclusions will be dealt with in turn.

In primitive times there was little or no dramatic criticism, since there was scarcely any written drama for reflective minds to ponder. The chief risk run by the aboriginal actor was to violate a religious taboo in a tribal ritual, which might cost him ostracism from the tribe, if not his life.

Dramatic criticism, like so much of modern culture, began with the classical Greeks. Himself a gifted writer of comedy, Aristophanes praises the tragedian Euripides for his sense of dramatic form, his realistic scenes, and his use of dialogue by all characters but he criticizes Euripides for tiresome exposition, affected diction, and constant use of unpleasant plots.

Why is Aristotle often considered to be the greatest drama critic of all time? Aristotle saw that not only drama but all of literature derived its force from the pleasure human beings experience in seeing a representation of human life expressed in language which itself is pleasurable to contemplate. Basing his analysis upon great plays he had seen, chiefly those by Sophocles, Aristotle evolved a definition of tragedy that was so comprehensive that few succeeding critics could ever improve on it, and many critics used his format in trying to define other dramatic genres. Since he considered plot to be the "soul" of tragedy, Aristotle gave special attention to the factors creating an excellent plot. Some of his key terms were catharsis, discovery, necessity, probability, and reversal. He also discussed character in some detail, particularly the nature of the tragic hero.

Roman criticism, like Roman drama, was weaker than its Greek counterpart. Cicero wrote about the proper types of character in comedy, and he attacked the Roman love for spectacle as well as the Roman tendency to mix tragedy and comedy.

Rome's most influential critic, Horace, was chiefly concerned about keeping decorum in drama. This meant to him that nothing violent or disgusting would be depicted on stage, tragedy and comedy would not be mixed, and the four stages of character would be decorously observed (playful childhood, unstable youth, ambitious adulthood, and reminiscent age). Horace also prescribed five acts for plays, iambic verse (to be more easily heard in a noisy theater), and the opening of the play in the midst of the plot's action.

More so than the Greeks, Roman critics shaped what came to be called classical dramatic criticism in later centuries, namely, the preference of the ordinary to the unusual, the use of types of generalizations rather than eccentric or highly individualized characters, and the adherence to tried and approved dramatic traditions.

Medieval times produced even less dramatic criticism than it did drama. The Christian church opposed the theater first because Roman plays had often lampooned Christians, and second because the stage was considered to be an immoral influence upon society. Church fathers like Tertullian and Augustine were outspoken in their attacks upon the theater. A refreshingly new approach came in the tenth century with the Benedectine abbess, Hrosvitha, who not only wrote some criticism but also rewrote six of Terence's plays, endowing them with Christian subjects.

European drama grew out of two sources, medieval church drama and secular mimes. In 1207 Pope Innocent III banned popular plays from church premises. Thereafter the church encouraged the performance of miracle and mystery plays. The chief topic of a thousand years of medieval criticism—even then it was quite poorly done—was to try to define the differences between comedy and tragedy.

Modern dramatic criticism can be said to have begun with the Italian Renaissance. In the sixteenth century a number of commentators on Aristotle sparked the interest that led to modern criticism. Francisco Robortello added two new concepts for the evaluation of plays: admiration, or amazement at the unexpected or the marvelous, and "difficulty overcome," the idea that the playwright who surmounts the greatest obstacle has made the greatest contribution. Gianmaria Cecchi dealt at great length with farce, and Giambattista Guarini defined tragicomedy. Minturno, Bishop of Ugento, said that an important effect of a play is its ability to "transport" the viewer, that is, move him emotionally.

The most influential Italian critic of the period was Lodovico Castelvetro, who placed great stress upon audience reaction. It was Castelvetro who formulated the doctrine of the Three Unities that a play should observe, those of action, time, and place. Thus the plot should represent one action, the time duration of the play should be no more than one day, and the setting should be one place (later expanded to include one city). Although the Three Unities tend to give a play compactness and tension, they clearly have been gloriously ignored in some of the best plays.

Interestingly, early French criticism opposed iron-clad rules. Jacques Grévin objected both to the concept of the Three Unities and to the five-act format for plays. Alexandre Hardy vigorously defended tragicomedy, and François Ogier attacked classical drama as an offence against nature because of its improbability. Jean de la Taille, however, brought the doctrine of the Three Unities to France; for several centuries French critics reveled in the role as lawgivers.

Renaissance English clergymen continued to attack the theater as an immoral force. The first serious English critic, Sir Philip Sidney, was greatly influenced by Italian critics. Although he made an impassioned plea in defense of drama and other literature, Sidney accepted the Three Unities and opposed the use of tragicomedy. Ben Jonson, a greater critic than Sidney, said that a dramatist was justified in violating rules to achieve a higher artistic purpose. Jonson developed the theory and practice of the comedy of humours, which portrayed characters overcome by an imbalance of personality factors. Comedy, to Jonson, had a purpose as a social purgative.

Almost from the start, Spanish criticism stressed the importance of audience reaction. As in other European countries,

Spain had critics who had been influenced by Aristotle and the Italian writers. There was also church pressure against the stage, with theaters being closed by governmental decree in 1597-98 and 1644-49.

The most influential Spanish critic was the dramatist Lope de Vega. In *The New Art of Writing Plays* in 1609, de Vega said that since the public pays the bill, it calls the tune. Thus he advocated simple diction, much mystery and suspense, a lot of variety, and such crowd-pleasing devices as dressing women in men's clothes. In his hundreds of popular plays de Vega carried out his theory.

Cervantes switched from a classical position to one admitting the shrewdness of de Vega's stance. Another playwright, Tirso de Molina, defended de Vega on the grounds of common sense and probability. Also on his side were the adherents of Elizabethan drama, for it was recognized that no set of rules could produce such great works as the plays of Shakespeare. Chief opposition to de Vega came from Spanish critics under French influence, where the doctrine of neoclassicism was being formulated.

In 1636 Pierre Corneille published *Le Cid*, a play that evoked great controversy. So great was the pressure upon Corneille for having violated the rules and used irregularities improper in classical drama that he had to confess his error. The Abbé d'Aubignac codified countless dramatic rules, all in the name of "reason." Nicolas Boileau became a latter-day Horace, using "nature" as his esthetic norm. René Rapin synthesized classicism, rationalism, and good taste, adding the mercurial *je ne sais quoi* that eventually undid classicism. Charles de Saint-Évremond had the good sense to know the rules but also their limitations.

During the Commonwealth period, English theaters were closed. Interested in drama, John Milton asked for Christian drama inspired by the Holy Spirit. One of drama's great critics, John Dryden, had originality, good taste, and a wide knowledge of drama and of criticism. Dryden further refined ideas concerning the tragic hero, tragicomedy, and the use of poetry in drama.

A lover of the ancients, Thomas Rymer attacked Shakespeare for improbabilities and sentimentality. Rymer first named the concept of poetic justice in drama. A thorough critic, Rymer applied Aristotelian terms minutely in analyzing a play, but he unfortunately possessed poor taste and little judgment. John Dennis began as Rymer's opponent, but engulfed by neoclassical standards he ended up attacking Shakespeare for violating dramatic rules.

Incensed at the immorality of Restoration drama, Jeremy

Collier unleashed a powerful attack against the theater in 1698, based on esthetic as well as moral grounds. The influential Joseph Addison opposed the use of rhyme in plays, as well as long speeches, poetic justice, and elaborate staging effects. The novelist Henry Fielding, who also wrote plays, satirized heroic tragedy (such as Dryden wrote) and neoclassical rigidity.

It was Samuel Johnson who pronounced the death sentence to dramatic rules, stating "the drama's laws the drama's patrons give." Although this was the position of Lope de Vega a century and a half earlier, Johnson added both logic and convincing examples so forcefully that no neoclassical critic could feel comfortable thereafter.

Lord Kames, for example, now accepted mixed genres. Oliver Goldsmith held out for pure comedy rather than the sentimental comedy which mixed laughter and tears. In his play *The Critic*, Richard Sheridan made fun of a myriad of dramatic ineptitudes, such as clumsy exposition, asides, improbability, unrelated double plots, and melodramatic stage effects.

In France, neoclassicism died more slowly. Voltaire called Shakespeare's tragedies "monstrous farces" since they did not obey a single rule, he said. He preferred Racine's plays because of their style, clarity, and adherence to the Three Unities. Rousseau considered the theater to be immoral. Denis Diderot initially felt that drama would reform the public's morals but in later life he doubted whether it could. When Beaumarchais discovered the public's reluctance to accept serious drama, he disgustedly gave them the "ridiculous citizens and unhappy kings" they wanted in *The Barber of Seville* and *The Marriage of Figaro*.

Shakespeare's rise in critical esteem paralleled the decline of neoclassical critical laws. Samuel Johnson settled the matter of Shakespeare's irregularities decisively when he announced that each deviation from dogma needed to be evaluated in terms of its ultimate esthetic effect. On these grounds it was found that the so-called irregularities generally enhanced rather than interfered with the overall esthetic pattern. Previously, of course, Shakespeare had been defended by such worthies as Ben Jonson, Milton, and Dryden. Work by textual critics helped to recover Shakespeare's original intent. By the late eighteenth century it was nearly unanimous that Shakespeare was England's (and probably the world's) greatest playwright. Critics like Lord Kames now saw him as a great psychologist, giving viewers and readers insight into characters the like of which no previous drama had ever created.

German drama and dramatic criticism lagged behind that of southern Europe. Boileau and neoclassical rules were brought to Germany by Johann Gottsched. Germany's best dramatic critic has been Gotthold Lessing, whose wide reading background and perceptive judgment provided one of the most systematic approaches ever seen in the discussion of plot, character, unity, and catharsis.

Goethe's contributions to dramatic criticism were his consideration of the inner form of a play, and his discussion of the organic unity of subjective and objective factors in the play's structure. For Johann von Schiller theater was a civilizing force: as we see the struggle for freedom depicted in a tragedy, we can better endure our fate when life's forces crush us, Schiller said.

The Schlegel brothers played an important role in popularizing the rising Romanticism in Germany. In addition, Friedrich von Schlegel discussed dramatic irony comprehensively, and his brother August Wilhelm recommended the use of fantasy and caprice in comedy, since realistic comedy, he felt, really was not very funny. Ludwig Tieck placed great stress upon experimental stage techniques, and Adam Müller argued for a return to religious drama.

Friedrich Hebbel, the playwright who championed the cause of bourgeois drama, saw Western civilization at a great breaking point in its history. Its first two crises had been the Greek shift from reliance on gods to submission to fate, and the transition from medieval groupism to Renaissance individualism. In the current crisis, Hebbel said, mankind is evolving towards some new form of humanity, and so drama's role nowadays is to provide the forum for a radical re-examination of all existing institutions. Eric Bentley hailed Hebbel as a modern-day prophet for this insight into the modern condition of man.

The nineteenth century witnessed a growing disregard for dramatic rules in France. Madame de Staël stressed the free expression and spontaneity loved by all Romantic critics. In his preface to *Cromwell* in 1827 Victor Hugo sounded the battle cry: follow nature, not the rules, said Hugo, and thus feel free to mix tragedy and comedy, the beautiful and the ugly, the evil and the good, just as life does. Charles Sainte-Beuve recommended a study of the dramatist's biography and psychology in an effort to determine his predominant interests.

Francisque Sarcey has been called "the Aristotle of the well-made play," which has four acts, as follows: exposition, complication, crisis, and resolution. Sarcey stressed much action, plot "preparations" that sow probability, and the *scène à faire*, meaning the dramatist's obligation to depict on stage the central plot scene.

Influenced by Darwin, Ferdinand Brunetière stated that dramatic genres, like biological species, evolve, flower, and wane. Brunetière defined the law of the theater as a conscious will encountering conflict. Meanwhile playwrights Henry Becque and Émile Zola asked for slice-of-life naturalism, and Stéphane Mallarmé and Maurice Maeterlinck defended symbolism as the best way to get at life's inner meaning.

The Romantic movement in England produced some of that country's best dramatic criticism. For Coleridge, the imagination was the creative shaping power mediating between the mundane understanding and the higher-ranking reason. Drama he saw as a will struggling with fate, generally in the form of a higher will. With no pre-determined iron-clad dogma, Coleridge approached each play as an individual art work, hoping to find at its core the organic unity of form and content.

Charles Lamb and William Hazlitt brought three new techniques into dramatic criticism. They tried in their writing to evoke the author's style, they sought to coin appropriate metaphors, and they indulged in personal impressions designed to capture the play's quintessence. Though desultory, Lamb's style and substance were very influential. Hazlitt gave special attention to a careful analysis of comedy's effects. The critic Leigh Hunt gave major stress to analyzing acting.

The new drama, headed by Ibsen, split critics into competing camps. William Archer, who had translated Ibsen, supported the problem play. To Archer crisis, not conflict, was the chief factor in drama. The playwright Henry Arthur Jones reconciled Archer and Brunetière by saying that the crises which are dramatic are those accompanied by conflict.

George Bernard Shaw boldly attacked Shakespeare, saying he is often vulgar, melodramatic, platitudinous, and unoriginal in plots, but he quickly added that Shakespeare's great strengths outshone those of other dramatists. Shaw believed that following Wagner's fusion of music and drama, the only function left for non-musical drama was the area of the problem play.

In America the colonial atmosphere was hostile towards the theater. So deeply was the stage considered to be immoral that one of the first acts of the Continental Congress was to pass a recommendation that stage plays be abolished.

Edgar Allan Poe asked for verisimilitude in drama in opposition to asides, soliloquies, and preachments. Considering the theater to be democracy's school, Walt Whitman asked for American plays and American actors to replace European imports.

By the 1850's, when French influence was marked upon American drama, a group of newspaper critics constituted America's first organized set of dramatic critics. Henry Clapp, Junior, asked for a full drama which incorporated all types of entertainment, including music, ballet, and pantomime. The brilliant young Edward G.P. Wilkins attacked the star system, in which a star actor traveled to community theaters playing the lead role. An opponent of Ibsen and Shaw, William Winter enjoyed a long tenure as a critic, analyzing acting and protecting what he felt were society's morals. Andrew C. Wheeler not only echoed the critical views of Sainte-Beuve and Hippolyte Taine but he also heralded the new French drama.

Many American playwrights of this period wrote criticism designed to educate playgoers about the intent of their plays. Chief among these were Dion Boucicault, Augustin Daly, Stephen Ryder Fiske, and Bronson Howard. By the turn of the century American colleges were offering courses in drama, and several prominent academic critics did much for drama. Brander Matthews wrote widely on the new drama and helped introduce the public to many new dramatists. George Pierce Baker turned out countless gifted actors and playwrights in his courses at Harvard and Yale. Joel Spingarn dissected the "well made" play and found it wanting; Spingarn asked for creative criticism of the sort practiced by Lessing, Goethe, and Coleridge. By World War I, when theaters were put into army camps, the United States had officially accepted drama. Responsible for the change in attitude since Revolutionary War days were such factors as college courses, the Little Theater movement, the influence of European drama, and the work of a small corps of unheralded but persistent drama critics.

Russia, which had no Reformation and only a delayed Renaissance, had no well developed body of medieval church drama and consequently no dramatic criticism until relatively recent times. The first Russian tragedian, Alexander Sumarokov, wrote the first serious dramatic criticism, a paraphrase of the ideas of Boileau, around 1750. The German influence was felt about 1800, when August von Kotzebue directed the German theater in St. Petersburg.

Alexander Pushkin, who wrote some excellent plays, attacked Sumarokov and French rules but praised Shakespeare for his free and unshackled genius. Russia's greatest comic writer, Nikolai Gogol, said that the function of the theater is to educate the public. Gogol argued, like Ben Jonson, that comedy had a serious purpose, to serve as a social purgative. Vissarion Belinsky agreed with Gogol's theories, although his famous letter attacked Gogol for having deserted his own principles.

The popular drama of Alexander Ostrovsky occasioned a critical war. His leading defendant, Apollon Grigoriev, praised Ostrovsky's realism. The liberal critic Nikolay Dobrolyubov, however, found in Ostrovsky a weak defender of the status quo. Ostrovsky and other dramatists wrote many historical plays educating theatergoers about Russia's past.

Leo Tolstoy attacked Shakespeare for not inculcating morals and Chekhov for plots lacking action. Influential as he was as a dramatist, Chekhov wrote little criticism, mainly letters to fellow playwrights recommending honesty, realism, simplicity, and discipline.

Beginning the new century a wave of symbolist dramatists and writers wrote candidly about the role of the theater. Valery Bryusov demanded simple sets rather than the detailed realism of the Moscow Art Theater. Andrey Bely stated that Chekhov had surprisingly captured life's deep meaning by strategic use of silences and symbolic effects. Alexander Blok praised Ibsen and Leonid Andreev for their combination of symbolism and realism. Andreev praised Chekhov for what he called "panpsychism," a technique in which every little thing in a play seemed to come alive.

Vyacheslav Ivanov felt that the only hope for the theater was for it to return to its role as religious rite. Feeling that the theater was too literary and that gestures communicate better than words, Nikolay Evreinov asked for monodrama, a return to the theater of Thespis, when only one actor was used. Vsevolod Meyerhold said that the ultimate failure of both Chekhov and symbolist drama could be attributed to their lack of theatricality.

The first decade of communism in Russia saw every manner of experiment in all the art forms, including drama. Expressionism, futurism, lyricism, and many other modes were tried out. The first Commissar of Education, Anatoly Lunacharsky, himself a dramatist, tried to walk the tightrope between enforcing Marxist ideology and giving the stage and other art forms the freedom necessary for creative achievement.

The dogmatic pronouncement of the doctrine of socialist

realism in 1934 pretty well ended creativity in modern Russian art forms. Dramatists feared Siberia, directors did not dare to express their esthetic concepts, and actors worried that their interpretations might not be tendential enough to please a party censor.

In 1939 Meyerhold bravely declared his conviction that perhaps outlawed formalism was not so bad, since it at least produced better works than the socialist realism fare on current Moscow stages. Needless to say, Meyerhold disappeared and was not heard from again.

Stalin's death in 1953 raised hopes that perhaps drama would be given something like the freedom it enjoys in the West. Indeed, for several years both plays and critics challenged not only the concept of socialist realism but also the "no conflict" theory, that is, the idea that in a socialist country conflict never exists because all men are brothers.

The Hungarian revolt of 1956 ended the thaw in cultural ideology, particularly when Nikita Khrushchev found out that dramatists and other writers had been helping fan the fire of rebellion. Never having had a free drama, however, Russian playwrights cannot point to the Czarist period as one to which they aspire. Russian drama has always been tendential. Pushkin craved freedom, Gogol spoke of educating the masses, and Belinsky wanted drama to defend the dignity of man. In Russia perhaps only Chekhov's plays have not been tendential, and they are so unique in concept and structure that they have spawned few if any legitimate offspring.

As the twentieth century dawned in England, the playwright George Calderon wrote one of the best critical analyses ever penned on Chekhov's drama. Calderon listed Chekhov's singular contributions as subtle exposition of plot and character, disconnected dialogue, artful stage pictures, creation of mood or atmosphere, and the use of a centrifugal plot, that is, a plot in which attention is directed away from the particular plight of the characters, outward toward the larger questions of man and his place in the universe.

Swedish playwright August Strindberg described and defended his own dramatic innovations as chamber drama (fantasy or dream plays), conglomerate characters in whom disunity is structural, and expressionism, a deliberate departure from realism in order to achieve a specific esthetic effect.

The German poet and dramatist Bertolt Brecht wrote what he called Epic Drama, plays that intentionally kept viewers from identifying with the characters in order that social and political problems might be presented more objectively.

The existentialist philosopher Jean-Paul Sartre expounded his metaphysics in plays in which subjectivity is so paramount that compactness and tension are produced in a way reminiscent of the Three Unities. Jacques Copeau created a Wagnerian synthesis of art forms in his theater. Meanwhile in Italy, reflecting the age of relativity in science, professor Luigi Pirandello wrote grotesque plays in which the viewpoint is shifting, impermanent, with values relative to the observer. In Hungary Marxist critic George Lukacs said that modern bourgeois drama shows the alienation produced by capitalistic individualism.

A number of modern dramatists have tried to restore poetry to drama. William Butler Yeats sought for a unifying myth in Irish folklore. Yeats wanted poetry to restore drama's native dignity, and so he recommended less emphasis on acting and scenery and more upon language.

T.S. Eliot felt that drama's reaction to the debasement of modern materialism should be to return to poetic language and religious themes. Christopher Fry agreed, although he did not necessarily wish to restore the Three Unities, as Eliot did.

The Polish director Jerzy Grotowski created a Theater of the Poor, in which actors discipline themselves to wholly surrender themselves to their roles. Since the church is obsolescent, Grotowski said, theater must replace religion in our time. The Swiss dramatist Friedrich Duerrenmatt felt that tragedy implies guilt, but we moderns feel no guilt but rather consider ourselves to be victims. Comedy is the proper dramatic form, said Duerrenmatt, for a grotesque chaotic world, a world about to fade, in his opinion.

The Theater of the Absurd has probably been the most important dramatic movement of the twentieth century. Eugène Ionesco says that cut off from his religious and metaphysical roots, man is lost and his actions become meaningless and absurd.

The King Ubu character created by Alfred Jarry in 1896 used violence that shocked playgoers, but his violence was tame compared to that of Hitler and Stalin a few years later. Jarry used what he called pataphysics, which is strict logic employed to arrive at absurd conclusions.

Samuel Beckett says that the honest playwright must depict the mess which constitutes the modern world. Beckett uses many innovative dramatic techniques to depict the absurdity of modern life. He despairs at our loss of human dignity, yet he insists that even the world vision of *Waiting for Godot* is not defeatist. Life, he says, is aimless, but humans never lose hope.

Ionesco agrees that man's plight, however grim, is not hopeless. He feels that depicting modern absurdity is one way to get rid of it. To shock people into seeing through the falseness and emptiness of their lives, Ionesco coined many dramatic tricks, chiefly linguistic ones, for his plays. His play *The Bald Soprano*, he says, shows the emptiness of a world lacking a metaphysical base. *The Chairs*, he explains, shows the vacuum of modern life; in the absence of God there exists a deeply felt spiritual rootlessness.

French playwright Antonin Artaud said that the only ways out of the contemporary crisis are purification or death. Artaud wants purification, achieved through what he called the Theater of Cruelty—not cruelty in the sense of harming fellow humans but in the sense of frankly attacking the baseness and hypocrisy of the modern world. Technically, Artaud downgrades plot, acting, and language, and upgrades dance, gesture, lighting, music, and scenery. Like the Balinese theater which he admired so greatly, Artaud said that modern drama must once again incorporate religious myth and ritual if we are to survive.

Harold Pinter in England depicts the tragedy of lost integrity in his Absurdist drama. In the United States, Edward Albee shows the selling-out of the American dream of universal democracy. The Russian émigré Arthur Adamov, who writes Absurdist plays, says, "The crisis of our time is essentially a religious crisis. It is a matter of life or death."

Critics have been divided in their reaction to the Theater of the Absurd. Frederick Lumley believes that its static plots constitute antitheater. David Grossvogel avers that it requires much more than nausea to produce art. Kenneth Tynan acknowledges the honesty and the cleverness of Absurdist drama, but says that great art must also address itself to the healing function.

But Polish critic Jan Kott says that Absurdist drama best portrays the modern condition. "When all established values—God, Nature and History—have been overthrown," he says, "all that is left is the clown."

The leading interpreter of Absurdist drama, Martin Esslin, says that this movement is the closest thing to an authentic religious quest in our time. Not only is God dead, says Esslin, but the substitutes erected in His place—war, advertising, nationalism, materialism—are even worse. A return to the theater as mystery, Absurdist drama is an intelligent effort to somehow relate man to the cosmos, he feels. If nothing else, in his opinion, it represents the best modern protest against man's inhumanity to man.

America has produced some excellent critics since 1920. Brilliant if at times unreliable, George Jean Nathan produced a great deal of impressionistic criticism that helped introduce European dramatists to the American public. Stark Young translated Chekhov, introduced Japanese drama, and wrote much intelligent and insightful criticism. Bemoaning our loss of the tragic vision, Joseph Wood Krutch felt we had thereby been robbed of the dignity that helps us transform despair into joy.

The playwright Maxwell Anderson found his religion in the theater. Calling the theater "a church without a creed," Anderson said that the message of great drama is always the same: God Himself (by which Anderson meant man's perception of God) must grow and change if He is to avoid injustice.

Thornton Wilder believed that the theater's charm lay in the fact that stage action is a perpetual present tense—it is always "now" in the theater. Influenced by Chekhov, Tennessee Williams fuses lyricism and naturalism tenderly. Williams believes that drama asserts not so much man's dignity as his ambiguity. Arthur Miller stouthcartedly defends the notion that common people, as well as kings, are fit subjects for tragedy.

One of the best modern critics, Brooks Atkinson, regretted the minuteness of modern drama compared to the challenges of the atomic age. This is no time for great drama, Atkinson said. We are all "waiting for the other shoe to drop." In another century, if there is anything left of civilization, predicted Atkinson, there will be ample themes for great drama for a long time.

One who likes the theater of ideas, Eric Bentley has fostered Brecht, Shaw, and Strindberg but attacked O'Neill. Francis Fergusson said that in a society lacking an idea of a theater, a climate favorable to drama, grounded in an accepted myth, the playwright cannot be expected to produce great plays. A leading anthologizer of drama, John Gassner served as a catalyst to a number of modern playwrights. Louis Kronenberger made a careful analysis of comedy, and asked for a high-grade repertory theater that could sponsor artistic plays that lack commercial appeal.

Walter Kerr reminds us not to ask drama to do what religion, psychology, or politics cannot accomplish. With an excellent background, Kerr spies into hidden corners of plays, revealing significant flaws or beauties that the uninitiated might overlook.

Robert Brustein says that the revolt in the modern theater is an extension of the Romantic revolution in literature. He traces the relativism of modern values in contemporary drama to Einstein.

Speaking of recent playwrights, Richard Eder says that Sam Shepard understands the United States today as being in a period of spiritual starvation. David Mamet, Eder feels, shows real promise because of his energetic language and good command of mood and character.

After a long career in the theater as director and critic, Harold Clurman found modern dramatists to be tentative and unsure in their approach, as if standing on shifting ground. Their work, he felt, too often betrays haste and lack of careful craftsmanship. But his faith in drama's recovery never wavered. Some loving words of care, he said, would enable the theater's tremendous vitality to renew itself.

Margaret Croyden interprets the sterility of modern drama as a product of the revolt of the 1960's. The language of the plays of that period was weakened in deference to sound, movement, and image, she feels. The directors were able to show their virtuosity, but "a whole generation of writers may have been lost in the process," she believes. Modern dramatists dispense with traditional plots in favor of nonlinear construction, she says, but so far the experiments have borne little fruit. For serious drama to survive, she states, "it must combine grand themes and emotional depth with new visual and aural techniques."

Motion pictures, in a sense, have democratized American culture. When theater tickets cost too much for the average person and when stage plays were not accessible except in larger towns and cities, cinema brought its form of drama to small towns as well as big cities, at a price most persons could afford to pay. Because of huge production costs, cinema has always had to count upon a large market, and hence its fare is geared for mass appeal.

The poet Vachel Lindsay was the first important movie critic. To Lindsay cinema would be the paramount art form for the common man. In an effort to isolate its peculiar strength, Lindsay enumerated thirty differences between cinema and theater. Whereas the theater depends upon passion and character, he said, cinema relies chiefly upon splendor and speed.

The first important director was D.W. Griffith. Among his contributions to the new art of cinema were camera angles, crowd shots, montage, and special scenic effects. Sergei Eisenstein was another director whose films drew critical acclaim. He further developed montage as crosscutting of images to represent complex ideas, and he also employed typage, or the use of amateur actors who seemed to be just what the roles required. Eisenstein said that his masterpiece *Potemkin* was a film based upon Hegelian dialectic. His fellow Russian, Vsevolod Pudovkin, created films synthesizing the best work of Griffith, Eisenstein, and Stanislavsky.

Walt Disney pioneered in a number of film areas, including sound cartoons, three-color process film, and directional stereophonic sound.

Several critics were important in defining cinema's powers and limitations. Rudolf Arnheim correlated camera effects with the psychology of the viewer. André Bazin was expert in photography. Saying viewers are really voyeurs (because of the darkened movie house), Bazin stated that cinema was more individualistic and more powerful in impact than theater. In a study which analyzed the differences between theater and cinema, Erwin Panofsky found that cinema's particular fortes were to make space dynamic, and to space out time in accordance with the film's psychology. Siegfried Kracauer studied German expressionist films and correlated them with the theater of the grotesque.

The French director François Truffaut said that ultimate power must be granted the director, since he, rather than the writer, was the true author of the film. American critic Andrew Sarris supported this view, which is called "the auteur theory." American philosopher Mortimer Adler pointed out that although the cinema can be neither as realistic as theater nor as fantastic as the novel, its triumph is that it can at the same time be more realistic and more fantastic than either theater or the novel.

The United States has had a number of interesting film critics. An early one, James Agee, was one of the best, since his skillful writing made it possible for the reader to visualize the film being reviewed. John Simon has shown a steady esthetic approach, just as Robert Warshow has used a sociological perspective. Pauline Kael has been perhaps our most popular movie critic. Vernon Young analyzes films in terms of each country's ethos. Stanley Kauffmann employs a modified Aristotelian approach. Dwight Macdonald defined the criteria for excellence in Bible spectacles.

To Parker Tyler, cinema was not art but myth. Films, he said, appeal to the viewer's buried desires. Thus, he felt, films play a valuable therapeutic function in our society. Actors and actresses are our counterpart of the ancient Greek gods, Tyler said, and we cannot afford to be without them.

Siegfried Kracauer, on the other hand, found a more serious function for cinema. In a world that is ideologically shelterless, he said, it was the role of modern cinema to "redeem the time."

This historical survey of the highlights of theater and film criticism shows how slowly valuable new critical insights develop. Much of what is being said today is implicit in Aristotle's *Poetics*. Nevertheless, modern drama, a radical departure from older dramaturgy, has sent a healthy ferment through contemporary critics, many of whom have responded with brilliant insights and interpretations. Although an assumption seems to be that the older Aristotelian criticism is the wrong measuring-stick to apply to the new dramatic art, thus far no modern critic has volunteered to do the necessary but difficult job of formulating the *Poetics* of modern drama.

Some of the recent developments in drama that cannot be satisfactorily accounted for in Aristotelian terms are: the development of middle genres; dramatic atmosphere, as created by Chekhov; the synthesis of art forms (what Wagner called the *Gesamtkunstwerk*); the combinations of realism and nonrealism; tragedy among common people; a general theory of comedy; the plotless play; symbolism; fantasy; non-representational drama; expressionism; and Absurdist drama. Simply to list these terms suggests that they may be so diverse as to be incapable of fitting into any modern *Poetics*. If this is true, we need not wait for a modern Aristotle, but turn to the chief expositor in each of these avenues of development. This book is intended to help readers in that particular quest.

Another kind of summary is to show the relationship between the history of dramatic criticism and the broader history of ideas, of which dramatic criticism is but a small part. This sort of summary would stress some of the following matters. First, perhaps, comes the generalization that great drama seems to precede great criticism, so that if any causal connection can be established, it would seem that inspired criticism will seldom produce outstanding plays, but that artful drama often has inspired penetrating criticism. Another generalization relates to the theatrical experience of the better critics. Most of the best commentators on drama have had some experience in the theater. Witness Ben Jonson, Lope de Vega, Corneille, Molière, Dryden, Lessing, Coleridge, Eliot. But so far as we know,

Aristotle never wrote a play, and he surely stands as the greatest drama critic of all time. Thus once again a categorical "rule" of dramatic criticism had better not be formulated. In fact, a third general principle might be that dramatic "rules" have seldom fostered great drama. A corollary might be that "rules" of dramatic criticism are every bit as useless.

The history of ideas will educidate much that has happened in drama and dramatic criticism. New insight can be obtained into Aristotle's discussion of parts of the plot, if we understand how Greek tragic form derived from the form of a religious ritual. The historic opposition of the Christian Church to drama can be understood when we are acquainted with the lewd lampooning given early Christians by the Romans. The extraordinary insights into human character achieved in Renaissance drama can be placed in the pattern of the wholesale enshrinement of the individual which that historic epoch worked constantly to achieve. The "heavenly city" of the eighteenth century philosophers is reflected not only in Mozart and Watteau, but in such neoclassical critical precepts as decorum, conformity to rule, and reasoned restraint upon imagination. The political and social revolutions later in the century roughly parallel the radical overthrow of critical "rules." In the nineteenth century, the earth-shaking concept of evolution influenced Brunetière to see a similar evolution of dramatic genres from simple, undifferentiated types to complex, intermingled entities, and Nietzsche to prefer the occasional superior genius in the theater to the continual effort to raise the common mass.

But the most fascinating of all correlations between dramatic criticism and the *Zeitgeist* comes in the twentieth century. Dramatic forms have evolved (and thus need to be interpreted) in a whole Disneyland of ideologies. Some of the contributing skeins are the following. Relativity and the pluralism of pragmatism are reflected in plays and criticism by Pirandello and Strindberg, Chekhov, Maeterlinck, and Tennessee Williams. Tendential drama, particularly the social protest plays of "socialist realism," has been written, but interestingly enough most of these plays are better off judged as political rhetoric than as art. The continued spread of democratic concepts is reflected in modern "bourgeois tragedy," which is based on the theory that "little" people can suffer tragic hurts as much as royalty.

But even more desperate, in this Age of Survival, has been the dramatic depiction of man's loss of an absolute. "God is dead!"

Nietzsche triumphantly declared, but the theater has evinced no kindred sense of exaltation. For after all, drama at its best has generally been closely connected with religion, for both of them depend for their ultimate effect upon certain non-demonstrable realities of faith. When the poet of the theater has no myth, no common frame of reference in which to ground his symbols of value, he is thrown back into self-expression or virtuostic exhibitionism. In such cases, he cannot disguise his disgust, his frustration, and his artificiality. Some of the modern reflections in drama and its criticism of this search for individual values are Sartre's dramas of existentialism, the theater of fantasy, the Theater of the Absurd, and the beginning of an interest in Oriental drama and its underlying philosophy.

Finally, one may ask, what light is shed upon mankind's plight in the Age of Survival by an understanding of the development of a significant body of dramatic criticism?

First of all, drama originates in religion. Divorced from its religious roots, drama is at best tentative and ephemeral. Arnold Toynbee in *A Study of History* has shown that of all literary forms, drama is paramount in the mature stage of a nation's cultural cycle. This can be verified by looking at classical Greece; Renaissance England, France, and Spain; and modern America. As a nation loses its political and military power, its drama wanes.

In the mature stage of a cultural cycle, Toynbee says, science and religion achieve a type of symbiotic relationship. There are signs of this search for synthesis in almost all parts of the contemporary world.

The jeremiads of drama critics concerning the relatively low status of modern drama cannot thus be taken lightly. Nor can the admonitions that for drama and its parent culture to be healthy, religion lies at the base of the mimetic urge.

The honest search for alternatives to God in existentialist theater, the Theater of the Absurd, and other modern drama forms has revealed a depressing vacuum. When Ionesco says that without God, man, his culture, and his drama are absurd and meaningless, it never seems to dawn on him and fellow Absurdists that one way back to sanity and meaningfulness is to search again for the everlasting Creator—to overcome the alienation between the product and his Maker, in order to once again give life meaning, purpose, and dignity.

There is too much potential strength in contemporary drama

in all its forms—radio, television, theater, motion picture—for one to believe that the modern world cannot recover the idea of a theater that Francis Fergusson recommends. True, drama cannot be expected to solve political, social, and religious problems. But what drama can do—indeed, must do if it and our culture are once again to be healthy—is to help spearhead cultural renewal through a re-involvement with the great religious and metaphysical themes that interest our species. At the time when classical writers invoked the help of the gods in producing great masterpieces, the invocation was not merely literary convention.

Drama and dramatic criticism are anything but dead in our time. They may mirror our confusion, our chaos, our multiplicity—as they should. "The function of the dramatist," said Chekhov, "is not to solve life's problems, but to be talented." The function of the drama critic is to interpret that talent. If modern drama criticism can combine the practicality of the journalistic critic (who is concerned about the final cause of drama, audience effect) with the theoretic interest of the academic critic (who concerns himself chiefly with the formal cause of drama, its artistic form), then the twentieth century might see what has rarely happened—a body of criticism worthy of the drama of its time.

References

See Bibliography, following, for full citations.

Chapter 1

1. Cheney, *The Theatre: Three Thousand Years ...*, p. 23.
2. Havemeyer, *Drama of Savage Peoples as Revealed in Their Rites*, p. 9.
3. Jane Harrison, *Ancient Art and Ritual* (New York: Holt, 1913), p. 127.
4. Sam R. Littlewood, in Hartnoll, *The Oxford Companion to the Theatre* (1st ed., 1951), p. 196.
5. Nicoll, *The Theatre and Dramatic Theory*, p. 91.
6. Cheney, p. 108.

Chapter 2

1. Saintsbury, *A History of Criticism ... in Europe*, vol. I, p. 24.
2. *Ibid.*, p. 22.
3. *Ibid.*, p. 59.
4. Aristotle, *The Poetics*, p. 1449b.
5. *Ibid.*
6. Atkins, *Literary Criticism in Antiquity*, vol. II, p. 9.
7. *Ibid.*, p. 38.
8. Cicero, *Offices, Essays, and Letters* (London: J.M. Dent, 1949), p. 275.
9. Atkins, *Literary Criticism in Antiquity*, vol. II, p. 140.
10. Clark, *European Theories of the Drama*, p. 28.
11. Herrick, *The Poetics of Aristotle in England*, p. 2.
12. Saintsbury, vol. I, p. 229.
13. Clark, *European Theories of the Drama*, p. 425.

Chapter 3

1. Hunningher, *The Origin of the Theater*, p. 71.
2. Atkins, *English Literary Criticism: The Medieval Phase*, pp. 17-18.

3. Littlewood, *The Art of Dramatic Criticism*, p. 11.
4. Wickham, *The Medieval Theatre*, p. 128.
5. Walter Kerr, in R.M. MacIver, *New Horizons in Creative Thinking* (New York: Harper, 1954), p. 110.
6. Chambers, *The Medieval Stage*, vol. II, p. 102.
7. Clark, *European Theories of the Drama*, p. 43.
8. *Ibid.*
9. *Ibid.*, p. 45.
10. *Ibid.*, p. 47.
11. Atkins, *English Literary Criticism: The Medieval Phase*, p. 32.
12. Tydeman, *The Theatre in the Middle Ages*, pp. 245-46.

Chapter 4

1. Gilbert, *Literary Criticism: Plato to Dryden*, p. 254.
2. Smith and Parks, *The Great Critics*, p. 668.
3. Clark, *European Theories of the Drama*, p. 66.
4. Gilbert, p. 524.
5. *Ibid.*, p. 512.
6. *Ibid.*
7. Saintsbury, vol. II, p. 89.
8. Clark, *European Theories of the Drama*, p. 75.
9. *Ibid.*, p. 70.
10. Smith and Parks, p. 269.
11. Nitze and Dargan, *A History of French Literature*, p. 247.
12. Hall, *Renaissance Literary Criticism*, p. 174.
13. Littlewood, *The Art of Dramatic Criticism*, p. 30.
14. *Ibid.*, p. 31.
15. *Ibid.*, p. 32.
16. Atkins, *English Literary Criticism: The Renascence*, p. 230.
17. G. Gregory Smith, *Elizabethan Critical Essays*, vol. I, p. 59.
18. Atkins, *English Literary Criticism: The Renascence*, p. 241.
19. Clark, *European Theories of the Drama*, p. 100.
20. Atkins, *English Literary Criticism: The Renascence*, p. 243.
21. Littlewood, *The Art of Dramatic Criticism*, p. 73.
22. *Hamlet*, Act III, Scene 2, lines 24-28.
23. Herrick, *The Poetics of Aristotle in England*, p. 43.

Chapter 5

1. Saintsbury, vol. II, p. 332.
2. Jacob Isaacs, "Dramatic Criticism," *Encyc. Britannica*, 1971 ed., p. 652.
3. *Ibid.*
4. Chaytor, *Dramatic Theory in Spain*, p. 30.
5. Saintsbury, vol. II, p. 342.
6. Babbitt, *The Masters of Modern French Criticism*, p. 338.
7. Clark, *European Theories of the Drama*, p. 82.

Chapter 6

1. A.F.B. Clark, *Boileau and the French Classical Critics in England, 1660–1830*, p. 240.
2. Saintsbury, vol. II, p. 407.
3. Nitze and Dargan, p. 249.
4. Clark, *European Theories of the Drama*, p. 155.
5. *Ibid.*, p. 156.
6. Saintsbury, vol. II, p. 572.
7. Smith and Parks, p. 270.
8. Adams and Hathaway, *Dramatic Essays of the Neoclassic Age*, p. 121.
9. Littlewood, *The Art of Dramatic Criticism*, pp. 70–71.
10. *Ibid.*, p. 70.
11. *Ibid.*, p. 69.
12. Clark, *European Theories of the Drama*, p. 171.
13. Schorer et al., *Criticism*, p. 246.
14. *Ibid.*, p. 247.
15. Atkins, *English Literary Criticism: 17th and 18th Centuries*, p. 64.
16. *Ibid.*, p. 61.
17. Herrick, *The Poetics of Aristotle in England*, p. 61.

Chapter 7

1. Adams and Hathaway, p. xvii.
2. Atkins, *English Literary Criticism: 17th and 18th Centuries*, p. 156.
3. Wellek, *A History of Modern Criticism*, vol. I, p. 150.
4. Loftis, *Restoration Drama*, p. x.
5. Herrick, *The Poetics of Aristotle in England*, p. 113.
6. Atkins, *English Literary Criticism: 17th and 18th Centuries*, p. 216.
7. Nicoll, *The Theatre and Dramatic Theory*, p. 56.
8. Clark, *European Theories of the Drama*, p. 231.
9. Littlewood, *The Art of Dramatic Criticism*, p. 105.
10. Clark, *European Theories of the Drama*, p. 234.
11. Atkins, *English Literary Criticism: 17th and 18th Centuries*, p. 342.
12. Moulton, *Shakespeare as a Dramatic Artist*, p. 9.
13. Lounsbury, *Shakespeare and Voltaire*, p. 318.
14. *Ibid.*, p. 143.
15. *Ibid.*, p. 144.
16. *Ibid.*, p. 346.
17. Saintsbury, vol. II, p. 524.
18. Adams and Hathaway, p. 365.

Chapter 8

1. Bate, *Criticism: The Major Texts*, p. 149.
2. *Ibid.*

3. Green, *Neoclassic Theory in Tragedy in England during the Eighteenth Century*, p. 99.
4. Smith, *Shakespeare Criticism*, p. xiv.
5. Patricia M. Spacks, ed., *Late Augustan Prose* (Englewood Cliffs, N.J.: Prentice-Hall, 1971), p. 147.
6. Smith, *Shakespeare Criticism*, p. xii.
7. Clark, *European Theories of the Drama*, p. 234.
8. Spacks, p. 180.
9. *Ibid.*, p. 150.
10. *Ibid.*, p. 155.
11. *Ibid.*, p. 148.
12. Wellek, p. 151.

Chapter 9

1. Jules Isaac, "Dramatic Criticism," *Encyclopaedia Britannica*, 14th ed., p. 619.
2. Robertson, *Lessing's Dramatic Theory*, p. 490.
3. Littlewood, *The Art of Dramatic Criticism*, p. 50.
4. A.W. von Schlegel, in Spingarn, *Creative Criticism*, p. 74.
5. Sandys, *A History of Classical Scholarship*, vol. III, p. 92.
6. *Ibid.*, p. 98.
7. Witkowski, *The German Drama of the Nineteenth Century*, p. 40.
8. *Ibid.*, p. 47.
9. *Ibid.*, p. 38.
10. Bentley, *The Playwright as Thinker*, pp. 299–300.
11. Littlewood, *The Art of Dramatic Criticism*, p. 64.
12. Witkowski, p. 126.
13. Block and Shedd, *Masters of Modern Drama*, p. 6.
14. Witkowski, p. 33.
15. Bentley, pp. 26–27.
16. Witkowski, p. 71.
17. *Ibid.*, p. 82.
18. *Ibid.*, p. 86.
19. *Ibid.*, p. 120.
20. *Ibid.*, p. 151.
21. *Ibid.*, p. 165.
22. Block and Shedd, p. 127.
23. *Ibid.*, p. 7.
24. Bentley, p. 301.
25. *Ibid.*, p. 265.

Chapter 10

1. Babbitt, p. 2.
2. Saintsbury, vol. III, p. 137.

3. Nitze and Dargan, p. 555.
4. Spingarn, *Creative Criticism*, p. 78.
5. Nitze and Dargan, p. 717.
6. *Ibid.*, p. 721.
7. Halliday, *Shakespeare and His Critics*, p. 254.
8. *Ibid.*, p. 256.
9. Herrick, *The Poetics of Aristotle in England*, p. 144.
10. Wellek, vol. II, p. 187.
11. Tillyard, *Lamb's Criticism*, p. xiii.
12. Littlewood, *The Art of Dramatic Criticism*, p. 93.
13. Edmund D. Jones, ed., *English Critical Essays: Nineteenth Century* (London: Oxford University Press, 1916), pp. 98-99.
14. Littlewood, *The Art of Dramatic Criticism*, p. 93.
15. *Ibid.*, p. 97.
16. Herrick, *The Poetics of Aristotle in England*, p. 156.
17. *Ibid.*, p. 166.
18. *Ibid.*, p. 169.
19. Bentley, p. 313.
20. Littlewood, *The Art of Dramatic Criticism*, p. 124.
21. *Ibid.*, p. 125.
22. Archer, *Play-Making: A Manual for Craftsmanship*, p. 226.
23. Littlewood, *The Art of Dramatic Criticism*, p. 127.
24. *New Statesman and Nation*, May 2, 1953, p. 520.
25. Block and Shedd, p. 5.
26. Spingarn, *Creative Criticism*, p. 79.
27. Littlewood, *The Art of Dramatic Criticism*, p. 132.

Chapter 11

1. Wilson, *Three Hundred Years of American Drama and Theatre*, p. 9.
2. *Ibid.*, p. 16.
3. *Ibid.*, p. 14.
4. Arthur Hobson Quinn, in *The Cambridge History of American Literature*, vol. I, p. 217.
5. Moses and Brown, *The American Theatre as Seen by Its Critics, 1752-1934*, p. 24.
6. Miller, *Bohemians and Critics: American Theatre Criticism in the Nineteenth Century*, p. 3.
7. Wilson, p. 45.
8. Miller, p. 2.
9. *Ibid*.
10. *Edgar Allan Poe*, ed. by Margaret Alterton and Hardin Craig (New York: American Book Co., 1935), p. xliii.
11. *Ibid.*, p. xliv.
12. Miller, p. 7.
13. Moses and Brown, p. 60.
14. *Ibid.*, p. 61.

15. *Ibid.*, p. 65.
16. Miller, p. 8.
17. Moses and Brown, p. 67.
18. *Ibid.*, p. 68.
19. Miller, p. 9.
20. Ambrose Bierce, *The Devil's Dictionary* (New York: Dover, 1958), p. 32.
21. Quinn, p. 223.
22. Miller, p. 67.
23. *Ibid.*, p. 62.
24. Wilson, p. 98.
25. Winter, *Shakespeare on the Stage, Second Series*, p. 205.
26. Miller, p. 85.
27. *Ibid.*, p. 88.
28. *Ibid.*, p. 89.
29. *The Cambridge History of American Literature*, vol. III, p. 128.
30. Miller, p. 99.
31. *Ibid.*, p. 117.
32. *Ibid.*, p. 124.
33. *Ibid.*, p. 125.
34. *Ibid.*, p. 145.
35. *Ibid.*, p. 157.
36. *Ibid.*
37. James Russell Lowell, *Literary Essays* (Boston: Houghton Mifflin, 1890), vol. III, p. 34.
38. *Ibid.*, p. 93.
39. *Ibid.*
40. Sandys, vol. III, p. 462.
41. *Ibid.*
42. Moses and Brown, p. 123.
43. *Ibid.*, p. 135.
44. Miller, p. 86.
45. Wilson, p. 164.
46. *Ibid.*
47. *Ibid.*
48. Spingarn, *Creative Criticism*, pp. 84–85.
49. Moses and Brown, pp. 151–52.
50. Wilson, p. 236.
51. Moses and Brown, p. 174.
52. *Ibid.*, p. 149.
53. *Ibid.*

Chapter 12

1. Senelick, *Russian Dramatic Theory from Pushkin to the Symbolists*, p. xvii.
2. *Ibid.*, p. xviii.
3. Mirsky, *A History of Russian Literature*, p. 111.

4. Senelick, p. xxi.
5. *Ibid.*, p. 11.
6. *Ibid.*, p. xxii.
7. Mirsky, p. 154.
8. Senelick, p. 21.
9. *Ibid.*, p. xxvii.
10. *Ibid.*, p. 64.
11. *Ibid.*, p. 65.
12. Matlaw, *Belinsky, Chernyshevsky, and Dobrolyubov: Selected Criticism*, p. 29.
13. Mirsky, p. 235.
14. *Ibid.*, p. 238.
15. Leo Wiener, *The Contemporary Drama of Russia* (Boston: Little, Brown, 1924), p. 87.
16. *Ibid.*, p. 89.
17. West, *Russian Symbolism*, p. 25.
18. Senelick, pp. 11–12.
19. Constance Garnett, *Letters of Anton Chekhov to His Family and Friends* (New York: Macmillan, 1920), p. 408.
20. Senelick, p. xxxvi.
21. *Ibid.*
22. *Ibid.*, p. 90.
23. West, p. 154.
24. Senelick, p. 164.
25. *Ibid.*, p. 150.
26. *Ibid.*, p. 165.
27. *Ibid.*, p. 106.
28. West, p. 141.
29. Senelick, p. 137.
30. West, p. 142.
31. *Ibid.*, p. 141.
32. Senelick, p. 188.
33. *Ibid.*, p. liv.
34. *Ibid.*, p. 240.
35. *Ibid.*, pp. 240–41.
36. *Ibid.*, p. 271.
37. Bentley, pp. 66–67.
38. Senelick, p. 202.
39. A.M. Egolin, *The Ideological Content of Soviet Literature* (Washington, D.C.: Public Affairs Press, 1946), p. 14.
40. *Ibid.*
41. Dukore, *Dramatic Theory and Criticism: Greeks to Grotowski*, p. 958.
42. *Ibid.*, p. 953.
43. *Ibid.*, p. 956.
44. *Ibid.*, p. 963.
45. *Ibid.*
46. *Ibid.*, p. 967.
47. *The Saturday Review*, February 10, 1951, p. 28.

48. *Ibid.*
49. *Ibid.*
50. *Ibid.*
51. *Ibid.*
52. Egolin, pp. 8–9.
53. *Ibid.*, p. 9.
54. *Ibid.*, p. 19.
55. Weiss, *Drama in the Modern World: Plays and Essays*, p. 547.
56. *The Saturday Review*, January 30, 1954, p. 31.
57. *Ibid.*
58. *New York Times*, Drama Section, February 26, 1956, p. 3.
59. *New York Times Magazine*, September 29, 1957, p. 69.
60. Harrison E. Salisbury, *The Soviet Union: The Fifty Years* (New York: New American Library, 1968), p. 190.

Chapter 13

1. *New York Times Book Review*, May 13, 1956, p. 19.
2. Barnet et al., *Types of Drama: Plays and Essays*, p. 17.
3. *Ibid.*, p. 112.
4. *Ibid.*
5. Ronald Hayman, *Theatre and Anti-Theatre: New Movements Since Beckett* (New York: Oxford University Press, 1979), p. 167.
6. Block and Shedd, p. 842.
7. Bentley, p. 192.
8. *Ibid.*, p. 193.
9. Benedikt and Wellwarth, *Modern French Theatre*, p. 99.
10. Barnet, p. 9.
11. Dukore, p. 937.
12. *Ibid.*, p. 934.
13. *Ibid.*, p. 941.
14. Bentley, p. 277.
15. Littlewood, *The Art of Dramatic Criticism*, p. 166.
16. Bate, p. 535.
17. Corrigan and Rosenberg, *The Context and Craft of Drama*, p. 166.
18. *New York Times Magazine*, March 12, 1950, p. 61.
19. *Ibid.*, p. 63.
20. Hartnoll, *The Oxford Companion to the Theatre*, p. 101.
21. Loftis, p. 27.
22. *Ibid.*
23. *New York Times Magazine*, October 20, 1957, p. 25.
24. *Ibid.*, p. 26.
25. *Ibid.*
26. Corrigan and Rosenberg, pp. 265–66.
27. *Ibid.*, p. 267.
28. *Ibid.*, p. 273.
29. *Ibid.*

References 257

30. Dukore, p. 988.
31. *Ibid.*, p. 993.
32. *Ibid.*
33. *New York Times*, Arts Section, August 17, 1980, p. 5.
34. *Ibid.*
35. *Ibid.*
36. *Ibid.*, July 10, 1977, p. 8.
37. *Ibid.*

Chapter 14

1. Block and Shedd, p. 7.
2. *Ibid.*
3. Esslin, *The Theatre of the Absurd*, p. 257.
4. *Ibid.*, p. 258.
5. Smallwood, *Elements of the Existentialist Philosophy in the Theatre of the Absurd*, p. 15.
6. Esslin, p. xx.
7. *Ibid.*, p. xix.
8. *Ibid.*, p. 48.
9. *Ibid.*, p. 51.
10. *Ibid.*, p. 290.
11. *Ibid.*
12. *Ibid.*, p. 303.
13. *Ibid.*, p. 92.
14. Artaud, *The Theater and Its Double*, p. 14.
15. Esslin, p. 291.
16. *Ibid.*, p. 293.
17. *Ibid.*, p. 314.
18. *Ibid.*, p. 138.
19. Styan, *The Dark Comedy: The Development of Modern Comic Tragedy*, p. 282.
20. *Ibid.*, p. 283.
21. Esslin, p. 236.
22. *Ibid.*, p. 299.
23. Weiss, p. 505.
24. *Ibid.*, p. 506.
25. *Ibid.*
26. *Ibid.*, p. 507.
27. *Ibid.*
28. *Ibid.*, p. 508.
29. Esslin, p. 294.
30. Reiter, *World Theater: The Structure and Meaning of Drama*, p. 227.
31. *New York Times*, Arts Section, April 19, 1981, p. 5.
32. *Ibid.*
33. Esslin, p. 133.
34. Corrigan and Rosenberg, p. 286.

References

35. *Ibid.*, p. 287.
36. Weiss, p. 481.
37. Esslin, p. 100.
38. Weiss, p. 481.
39. Esslin, p. 132.
40. Corrigan and Rosenberg, p. 285.
41. Weiss, p. 482.
42. *Ibid.*, p. 483.
43. *Ibid.*, p. 484.
44. *Ibid.*
45. *Ibid.*
46. *Ibid.*
47. *Ibid.*, p. 486.
48. *Ibid.*
49. Artaud, p. 8.
50. *Ibid.*, p. 27.
51. *Ibid.*
52. *Ibid.*, p. 31.
53. *Ibid.*, pp. 31–32.
54. *Ibid.*
55. *Ibid.*, p. 44.
56. *Ibid.*, p. 46.
57. *Ibid.*, p. 59.
58. *Ibid.*, p. 70.
59. *Ibid.*, p. 77.
60. *Ibid.*, p. 78.
61. *Ibid.*, p. 79.
62. *Ibid.*
63. *Ibid.*, p. 114.
64. *Ibid.*, p. 104.
65. *Ibid.*, p. 122.
66. *Ibid.*, p. 123.
67. *Ibid.*, p. 90.
68. *Ibid.*, p. 99.
69. *Ibid.*, p. 82.
70. Esslin, p. 216.
71. *New York Times*, Arts Section, November 21, 1976, p. 3.
72. Esslin, p. 217.
73. Reiter, p. 215.
74. *Ibid.*, pp. 215–16.
75. *New York Times*, Arts Section, August 7, 1977, p. 22.
76. *Ibid.*
77. *Ibid.*, March 28, 1982, p. 28.
78. *Ibid.*
79. *Ibid.*
80. Grossvogel, *The Blasphemers*, p. 178.
81. *Ibid.*
82. Lumley, *New Trends in 20th Century Drama*, p. 208.

References 259

83. Barnet, p. 652.
84. Esslin, p. 308.
85. *Ibid.*, p. 310.
86. *Ibid.*, p. 315.

Chapter 15

1. Moses and Brown, p. 203.
2. *Ibid.*, p. 202.
3. *Ibid.*
4. *Ibid.*, p. 119.
5. *Ibid.*, p. 121.
6. *Ibid.*, p. 196.
7. *Ibid.*, p. 197.
8. Angoff, *The World of George Jean Nathan*, p. 304.
9. *Ibid.*, p. 305.
10. George Jean Nathan, *The Critic and the Drama* (Rutherford, N.J.: Fairleigh Dickinson University Press, 1972), p. 16.
11. Moses and Brown, p. 257.
12. *Ibid.*, p. 325.
13. Schorer, p. 80.
14. *Ibid.*, p. 84.
15. Weiss, p. 284.
16. *Ibid.*, p. 285.
17. Eugene O'Neill, *Nine Plays* (New York: Modern Library, 1941), p. xvii.
18. John Gassner et al., *A Treasury of the Theater: Ibsen to Odets* (New York: Simon and Schuster, 1940), p. 133.
19. John Gassner, *Best American Plays, Third Series, 1945–1951* (New York: Crown, 1952), p. xx.
20. Anderson, *Off Broadway: Essays about the Theatre*, p. 28.
21. *Ibid.*, p. 31.
22. *Ibid.*, p. 33.
23. *Ibid.*, p. 35.
24. *American Literature*, May, 1944, p. 81.
25. Moses and Brown, p. 223.
26. *Ibid.*, p. 252.
27. *New York Times*, Drama Section, January 13, 1957, p. 1.
28. *Ibid.*
29. *Ibid.*
30. *New York Times Book Review*, November 8, 1981, p. 43.
31. *Ibid.*, p. 42.
32. *Ibid.*, p. 43.
33. Dukore, p. 892.
34. Jim Gaines, *The Saturday Review*, April 29, 1972, p. 29.
35. *Ibid.*
36. Block and Shedd, p. 989.
37. *New York Times*, Drama Section, March 8, 1959, p. 3.

38. *Ibid.*
39. *New York Times Book Review*, November 26, 1961, p. 1.
40. *Ibid.*, p. 36.
41. Kerr, *Pieces at Eight*, p. 125.
42. *Ibid.*, p. 126.
43. Gaines, p. 29.
44. Barnet, p. 257.
45. *New York Times*, Drama Section, February 5, 1950, p. 3.
46. *Ibid.*, Arts Section, September 28, 1980, p. 32.
47. *Ibid.*
48. *Theatre Arts*, March, 1942, p. 176.
49. *New York Times Magazine*, November 27, 1949, p. 28.
50. *Ibid.*, October 30, 1949, p. 18.
51. *Ibid.*, p. 20.
52. *New York Times*, Drama Section, September 13, 1953, p. 1.
53. *Ibid.*
54. *Ibid.*
55. *The Saturday Review*, December 24, 1949, p. 24.
56. *Ibid.*, p. 25.
57. *Ibid.*, p. 26.
58. *Ibid.*, March 1, 1952, pp. 20–22.
59. *Poetry*, April, 1951, p. 43.
60. Weiss, p. 288.
61. Bentley, p. 244.
62. Ray B. West, *Essays in Modern Literary Criticism* (New York: Rinehart, 1952), p. 570.
63. Bentley, p. 33.
64. Fergusson, *The Idea of a Theater*, p. 239.
65. Barnet, p. 644.
66. *Ibid.*, p. 261.
67. *Ibid.*, p. 262.
68. *Theatre Arts*, September, 1951, p. 12.
69. *Ibid.*
70. *Ibid.*
71. *Ibid.*
72. Kerr, p. 58.
73. Louis Kronenberger, *Cavalcade of Comedy* (New York: Simon and Schuster, 1953), pp. xi–xii.
74. *New York Times*, Drama Section, March 30, 1952, p. 1.
75. *Ibid.*, Arts Section, October 14, 1979, p. 4.
76. *Ibid.*
77. Corrigan and Rosenberg, p. 153.
78. *The Saturday Review*, April 29, 1972, p. 64.
79. *New York Times*, Arts Section, August 12, 1979, p. 5.
80. *Ibid.*, September 25, 1977, p. 4.
81. *Ibid.*, January 18, 1981, p. 4.
82. *Ibid.*, May 9, 1982, p. 4.
83. *Ibid.*

84. *Ibid.*
85. *Ibid.*, July 29, 1979, p. 22.
86. *Ibid.*
87. *Ibid.*, May 2, 1982, p. 6.
88. *Ibid.*
89. Engel, *The Critics*, p. 97.
90. *Ibid.*, p. 93.
91. *New York Times*, Arts Section, April 5, 1981, p. 4.
92. *Ibid.*
93. *Ibid.*
94. *Ibid.*, June 20, 1982, p. 33.
95. *New York Times Magazine*, November 23, 1980, p. 58.
96. *Ibid.*
97. *Ibid.*, p. 122.
98. Wilson, p. 474.
99. *New York Times*, Arts Section, March 4, 1979, p. 27.
100. *Ibid.*, p. 1.
101. Vos, *The Drama of Comedy: Victim and Victor*, pp. 7–8.
102. *New York Times*, Arts Section, March 9, 1980, p. 9.
103. *Ibid.*
104. *Ibid.*
105. *Ibid.*
106. *Ibid.*, June 20, 1982, p. 33.
107. *Ibid.*

Chapter 16

1. "Motion Pictures," *Encyclopaedia Britannica*, 1971 ed., p. 905.
2. *Ibid.*, p. 901.
3. *Ibid.*, p. 913.
4. *Ibid.*
5. Bazin, *What Is Cinema?*, p. 57.
6. Lindsay, *The Art of the Moving Picture*, pp. 94–95.
7. *Ibid.*, p. 317.
8. *Ibid.*, p. 161.
9. *Ibid.*, p. 189.
10. "David Wark Griffith," *Encyclopaedia Britannica*, 1971 ed., p. 925.
11. Murray, *Nine American Film Critics*, p. 225.
12. *Ibid.*, p. 73.
13. *Ibid.*
14. Eisenstein, *Film Form*, pp. 193–94.
15. *Ibid.*, p. 234.
16. *Ibid.*, p. 206.
17. Bazin, p. 25.
18. *Ibid.*, p. 24.
19. "Motion Pictures," *Encyclopaedia Britannica*, p. 905.
20. Eisenstein, p. 38.

21. Pudovkin, *Film Technique and Film Acting*, p. 157.
22. "Motion Pictures," *Encyclopaedia Britannica*, p. 906.
23. Arnheim, *Film as Art*, p. 154.
24. *Ibid.*, p. 119.
25. *Ibid.*, p. 225.
26. Bazin, p. 14.
27. *Ibid.*
28. *Ibid.*, p. 16.
29. *Ibid.*, p. 99.
30. *Ibid.*, p. 92.
31. *Ibid.*, p. 50.
32. *Ibid.*, p. 29.
33. *Ibid.*
34. Artaud, p. 144.
35. *Ibid.*, p. 142.
36. Bazin, p. 33.
37. *Ibid.*, p. 36.
38. Murray, *Nine American Film Critics*, p. 64.
39. *Ibid.*, p. 158.
40. "Motion Pictures," *Encyclopaedia Britannica*, p. 903.
41. *New York Times Book Review*, June 27, 1982, p. 29.
42. Murray, *Nine American Film Critics*, p. 201.
43. *Ibid.*, p. 164.
44. *Ibid.*, p. 103.
45. *Ibid.*, p. 65.
46. *New York Times*, Drama Section, December 9, 1951, p. 9.
47. Murray, *Nine American Film Critics*, pp. 149–50.
48. Mortimer Adler, *Art and Prudence* (New York: Longmans, Green, 1937), p. 568.
49. *Ibid.*, p. 569.
50. *Ibid.*, p. 570.
51. *Ibid.*, p. 571.
52. Murray, *Nine American Film Critics*, p. 50.
53. *Ibid.*, p. 40.
54. *Ibid.*
55. Eric Bentley, *The Play: A Critical Anthology* (New York: Prentice-Hall, 1951), p. 769.
56. Murray, *Nine American Film Critics*, p. 230.
57. *Ibid.*, p. 214.
58. *Ibid.*, p. 225.
59. *New York Times*, Arts Section, January 9, 1983, p. 22.
60. *Arizona Republic*, January 10, 1983, p. C9.
61. Murray, *Nine American Film Critics*, p. 72.
62. *Ibid.*, p. 70.
63. *Ibid.*, p. 71.
64. *Ibid.*
65. *Ibid.*
66. *Ibid.*, p. 34.

67. *Ibid.*
68. *Ibid.*, p. 35.
69. *Ibid.*, p. 91.
70. *Ibid.*, p. 114.
71. *New York Times Book Review*, November 14, 1982, p. 9.
72. Murray, *Nine American Film Critics*, p. 177.
73. *Ibid.*, p. 179.
74. *Ibid.*, p. 185.
75. *Ibid.*, p. 147.
76. *Ibid.*, p. 151.
77. *Ibid.*, p. 150.
78. *New York Times*, Arts Section, June 20, 1982, p. 21.
79. Murray, *Nine American Film Critics*, p. 169.
80. *New York Times*, Arts Section, April 25, 1982, p. 1.
81. *Ibid.*, p. 30.
82. *Ibid.*
83. *Ibid.*
84. *Ibid.*
85. Murray, *Nine American Film Critics*, p. 231.

Throughout the book indebtedness is acknowledged to the past forty years of issues of the following publications:
New York Times, Arts and Drama Sections
New York Times Book Review
New York Times Magazine
The Saturday Review
Theatre Arts

Bibliography

Note: This bibliography is fully indexed
(to entry numbers) beginning on page 295.

1. Adams, Henry H. and Baxter Hathaway, eds. *Dramatic Essays of the Neoclassic Age.* New York: Columbia University Press, 1950. This work includes criticism from Joseph Addison, Beaumarchais, William Congreve, John Dennis, Denis Diderot, Sebastien Mercier, and Voltaire, among others. The contrasting approaches provide an excellent picture of the battle waged over dramatic rules.
2. Agate, James, ed. *The English Dramatic Critics.* New York: Hill & Wang, 1958. The period covered is from 1660 to 1932. Among the critics represented are William Archer, Ivor Brown, Oliver Goldsmith, William Hazlitt, Leigh Hunt, Charles Lamb, Desmond MacCarthy, Clement Scott, and Richard Steele.
3. Anderson, Maxwell. *Off Broadway: Essays About the Theater.* New York: William Sloan, 1947. Calling the theater "a church without a creed," Anderson says that its purpose is to exalt mankind's spirit. He gives "the rules of playwriting," including the belief that the proper subject of a play is the conflict between good and evil within the protagonist.
4. Angoff, Charles ed. *The World of George Jean Nathan.* New York: Knopf, 1952. "What interests me in life is the surface: life's music and color, its charm and ease, its humor and its loveliness. The great problems of the world do not concern me in the slightest," said Nathan. Modern dramatic criticism, as revealed in this collection of his writings, has no better

example of the brilliance and the inadequacy of impressionistic commentary on drama.
5   Archer, William. *Play-Making: A Manual for Craftsmanship.* Boston: Small, Maynard, 1925. Among the many practical suggestions to playwrights, Archer gives an extended treatment to conditions underlying the employment of the "obligatory scene" (*scène à faire*).
6   Aristotle, *Poetics.* There are many translations. One I recommend is: *Poetics*, translated by S.H. Butcher. New York: Hill & Wang, 1965. This is the fundamental document of dramatic criticism. Aristotle early put criticism on a systematic basis. No idle theorist, he gave concrete examples of excellence, chiefly from the plays of Sophocles. Aristotle grounded his approach on the assumption that the goal of all art is pleasure. He showed a marvelous command of the subtle blendings and distinctions of art and nature. Confining himself to a treatment of tragedy, he gave special attention to plot, which he called the "soul" of drama.
7   Arnheim, Rudolf. *Film as Art.* Berkeley: University of California Press, 1967. Creating a theory of film, Arnheim describes how silent films built their art around their limitations. He sets up criteria for evaluating sound films. His approach is to study the varying possibilities of camera effects and correlate them with their corresponding psychological effects.
8   Artaud, Antonin. *The Theater and Its Double.* Translated from the French by Mary Caroline Richards. New York: Grove Press, 1958. The founder of the "Theater of Cruelty" vividly explains his position. He states that unless mankind restores theater as expression of the core of its metaphysical beliefs, the human race is doomed.
9   Arvin, Newton C. *Eugène Scribe and the French Theatre, 1815-1860.* Cambridge, Mass.: Harvard University Press, 1924. Arvin traces the development of the so-called "well made" play. He says that virtually every reform in nineteenth-century drama originated with Scribe, an obvious overstatement.
10 Atkins, J.W.H. *English Literary Criticism: The Medieval Phase.* Cambridge, England: Cambridge University Press, 1943. Although most of this book relates to literary rather than dramatic criticism, Atkins has some good material on the attack of the Church Fathers upon the theater.

11 _____. *English Literary Criticism: The Renascence*. 2nd ed. London: Methuen, 1951. This informative work shows the contributions of humanists, major critics, and minor critics. It demonstrates how a reconsideration of the classics laid the foundation for the development of native English literature and drama of high quality.

12 _____. *English Literary Criticism: 17th and 18th Centuries*. Cambridge, England: Cambridge University Press, 1950. Atkins shows the French influence upon English critics, as well as the challenges to neoclassicism. He gives chief attention to John Dryden, Samuel Johnson, and the Shakespearian critics.

13 _____. *Literary Criticism in Antiquity*. 2 vols. Cambridge: Cambridge University Press, 1934. Atkins has a volume on Greek and a volume on Roman critics. Although his topic is literary criticism, he provides a good deal of material on comedy and tragedy.

14. Babbitt, Irving. *The Masters of Modern French Criticism*. New York: Farrar, Straus and Giroux, 1940. Babbitt summarizes the contributions of Brunetière, Sarcey, Sainte-Beuve, and other leading nineteenth-century French critics.

15 Babcock, R.W. *The Genesis of Shakespeare Idolatry, 1766–1799*. Chapel Hill: University of North Carolina Press, 1931. After giving a good overview of Shakespearian criticism from the beginning, this book focuses on the criticism which appeared after Samuel Johnson's *Preface to Shakespeare*. The book has an extensive bibliography on Shakespearian criticism.

16 Baker, Blanch M. ed. *Theatre and Allied Arts*. New York: H.W. Wilson, 1952. This is an annotated bibliography of books dealing with the history, criticism, and technique of drama and theater. In some cases brief reviews are given for the book being summarized.

17 Baker, George Pierce. *Dramatic Technique*. Boston: Houghton Mifflin, 1919. The well-known drama professor writes a handbook for dramatists to follow in building a play. Each dramatic ingredient is analyzed both from the artistic and the box-office viewpoint.

18 Barnet, Sylvan, Morton Berman, and William Burto, eds. *Types of Drama*. Boston: Little, Brown, 1972. This anthology of plays from Sophocles to Ionesco includes a number of critical essays plus a glossary of dramatic terms.

19 Bate, Walter J., ed. *Criticism: The Major Texts*. New York:

Harcourt Brace Jovanovich, 1970. This excellent collection includes many of the standard classics of dramatic criticism. The introductory essays and the footnotes are also helpful.

20 Bazin, André. *What Is Cinema?* Translated by Hugh Gray. Berkeley: University of California Press, 1967. France's best film critic, Bazin gives original comments in a readable style. His main idea is that the cinema is the most objective of all the arts. He combines critical insight with knowledge of modern science, literature, philosophy, and religion.

21 Bell, A.F.G. *Contemporary Spanish Literature.* New York: Knopf, 1928. This book has a section on drama and a chapter on criticism. A list of authors and their works is also provided.

22 Benedikt, Michael and George E. Wellwarth, eds. *Modern French Theatre.* New York: Dutton, 1966. This collection has avant-garde, dadaist, and surrealist plays. The introduction to the book and a number of the prefaces to the plays contain useful criticism of these kinds of drama.

23 Bennett, Benjamin. *Modern Drama and German Classicism.* Ithaca, N.Y.: Cornell University Press, 1979. Bennett argues that the dramatic movement in Germany from Lessing to Nietzsche was a unique combination of elements of German classicism and romanticism. He shows how "the assault upon the audience" of modern drama relates to that German dramatic movement.

24 Bentley, Eric. *The Playwright as Thinker.* New York: Meridian Books, 1955. Bentley gives many perceptive insights in his defense of drama as an intellectual enterprise. He is especially good on German plays and criticism.

25 Bernbaum, Ernest. *The Drama of Sensibility.* Magnolia, Mass.: Peter Smith, 1958. Bernbaum gives the history of English sentimental comedy and domestic tragedy from 1696 to 1780. He finds these plays, such as those by Colley Cibber and Richard Steele, to be based upon the concept of man's natural goodness.

26 Blades, Joseph D., Jr. *A Comparative Study of Selected American Film Critics, 1958-74.* New York: Arno, 1976. This Ph.D. dissertation at Bowling Green State University analyzes the style, tone, biases, emphases, and approaches to film criticism of Vincent Canby, Judith Crist, Pauline Kael, Stanley Kauffmann, Andrew Sarris, and John Simon.

27 Block, Haskell M. and Robert G. Shedd, eds. *Masters of*

Modern Drama. New York: Random House, 1962. Probably the best anthology of modern drama, this book has excellent introductory sections on playwrights from Ibsen to Max Frisch.

28 Boileau-Despréaux, Nicolas. *Selected Criticism.* Translated by Ernest Dilworth. New York: Irvington, 1965. Friendly toward Racine and Molière, Boileau frequently censures Corneille. His method is largely negative, showing dramatists what to avoid. Horatian in doctrine, he recommends a short introduction, observance of the Three Unities, avoidance of the incredible, and total relevance of every device to the overall effect.

29 Bowra, C.M. *Sophoclean Tragedy.* Oxford: Clarendon Press, 1944. Bowra shows the importance of ideas in seven tragedies by Sophocles. In speculating upon the nature of Sophoclean tragedy, Bowra sheds much light on the nature of tragedy in general.

30 Bradley, Andrew C. *Shakespearean Tragedy.* New York: Fawcett, 1977. Originally published in 1904, this work showed Bradley to be a leading modern interpreter of Shakespeare. Bradley felt that a clue to Shakespeare's masterful presentation of character was his technique of holding back some of his knowledge of a character from the stage presentation.

31 Brockett, Oscar G. *Perspectives on Contemporary Theatre.* Baton Rouge: Louisiana State University Press, 1971. Brockett shows the background of ideas underlying contemporary drama. He finds the themes of impersonality and irrationality to underly most of the Absurdist plays.

32 Brown, Edward J. *Russian Literature Since the Revolution.* New York: Collier Books, 1963. Brown explains the relationship of Soviet ideology to Soviet drama. He shows the purpose of the Proletcult to be the training of working-class writers to produce a specifically proletarian class literature.

33 Brunetière, Ferdinand. *The Law of the Drama.* Translated by Philip M. Hayden. New York: Columbia University Press, 1914. Brunetière distinguishes between rules, which he shuns, and laws, which he feels state eternal principles underlying drama. The fundamental law that every good play observes, he believes, is the depiction of a conscious will striving towards a goal, endeavoring to overcome obstacles.

34 Brustein, Robert. *The Theatre of Revolt.* Boston: Atlantic

Monthly Press, 1964. Brustein analyzes the work of eight playwrights: Brecht, Chekhov, Genet, Ibsen, O'Neill, Pirandello, Shaw, and Strindberg. He shows how their attitudes towards the common theme of revolt determines their approaches to plot, character, and language.

35 Calderon, George. *Two Plays by Chekhov*. London: Grant Richards, 1912. Calderon, the English dramatist, wrote an introductory essay to this book which was the most important criticism of Chekhov written in English. Among Calderon's critical contributions were the centrifugal plot, mood achieved through group emotions, realism in character concept and technique of portrayal, disconnected dialogue, symbolism, and Chekhov's unique type of tragicomedy.

36 Calderwood, James L., and Harold E. Toliver, eds. *Essays in Shakespearean Criticism*. Englewood Cliffs, N.J.: Prentice-Hall, 1970. Of the 38 essays given, 31 comment on Shakespeare's plays. Approaches represent textual criticism, history of ideas, imagery, sources of the plays, structure and texture of the plays, and their relationship to ritual and myth.

37 Chambers, E.K. *The Medieval Stage*. 2 vols. London: Oxford University Press, 1903. Chambers gives an exhaustive account of minstrelsy, folk drama, and religious drama of the medieval period. He shows how the secularization of church drama led to the development of Renaissance non-religious drama.

38 Chandler, Frank W. *Aspects of Modern Drama*. New York: Macmillan, 1914. Chandler studies modern drama from the standpoint of ideas and technique. His bibliography contains extensive critical references on such dramatists as Eugène Brieux, Gerhart Hauptmann, Henrik Ibsen, Maurice Maeterlinck, Arthur Schnitzler, August Strindberg, Hermann Sudermann, and others.

39 Charlton, H.B. *Castelvetro's Theory of Poetry*. Manchester, England: University Press, 1913. This is an extensive treatment of the work of the critic generally considered responsible for formulating the doctrine of the Three Unities. Castelvetro, however, was no servile follower of Aristotle. He gives major consideration to the ways plays are affected by audience reactions, and he states, in a manner that sounds most modern, that both tragedy and comedy can have either a happy or a sad ending.

40 Chaytor, Henry J. *Dramatic Theory in Spain*. Cambridge, England: Cambridge University Press, 1925. Chaytor points out that Aristotle and Horace were known in Spain before they were known in France. He also indicates that nationalism was a far greater influence upon dramatists than was classicism. This book is the best work of its kind in its field.

41 Cheney, Sheldon. *The Theatre: Three Thousand Years of Drama, Acting and Stagecraft*. New York: Tudor Pub., 1935. Although his broad survey covers three millennia of theatrical history, Cheney has especially good material on primitive and early Greek drama.

42 Clark, A.F.B. *Boileau and the French Classical Critics in England, 1660-1830*. Paris: Edouard Champion, 1925. Clark finds that French classicism received a generally hostile reception in England. He states that d'Aubignac was probably the French critic who was most influential in England.

43 Clark, Barrett H., ed. *European Theories of the Drama*. Rev. ed. New York: Crown, 1947. This has been the standard anthology in the field of dramatic criticism. Though it has little on the twentieth century and is somewhat outdated by more recent scholarship, it remains an extremely useful work in depicting the growth and development of critical concepts in drama.

44 Cole, Toby, ed. *Playwrights on Playwriting*. New York: Hill & Wang, 1960. Cole analyzes the theory and practice of many modern dramatists. In a perceptive introduction, John Gassner warns readers to judge a play on its independent merits rather than by how fully it carries out its author's stated intentions.

45 Coleridge, Samuel T. *Coleridge's Principles of Criticism*. Philadelphia: Richard West, 1904. Somewhat indebted to the German critics, Coleridge in his comments on Shakespeare uncovered some original insights into the nature of dramatic art. He is especially good on the role of the imagination in shaping an esthetic whole which possesses organic unity.

46 Comtois, M.F., and Lynn F. Miller. *Contemporary American Theatre Critics*. Metuchen, N.J.: Scarecrow Press, 1977. This is a dictionary and anthology of the works of many current critics.

47 Cooper, Lane. *The Poetics of Aristotle: Its Meaning and Influence*. Westport, CT: Greenwood, 1972. Cooper shows

how writers in various periods have reacted to this seminal work. The *Poetics* can help a great writer produce artistic work, Cooper says, since it is "one of the great constructive efforts of a scientific imagination that is sister to the poetic genius."

48 Corrigan, Robert W. and James L. Rosenberg, eds. *The Context and Craft of Drama*. San Francisco: Chandler Publishing Company, 1964. Thirteen critics and playwrights discuss drama as an art form, and sixteen critics, directors, and stage designers discuss theater as applied stagecraft.

49 Crane, Ronald S., ed. *Critics and Criticism: Ancient and Modern*. Chicago: University of Chicago Press, 1952. This comprehensive collection is especially rich in neo-Aristotelian criticism. It has, however, relatively little on drama.

50 Crawford, James P. *Spanish Drama before Lope de Vega*. Rev. ed. Philadelphia: University of Pennsylvania Press, 1937. This is an excellent study of early drama, including farces, tragedies, and religious plays. The extensive footnotes and bibliography are very useful.

51 Dean, Leonard F., ed. *Shakespeare: Modern Essays in Criticism*. Rev. ed. London: Oxford University Press, 1967. These essays offer fresh and provocative insights into individual plays. Some of the topics discussed are patterns of imagery, the structure of ironic drama, Renaissance modes of thought, and the esthetics of drama.

52 Deane, C.V. *Dramatic Theory and the Rhymed Heroic Play*. London: Frank Cass, 1967. Deane discusses Dryden's advocacy of this type of play, in the light of French and English critical comments on it. Critical rules as applied to heroic drama existed less as a restriction than as guideposts to develop excellence within the genre, Deane feels.

53 Denby, David, ed. *Awake in the Dark: An Anthology of American Film Criticism, 1915-77*. New York: Random House, 1977. This excellent anthology covers the definition of cinema, cinema as an art form, movie criticism, actors, directors, and other topics. Included are writings by James Agee, Otis Ferguson, Pauline Kael, Vachel Lindsay, Erwin Panofsky, Gilbert Seldes, John Simon, Robert Warshow, and others.

54 Driver, Tom F. *Romantic Quest and Modern Query*. New York: Delacorte, 1970. Many critical issues are raised in this history

of the modern theater. Driver believes that the soul-searching of contemporary drama is a continuation of the quest of the great Romantic poets. Driver points out the religious and philosophical significance of modern drama. He also finds interesting parallels between Beckett and Chekhov.

55 Dryden, John. *Selected Criticism.* Edited by James Kinsley and G.A. Parfitt. London: Oxford University Press, 1970. Dryden was so prolific as a writer and critic that he was bound to have made some poor choices. And yet what he said of Shakespeare applies equally to himself: "He is always great when some great occasion is presented to him."

56 Duckworth, George E. *The Nature of Roman Comedy.* Princeton: Princeton University Press, 1971. After describing the essence of the comedy of Plautus and Terence, Duckworth shows their influence upon Renaissance drama.

57 Dukes, Ashley. *Modern Dramatists.* Freeport, N.Y.: Books for Libraries Press, 1967. Reprint of 1912 edition. Dukes provides an overview of modern playwrights and their work. He finds Ibsen to be the most profound influence upon them, dismissing Chekhov with the comment that "by no stretch of imagination can Chekhov be called a great dramatist."

58 Dukore, Bernard F., ed. *Dramatic Theory and Criticism: Greeks to Grotowski.* New York: Holt, Rinehart, and Winston, 1974. This comprehensive anthology is arranged chronologically by countries. Although Dukore has nothing on Oriental criticism, his book is especially rich in excerpts of Soviet dramatic criticism.

59 Dunlap, William. *History of the American Theatre.* New York: Burt Franklin, 1963. Reprint of the 1833 edition. The playwright and manager gives an invaluable account of the early American theater.

60 Dunn, Esther C. *Shakespeare in America.* New York: Benjamin Blom, 1968. This book includes material on play performances in America as well as editorial and textual criticism. It also shows the attitude towards Shakespeare by Emerson, Thoreau, Whitman, and other American writers.

61 Eisenstein, Sergei. *Film Form.* Edited and translated by Jay Leyda. New York: Harcourt Brace, 1949. The great Soviet director discusses film theory, including such key concepts as montage, typage, and historical realism. He makes clear his indebtedness to the work of D.W. Griffith.

62 *Encyclopaedia Britannica*, "Motion Pictures." In, for example, vol. 15, pp. 898–918, of the 1971 edition. Chicago. A detailed history of the origin of motion pictures, giving credit to those who made the most significant contributions.

63 Engel, Lehman. *The Critics*. New York, Macmillan, 1976. Engel discusses recent American newspaper drama critics. He calls George Jean Nathan "a sophomoric harlequin who used barbs that seemed witty at the time but today are a pathetic waste of newsprint." But Walter Kerr's reviews are "significant contributions to the theater," for they "spy into hidden but significant corners, criticizing on the one hand, imparting a feeling of hopefulness on the other."

64 Esslin, Martin. *The Theatre of the Absurd*. Garden City, N.Y.: Anchor Books, 1961. This is the most penetrating and exhaustive analysis of Absurdist drama.

65 Evreinov, Nikolai. *The Theater in Life*. New York: Brentano, 1926. The proponent of monodrama vigorously defends his views. Feeling that gestures communicate better than words, Evreinov wants to return to the pre-dialogue theater of Thespis.

66 Fagin, N. Bryllion. *The Histrionic Mr. Poe*. Baltimore: Johns Hopkins University Press, 1949. Fagin studies the dramatic instinct in Poe, and the extent to which it affected all of his writings. Among other topics discussed is Poe's status as a drama critic.

67 Fergusson, Francis. *The Idea of a Theater*. Garden City, N.Y.: Anchor Books, 1953. Fergusson argues that great drama can be found only in societies that take drama seriously. He urges moderns to create the conditions for a theater in which the stage represents "the human situation which the whole culture embodies."

68 Flickinger, R.S. *The Greek Theater and Its Drama*. 4th ed. Chicago: University of Chicago Press, 1960. This book shows how the conditions of the Greek theater affected the development of Greek drama.

69 Fowlie, Wallace. *Dionysus in Paris: A Guide to Contemporary French Theater*. Gloucester, Mass.: Peter Smith, 1971. Fowlie gives insightful criticism of the leading modern French dramatists.

70 Frank, Grace. *The Medieval French Drama*. Oxford: Clarendon Press, 1954. This scholarly work shows the growth of religious

drama, as well as of farces and comedies. It traces the influences of medieval drama upon subsequent theater.

71 Frenz, Horst, ed. *American Playwrights on Drama.* New York: Hill & Wang, 1965. This book presents interesting comments on their craft by Edward Albee, Maxwell Anderson, Paul Green, William Inge, John Howard Lawson, Arthur Miller, Eugene O'Neill, Thornton Wilder, Tennessee Williams, and others.

72 Freytag, Gustav. *Technique of the Drama.* Translated from the 6th German edition by Elias J. MacEwan. New York: Arno, 1968. Like Sarcey, Freytag was a playwright with a predilection for the "well made" play, and hence he tends to stress theatrical considerations over dramatic ones. His chief critical contribution is his advice on how to build the pyramidal plot.

73 Fujimura, Thomas H. *The Restoration Comedy of Wit.* Princeton, N.J.: Princeton University Press, 1952. Fujimura has a good treatment of the esthetics of wit comedy. He differentiates this genre from other comedy by its stress upon ideas and words rather than upon people and action.

74 Garten, H.F. *Modern German Drama.* Fairlawn, N.J.: Essential Books, 1959. This study of German naturalism and expressionism is descriptive rather than critical. It is enriched by Garten's intimate knowledge of the German theater of the 1920's.

75 Gassner, John, ed. *Ideas in the Drama.* New York: Columbia University Press, 1964. In addition to editing this book, Gassner summarizes Shaw's criticism of Ibsen's ideas. Articles by other writers show the role of ideas in Greek drama and in the plays of Brecht, O'Neill, and Sartre, and how myths, through drama, express ideas which ultimately return to their mythic form.

76 Gilbert, Allan H., ed. *Literary Criticism: Plato to Dryden.* New York: American Book Company, 1940. This comprehensive anthology contains dramatic criticism by Cinthio, Corneille, Dryden, Guarini, Jonson, Minturno, Saint-Évremond, Trissino, Lope de Vega, and others. The detailed index is especially helpful.

77 Goethe, Johann Wolfgang von. *Conversations of Goethe.* Recorded by Johann Peter Eckermann. New York: Tudor Pub. Co., 1949. "The epoch of world literature is at hand," Goethe declared. Accordingly, he shows catholic taste and

discriminating judgment in speaking of dramatists and their works. His native love of Greek classics is tempered by a romantic flair for fire and for free invention. It is ironic that a man who was better as a drama critic than a literary critic should write drama valued more for its literary than its dramatic quality.

78 Gorchakov, Nikolai. *The Theatre in Soviet Russia*. New York: Columbia University Press, 1958. A Russian émigré argues that even extreme political repression cannot keep the Russian people from loving the theater.

79 Gray, Charles H. *Theatrical Criticism in London to 1795*. New York: Benjamin Blom, 1964. This is a thorough and readable summary of London drama critics of the period.

80 Green, C.C. *Neoclassic Theory of Tragedy in England during the Eighteenth Century*. Cambridge, Mass.: Harvard University Press, 1934. Green demonstrates that English critics and dramatists evolved their own unique form of classicism during this century. Rationality led to distrust of the imagination, but by the end of the century the rules were dying, if not dead.

81 Grein, J.T. *Dramatic Criticism: 1903*. New York: Benjamin Blom, 1969. The founder of the Independent Theater in London issues one of his annual summaries of his periodical dramatic criticism. He calls for creation of a repertory theater. He gives much attention to acting and to Continental drama.

82 Grimsted, David. *Melodrama Unveiled: American Theatre and Culture, 1800–1850*. Chicago: University of Chicago Press, 1968. Grimsted shows the important role played by melodrama in the formation of American culture.

83 Grossvogel, David I. *The Blasphemers*. Ithaca, N.Y.: Cornell University Press, 1962. Grossvogel underlines the weaknesses of Absurdist drama without doing justice to its strengths. He ignores both its innovative dramatic technique and its bold, if indirect, call for social reform.

84 ———. *The Self-conscious Stage in Modern French Drama*. New York: Columbia University Press, 1958. In analyzing modern French and Belgian drama, Grossvogel argues that each sensitive playgoer is as much a participant in the play as the author, actor, or director, and that the success of the play depends ultimately upon the playgoer.

85 Grotowski, Jerzy. *Towards a Poor Theater*. London: Methuen, 1969. Grotowski focuses upon the theater's close relationship

between actor and spectator, aiming to get the spectator to confront his complexes emanating from the collective unconscious. Since it cannot be as lavish as motion pictures or television, the theater should turn its relatively "poor" status into a strength, by building an extraordinary bridge of closeness between actor and spectator.

86 Hall, Vernon, Jr. *Renaissance Literary Criticism*. New York: Columbia University Press, 1945. Hall discusses theories of the drama in Renaissance England, France and Italy. He relates dramatic theory to its background in intellectual history. Some of his topics are the fight for the vernacular, scorn for the people, and the writer and his purpose.

87 Halliday, F.E. *Shakespeare and His Critics*. Rev. ed. London: Duckworth, 1958. This is a good discussion of Shakespeare's critics, with excerpts quoting reviews on specific plays. Unfortunately some of the excerpts are not translated, and the index is rather confusing.

88 Hamilton, Clayton. *The Theory of the Theatre, and Other Principles of Dramatic Criticism*. Rev. ed. New York: Octagon Books, 1976. Hamilton stresses action over dialogue in this handbook of practical stagecraft. His overstress on the importance of the audience led to his formulating dramatic principles that are either hackneyed or shallow.

89 Hardison, O.B. Jr., ed. *English Literary Criticism: The Renaissance*. New York: Appleton-Century-Crofts, 1963. This collection includes such works as Stephen Gosson's *School of Abuse*, Thomas Heywood's *An Apology for Actors*, and Ben Jonson's *Timber, or Discoveries*. Hardison shows the great influence of Italian critics upon English dramatists and critics.

90 Hartnoll, Phyllis, ed. *The Oxford Companion to the Theatre*. 3rd ed. London: Oxford University Press, 1967. This is a useful compendium of articles on topics from Henry Abbey to Carl Zuckmayer. A brief bibliography on dramatic criticism is included, as well as a rich collection of photographs illustrating plays and theatrical effects.

91 Havemeyer, Loomis. *Drama of Savage Peoples as Revealed in Their Rites*. New York: Haskell, 1969. Reprint of 1916 edition. This book shows the importance of drama in the everyday life of non-literate peoples.

92 Hayman, Ronald. *Theatre and Anti-Theatre: New Movements since Beckett*. New York: Oxford University Press, 1979.

Hayman gives a sympathetic account of the purposes and achievements of Absurdist drama.

93 Hazlitt, William. *Hazlitt on Theatre.* Edited by William Archer and Robert Lowe. Westport, Conn.: Hyperion Conn, 1979. Though unsystematic, Hazlitt's comments on plays often give the reader a sense of discovery. He felt that it was hard to write modern comedy because the universal human foibles which are comedy's true subject have been often well lampooned in previous comedy.

94 Heitner, Robert R. *German Tragedy in the Age of Enlightenment.* Berkeley: University of California Press, 1963. Although this work primarily studies the tragedies written in the period from 1724 to 1768, there is much discussion of dramatic theory and criticism. An excellent bibliography on 18th century German drama is presented.

95 Herrick, Marvin T. *Comic Theory in the Sixteenth Century.* Urbana: University of Illinois Press, 1964. Herrick deals with various theories of the risible, and shows the importance of many commentators of Terence. He gives detailed consideration to concepts of comic plot and comic character.

96 _____. *The Poetics of Aristotle in England.* New Haven: Yale University Press, 1930. Herrick shows the evolution of understanding of Aristotle's terms from the Middle Ages to the beginning of this century. He illustrates that every great English critic was influenced by the *Poetics* in some way.

97 Hobson, Harold. *The French Theatre of Today.* New York: Arno, 1953. Hobson has especially good chapters on Anouilh, Henry de Montherlant, Armand Salacrou, and Sartre.

98 Hocking, Elton. *Ferdinand Bruentière: The Evolution of a Critic.* Madison: University of Wisconsin Press, 1936. Hocking shows how Darwin's theory of evolution affected Brunetière's dramatic views.

99 Horace. *The Art of Poetry.* In *The Complete Works of Horace,* edited by Casper J. Kraemer, Jr.; translated by Edward Henry Blakeney. New York: Modern Library, 1936. Quintus Horatius Flaccus was the most important Roman literary critic. *The Art of Poetry* is so brilliantly phrased that many of its lines have become commonplaces of criticism. His stress on decorum gave the critical dicta of Horace a frigidity when later interpreters made a critical dictator out of one who aspired to be merely a guide.

100 Hughes, Leo. *A Century of English Farce*. Princeton, N.J.: Princeton University Press, 1950. Hughes provides a well-documented study of London farces from 1750 to 1850.

101 Hunningher, Benjamin. *The Origin of the Theater*. The Hague: Martinus Nijhoff, 1955. Hunningher sees the origin of the modern theater not so much in medieval church drama as in the comic interludes of that drama, and in the secularization of forms of the church drama.

102 Hunt, Leigh. *Leigh Hunt's Dramatic Criticism, 1808-1831*. Edited by Lawrence H. Houtchens and Carolyn W. Houtchens. New York: Columbia University Press, 1949. This is a representative selection of Hunt's periodical criticism. It includes an appendix on Hunt's reaction to William Hazlitt's *Characters of Shakespeare's Plays*.

103 Hyde, Mary C. *Playwriting for Elizabethans*. New York: Columbia University Press, 1949. Hyde includes material on Horace and Lope de Vega as well as on English dramatists.

104 Ionesco, Eugène. *Notes and Counter Notes*. New York: Grove Press, 1964. One of its leading playwrights demonstrates that the absurd conditions of modern life underly Absurdist drama.

105 Jelagin, Juri. *Taming of the Arts*. New York: Dutton, 1951. Jelagin describes censorship curbs used by Soviet political leaders. He gives a detailed account of Vsevolod Meyerhold's courageous protest against socialist realism in the Soviet theater.

106 Johnson, Samuel. *The Critical Opinions of Samuel Johnson*. Edited by Joseph E. Brown. New York: Russell and Russell, 1961. This work has the opinions listed by topic headings. Johnson's comments on criticism, drama, and on specific dramatists are thus readily found.

107 Jonson, Ben. *Ben Jonson: Selected Works*. Edited by Harry Levin. New York: Random House, 1938. Joel Spingarn calls Jonson "the first Englishman with the critical temper." Possessed with common sense, great learning, fearlessness, and a penetrating insight, Jonson brought more natural ability to the office of critic than virtually anyone before him or since. Included here is some of his most important criticism, taken from his plays and from *Timber* and *Conversations with William Drummond of Hawthornden*.

108 Jourdain, Eleanor. *The Drama in Europe in Theory and*

Practice. New York: Haskell, 1972. Reprint of 1924 edition. This is a brief study of the influence of theory upon the development of stagecraft. It relates specific plays and dramatists to the broader background of ideas in which they flourished.

109 Kauffmann, Stanley and Bruce Henstell, eds. *American Film Criticism.* Westport, Conn.: Greenwood, 1979. This is a useful collection of film reviews from Edison's Vitascope in 1896 until *Citizen Kane* in 1941. Although most of the articles concern specific films, some of them deal with general criticism of motion pictures as an art form.

110 Kerr, Walter. *Pieces at Eight.* New York: Simon and Schuster, 1957. Kerr looks at total theater — plays, playwrights, actors, directors, and the box-office. He shows a sensitive and an informed taste in making critical judgments.

111 Kitto, H.D.F. *Poiesis: Structure and Thought.* Berkeley: University of California Press, 1966. A distinguished scholar endeavors to lay a solid basis for criticism. In analyzing the structure of tragedy, he gives chief attention to the works of Aeschylus and Sophocles.

112 Klein, David. *Elizabethan Dramatists as Critics.* New York: Philosophical Library, 1963. Organized by topics, this book gives brief quotations from the dramatists. Shakespeare and Ben Jonson are given special consideration.

113 Kracauer, Siegfried. *From Caligari to Hitler.* Princeton, N.J.: Princeton University Press, 1947. This is a psychological history of early German cinema. Kracauer shows how German movies reflected deep psychological trends that led to the Nazi take-over. The book has illustrations from the motion pictures under discussion.

114 Krook, Dorothea. *Elements of Tragedy.* New Haven, Conn.: Yale University Press, 1969. The four elements of tragedy, Krook says, are the act of shame, the suffering, knowledge, and affirmation. The act of shame must be one that anyone could commit. The suffering must be intense, fatal, and conscious. Not necessarily self-insight, the knowledge might be perceived more by the audience than by the protagonist. The affirmation is Aristotelian catharsis — our faith in mankind is not undermined but fortified.

115 Krutch, Joseph Wood. *The Modern Temper.* New York: Harcourt Brace, 1956. Longtime drama critic for *The Nation*,

Krutch here bewails the loss of "the tragic vision," which alone can put meaning and purpose into life. Alienated from the universe by modern thought, modern man can find only in his pursuit of knowledge the affirmation his soul requires, says Krutch.

116 Lamb, Charles. *Lamb's Criticism*. Edited by E.M. Tillyard. Cambridge, England: Cambridge University Press, 1923. This brief collection is well selected to illustrate the range of Lamb's critical writings. Tillyard's introduction weighs Lamb's strengths and weaknesses as a critic.

117 Lancaster, H.C. *The French Tragicomedy*. Staten Island, N.Y.: Gordian Press, 1966. Reprint of 1907 edition. Lancaster shows how this form, in its origin and development from 1552 to 1628, provided a striking contrast to neoclassical theories of drama as they were being formulated in France during this period.

118 _____. *A History of French Dramatic Literature in the 17th Century*. 9 vols. Staten Island, N.Y.: Gordian Press, 1966. An exhaustive account of French dramatists and plays from 1610 to 1700, Lancaster covers from the pre-classical period through Racine.

119 Leites, Nathan and Martha Wolfenstein. *Movies: A Psychological Study*. Glencoe, Ill.: The Free Press, 1950. This book contains interesting analyses of many movies from a psychological viewpoint. It shows changing American tastes concerning such things as morals, values, beauty, and sex.

120 Lessing, Gotthold. *Hamburg Dramaturgy*. New York: Dover, n.d. Lessing's broad scholarship gave him a good base to attack Racine and especially Corneille for their false adherence to neoclassical standards. Nevertheless he praised Molière and Diderot for their honesty and their art. He believed that tragedy's pity and fear should be translated into altruistic action by the playgoer.

121 Lever, Katherine. *The Art of Greek Comedy*. London: Methuen, 1956. Lever traces the rise of Greek comedy, from its beginnings in Dionysian rites through the Old Comedy of Aristophanes to the New Comedy of Menander. She gives incisive analysis of each type of comedy.

122 Levin, Richard, ed. *Tragedy: Plays, Theory, and Criticism*. New York: Harcourt Brace & World, 1960. Theories of tragedy included in this work are by Aristotle, Andrew C.

Bradley, David Hume, Joseph Wood Krutch, Arthur Miller, and Richard B. Sewall. Among the critics quoted are C.M. Bowra, Cleanth Brooks, Francis Fergusson, Robert B. Heilman, H.L. Mencken, and George Bernard Shaw.

123 Lindgren, Ernest. *The Art of the Film.* New York: Macmillan, 1963. This basic book on film technique has good illustrations and a useful glossary of film terms.

124 Lindsay, Vachel. *The Art of the Moving Picture.* New York: Liveright, 1970. First published in 1915, this was America's first book of esthetic film criticism. It was used in many early college film classes. It is surprising how many of its insights remain valid today.

125 Littlewood, Sam R. *The Art of Dramatic Criticism.* London: Pitman, 1952. Although he gives attention to every period, Littlewood is especially good on nineteenth century English dramatic criticism. He himself was a periodical drama critic in London for over forty years.

126 Loftis, John, ed. *Restoration Drama.* London: Oxford University Press, 1966. This collection of eighteen modern critical essays has an introduction which contains an excellent summary of the critical issues concerning Restoration drama.

127 Lounsbury, Thomas R. *Shakespeare and Voltaire.* New York: Benjamin Blom, 1968. Lounsbury gives not only a detailed chronological account of Voltaire's criticism of Shakespeare but also relates that criticism to its background in both England and France.

128 Lumley, Frederick. *New Trends in 20th Century Drama.* London: Barries and Rockliff, 1967. In his attack on Absurdist drama, Lumley shows little understanding of its goals. He misses the theatricality of Absurdism's anti-theater.

129 Mantzius, Karl. *A History of Theatrical Art in Ancient and Modern Times.* 6 vols. London: Duckworth, 1903-21. Mantzius includes material on the Oriental theater, Shakespearian criticism, and is especially rich on acting. Illustrations and indexes make the work very usable. The final volume ends with the Romantic period.

130 Marshall, Norman. *The Other Theatre.* London: John Lehmann, 1948. Marshall gives a personal account of the experimental theater in England between World War I and World War II.

131 Matlaw, Ralph E., ed. *Belinsky, Chernyshevsky, and*

Dobrolyubov: Selected Criticism. New York: Dutton, 1962. This book consists of standard critical works by three leading Russian critics. All three stress the social function of criticism, in opposition to the pietism, mysticism, and nationalism of Slavophile writers and critics.

132 Matthews, Brander. *A Study of the Drama.* Boston: Houghton Mifflin, 1910. Matthews focuses upon the art of writing a play, particularly as it is affected by audience considerations. He includes, however, material on acting, dramatic conventions, poetry in the theater, and dramatic criticism.

133 Meyerhold, Vsevolod. *Meyerhold on Theatre.* Edited and translated by Edward Braun. London: Methuen, 1968. The great Soviet director explains his approach, showing his agreement and differences with the Stanislavsky technique.

134 Miller, Tice L. *Bohemians and Critics: American Theatre Criticism in the Nineteenth Century.* Metuchen, N.J.: Scarecrow Press, 1981. Although chiefly an account of the criticism of Henry Clapp, Jr., Stephen Ryder Fiske, Andrew C. Wheeler, Edward G.P. Wilkins, and William Winter, this book has other excellent material on the nineteenth century American theater. The footnotes and bibliography are useful to the serious student.

135 Mirsky, D.S. *A History of Russian Literature.* Edited by Francis J. Whitfield. New York: Knopf, 1949. This standard history contains much useful material on Russian drama and theater.

136 Montague, Charles E. *Dramatic Values.* 2nd ed. London: Methuen, 1911. A writer of fiction, Montague served as drama critic for the *Manchester Guardian.* In this work he gives much attention to plot, including a discussion of good and bad subjects for play plots.

137 Moses, Montrose J., and John Mason Brown, eds. *The American Theatre as Seen by Its Critics, 1752-1934.* New York: Cooper Square Publishers, 1967. This book is an anthology of the writings of New York newspaper critics, chosen for the typical insights they gave concerning the theater of their time. The appendix gives biographical sketches of actors, playwrights, and critics for the period covered by the book.

138 Moulton, Richard G. *The Ancient Classical Drama.* 2nd rev. ed. New York: Russell and Russell, 1968. Reprint of 1898

edition. Moulton provides a detailed analysis of the development of Greek and Roman drama. The appendix contains a critique of classical plays using classical principles of dramatic criticism.

139 _____. *Shakespeare as a Dramatic Artist.* Oxford: Clarendon Press, 1885. Moulton tried to establish dramatic criticism on a scientific basis by relating it to historical authenticity and to inductive logic. In chapter 11 he studies dramatic criticism as an inductive science.

140 Murray, Edward. *The Cinematic Imagination.* New York: Frederick Ungar, 1972. This book studies the impact of films upon the theater. It also describes how the novel has influenced cinema and how cinema has influenced the novel.

141 _____. *Nine American Film Critics.* New York: Frederick Ungar, 1975. Murray evaluates the film criticism of James Agee, Pauline Kael, Stanley Kauffmann, Dwight Macdonald, Andrew Sarris, John Simon, Parker Tyler, Robert Warshow, and Vernon Young. The appendix has an interesting summary of film directors' reactions to film critics.

142 Murray, Gilbert. *Aeschylus, Creator of Tragedy.* Westport, Conn.: Greenwood, 1978. Murray discusses the stage technique, the language, and the ideas of the first great writer of tragedy. He includes an appendix consisting of a scenario of *Agamemnon*.

143 _____. *Euripides and His Age.* New York: Henry Holt, 1913. After showing how the plays of Euripides reflect changes in Greek thought, the famous classical scholar devotes two chapters to an analysis of the dramatic art expressed in the plays.

144 Nicoll, Allardyce. *Film and Theatre.* New York: Crowell, 1936. Nicoll argues that camera close-ups require that cinema characters be more highly individualized than their stage counterparts, and that only some type of poetic diction, even Maxwell Anderson's in *Winterset*, can give films the depth and staying power that they, at their best, deserve.

145 _____. *Masks, Mimes and Miracles.* New York: Cooper Square Publishers, 1963. This work is excellent on medieval religious drama, on mimes, and on *commedia dell'arte*. It is interestingly written and profusely illustrated.

146 _____. *The Theatre and Dramatic Theory.* London: George Harrap, 1962. Nicoll believes that drama is peculiarly sensitive

to the impact of critical theory upon it. He also feels that middle-class drama, built according to the precepts of Beaumarchais, Denis Diderot, and Hermann Hettner, has become the prevailing mode in the theater, despite the fact that it fails to satisfy the deep needs of the audience as traditional tragedy and comedy have done. His final chapter is a brief history of dramatic criticism.

147 _____. *The Theory of Drama*. New York: Benjamin Blom, 1966. This book deals much more with drama than with dramatic criticism. In the definition and illustration of specific dramatic genres, however, much criticism, especially of a historical nature, is presented.

148 Nietzsche, Friedrich. *The Birth of Tragedy and The Case of Wagner*. Translated by Walter Kaufmann. New York: Vintage Books, 1967. After praising Richard Wagner for his rebirth of Greek tragedy, Nietzsche reconsiders and accuses Wagner of undisciplined neurotic romanticism.

149 Nitze, William A. and E. Preston Dargan. *A History of French Literature*. 3rd ed. New York: Henry Holt, 1938. This work includes much on drama and dramatic criticism. The extensive bibliography is broken down into the same historical periods as the book itself.

150 Norwood, Gilbert. *The Art of Terence*. New York: Russell and Russell, 1965. Norwood analyzes not only the plays of Terence but Roman comedy generally.

151 Olson, Elder. *Tragedy and the Theory of Drama*. Detroit: Wayne State University Press, 1961. Olson gives a dramatist's viewpoint of plot, incident, character, stage representation, and dialogue. The last four chapters analyze plays from Aeschylus to T.S. Eliot.

152 Phelps, William Lyon. *The Twentieth Century Theatre*. Port Washington, N.Y.: Kennikat Press, 1968. Reprint of 1918 edition. The Yale professor discusses dramatic criticism, acting, the Drama League, and other topics.

153 Phillips, Henry. *The Theatre and Its Critics in Seventeenth-Century France*. New York: Oxford University Press, 1980. This book is especially valuable for its moral and religious criticism of the drama of the period.

154 Pirandello, Luigi. *Naked Masks*. Edited and translated by Eric Bentley. New York: Dutton, 1952. Pirandello says that we all play behind masks, not knowing our true selves. The concern

in his drama and criticism for identity (and its corollary, the multiple personality) paralleled the rise of modern subjective psychology. His striking discard of the "well made" plot to show that characters can exist outside of their play has been vastly influential in modern drama.

155 Pollard, Percival. *Masks and Minstrels of New Germany*. Boston: John W. Luce, 1911. The chief value of this book is its portrayal of the German popular theater in the period around 1900. There is no index or bibliography.

156 Pudovkin, Vsevolod I. *Film Technique and Film Acting*. Edited and translated by Ivor Montagu. New York: Grove Press, 1960. Pudovkin synthesized the contributions of Griffith, Eisenstein, and Stanislavsky to produce many excellent films, which he describes in this work.

157 Ralli, Augustus. *A History of Shakespearian Criticism*. 2 vols. New York: Humanities Press, 1965. This is a detailed account, chronological and by country, of Shakespearian criticism from 1598 to 1925. Although not very readable, it is objective and comprehensive.

158 Reiter, Seymour. *World Theater: The Structure and Meaning of Drama*. New York: Horizon Press, 1973. Reiter's broad scope includes material on Oriental and Sanskrit drama. He points out the submerged plot structure of many modern plays, including Beckett's *Waiting for Godot*.

159 Rennert, Hugo A. *The Spanish Stage in the Time of Lope de Vega*. New York: Hispanic Society of America, 1909. This extensive work deals with autos, comedias, and other dramatic works of the period. A comprehensive list of biographies of Spanish actors from 1560 to 1680 is presented.

160 Ridgeway, William. *The Drama and Dramatic Dances of Non-European Races*. New York: Arno, 1963. Ridgeway shows the dramatic elements of ritualistic dances in ancient Egypt, Java, India, Japan, and Polynesia. He relates these rites to the origin of tragedy in Greece. In an appendix he deals with the origin of Greek comedy. The book's illustrations and photographs make it very readable.

161 _____. *The Origin of Tragedy*. New York: Benjamin Blom, 1966. Reprint of 1910 edition. Using an anthropological approach, Ridgeway traces the beginnings of tragedy in Asiatic lands and in early Greece. He avers that tragedy arose not from the cult of a particular deity, but from beliefs

concerning the dead which are universal throughout human society.

162 Robertson, J.G. *Lessing's Dramatic Theory*. New York: Benjamin Blom, 1965. Admitting that many of Lessing's contributions are overrated and outdated, Robertson asserts that *Hamburg Dramaturgy* was nonetheless the greatest treatise on dramatic theory written in the eighteenth century. Lessing's chief contributions are seen to be esthetic theory and an addendum to the theory of tragedy.

163 Russell, Trusten W. *Voltaire, Dryden, and Heroic Tragedy*. New York: AMS Press, 1966. Although begun as a study of Dryden's influence upon Voltaire, this work developed into a study of the effect of epic theory upon Voltaire's drama and criticism. Included are chapters on French and English dramatic theory and criticism in the seventeenth and eighteenth centuries. Many French passages are not translated.

164 Saintsbury, George. *A History of Criticism and Literary Taste in Europe*. 3 vols. Edinburgh: Blackwood, 1900. Saintsbury's three volumes are devoted to classical, Renaissance, and post-Renaissance literary and dramatic criticism. Although dated, the approach is sensible and well documented.

165 Sandys, John Edwin. *A History of Classical Scholarship*. 3 vols. New York: Hafner Pub. Co., 1958. Sandys studies classical scholarship from the sixth century B.C. until the nineteenth century. Although his range is extensive, including, for example, discussion of Scandinavian and Dutch scholars, his treatment of individual works lacks substance and depth.

166 Sarcey, Francisque. *A Theory of the Theater*. Translated by Hatcher H. Hughes. New York: Columbia University Press, 1916. Sarcey has been called "the Aristotle of the 'well made' play." A drama critic for forty years, he made the audience the key factor in determining a play's worth. As public taste shifted away from the classics, Sarcey condoned the shift. He placed great stress upon the *scène à faire*, the central plot situation which he felt the dramatist was obliged to represent on the stage.

167 Sayler, Oliver M. *Inside the Moscow Art Theatre*. New York: Brentano, 1925. Saylor analyzes the technique that brought this theater world fame.

168 Schlegel, August Wilhelm von. *Lectures on Dramatic Art and Literature*. 2nd ed. Translated by John Black. London: Bohn

Library, 1914. In these essays Schlegel introduces Shakespeare and Spanish drama into Germany. He writes perceptively about drama as an art form. These essays influenced Coleridge and other English critics.

169 Schorer, Mark, Josephine Miles, and Gordon McKenzie, eds. *Criticism*. New York: Harcourt Brace & World, 1958. This anthology of criticism from Aristotle to Francis Fergusson contains many of the best critics, new and old. The book is organized to answer three questions about literature and drama: where does art come from, how does it become what it is, and what does it accomplish?

170 Schwab, Arnold T. *James Gibbon Huneker: Critic of the Seven Arts*. Stanford, Calif.: Stanford University Press, 1965. Schwab gives an interesting study of the writings of an important eclectic critic.

171 Segal, Erich, ed. *Euripides: A Collection of Critical Essays*. Englewood Cliffs, N.J.: Prentice-Hall, 1968. Articles in this collection deal with ideas in the plays of Euripides, the relation of tragedy to religion, and analysis of specific plays. Segal boldly asserts that the greatest contemporary admirer of Euripides was Aristophanes, since he imitated in comic form what Euripides was brave enough to put into serious form.

172 Senelick, Laurence, editor and translator. *Russian Dramatic Theory from Pushkin to the Symbolists*. Austin: University of Texas Press, 1981. Senelick's comprehensive anthology is the best in the field for the period it covers.

173 Shaw, George Bernard. *Dramatic Opinions and Essays*. New York: Brentano, 1913. As a critic, Shaw is always readable and often perceptive. As a dramatist, he often ignored his own criticism. Evaluating Sheridan, Shaw says that the test of a great play is whether it is grounded in universal human nature. Evaluating Shakespeare, Shaw impertinently but properly puts his finger on the Bard's weaknesses – and then reluctantly confesses Shakespeare's great art.

174 Sherbo, Arthur. *English Sentimental Comedy*. East Lansing: Michigan State University Press, 1957. Unsympathetic towards sentimental comedy, Sherbo seeks to derive a definition of the type by examining the plays and contemporary comments on them.

175 Sidney, Philip. *Apology for Poetry*. Edited by Geoffrey Shepherd. New York: Barnes & Noble, 1965. Sidney's critical

position is largely that of the Italian commentators on Aristotle—Minturno, Scaliger, and Castelvetro. Sidney preferred Roman dramatists to the Greek masters. He first introduced Aristotle to English literature on a wide scale, and he gave a high place to the Three Unities. Despite its weaknesses, this impassioned defence of drama and poetry gave both forms great support when they were under attack.

176 Smallwood, Clyde G. *Elements of the Existentialist Philosophy in the Theatre of the Absurd.* Dubuque, Iowa: William C. Brown, 1966. Smallwood describes four existentialist concepts that are found in Absurdist drama: man is what he makes of himself; his constant instability leads man to anguish; reason is impotent to make sense out of the human condition; and man has within himself the power to be, but only through the "bounding leap" of a supreme effort.

177 Smith, David Nichol, ed. *Shakespeare Criticism.* London: Oxford University Press, 1916. This is a good introduction to the major Shakespearian critics, giving excerpts from their works.

178 Smith, G. Gregory, ed. *Elizabethan Critical Essays.* 2 vols. London: Oxford University Press, 1937. This comprehensive collection includes George Whetstone's Dedication to *Promos and Cassandra.* The book has a good introduction and index, and is well annotated.

179 Smith, James Harry, and Edd W. Parks, eds. *The Great Critics.* Rev. ed. New York: Norton, 1939. With excerpts of critics from Plato to Walter Pater, this collection features major figures such as Aristotle, Horace, Ben Jonson, Dryden, Lessing, and Coleridge. Italian Renaissance critics are well represented. The book has a very usable index.

180 Smith, Winifred. *The Commedia dell'Arte.* New York: Columbia University Press, 1912. This is a readable and scholarly account of the origin and development of this Italian theater of improvisation. A scenario of typical plots is presented, as well as a comprehensive bibliography. There is also an appendix on the influence of Italian comedy in England.

181 Spingarn, Joel E. *Creative Criticism.* Westport, Conn.: Hyperion Conn, 1979. There is something refreshing about Spingarn's rejection of traditional rules, genres, moral judgments, and sociological evaluations—something valuable in his insistence, following Benedetto Croce, that an esthetic

work should be judged solely by a sensitive critic's creative identification with the work itself. The chapter on "Dramatic Criticism" constitutes a good brief history of the subject.

182 _____. *Critical Essays of the Seventeenth Century*. 3 vols. London: Oxford University Press, 1908-09. This collection of writings by English critics includes minor as well as major figures. Volume II, with material from William Davenant, Richard Flecknoe, Robert Howard, and Thomas Rymer, is particularly rich in dramatic criticism.

183 _____. *A History of Literary Criticism in the Renaissance*. 2nd ed. New York: Columbia University Press, 1908. Spingarn shows the growth of key concepts in Renaissance dramatic criticism in England, France, and Italy. He reveals how neoclassicism developed as a French version of the critical positions laid down by the Italian commentators on Aristotle.

184 Stack, R.H. *Russian Literary Criticism, A Short History*. Syracuse, N.Y.: Syracuse University Press, 1974. Although not confined to drama, this book includes some valuable material on Russian dramatic criticism. Included are studies of Russian formalism, futurism, realism, and symbolism.

185 Stanislavksy, Konstantin. *My Life in Art*. Boston: Little, Brown, 1924. The noted actor and director describes his method of achieving artistic unity in a play.

186 Steiner, George. *The Death of Tragedy*. Lawrence, Maine: Merrimack Book Service 1961. Steiner says that tragedy assumes either a malevolent God or a mocking blind fate. Since both assumptions are alien to Christianity and Marxism, the two reigning intellectual concepts, there can be no modern tragedy, he feels. The lack of poetry in modern drama is a further limiting factor in the development of contemporary tragedy.

187 Styan, J.L. *The Dark Comedy: The Development of Modern Comic Tragedy*. 2nd ed. Cambridge, England: Cambridge University Press, 1968. Styan sees Absurdist drama as didactic theater, determined more to educate than to entertain the public. Since modern life provides laughter only through tears, this drama strives for a stage reconciliation of the forces of comedy and tragedy.

188 _____. *Modern Drama in Theory and Practice*. 3 vols. Cambridge, England: Cambridge University Press, 1981. Styan covers the dramatic movements of realism, naturalism,

symbolism, surrealism, the Absurd, expressionism, and Epic Theater. His comprehensive volumes have good bibliographies, as well as charts relating events outside the theater to happenings inside the theater.

189 Tave, Stuart M. *The Amiable Humorist*. Chicago: University of Chicago Press, 1960. Tave summarizes comic theory and criticism of the eighteenth and early nineteenth centuries.

190 Thompson, Alan Reynolds. *The Anatomy of Drama*. 2nd ed. Berkeley: University of California Press, 1946. A professor at Berkeley, Thompson gives extensive treatment to such plot matters as surprise, irony, and suspense. He also studies the contrast between melodrama and tragedy.

191 Thorndike, Ashley H. *English Comedy*. New York: Macmillan, 1929. Thorndike finds it amusing that comedy has such unlikely bedfellows: tragedy, pity, morality, love, sentimentality. He gives a good introduction to the field of comedy.

192 Towse, John Rankin. *Sixty Years of the Theater*. New York: Funk & Wagnalls, 1916. Towse recounts the highlights of his life as a newspaper drama critic in New York City.

193 Tydeman, William. *The Theatre in the Middle Ages*. Cambridge, England: Cambridge University Press, 1978. Tydeman describes stage conditions in Britain, France, Germany, and Spain from 800 to 1576. He shows that the assumption of a steady evolution of liturgical drama throughout this period, as postulated by E.K. Chambers and Karl Young, probably represents an oversimplification, since there were many false starts, blind alleys, and uncharted influences.

194 Tynan, Kenneth. *Curtains*. New York: Atheneum, 1961. These excerpts from the periodical criticism of a leading British critic illustrate his change in taste, from a preference of plays of shock and fantasy to those conveying a political or social message.

195 Valency, Maurice. *The End of the World: An Introduction to Contemporary Drama*. London: Oxford University Press, 1980. Valency interprets modern dramatists as symbolically portraying the chaos, savagery, and inhumanity of a world about to destroy itself.

196 Van Thal, Herbert, ed. *James Agate: An Anthology*. New York: Hill & Wang, 1961. This is a collection of periodical criticism by the man who served as critic for the *Manchester Guardian*, *Saturday Review*, and the *Times* (London). Agate

helped introduce British theatergoers to many Continental playwrights.

197 Vega, Lope de. *The New Art of Writing Plays in This Age.* Translated by William T. Brewster. New York: Columbia University Press, 1914. "Why bore the audience with the classics?" asks Lope. Instead, give them suspense and mystery, let women wear men's clothes, and mix comedy and tragedy, as life does. Lope's practical advice, based on the experience of writing over 2000 plays, was a healthy antidote to the sycophantic worship of Aristotle's views during the Renaissance and eighteenth century.

198 Vos, Nelvin. *The Drama of Comedy: Victim and Victor.* Richmond, VA.: John Knox Press, 1966. Vos analyzes the comic victor in Thornton Wilder's plays, the comic victim in Ionesco's plays, and the comic victim-victor in Christopher Fry's plays. He says: "My argument is that the structure of dramatic comedy and the structure of Christ's passionate action bear an analogical relation to each other and that a study of these two may deepen our perception of the essential meaning of comedy and of the Christian account of human existence."

199 _____. *The Great Pendulum of Becoming.* Grand Rapids, Mich.: Eerdmans, 1980. Vos states that due to its communal character, drama reflects an era's moral and religious character better than any other art form. He interprets the chaos, bestiality, and impotence depicted in modern drama as signs of the restlessness and meaninglessness of modern man's outlook on the universe.

200 Ward, A.C., ed. *Specimens of English Dramatic Criticism, 17th to the 20th Centuries.* London: Oxford University Press, 1945. This book has excerpts from British critics from Samuel Pepys to Alan Dent. The lengthy descriptive index makes the work very usable.

201 Weiss, Samuel A., ed. *Drama in the Modern World: Plays and Essays.* New York: D.C. Heath, 1964. Weiss presents fourteen modern plays, from Ibsen to Beckett, with critical essays on each play. Critics include Eric Bentley, Maxim Gorky, Joseph Wood Krutch, Pirandello, Strindberg, John M. Synge, Kenneth Tynan, and Yeats.

202 Wellek, René. *A History of Modern Criticism.* 5 vols. New Haven, Conn.: Yale University Press, 1955-65. Wellek

carefully studies criticism from neoclassicism to contemporary. Much of his work relates to drama and dramatic criticism. His footnotes are helpful, albeit frequently in a foreign tongue.

203 Wellwarth, George. *The Theater of Protest and Paradox*. Rev. ed. New York: New York University Press, 1971. Wellwarth believes that much modern drama uses the shock of paradox as a technique to call attention to its protest against the inhumanity of modern life.

204 West, James. *Russian Symbolism*. London: Methuen, 1970. This is a good study of the Russian symbolist Vyacheslav Ivanov and of the esthetics of the Russian symbolists, such as Andrey Bely, Alexander Blok, Valery Bryusov, and Fyodor Sologub. Many of the footnotes and bibliography entries are in Russian.

205 Whitman, Cedric H. *Aristophanes and the Comic Hero*. Cambridge, Mass.: Harvard University Press, 1964. Whitman makes a strong case for the consideration of the Old Comedy of Aristophanes as fundamentally fantasy rather than satire. He sees Old Comedy as a heroic form, in which the hero usually succeeds in asserting the dethronement of limits, of reason, or of the gods themselves.

206 Wickham, Glynne. *The Medieval Theatre*. New York: St. Martin's Press, 1974. This book shows the influences of religion, recreation, and commerce upon the development of European drama between the tenth and sixteenth centuries. Drawings and photographs make the book interesting and informative.

207 Wiles, Timothy J. *The Theater Event: Modern Theories of Performance*. Chicago: University of Chicago Press, 1980. Wiles calls the creative interaction of literary text, actor's part, and spectator participation "the theater event." He describes three modern acting schools: Stanislavsky and his catharsis of characters; Brecht and his catharsis of incident; and Artaud and Grotowski with their catharsis of actor and audience.

208 Wilson, Garff B. *Three Hundred Years of American Drama and Theatre*. Englewood Cliffs, N.J.: Prentice-Hall, 1973. This illustrated survey has more material on theater than on drama and criticism. There is extensive criticism, however, of American acting.

209 Winter, William. *Old Friends*. New York: Moffat, Yard, 1914.

America's most noted nineteenth century periodical dramatic critic recalls outstanding theatrical experiences.

210 _____. *Shakespeare on the Stage, Second Series*. New York: Moffat, Yard and Company, 1915. Winter gives detailed information on various plays, including sources, early performances, leading actors, and his own criticism of American performances. The book has a good index and numerous illustrations.

211 Witkowski, Georg. *The German Drama of the Nineteenth Century*. Translated by L.E. Horning. New York: Benjamin Blom, 1968. In summarizing the highlights of the drama of the period, Witkowski provides critical analysis in support of his judgments. His final chapter contains a record of the number of performances of German plays during the period 1899-1905.

212 Yarmolinsky, Avraham, ed. *Letters of Anton Chekhov*. New York: Viking Press, 1973. This excellent edition of Chekhov's letters has a useful index with many references to plays, playwrights, and critics.

213 Yeats, William Butler. *Essays and Introductions*. New York: Macmillan, 1961. In this work Yeats provides a good general introduction to his writings, as well as a consideration of the plays of John M. Synge, Japanese drama, and poetic drama.

214 Young, Karl. *The Drama of the Medieval Church*. 2 vols. Oxford: Clarendon Press, 1933. This work provides comprehensive treatment of its subject, with footnotes, bibliography, and appendices on such things as medieval records pertaining to church drama and extracts from comments by reformers (some of which is in Latin).

215 Young, Stark. *The Theatre*. New York: Hill & Wang, 1958. Young shows what art is in all levels of theater—writing, acting, directing, and stagecraft. The test of art in the theater, he says, is not so much that everyone understands the work, as that to those who do its meaning is lofty and significant.

Index to Bibliography

References are to entry numbers.

Abbey, Henry 90
acting 41, 53, 81, 85, 110, 129, 132, 137, 152, 159, 185, 207, 208, 209, 210, 215
Adams, Henry H. 1
Addison, Joseph 1
Aeschylus 111, 142, 151
Agamemnon 142
Agate, James 2, 196
Agee, James 53, 141
Albee, Edward 71
American criticism 3, 4, 17, 31, 34, 38, 44, 46, 48, 49, 57, 58, 60, 63, 66, 67, 69, 71, 75, 82, 83, 84, 88, 110, 114, 115, 121, 132, 134, 137, 151, 152, 158, 167, 170, 171, 174, 176, 181, 190, 191, 192, 198, 199, 203, 207, 208, 209, 215
American drama 4, 59, 71, 75, 82, 208, 209, 210
Anderson, Maxwell 3, 71, 144
Angoff, Charles 4
Anouilh, Jean 97
anti-theater 92, 128
Archer, William 1, 5, 93
Aristophanes 121, 171, 205
Aristotle 6, 13, 39, 40, 47, 49, 96, 114, 122, 166, 169, 175, 179, 183, 197
Arnheim, Rudolf 7
Artaud, Antonin 8, 207
Arvin, Newton C. 9
Atkins, J.W.H. 10, 11, 12, 13
auto 159

Babbitt, Irving 14
Babcock, R.W. 15
Baker, Blanch M. 16
Baker, George Pierce 17
Barnet, Sylvan 18
Bate, Walter J. 19
Bazin, André 20
Beaumarchais, Pierre de 1, 146
Beckett, Samuel 54, 92, 64, 158, 201
Belgian drama 84
Belinsky, Vissarion 131
Bell, A.F.G. 21
Bely, Andrey 204
Benedikt, Michael 22
Bennett, Benjamin 23
Berman, Morton 18
Bernbaum, Ernest 25
Black, John 168
Blades, Joseph D., Jr. 26
Blakeney, Edward H. 99
Block, Haskell M. 27
Blok, Alexander 204
Boileau (Boileau-Despréaux), Nicolas 28, 42
Bowra, C.M. 29, 122
Bradley, Andrew C. 30, 122
Braun, Edward 133
Brecht, Bertolt 34, 207
Brewster, William T. 197
Brieux, Eugène 38
Brockett, Oscar G. 31

Brooks, Cleanth 122
Brown, Edward J. 32
Brown, Ivor 2
Brown, John Mason 137
Brown, Joseph E. 106
Brunetière, Ferdinand 14, 33, 98
Brustein, Robert 34
Bryusov, Valery 204
Burto, William 18
Butcher, S.H. 6

The Cabinet of Dr. Caligari 113
Calderon, George 35
Calderwood, James L. 36
Canby, Vincent 26
Castelvetro, Lodovico 39, 175
Chambers, E.K. 37, 193
Chandler, Frank W. 38
character 30, 34, 35, 95, 102, 151, 154, 207
Charlton, H.B. 39
Chaytor, Henry J. 40
Chekhov, Anton 34, 35, 54, 57, 212
Cheney, Sheldon 41
Chernyshevsky, Nikolai 131
Christ 198
Cibber, Colley 25
cinema *see* motion pictures
Cinthio, Giambattista Giraldi 76
Citizen Kane 109
Clapp, Henry, Jr. 134
Clark, A.F.B. 42
Clark, Barrett H. 43
Cole, Toby 44
Coleridge, Samuel T. 45, 168, 179
comedia 159
comedy 13, 39, 56, 70, 93, 95, 121, 146, 150, 160, 180, 187, 189, 191, 198, 205
comedy, dark 187
comedy, sentimental 25, 174, 191
commedia dell'arte 145, 180
Comtois, M.F. 46
Congreve, William 1
Cooper, Lane 47
Corneille, Pierre 28, 76, 120
Corrigan, Robert W. 48
Crane, Ronald S. 49
Crawford, James P. 50
Crist, Judith 26
Croce, Benedetto 181

Dadaism 22
Dargan, E. Preston 149
Darwin, Charles 98
d'Aubignac, Abbé (François Hédelin) 42
Davenant, William 182
Dean, Leonard F. 51
Deane, C.V. 52
decorum 99
Denby, David 53
Dennis, John 1
Dent, Alan 200
dialogue 34, 35, 86, 88, 142, 144, 151
Diderot, Denis 1, 120, 146
Dilworth, Ernest 28
Dionysus 121
director 48, 53, 59, 61, 110, 133, 141, 185, 215
Dobrolyubov, Nikolai 131
Drama League 152
drama, middle-class 146
dramatic dances of non-European cultures 160
Driver, Tom F. 54
Dryden, John 12, 52, 55, 76, 163, 179
Duckworth, George E. 56
Dukes, Ashley 57
Dukore, Bernard F. 58
Dunlap, William 59
Dunn, Esther C. 60
Dutch critics 165

Eckermann, Johann 77
Edison, Thomas A. 109
Eisenstein, Sergei 61, 156
Eliot, T.S. 151
Emerson, Ralph Waldo 60
Engel, Lehman 63
English criticism 1, 2, 5, 10, 11, 12, 15, 19, 25, 29, 30, 35, 36, 37, 38, 42, 43, 45, 49, 51, 52, 55, 58, 75, 76, 79, 80, 81, 86, 87, 89, 93, 96, 102, 103, 106, 107, 112, 116, 125, 126, 127, 128, 130, 136, 146, 147, 163, 175, 177, 178, 182, 183, 187, 188, 194, 195, 196, 200
English drama 25, 36, 81, 100, 103, 112, 126, 130, 163, 174
Epic Theater 188
Esslin, Martin 64
Euripides 143, 171
Evreinov, Nikolai 65

Index to Bibliography 297

existentialism 176
expressionism 74, 188

Fagin, N. Bryllion 66
fantasy 194, 205
farce 50, 70, 100
Ferguson, Otis 53
Fergusson, Francis 67, 122, 169
film *see* motion pictures
Fiske, Stephen Ryder 134
Flecknoe, Richard 182
Flickinger, R.S. 68
folk drama 37
formalism 184
Fowlie, Wallace 69
Frank, Grace 70
French criticism 14, 22, 42, 43, 49, 52, 76, 86, 98, 127, 149, 153, 163, 166, 183
French drama 22, 69, 70, 84, 97, 117, 118, 149, 153, 163
Frenz, Horst 71
Freytag, Gustav 72
Frisch, Max 27
Fry, Christopher 198
Fujimura, Thomas H. 73
futurism 184

Garten, H.F. 74
Gassner, John 44, 75
Genet, Jean 34
German criticism 45, 49, 58, 72, 74, 76, 78, 94, 120, 162, 168
German drama 23, 24, 72, 74, 94, 155, 211
Gilbert, Allan H. 76
Goethe, Johann von 77
Goldsmith, Oliver 2
Gorchakov, Nikolai 78
Gorky, Maxim 201
Gosson, Stephen 89
Gray, Charles H. 79
Gray, Hugh 20
Greek criticism 13, 43, 49, 58, 76, 138, 165
Greek drama 6, 13, 29, 41, 68, 75, 77, 111, 121, 129, 138, 142, 143, 148, 160, 165, 171, 175
Green, C.C. 80
Green, Paul 71

Grein, J.T. 81
Griffith, D.W. 61, 156
Grimsted, David 82
Grossvogel, David 83, 84
Grotowski, Jerzy 58, 85, 207
Guarini, Giambattista 76

Hall, Vernon, Jr. 86
Halliday, F.E. 87
Hamilton, Clayton 88
Hardison, O.B., Jr. 89
Hartnoll, Phyllis 90
Hathaway, Baxter 1
Hauptmann, Gerhart 38
Havemeyer, Loomis 91
Hayden, Philip M. 33
Hayman, Ronald 92
Hazlitt, William 2, 93, 102
Heilman, Robert B. 122
Heitner, Robert R. 94
Henstell, Bruce 109
hero (protagonist) 3, 205
heroic play 52, 163
Herrick, Marvin T. 95, 96
Hettner, Hermann 146
Heywood, Thomas 89
Hitler, Adolf 113
Hobson, Harold 97
Hocking, Elton 98
Horace 13, 28, 40, 99, 103, 179
Horning, L.E. 211
Houtchens, Carolyn W. 102
Houtchens, Lawrence H. 102
Howard, Robert 182
Hughes, Hatcher H. 166
Hughes, Leo 100
Hume, David 122
Huneker, James G. 170
Hunningher, Benjamin 101
Hunt, Leigh 2, 102
Hyde, Mary C. 103

Ibsen, Henrik 27, 34, 38, 57, 75, 201
imagery 36, 51
impressionism 4
Inge, William 71
Ionesco, Eugène 18, 64, 104, 198
Irish criticism 213
Italian criticism 39, 43, 49, 58, 76, 86, 89, 154, 175, 179, 183

Italian drama 154, 180
Ivanov, Vyacheslav 204

Japanese drama 213
Jelagin, Juri 105
Johnson, Samuel 12, 15, 106
Jonson, Ben 76, 89, 107, 112, 179
Jourdain, Eleanor 108

Kael, Pauline 26, 53, 141
Kauffmann, Stanley 26, 109, 141
Kaufman, Walter 148
Kerr, Walter 63, 110
Kinsley, James 55
Kitto, H.D.F. 111
Klein, David 111
Kracauer, Siegfried 113
Kraemer, Casper J., Jr. 99
Krook, Dorothea 114
Krutch, Joseph Wood 115, 122, 201

Lamb, Charles 2, 116
Lancaster, H.C. 117, 118
language *see* dialogue
Lawson, John Howard 71
Leites, Nathan 119
Lessing, Gotthold 23, 120, 162, 179
Lever, Katherine 121
Levin, Richard 122
Leyda, Jay 61
Lindgren, Ernest 123
Lindsay, Vachel 53, 124
literature 10, 11, 12, 13, 19, 20, 21, 32
Littlewood, Sam R. 125
Loftis, John 126
Lounsbury, Thomas R. 127
Lowe, Robert 93
Lumley, Frederick 128

MacCarthy, Desmond 2
Macdonald, Dwight 141
MacEwan, Elias J. 72
McKenzie, Gordon 169
Maeterlinck, Maurice 38
Mantzius, Karl 129
Marshall, Norman 130

Marxism 130
mask 145, 154, 155
Matlaw, Ralph E. 131
Matthews, Brander 132
medieval drama 10, 37, 70, 101, 145, 193, 206, 214
melodrama 82, 190
Menander 121
Mencken, H.L. 122
Mercier, Sebastian 1
metaphysics 8
Meyerhold, Vsevolod 105, 133
Miles, Josephine 169
Miller, Arthur 71, 122
Miller, Lynn F. 46
Miller, Tice L. 134
mime 145
Minturno (Antonio Sebastiano) 76, 175
Mirsky, Prince D.S. 135
Molière, Jean B.P. 28, 120
monodrama 65
montage 61
Montagu, Ivor 156
Montague, Charles E. 136
Montherlant, Henry de 97
Moscow Art Theater 167
Moses, Montrose J. 137
motion pictures 7, 20, 26, 53, 61, 62, 109, 113, 119, 123, 124, 140, 141, 144, 156
Moulton, Richard G. 138, 139
Murray, Edward 140, 141
Murray, Gilbert 142, 143
mysticism 131

Nathan, George Jean 4, 63
naturalism 74, 188
neoclassicism 1, 11, 12, **23**, 28, 40, 42, 80, 117, 120, 164, 183, 202
Nicoll, Allardyce 145, 146, 147
Nietzsche, Friedrich 23, 148
Nitze, William A. 149
Norwood, Gilbert 150

obligatory scene 5, 166
Olson, Elder 151
O'Neill, Eugene 34, 71
Oriental drama 129, 158

Panofsky, Erwin 53
Parfitt, G.A. 55
Parks, Edd W. 179
Pater, Walter 179
Pepys, Samuel 200
Phelps, William Lyon 152
Phillips, Henry 153
philosophy 20, 54
Pirandello, Luigi 34, 154, 201
Plato 76, 179
Plautus 56
plot 6, 9, 34, 35, 36, 72, 95, 136, 151, 158, 166, 190
plot, catharsis 114, 207
Poe, Edgar Allan 66
poetry 132, 144, 175, 186, 213
Pollard, Percival 155
primitive drama 41, 91
Proletcult 32
Promos and Cassandra 178
psychology 154
Pudovkin, Vsevolod 156
Pushkin, Alexander 172

Racine, Jean 28, 118, 120
Ralli, Augustus 157
realism 61, 184, 188
Reiter, Seymour 158
religion 3, 8, 10, 20, 37, 50, 54, 70, 101, 145, 153, 160, 161, 171, 186, 193, 198, 199, 206, 214
Renaissance 11, 37, 51, 56, 86, 89, 103, 164, 183, 197
Rennert, Hugo A. 159
Richards, Mary Caroline 8
Ridgeway, William 160, 161
Robertson, J.G. 162
Roman criticism 13, 43, 49, 58, 99, 138, 165
Roman drama 56, 129, 138, 150, 165, 175
romanticism 23, 54, 78, 129, 148
Rosenberg, James L. 48
Russell, Trusten W. 163
Russian criticism 43, 58, 65, 78, 105, 131, 133, 135, 172, 184, 185, 212
Russian drama 32, 65, 78, 135, 167, 204, 212
Rymer, Thomas 182

Sainte-Beuve, Charles 14
Saint-Évremond, Charles de 76

Saintsbury, George 164
Salacrou, Armand 97
Sandys, John Edwin 165
Sanskrit drama 158
Sarcey, Francisque 14, 72, 166
Sarris, Andrew 26, 141
Sartre, Jean-Paul 97
Sayler, Oliver M. 167
Scaliger, Julius Caesar 175
Scandinavian critics 165
Schlegel, August von 168
Schnitzler, Arthur 38
Schorer, Mark 169
Schwab, Arnold T. 170
science 20, 47, 139
Scott, Clement 2
Scribe, Eugène 9
Segal, Erich 171
Seldes, Gilbert 53
Senelick, Laurence 172
Sewall, Richard B. 122
Shakespeare, William 12, 15, 30, 36, 45, 51, 55, 60, 87, 102, 112, 127, 129, 139, 157, 168, 173, 177
Shaw, George Bernard 34, 75, 122, 173
Shedd, Robert G. 27
Shepherd, Geoffrey 175
Sherbo, Arthur 174
Sheridan, Richard Brinsley 173
Sidney, Sir Philip 175
Simon, John 26, 53, 141
Slavophiles 131
Smallwood, Clyde 176
Smith, David Nicol 177
Smith, G. Gregory 178
Smith, James H. 179
Smith, Winifred 180
socialist realism 105
Sologub, Fyodor 204
Sophocles 6, 18, 29, 111
Spanish criticism 40, 43, 50, 58, 76, 197
Spanish drama 21, 40, 50, 159, 168, 197
Spingarn, Joel 107, 181, 182, 183
Stack, R.H. 184
stagecraft 16, 41, 59, 90, 108, 129, 167, 185, 188, 208, 215
stage designer 48
Stanislavsky, Konstantin 133, 156, 185, 207
Steele, Richard 2, 25
Steiner, George 186
Strindberg, August 34, 38, 201
Styan, J.L. 187, 188
Sudermann, Hermann 38

300 Index to Bibliography

surrealism 22, 188
symbolism 35, 172, 184, 188, 195, 204
Synge, John M. 201, 213

Tave, Stuart M. 189
Terence 56, 95, 150
theater, attacks upon the 10
Theater of Cruelty 8
Theater of the Absurd 8, 31, 64, 83, 92, 104, 128, 176, 187, 188
Theater of the Poor 85
theme (thought) 3, 24, 29, 31, 36, 51, 73, 75, 142, 143, 171
Thespis 65
Thompson, Alan R. 190
Thoreau, Henry D. 60
Thorndike, Ashley H. 191
Tillyard, E.M. 116
Toliver, Harold E. 36
Towse, John Rankin 192
tragedy 6, 13, 29, 39, 50, 80, 94, 111, 114, 115, 120, 122, 142, 146, 148, 151, 160, 161, 162, 171, 186, 187, 190, 191
tragedy, domestic 25
tragicomedy 35, 117
Trissino, Giangiorgio 76
Tydeman, William 193
Tyler, Parker 141
Tynan, Kenneth 194, 201
typage 61

Unities, Three 28, 39, 175

Valency, Maurice 195
Van Thal, Herbert 196
Vega, Lope de 40, 50, 76, 103, 197
Vitascope 109

Voltaire (François Marie Arouet) 1, 27, 163
Vos, Nelvin 198, 199

Wagner, Richard 148
Waiting for Godot 158
Ward, A.C. 200
Warshow, Robert 53, 141
Weiss, Samuel A. 201
Wellek, René
"well made" play 9, 72, 154, 166
Wellwarth, George E. 22, 203
West, James 204
Wheeler, Andrew C. 134
Whetstone, George 178
Whitfield, Francis J. 135
Whitman, Cedric H. 205
Whitman, Walt 60
Wickham, Glynne 206
Wilder, Thornton 71, 198
Wiles, Timothy J. 207
Wilkins, Edwin G.P. 134
Williams, Tennessee 71
Wilson, Garff B. 208
Winter, William 134, 209, 210
Winterset 144
wit 73
Witkowski, Georg 211
Wolfenstein, Martha 119

Yarmolinsky, Avrahm 212
Yeats, William Butler 201, 213
Young, Karl 193, 214
Young, Stark 215
Young, Vernon 141

Zuckmayer, Carl 90

Index to Text

References are to page numbers.

Abbey Players 142
Abe Lincoln in Illinois 183
Abrams, M.H. 226
Absolute, Sir Anthony 111
Accius, Lucius 14
Acolastus 30
acting 64, 65, 78, 79, 80, 81, 82, 91, 93, 94, 98, 101, 103, 104, 106, 108, 109, 111, 116, 117, 118, 120, 121, 125, 126, 129, 145, 146, 148, 150, 153, 155, 157, 180, 185, 196, 198, 205, 206, 207, 213, 236, 237, 239, 240, 241
Actors Studio 198
Adamov, Arthur 160, 241
Adams, Charles 98
Adams, John 98
Addams, Jane 204
The Adding Machine 177, 188
Addison, Joseph 47, 53, 56, 57, 59, 73, 99, 234
Adler, Mortimer 220, 244
The Admirable Crichton 95
Admiral Nakhimov 213
Aeschylus 5, 6, 7, 14, 23, 64, 128, 182
Aetheria 16
Afinogenov, Alexander 133, 187
Agamemnon 28, 94
Agate, James 153
Agee, James 217, 229, 244
Aikhenvald, Yuly 125, 129
Aimatov, Chingiz 139, 140

Ajax 7
Akutagawa, Ryunosuke 218
Albee, Edward 164, 172, 198, 241
Alcestis 23
Alcuin 16
Aldrich, Thomas B. 102, 103
Alexander Nevsky 212
Alexander the Great 6
Alexis, Czar 115
Alfriend, E.M. 107
Alien Shadow 138
All for Love 50
All My Sons 186, 188
American Dramatists Club 110
The American Dream 172
American School of Playwriting 112
An American Tragedy 212
Amphitruo 10
anachronism 67, 68
Anastasyev, A. 138
Andelman, David 195
Anderson, Maxwell 177, 181, 182, 242
Andreev, Leonid 127, 128, 130, 131, 238
Androboros 97
Angilbert 16
Animal Crackers 216
Anna Ivanovna, Empress 131
Annensky, Innokenty 128
Anti-Christ 17
Antigone 79
Antigone 28, 78, 182

301

Antiphanes 6
anti-theater 174, 241
Antoine, Andre 88
Antonioni, Michelangelo 217, 218, 223, 227
Apache 2
Apollinaire, Guillaume 146, 147
Appia, Adolphe 80, 146
Aquinas, St. Thomas 18
Arbuzov, A. 138
Archer, William 91, 94, 95, 106, 191, 236
Argensola, Lupercio Leonardo de 39
Aristophanes 5, 6, 13, 64, 77, 180, 230
Aristophanes of Alexandria 13
Aristotle 6-10, 11, 12, 14, 19, 21, 22, 23, 25, 26, 27, 28, 29, 30, 31, 35, 36, 38, 40, 42, 43, 44, 47, 48, 51, 52, 53, 55, 57, 58, 60, 67, 74, 76, 77, 86, 87, 89, 90, 92, 96, 104, 109, 124, 126, 153, 178, 179, 185, 190, 191, 193, 215, 217, 226, 227, 230, 231, 232, 233, 235, 244, 245, 246
Arius 15
Arkadina 125
Armat, Thomas 203
Arnheim, Rudolf 214, 215, 244
Arnold, George 102
Arnold, Matthew 93
Arrabal, Fernando 164, 173
Artaud, Antonin 100, 160, 167-71, 198, 216, 241
The Ascent of Mt. Fuji 139
Ascham, Roger 30
aside 60, 99, 100, 237
The Assassin 192
Astor Place Riot 101
Astruc, Alexander 222
As You Like It 34, 179
Athanasius 15
Atkins, J.W.H. 32, 34
Atkinson, J. Brooks 183, 184, 185, 188, 189, 192, 242
Atlas, James 186, 187
Attack on a China Station 204
Augustine, Saint 14, 15, 168, 231
auteur policy 221, 225, 244
The Automobile Cemetery 173
Averkiev, Dmitry 124
Averroës 19
Awake and Sing 184
Aztecs 2

Bab, Julius 83
Babbitt, Irving 84
Bacon, Roger 30
Badius, Jodocus 26
Baïf, Lazare de 26
Baker, George Pierce 112, 193, 237
Balbis, Johannes de 19
The Bald Soprano 160, 165, 166, 241
Balinese theater 167, 169, 241
The Banker's Daughter 110
Bara, Theda 205
The Barber of Seville 64, 234
Barnett, Paul 187, 188
Barnum's Circus 107
Barreda, Francisco de la 39
Barry, Philip 112, 177, 189
Barrymore, Ethel 177
Barrymore, John 176, 177
Barrymore, Lionel 176, 177
Bateson, F.W. 153, 154
The Bathhouse 132, 138
Batteaux, Abbe 62
Bazin, André 205, 211, 215, 216, 222, 226, 244
Beattie, James 58
Beaumarchais, Pierre de 64, 234
Beaumont, Francis 33, 34, 80
The Beaux' Stratagem 55
Beckett, Samuel 162-65, 173, 174, 194, 196, 197, 240, 241
Becque, Henry 88, 236
The Bedbug 132, 138
Beerbohm, Max 95
Beggar on Horseback 177
The Beggar's Opera 145
Behrman, S.N. 86, 193
Belasco, David 105, 113
Belinsky, Vissarion 120, 121, 238, 239
Bellay, Joachim du 28-29
Bely, Andrey 126, 127, 238
Benavente, Jacinto 41
Benedek, Laslo 219
Ben Hur 209
Bennett, James Gordon 103
Bentley, Eric 79, 81, 82, 83, 142, 146, 190, 235, 242
Bentley, Gerald E. 179, 180
Bentley, Richard 57
Bergman, Ingmar 218, 219, 223
Bergman, Ingrid 218
Bergson, Henri 126, 148, 162, 179, 205
Bernhardt, Sarah 125, 203, 205
Bharata 2
Bible 2, 48

Bierce, Ambrose 102
The Birth of a Nation 208
Black Masks 130
Blackmore, Sir Richard 55
Block, Haskell 158
Blok, Alexander 127, 128, 238
The Blue Bird 130
Blunden, Edmund 90
Bodmer, Johann 73
Boeckh, August 78
Bogdanov, A.A. 132
Boileau (Boileau-Despréaux), Nicolas 40, 45, 46, 47, 49, 52, 53, 61, 73, 86, 87, 116, 233, 235, 237
Boker, George Henry 102
Boleslavsky, Richard 198
Booth, Edwin 101, 103, 104
Booth, John Wilkes 105
Boris Godunov 118, 120
Börne, Ludwig 78, 79
Borowsky, Marvin 208
Bosch, Hieronymous 154
Bosquet, Alain 165
Bossu, Le 51
Bossuet, Jacques B. 47, 60
Bouchet, Jean 27
Boucicault, Dion 102, 103, 105, 106, 110, 111, 237
Bow, Clara 209
Bowers, Faubion 4, 180
Boyl, Carlos 39
Bradley, A.C. 71, 152
Brady, John 228
Brando, Marlon 198
The Breasts of Tiresias 147
Brecht, Bertolt 145, 148, 166, 190, 198, 239, 242
Breitinger, J.J. 73
Brenman-Gibson, Margaret 183, 184
The Bride of Messina 76
Brook, Peter 201
The Brother of Our Lord 195
Brown, Ivor 153
Brown, John Mason 112, 188, 189
Browning, Robert 92
Bruce, Lenny 172
Brumoy, Pierre 65
Brunetière, Ferdinand 87, 88, 94, 236, 246
Brustein, Robert 172, 173, 187, 197, 243
Bruyère, Jean de la 47
Bryusov, Valery 126, 238
Buchner, Augustine 73
Büchner, Georg 81

Buckingham, Duke of 50
Bukharin, Nikolai 134
Bulgakov, Mikhail 194, 195
Bulgarin, Faddy 118
Bullough, Edward 148
Bulwer-Lytton, Edward 92, 93
Būnuel, Luis 223
Burbage, James 20
Burke, Edmund 56, 57
Burke, Kenneth 190
Bury the Dead 188
Butcher, S.H. 153
Butler, Samuel (1612–1680) 52, 53
Byron, Lord 92

The Cabinet of Dr. Caligari 213
Caecilius 13
Caesar, Julius 13
Cagney, James 177
Calderón (de la Barca), Pedro 41, 77, 99, 119, 131
Calderon, George 131, 143, 239
Caliban 68, 111
Camille 101, 183
Camille 102, 103, 108, 135
Camus, Albert 159
Canby, Vincent 223, 227
Candida 105, 177
Cannon, Gilbert 153
Cantor, Eddie 177
Capek, Karel 144
Capell, Edward 71
Captivi 30
Carlyle, Thomas 93
Carrillo, José 40
Carvallo, Luis Alfonso de 38
Cassirer, Ernst 223
Castelvetro, Lodovico 22, 25-26, 29, 31, 38, 44, 232
Castro, Fidel 173
Catherine the Great 116
Cato 73, 92
The Caucasian Chalk Circle 145
Cecchi, Gianmaria 23, 232
Celestina 27
Cenere 205
Cervantes, Miguel de 39, 131, 233
The Chairs 162, 166, 241
Chamber Drama 144
Chambers, E.K. 18
Chapelain, Jean 42, 44, 45, 52
Chaplin, Charlie 161, 205, 208, 218, 220

Chapman, George 34
character 9, 10, 11, 12, 14, 19, 25, 26, 28, 32, 33, 43, 51, 53, 57, 62, 64, 67, 68, 69, 70, 71, 72, 74, 75, 78, 82, 85, 91, 94, 98, 110, 112, 114, 118, 122, 125, 128, 130, 143, 144, 149, 150, 151, 157, 162, 164, 166, 171, 180, 184, 185, 197, 199, 200, 217, 228, 231, 232, 234, 235, 239, 243
Charlemagne 16
Chateaubriand, Vicomte de 72, 86
Chatsky 117
Chatterton 88
Chaussée, Nivelle de la 63
Chautauqua 114
Chaytor, H.J. 37, 39
Chekhov, Anton viii 88, 95, 114, 124, 125, 126, 127, 130, 140, 144, 149, 150, 151, 157, 162, 164, 166, 171, 180, 184, 185, 197, 199, 200, 217, 228, 231, 232, 234, 235, 239, 243
Cheney, Sheldon 2
Chernyshevsky, Nikolai 121
The Cherry Orchard 126, 143
Chiarelli, Luigi 147
Chicago 199
Chinese drama 3
Choephori 5
chorus 7, 10, 12, 22, 25, 27, 28, 29, 34, 35, 47, 52, 58, 76, 79, 93, 128, 129, 145, 192
Christ 2, 16, 18, 155, 173, 200
Christopherson, John 30
Christus Redivivus 30
Chrysostom, St. John 15
Churchill, Charles 59
Cicero 11, 12, 16, 18, 25, 30, 231
The Cid 28, 42, 43, 44, 233
Ciggarales de Toledo 39
cinema *see* motion pictures
CinemaScope 221
Cinematographe 203
Cinerama 221
Cinthio, Giambattista Giraldi 19, 22, 23, 28, 30
Citizen Kane 216, 217
Clapp, Henry Austin 111
Clapp, Henry, Jr. 102, 103, 237
claque 99
Clare, Ada 102
Clark, Barrett H. 179
Cléopâtre 28
closet drama 90, 125
Clurman, Harold 163, 177, 183, 187, 198, 200, 201, 243
Clytemnestra 11
Cocteau, Jean 146, 147, 148, 190, 191, 215
Coleridge, Samuel T. 72, 89-90, 96, 104, 109, 236, 237, 245
Collier, Jeremy 48, 55-56, 60, 61, 234
Colmenares, Diego de 39
Columbarius, Julius 39
commedia dell'arte 27, 131
comedy 6, 7, 11, 12, 16, 18, 19, 22, 23, 24, 28, 29, 30, 31, 32, 33, 34, 36, 38, 39, 47, 48, 50, 52, 53, 58, 60, 62, 63, 64, 70, 73, 77, 79, 84, 86, 91, 93, 98, 100, 116, 117, 119, 120, 121, 124, 148, 150, 151, 153, 154, 162, 165, 166, 173, 174, 179, 180, 183, 188, 189, 190, 192, 193, 200, 205, 208, 222, 231, 232, 235, 236, 238, 240, 242, 245
comedy, dark 161
comedy, sentimental 56, 57, 60, 234
comedy, situation 82
comedy, tearful 58, 60, 63, 64
Common Conditions 32
Comte, Auguste 82
Confucius 3
Congreve, William 50, 53, 90
The Connection 198
Connolly, Cyril 167
Connolly, Marc 177, 182
The Conquest of Granada 51
The Conquest of Mexico 170
constructivism 132
Conti, Prince de 60-61
The Contrast 98
The Converted Courtesan 127
Cook, Dutton 96
Cooper, Lane 11
Copeau, Jacques 146, 147, 159, 240
Copeland, Roger 199
Coquelin, Constant 203
Coriolanus 156
Corliss, Richard 228
Corneille, Pierre 42, 44, 45, 46, 47, 50, 51, 52, 61, 70, 102, 233, 245
Cornell, Katherine 177
Corrigan, Robert W. 194
Corry, John 197
costume 18-19, 53, 98, 119, 146, 171, 203
Courtney, W.L. 153
The Covetous Knight 120
Craig, Gordon 80, 129, 130, 146, 149, 176, 206
Crane, Ronald S. 191

Creizenach, William 152
Creon 79
Cricot 196
The Critic 60, 234
Croce, Arlene 217
Croly, Herbert 206
Cromwell 85, 235
Crowther, Bosley 217
Croyden, Margaret 195, 196, 199, 200, 201, 243
Cruz, Ramón de la 40
cubism 146
Cueva, Juan de la 38
Curse 199
Curtis, George William 109
Cushman, Charlotte 100, 101, 103, 104
Curtis, Robert 155, 156
Curtis, Susan 104
Czar Theodore 124

Dacier, André 47, 51, 52
Dadaism 196
Dahlstrom, C.E. 144
d'Aigaliers, Pierre de Laudun 27, 28
d'Alembert, Jean Le Rond 63
Daly, Arnold 105
Daly, Augustin 102, 110, 237
Dana, H.W.L. 187
Daniello, Bernardino 22
Dante 19, 21, 102
Darlington, W.A. 153
Darnton, Nina 195
Darwin, Charles 82, 87, 236
d'Aubignac, Abbé (François Hédelin) 43, 45, 51, 53, 233
Davenport, Jean 104
David, Harry and John 204
Death of a Salesman 186, 188, 219
Death of Caesar 27
Debussy, Claude 212
Decembrist uprising 117, 118
decorum 12, 13, 24, 32, 39, 43, 45, 51, 67, 69, 84, 112, 231, 246
DeForest, Lee 208, 209
Dekker, Thomas 34, 35
Delluc, Louis 205
Demetrius of Rostov 115
Dennis, John 52, 53, 57, 67, 92, 233
DePalma, Brian 225
Desire Under the Elms 177
detritus 28
Diaghilev, Sergei 146

dialogue 5, 8, 9, 10, 11, 12, 14, 16, 22, 23, 24, 25, 29, 30, 31, 32, 33, 36, 37, 39, 42, 49, 50, 51, 57, 61, 62, 64, 65, 67, 68, 69, 70, 71, 78, 80, 88, 90, 91, 98, 112, 116, 118, 125, 138, 143, 144, 150, 151, 162, 163, 165, 167, 168, 171, 172, 173, 174, 181, 183, 184, 185, 189, 190, 194, 197, 199, 200, 201, 212, 214, 227, 230, 231, 234, 240, 241, 243
Dickens, Charles 92, 211
Dickinson, Emily 179
Dickinson, Thomas H. 178
Diderot, Denis 61, 63-64, 74, 85, 106, 234
Didion, Joan 228
Diebold, Bernhard 82
Dio Chrysostom 14
Diomedes 18, 19, 26, 28
Dionysus 5, 128
director (stage manager) 10, 99, 106, 110, 120, 129, 132, 146, 166, 177, 180, 184, 190, 201, 207, 210, 212, 213, 215, 216, 217, 218, 219, 221, 222, 223, 225, 227, 228, 233, 239, 243, 244
Disney, Walt 209, 244
Distant Point 187
Dixon, Thomas 208
Dmitrevsky 116
Dobrolyubov, Nikolai 121, 122, 123, 238
documentary films 210
Dolce, Lodovico 22
Donatus 18, 19, 26, 28, 29, 38
Dostoevsky, Fyodor 122
Douglass, David 97, 98
Dowden, Edward 93
The Dream Play 144
Dreiser, Theodore 212
Drew, John 180
Drifters 210
Driver, Tom 162, 163, 197
Dryden, John 37, 40, 44, 46, 47, 48, 49-51, 52, 53, 55, 56, 59, 66, 67, 70, 85, 99, 233, 234, 245
Duerrenmatt, Friedrich 154, 155, 240
Dukes, Ashley 153
Dumas, Alexander (father) 78
Dumas, Alexander (son) 87, 88, 101
Dunlap, William 98
Dunne, John Gregory 228
Dupont, E.A. 213
Durán, Agustín 41
Durang, Christopher 172, 173, 200
D'Urfey, Thomas 55
Duse, Eleanora 108, 125, 180, 205
The Dutch Courtezan 34

Eagles, Jeanne 177
Eastman, Max 179
Eaton, Walter Pritchard 113
Echard 53
Eder, Richard 173, 195, 199, 200, 243
Edison, Thomas Alva 203
Egger, Emile 6
Egolin, A.M. 136
Egyptian drama 3
Ehrenburg, Ilya 137
Einstein, Albert 197, 243
Einstein on the Beach 197
Eisenstein, Sergei 210-12, 222, 227, 228, 244
Eizaguirre, José Echegaray y 41
Electra 186
Eliot, George 93
Eliot, T.S. 8, 51, 69, 89, 150, 151, 152, 190, 191, 240, 245
Elizabeth, Empress 116
Elizabeth the Queen 182
El Rufián Dichoso 39
Elyot, Sir Thomas 30
Emerson, Ralph Waldo 105
Encyclopedists 62, 63
The End of St. Petersburg 213
Engel, Lehman 197
Epic Theater 145, 148, 239
Esslin, Martin 159, 160, 161, 162, 164, 167, 171, 172, 173, 174, 175, 199, 241
Estragon 163, 164
E.T. 229
Ethelwold, Saint 17
Eumenides 7, 23
Euripides 5, 6, 8, 10, 14, 16, 23, 27, 43, 230
Evans, Maurice 143
Every Man in His Humour 35
Every Man Out of His Humour 35
Everyman 150
Evreinov, Nikolay 120, 129, 238
Exeter, Bishop of 30
existentialism 145, 159, 172, 199, 240, 247
expressionism 82, 132, 142, 144, 154, 177, 196, 213, 238, 239, 244, 245
The Extravagant Triumph 173

Fabricius, Georgius 73
Fairbanks, Douglas, Sr. 205, 208, 209
The Faithful Shepherdess 33
Falstaff, John 52, 71

Fantasia 209
fantasy 77, 95, 142, 144, 146, 147, 149, 159, 165, 189, 195, 199, 206, 218, 220, 235, 239, 247
Farber, Stephen 225
farce 27, 28, 32, 53, 57, 61, 71, 92, 93, 100, 124, 127, 133, 156, 165, 166, 180, 205, 232, 234
Farmer, Richard 70
Farquhar, George 53, 55
Farsa 23
Fashion 100
Fassbinder, Rainer Werner 227, 228
Faulkner, William 228
Fear 133, 187
Feast of Boys 17
Feast of Fools 17
Fellini, Federico 217, 223, 225, 227
Fergusson, Francis 8, 147, 190, 242, 248
Field, Sally 198
Fielding, Henry 57, 234
Fields, W.C. 162, 177
Fifth of July 199
Figueroa, Cristóbal Suarez de 39
Fiske, Harrison Grey 106
Fiske, Stephen Ryder 106, 107, 237
Fitch, Clyde 113, 114, 198
Fitzgerald, F. Scott 228
Fitzgerald, Percy 96
Flaherty, Robert J. 210
Flannery, James W. 194
Flaubert, Gustave 211
Flecknoe, Richard 49
Fletcher, John 33, 34
Flowers and Trees 209
folk drama 183
Fonda, Jane 198
Fontanne, Lynn 177, 188
Fontenelle, Bernard de 58
Fonvizin, Denis 116
formalism 135, 138, 141, 239
Forrest, Edwin 101, 103, 104
Fox, William 204
France, Anatole 16, 88
Francesca da Rimini 102
Frazer, James 223
Frederick the Great 75
Freeburg, Victor 206
Freie Bühne 81, 142
French Academy 42, 43, 85
Fresnaye, Vauquelin de la 29
Freud, Sigmund 126, 191, 223
Freytag, Gustav 80
Friedell, Egon 83

The Frogs 5, 35
The Front 136
Fry, Christopher 151, 189, 190, 200, 240
Fugard, Athol 196
Fujimura, Thomas H. 191
Fullonius 30
Furnivall, F.J. 93
futurism 126, 132, 238

Gable, Clark 177
Galsworthy, John 151
The Gamester 63
Garbo, Greta 218
Garfield, John 198
Garnier, Robert 28
Garrick, David 58, 60, 68-69
Gassner, John 181, 193, 242
Gate of Hell 218
Gaumont, Léon 203
Gazarra, Ben 198
Gehman, Richard 192
Gelber, Jack 198
Gellius 13
Genghis Khan 117
Genteel movement 108, 111
The Gentle People 188
Geoffroy, Julien-Louis 86, 88
George, Mlle. 117
George, Saint 17
Gerhoh of Reichersberg 17
Gershwin, George and Ira 177
Gerstenberg, Heinrich 75
Gessner, Niklaus 163
Ghéon, Henri 149
The Ghost Sonata 144
Ghosts 94, 105, 185
Gibney, Frank 218
Gilbert, John (1810–1889) 111
Gilbert, John (1897–1936) 209
Gildon, Charles 52, 57, 70
Gilman, Richard 187
Giraldi Cinthio *see* Cinthio
Girardoux, Jean 139
The Girl with the Green Eyes 114
Gish, Lillian 183
Glass, Philip 197
Globe Theater 20
Glowacki, Janusz 195
Godard, Jean-Luc 227
Goethe, Johann von 72, 74, 75, 76, 77, 78, 80, 83, 85, 109, 235, 237
Gogol, Nikolai 119, 120, 121, 125, 131, 140, 238, 239
Golden Boy 184
Goldsmith, Oliver 59, 60, 92, 234
The Good Woman of Setzuan 145, 166
Gorchakov, Nikolai 136
Gorky, Maxim 127, 128, 136
The Gospel According to Saint Matthew 223
Gosson, Stephen 31, 48
Gottsched, Johann 73, 75, 119, 235
Grabbe, Christian 78
Granville-Barker, Harley 143, 152
Gray, Hugh 204, 213, 215
Gray, Thomas 58
The Great Diamond Robbery 107
The Great Train Robbery 204
The Green Goddess 94
Green Pastures 182
Greg, W.W. 151, 152
Gregori, Dr. 115
Grein, J.T. 95
Grenier, Richard 227
Grévin, Jacques 27, 232
Griboyedov, Alexander 88, 117, 118, 127
Grierson, John 210
Griffith, D.W. 204, 206, 207, 208, 210, 211, 212, 228, 243, 244
Griffith, Elizabeth 71
Grigoriev, Apollon 122, 238
Grillparzer, Franz 80
Grimald, Nicholas 30
Grimm, Friedrich 64
Gromov, P. 136
Grossvogel, David 173, 241
grotesque 85, 142, 147, 154, 158, 166, 174, 196, 199, 240, 244
Grotowski, Jerzy 155, 195, 198, 201, 240
Group Theater 198
Gryphius, Andreas 73
The Guardsman 177
Guare, John 199
Guarini, Giambattista 22, 23, 232
The Guests 137
Guimerà, Angel 41
Gussow, Mel 164, 196
Gutzkow, Karl 78

Haeckel, Ernst 82
Hall, Joseph 33
Hall, Vernon, Jr. 29
Hallam, Lewis 97
Halline, Allan 182

Halliwell-Phillipps, J.O. 93
Hamilton, Clayton 179
Hamlet 13, 76, 103, 130, 182
Hamlet 34, 40, 61, 88, 130, 182
Hammond, Percy 113, 180
Hannele 130
Hapgood, Norman 113
A Hard Lot 123
Hardy, Alexandre 27, 28, 232
Hardy, Oliver 162
Harpe, Jean-François de la 62
Harrigan, Edward 111
Harris, Jed 192
Harris, Julie 198
Harrison, G.B. 152
Harrison, Jane 2
Hart, Moss 177
Hart, William S. 218
Harvard University 109
Hauptmann, Gerhart 82, 130, 178
Hauron, Louis Ducos du 202
Hawkins, Thomas 60, 70
Hayley, William 95
Hayman, Ronald 145
Hazlitt, William 69, 85, 89, 90, 91, 104, 153, 236
Hebbel, Friedrich 79, 80, 81, 235
Hédelin, François *see* d'Aubignac, Abbé
Hegel, Georg 79, 81, 211, 244
Heine, Heinrich 78
Heinsius, Daniel 35
Hellman, George 105
Hellman, Lillian 139
Hello, Dolly! 184
Henrietta Maria, Queen 48
Herder, Johann 72, 75
Hernani 91, 176
Herne, James A. 110
hero (protagonist) 9, 24, 47, 51, 59, 75, 77, 121, 123, 124, 128, 130, 149, 174, 182, 186, 192, 215, 227, 231, 233
Herod 17
Herodotus 2
heroic drama 50, 51, 57, 234
Heron, Matilda 101, 104
Herrad 17
Herrick, Marvin 12
Herrmann, Gottfried 78
Hettner, Hermann 79
Heywood, Thomas 34
High Tor 182
Hindu drama 3
history play 71
Hitchcock, Alfred 225

Hobbes, Thomas 25, 49, 58, 85
Hobson, Harold 151
Holiday 189
Hollaman, R.G. 203
the Holy Spirit 48, 233
The Homecoming 171
Homer 7, 25, 70, 86
Hood, Robin 17
Hope, Bob 177
Hopi 1
Hopkins, Arthur 176
Horace 12-13, 14, 19, 21, 22, 28, 29, 44, 45, 51, 67, 68, 73, 86, 231, 233
Horace 45
Hornblow, Arthur 107
House, Edward H. 102
Howard, Bronson 109, 110, 114, 237
Howard, Sir Robert 49
Howard, Sidney 112, 177
Howells, William Dean 102, 103, 105, 111, 113
Hows, J.W.S. 101
Hrosvitha 16, 231
Hubner, Zygmunt 195
Hugo, Victor 72, 78, 85, 86, 88, 91, 235
Hugutius 19
Hume, David 56
humour 32, 35, 36, 49, 50, 53, 59, 60, 91, 148, 232
Huneker, James 113, 178
Hunningher, Benjamin 15, 17
Hunt, Leigh 89, 91, 236
Hunter, Gov. Robert 97
Hurd, Richard 58
Huston, Walter 177
Hutcheson, Francis 58
Hutton, Laurence 111

Iago 13, 51
Ibsen, Henrik 41, 79, 80, 81, 83, 87, 94, 95, 96, 105, 108, 113, 114, 127, 139, 144, 178, 181, 192, 193, 236, 237, 238
The Iceman Cometh 186
Idiot's Delight 183
Ihering, Herbert 83
I-kher-nefert 2
Ilf, Ilya 137
imagery 151, 152, 189, 236, 243
The Importance of Being Earnest 180
impressionism 152, 178, 217, 236, 242
Ince, Thomas 207
Inchbald, Elizabeth 92

Index to Text 309

Independent Theatre 95, 142
The Informer 220
Innaurato, Albert 200
Innocent III, Pope 18, 231
The Inspector General 119
Intolerance 208, 212
Ionesco, Eugène 159, 161, 162, 165-67, 172, 173, 194, 200, 240, 241, 247
Irving, Henry 93, 94, 106, 188
Irving, Peter 98, 99
Irving, Washington 98, 99
Irwin, May 203
Isaac, Jules 74
Isidore of Seville 19
Ivan, Grand Duke of Moscow 119
Ivan the Terrible 212
Ivanov, Vyacheslav 128, 238

James, Henry 111, 113
James II, King 52
Japanese drama 4
Jarry, Alfred 147, 158, 159, 240
The Jazz Singer 209
Jefferson, Joe 103, 109
Jeffrey, Francis 85, 92
je ne sais quoi 43, 47
Jephtha 30
Job 2
Jodelle, Etienne 28
John of Damascus 16
John of Garland 19
John of Salisbury 19
Johnson, Samuel 58-59, 69-70, 84, 85, 90, 99, 104, 178, 234
Jolson, Al 209
Jones, Henry Arthur 94, 236
Jones, Robert Edmond 112, 176
Jonson, Ben 32, 34-36, 48, 49, 50, 52, 66, 67, 72, 79, 91, 99, 148, 179, 232, 234, 238, 245
jornada 38
Joyce, James 165
Juliet 184
Julius Caesar 52
Jullien, Jean 88
Jung, Carl 85, 223
Juvenal 14, 19

Kabuki 4, 180
Kael, Pauline 217, 225, 227, 244

Kafka, Franz 159
Kaiser, Georg 82, 144
Kakutani, Michiko 228
Kalidasa 3
Kalmus, Herbert T. 209
Kames, Lord 59, 68, 234
Kandinsky, Wassily 196
Kant, Immanuel 76
Kantor, Tadeusz 195, 196
Katayev, Valentin 133
Kauffmann, Stanley 217, 218, 219, 220, 226, 227, 229, 244
Kaufman, George S. 177
Kean, Charles 81, 100, 103, 142
Keaton, Buster 161, 205
Keats, John 197
Keene, Donald 4
Keene, Laura 104
Keown, Eric 153
Kerr, Alfred 83
Kerr, Walter 172, 186, 193, 197, 220, 242, 243
Kershner, Irvin 225
Key Largo 182
Khorev 116
Kinetoscope 203
King Ubu 147, 158, 159, 240
The Kiss 203
Kitto, H.D.F. 6, 153
Klopstock, Friedrich 74
Knight, Arthur 204, 217, 218
The Knight of the Burning Pestle 33
Knights, L.C. 153
Knipper, Olga 125
Kohout, Pavel 195
Komisarjevsky, Theodore 146
Kopit, Arthur 199
Korneichuk, Alexander 136, 137, 138
Kornfeld, Paul 144
Kosinski, Jerzy 228
Kott, Jan 174, 241
Kotzebue, August von 80, 117, 237
Kowalski, Stanley 195
Kracauer, Siegfried 228, 244, 245
Kronenberger, Louis 193, 242
Krook, Dorothea 192
Khrushchev, Nikita 138, 139, 239
Krutch, Joseph Wood 180, 181, 242
Kuleshov, Lev 211, 212
Kurosawa, Akira 218, 223
Kuzmin, Mikhail 127, 128
Kyd, Thomas 33

La Dolce Vita 217
Laius 9
Lamb, Charles 89, 90, 91, 104, 152, 153, 236
Lanciotto 102
Langbaine, Gerald 52
Langer, Susanne 192
language *see* dialogue
La Romanesca 23
La Strada 217
La Suivante 44
Laube, Heinrich 78
Laurel, Stan 162
Lavrenev, Boris 187
Lawson, John Howard 177
Lawson, Steve 196
Lear, King 60
Lee, Nathaniel 57
Leenhardt, Robert 222
Le Gallienne, Eva 177
Leipzig school of acting and criticism 73
Lemercier, Népomucène 84
Lenin, Nikolai 132, 133, 194
Lennox, Charlotte 70
Leonov, Leonid 136
Lermontov, Michael 131, 138
Leskov, Nikolai 121
Les Pauvres de Paris 102
Les Plaideurs 40
Lessing, Gotthold 40, 41, 72, 74, 75, 76, 79, 80, 89, 96, 124, 235, 237, 245
Lester, Elenore 198, 199
Levin, Elena 194
Levi-Strauss, Claude 223
Lewes, George Henry 93
Lewisohn, Ludwig 113, 177
Leyburn, Ellen D. 192
liaison des scènes 43, 112
The Life of Man 128
Lillian's Last Love 110
Lillo, George 63
Lindsay, Vachel 204, 206-07, 228, 243
literary attaché 110
Little Eyolf 182
The Little Foxes 182
Little Theater movement 114, 148, 177, 237
Littlewood, S.R. 48, 90, 92, 93, 94, 95
Livy 11
Locke, John 56
Lodge, Thomas 31
Loew, Marcus 204
Loman, Willy 219
The London Merchant 63

Longfellow, Henry W. 105
Longinus 14, 24, 52, 57, 69
Look Back in Anger 154
Lopakhin 143
Lopez, Alfonso 38
Lorca, Federico García 41, 190
Lowell, James Russell 109
The Lower Depths 128
Lucky 164
Lucretius 25
Ludwig, Otto 80, 81
Lugné-Poë, Aurelien-Marie 159
Luka 128
Lukacs, George 148, 149, 240
Lumière, Auguste & Louis 203
Lumley, Frederick 174, 241
Lunacharsky, Anatoly 133
Lunt, Alfred 177, 188
Luzán, Ignacio de 40
Lyly, John 33

Macaulay, Thomas B. 90, 153
Macbeth 176, 182, 226
MacCarthy, Desmond 153
Macdonald, Dwight 208, 222, 229, 244
Macgowan, Kenneth 176
McGuane, Thomas 228
MacKaye, Percy 114
McKerrow, R.B. 151, 152
Macpherson, James 75
Macready, William C. 101
Madame Bovary 211
Maeterlinck, Maurice 88, 126, 127, 130, 144, 149, 151, 236, 246
Maetius 11
Maggi, Vincenzo 22
Malinowsky, Bronislaw 223
Mallarmé, Stéphane 88, 159, 236
Malone, Edmond 71
Malraux, André 211
Mamet, David 164, 200, 243
Mamoulian, Rouben 180
Manly, Colonel 98
Mann, Thomas 205
Mans, Jacques Peletier du 28
Mansfield, Richard 105
Mantle, Burns 178, 180
Marat/Sade 139
Marey, Étienne 203
Margites 7
Mariamne 80
Mariana, Juan de 38

Index to Text 311

Marlowe, Christopher 32, 33
Marmontel, Jean-François 62
The Marriage of Figaro 64, 234
Marshall, Herbert 227
Marston, John 34
Martha the Seneschal's Wife 119
Martial 14
Martin, Theodore 96
Marx Brothers (Chico, Groucho, Harpo) 162, 164, 167, 177, 216
Marx, Karl 132, 133, 134, 138, 148, 238, 240
Mary of Scotland 182
mask 171, 183
The Mask and the Face 147
Mason, H.A. 146
Masquerade 131, 138
Massenet, Jules 16
Massine, Leonide 146
Master Harold...and the boys 196
The Matchmaker 184
Matthews, Brander 90, 111, 112, 114, 237
Maugham, W. Somerset 150, 177
Mayakovsky, Vladimir 132, 138
Mayhew, Edward 96
Meiningen Players 81, 82, 123, 142, 143
Meister, Wilhelm 76
Méliès, Georges 203, 207
melodrama 33, 41, 57, 60, 78, 94, 95, 100, 101, 102, 103, 117, 120, 147, 148, 191, 222, 226, 234, 236
Menander 13, 14
Mendelssohn, Moses 74
Menken, Adah Isaacs 102
Mercier, Sebastian 65
Meredith, George 93
The Merry Wives of Windsor 52
Mesa, Cristobal de 39
Mesnardière, La 43
Meyerhold, Vsevolod 80, 120, 131, 132, 133, 134, 135, 136, 138, 139, 140, 238, 239
A Midsummer Night's Dream 179
Miller, Arthur 139, 154, 185, 186, 187, 188, 196, 242
Miller, Marilyn 177
Miller, Tice L. 101, 103, 108
Milton, John 48, 52, 66, 181, 233, 234
mime 15, 16, 17, 27
Ming Huang 3
Minturno (Antonio Sebastiano) 22, 24, 25, 26, 29, 31, 232
miracle play 18, 20, 28, 115, 231
Mirandello, Pico della 33

Mirsky, Prince D.S. 115, 116, 118, 119, 122, 123, 136
Miss Julie 144, 190
The Mock Astrologer 50
Molière, Jean B.P. 45, 46, 47, 62, 77, 84, 86, 117, 120, 121, 124, 131, 179, 245
Molina, Tirso de 39, 40, 233
Molnar, Ferenc 177
Monkey Business 216
monodrama 120, 129, 130, 147, 238
monologue 29, 144, 152, 163
Monroe, Marilyn 198
montage 204, 207, 208, 210, 211-12, 213, 216, 222, 229, 244
Montagu, Elizabeth 71
Montagu, Ivor 212
Montiano y Luyando, Agustin de 40
Moody, William Vaughn 114
Moor, James 60
Moore, Edward 63
morality play 27, 174
Moratín, Leandro Fernández de 40
Moratín, Nicolas Fernández de 40
More, Sir Thomas 30
Morgan, Charles 152
Morgann, Maurice 71
Moscow Art Theater 23, 81, 123, 125, 126, 130, 140, 142, 143, 156, 194, 238
Moscow Imperial Dramatic Theater 123
Moscow Maly Theater 121
Moses, Montrose J. 109, 179, 183, 189
Mother 213
Mother Courage 145
motion picture eras 222
motion pictures 130, 131, 145, 149, 202-29, 243, 248
motion pictures, censorship 203
motion pictures, monopoly 205
Motte, Baron de la 61
Mowatt, Anna Cora Richie 100, 101
Mowbray, J.P. 108
Mowbray, Jennie Pearl 108
Mowbray, Morris 96
Mrs. Warren's Profession 105
Mukhamedzhanov, Kaltai 139
Mulgrave, Earl of 53
Müller, Adam 79, 235
Muni, Paul 177
Murray, Edward 208, 218, 221, 223, 224, 225, 229
Murray, Gilbert 8, 153, 223
Musaeus 25
Muybridge, Eadweard 203
Mystery Bouffe 132

mystery play 18, 20, 25, 28, 57, 115, 131, 161, 231

Naharro, Torres 38
Nanook of the North 210, 216
Napoleon Bonaparte 84
Nasarre, Blas de 40
Nashe, Thomas 33
Natasha 128
Nathan, George Jean 178, 181, 197, 242
naturalism 79, 82, 86, 87, 88, 126, 142, 144, 185, 236, 242
Nazimova, Alla 185
Negri, Pola 209
Nemirovich-Danchenko, Vladimir 125, 143
neoclassicism 8, 12, 24, 27, 28, 40, 41, 44, 46, 47, 48, 49, 50, 53, 54, 56, 57, 59, 60, 63, 64, 65, 66, 68, 72, 73, 74, 75, 84, 85, 86, 87, 88, 91, 99, 115, 119, 140, 233, 234, 235, 246
Neoptolemus of Parium 12
Neuber, Karoline 73
Neumeister, Erdmann 73
Newman, John Henry Cardinal 92
Newman, Paul 198
Nicholas I, Czar 118
nickelodeon 204
Nicole, Pierre 60
Nicoll, Allardyce 149
Nielsen, Asta 218
Nietzsche, Friedrich 80, 178, 223, 246, 247
Night and Day 196
Nightingale, Benedict 156
Nisard, Désiré 86
The Nixie 120
No Man's Land 172
No-play 4
Northbrooke, John 30

Obey, Andre 147
obligatory scene (*scène à faire*) 87, 94, 112, 236
O'Brian, Fitz-James 102
O'Casey, Sean 178, 194
The Octoroon 103
The Odd Couple 198
O'Dell, George 179
Odets, Clifford 183, 188, 196

Oedipe 62
Oedipus 9, 186, 208
Oedipus 94, 182
Ogier, François 28, 30, 43, 46, 232
Okhlopov, Nikolai 138, 139
Oldmixon, John 53
The Old Wives' Tale 33
Olivier, Laurence 156
Olson, Elder 192
O'Neill, Eugene 81, 112, 144, 177, 178, 181, 186, 190, 196, 198, 242
O'Neill-Barna, Anne 194
The Open City 217, 222
Opitz, Martin 73
Oresteia 182
The Orphan 97
Osborne, John 139, 154
Osiris 2
Ossian 75
Ostrovsky, Alexander 122, 131, 140, 238
Othello 93
Othello 51, 97
Otway, Thomas 97
Ozerov, Vladislav 119

Pacuvius, Marcus 14
Paisan 217
Palmer, John 153
Palsgrave, John 30
Panofsky, Erwin 205, 222, 244
pantomime 63, 103, 144, 169, 237
Papava, M. 137
Paphnutius 16
Parade 146
Paradjanov, Sergei 227
Paris Bound 189
parody 166
Pasolini, Pier Paolo 223
Passion of Christ 16
Pasternak, Boris 139
pastorale 27, 28
Pastor Fido 23
pataphysics 158, 240
Pazzi, Allesandro de' 21, 22
Pear Garden School of Acting 3
peasant play 41
Peasant Theatre 123
Peckinpah, Sam 225
Peele, George 33
Pemberton, Henry 53
Percy, Thomas 60
Perrault, Charles 60

Persius 19
Peter the Great 116
Petrarca's Sonnet 139
The Petrified Forest 183
Petronius 14
Petrov, Evgeny 137
Pfaff's Restaurant & Bier Saloon 102
The Phantom of the Opera 209
Philadelphia Story 189
Philaster 34
Philoctetes 14
Picasso, **Pablo** 146, 149
Pickford, Mary 208
Pinero, Sir Arthur 94, 105
Pinter, Harold 164, 171, 172, 196, 241
Pinto 84
Pirandello, Luigi 144, 147, 148, 240, 246
Pisarev, Dmitry 123
Piscator, Erwin 145
Pisemsky, Alexey 123
Placide, Henry 100
Plato 6, 16, 34, 128, 139
Plautus 10, 11, 19, 22, 23, 28, 30, 180
Plautus 53
Plavilshchikov, P.A. 117
Pléïde 27, 28, 29
Plekhanov, Georgi 132
plot 6, 8, 9, 12, 13, 14, 23, 25, 28, 33, 34, 36, 45, 48, 50, 53, 56, 60, 61, 62, 68, 70, 71, 74, 75, 78, 82, 87, 94, 102, 108, 112, 115, 116, 119, 121, 123, 124, 125, 131, 138, 143, 148, 151, 157, 164, 166, 174, 176, 180, 186, 191, 196, 199, 200, 220, 223, 226, 230, 231, 232, 234, 235, 236, 238, 241, 243, 245
plot, catharsis 8, 11, 23, 25, 26, 31, 36, 47, 48, 60, 74, 181, 185, 193, 220, 226-27, 231, 232, 235, 238, 239
plot, probability 9, 13, 14, 26, 28, 34, 42, 44, 45, 57, 60, 61, 62, 64, 75, 77, 98, 180, 227, 231, 233, 234, 236
Pluchek, Valentin 138, 139
Plutarch 13
Poe, Edgar Allan 99, 100, 237
The Poetaster 35
poetic justice 51, 52, 56, 108, 233, 234
poetry 12, 25, 26, 29, 34, 48, 50, 51, 61, 62, 67, 68, 80, 81, 85, 88, 90, 102, 114, 127, 129, 140, 145, 147, 150, 151, 174, 190, 191, 192, 199, 200, 206, 233, 234, 240, 243
Pogodin, Nikolai 139
Pollard, A.W. 151, 152
Pomerantsev, Vladimir 137

Pontanus, Jacobus 73
The Poor of Boston 102
The Poor of New York 102
Pope, Alexander 47, 67
Popkin, Henry 195
Porgy and Bess 180
pornography 226
Porter, Cole 177
Porter, Edwin S. 204, 207
Potemkin 210, 211, 220, 244
Pound, Ezra 4
Price, William T. 112
Pritchett, V.S. 174
problem play 81, 87, 95, 121, 147, 171, 236
Processional 177
The Prodigal 198
The Profligate 121
Prokopovich, Theophan 116
Proletcult 132
Promos and Cassandra 32
Prynne, William 48
psychic distance 131, 148
Pudovkin, Vsevolod 212, 213, 244
puppet theater 115
Pushkin, Alexander 88, 118-19, 120, 131, 136, 140, 237, 239
Pye, Henry James 60

Queen Elizabeth 205
Quem Quaeritis? (Whom Do You Seek?) 17
Quinn, Arthur Hobson 102, 179
Quintilian 13
Quo Vadis? 205

Rabe, David 173, 195, 199
Rachel, Mlle. 102
Racine, Jean 40, 44, 45, 61, 74, 81, 84, 86, 102, 116, 118, 119, 234
Rahv, Philip 187
Rain 177
Raleigh, Sir Walter (1861–1922) 89, 152
Ralph Roister Doister 32
Ranevsky, Madame 143, 195
Rapin, René 43, 46, 47, 51, 233
Rashomon 218, 223
Rattigan, Terence 151
realism 63, 78, 79, 87, 110, 123, 126, 127, 128, 134, 142, 145, 147, 149, 150, 159, 165, 171, 190, 191, 197, 199, 200, 205,

314 Index to Text

214, 215, 220, 221, 222, 230, 235, 238, 245
Red Desert 218
Redko, A.E. 129
The Rehearsal 51
Reinhardt, Max 146
Reiter, Seymour 162, 164
religion viii 1, 2, 8, 12, 15-19, 30, 48, 52, 79, 80, 107, 108, 115, 116, 124, 127, 128, 129, 146, 148, 151, 152, 155, 160, 161, 163, 166, 169, 170, 181, 182, 183, 200, 219, 223, 224, 235, 238, 240, 241, 242, 244, 246, 247, 248
Renoir, Jean 216
The Resistible Rise of Arturo Ui 145
Reunion in Vienna 183
The Rhinoceros 165
Rice, Elmer 177, 188
Rice, John 203
Rich, Frank 200
Richard II, King 120
Richard III, King 103
Richardson, Jack 198
Richardson, William 71
Richelieu, Cardinal 42, 93
Rip Van Winkle 109
Rip Van Winkle 108
The Rivals 111
The Road to Damascus 144
The Robe 221
Robertson, J.G. 74
Robertson, J.M. 152
Robinson, Edward G. 177
Robortello, Francesco 21, 22, 38, 232
Rocket to the Moon 184
Rodgers, Richard 177
Rodogune 74
Rogers, Will 177
romanticism 64, 75, 76, 77, 80, 84, 85, 86, 87, 88, 89, 90, 91, 93, 94, 96, 107, 117, 134, 148, 151, 197, 235, 236, 243
Romeo 104
Ronsard, Pierre de 29
The Rosciad 59
Rosenthal, Lewis 107
Rossellini, Roberto 217, 222, 227
Rousseau, Jean Jacques 63, 234
Rowdon, John 154
Rowe, Nicholas 67
Rudkin, David 156
Russell, John 146
The Russian Question 187
Rymer, Thomas 47, 51, 52, 53, 55, 57, 66, 67, 69, 233

Sainte-Beuve, Charles 45, 46, 86, 107, 150, 235, 237
Saint-Évremond, Charles de 47, 233
Saint Vladimir 116
Saintsbury, George 5, 6, 13, 44, 46, 49
Salas, Gonzales de 40
Salieri and Mozart 120
Saltykov-Shchedrin, Mikhail 194
Samson 2
Samson Agonistes 48, 52
Sandys, John Edwin 109
Santillana, Marquis de 38
Sarasin, Jean-François 43
Sarcey, Francisque 86, 87, 94, 191, 235
Sardanapalus 92
Sardou, Victorien 41, 87, 88, 94, 101, 123
Saroyan, William 178
Sarris, Andrew 217, 219, 221, 222, 225, 244
Sartre, Jean-Paul 145, 146, 159, 215, 240, 247
Satie, Eric 146
satyr play 27
Saurin, Bernard 63
Saxe-Meiningen, Duke of 81, 142
Scaliger, Julius Caesar 22, 25, 26, 29, 31, 46
scenery 48, 49, 80, 144, 146, 150, 207, 213, 238, 240, 241
Schelling, Friedrich von 40
Schepkin, Michael 121, 122
Schill 155
Schiller, Johann von 72, 76, 78, 80, 81, 83, 85, 120, 235
Schlegel, August von 40, 77, 85, 91, 118, 235
Schlegel, Friedrich von 40, 76, 77, 85, 235
Schlegel, Johann Elias 74
Scholiasts 6
The School for Scandal 111
Schopenhauer, Arthur 79
Schücking, L.L. 152
Schwartz, Harry 187
Scott, Clement 93, 94
Scott, Sir Walter 92
Scriabin, Alexander 212
Scribe, Eugène 41, 78, 87, 88, 102, 121, 123
Scudery, Georges de 42, 43
The Seagull 125, 126, 143
Sebastian y Latre 40
Sebastiano, Antonio *see* Minturno

Index to Text   315

Sebillet, Thomas 27
The Seduction 144
Segni, Bernardo 21, 22
Sejanus 35
Seneca 21, 22, 25, 26, 27, 29, 30, 31, 36
Senelick, Laurence 120, 124, 125, 130
Sennett, Mack 205
Sergeyev, Sergey 125
setting 7, 27, 53, 90, 110, 126, 146, 157, 171, 176, 207, 214
The Seventh Seal 219
Seymour, Charles B. 102
Shadows of Our Forgotten Ancestors 227
Shadwell, Thomas 49
Shaftesbury, Third Earl of 75
Shakespeare, William viii 26, 32, 34, 40, 44, 49, 51, 59, 60, 61, 62, 64, 66-72, 75, 76, 77, 78, 80, 81, 84, 85, 86, 89, 90, 91, 92, 93, 95, 96, 97, 100, 101, 103, 106, 109, 118, 119, 124, 126, 139, 142, 151, 152, 174, 180, 181, 188, 190, 197, 216, 233, 234, 236, 237, 238
Shaw, George Bernard 81, 95, 105, 148, 151, 152, 177, 178, 181, 190, 236, 237, 242
Shaw, Irwin 188, 192, 193
Shcheglov, Ivan 125
Shedd, Robert 158
Shenandoah 110
Shepard, Sam 164, 199, 243
The Shepherd's Chameleon 162
Sheridan, Richard Brinsley 60, 92, 111, 234
Sherwood, Robert 183
The Shoemaker's Holiday 34
Sholokhov, Mikhail 138
Shoot the Piano Player 222
Shylock 91
Sidney, Sir Philip 31, 35, 36, 39, 232
Simmel, Georg 144
Simon, John 200, 217, 219, 224, 225, 244
Simon, Neil 197
Simonov, Konstantin 136, 137, 138, 187
Simonov, Ruben 137
Simylus 6
Sir Clyomon and Sir Clamydes 32
Sister Mary Ignatius Explains It All For You 200
Sjöberg, Alf 218
Sjöström, Victor 218
Slavophiles 121, 122
Sleptsov, Vasily 121

Smallwood, Clyde 159
Smith, D. Nicol 69
Smith, G.A. 204
Snow White and the Seven Dwarfs 209
socialist realism 134, 140, 213, 238, 239, 246
Solger, Karl 77
soliloquy 68, 98, 99, 100, 237
Sologub, Fyodor 120, 129
Solovyov, Vladimir 128
Solzhenitsyn, Alexander 139
Song of Solomon 2
Sophocles vii 5, 6, 7, 9, 10, 14, 27, 45, 62, 64, 79, 80, 181, 190, 200, 231
Sorge, Reinhard 144
Sorge, Richard 82
Spears, Monroe 189, 190
spectacle 9, 10, 11, 60, 100, 116, 120, 130, 170, 171, 203, 223, 231, 244
Spingarn, Joel 12, 46, 112, 113, 237
Spurgeon, Caroline 152
Squaring the Circle 133
S.S. Glencairn 177
Staël, Madame de 72, 84, 107, 235
The Stag and the Camp Prostitute 139
stage directions 110
stage effects 63, 143, 146, 169, 176, 180, 185, 234, 244
stage picture 222, 239
Stalin, Joseph 134, 137, 159, 194, 239
Stallings, Lawrence 177
Stanford, Leland 203
Stanislavsky, Konstantin 125, 126, 131, 132, 135, 140, 143, 145, 146, 155, 198, 212, 213, 244
Stapleton, Maureen 198
Stanwyck, Barbara 177
Star Wars 229
Steamboat Willie 209
Steele, Richard 57, 99
Steevens, George 71
Steiger, Rod 198
Steiner, George 226
Stendhal (Henri Beyle) 84, 85
Sternberg, Josef von 212
Stevenson, Robert Louis 94
Sticks and Bones 173
Stiller, Mauritz 218
Stockwood, John 31
The Stone Guest 120
Stoppard, Tom 164, 196
Storm over Asia 213
Strasberg, Lee 198
Streamers 195

A Streetcar Named Desire 185, 195
Strindberg, August 82, 114, 143, 144, 178, 190, 218, 239, 242, 246
Sturm, Johann 73
Sturm und Drang 65, 72, 74, 75
Styan, J.L. 161
Sucksdorff, Arne 218
Sudermann, Hermann 105
Suetonius 19
Sumarokov, Alexander 116, 119, 237
The Sunshine Boys 198
The Suppliant Women 5, 8, 43, 128
surrealism 146, 162, 167, 196, 216
Sutter's Gold 212
Süvern, Johann 77
Suvorov 213
Swanson, Gloria 209
Swinburne, Algernon 93
symbolism 88, 91, 125, 126, 127, 146, 147, 148, 149, 150, 159, 169, 171, 173, 186, 199, 218, 236, 238, 245
syndicate, theatrical 107, 110

tableau 63, 145
Taille, Jean de la 29, 232
Taine, Hippolyte 82, 107, 237
Talley's Folly 199
Tamerlane 32
Tarasenkov, A. 137
Tartufe 45
Taylor, Edward 71
Taylor, Laurette 177
Technicolor 209
television 149, 156, 201, 202, 221, 223, 229, 248
The Tempest 34
Temple, Sir William 52
The Ten Commandments 209
Terence 10, 13, 16, 19, 22, 26, 35, 47, 58, 64, 231
Terry, Ellen 146, 188
Tertullian 14, 15, 231
Thaïs 16
theater, attacks upon the 14, 15, 16, 17, 18, 29, 30, 31, 38, 48, 55, 60, 63, 97, 98, 99, 231, 232, 233, 234, 236, 246
theater-in-the-round 171
A Theater Lets Out After the Performance of a New Comedy 119
Theater of Action 131
Theater of Cruelty 170, 241
theater of recreation 17

Theater of the Absurd 139, 158-75, 240, 241, 245, 247
Theater of the Poor 155, 240
Théâtre de l'Oeuvre 159
Théâtre du Vieux Colombier 146
Théâtre Libre 88, 142, 143
Theatres Act 92
theme (thought) 9, 10, 14, 26, 79, 80, 81, 82, 88, 94, 129, 143, 149, 150, 151, 154, 155, 166, 170, 176, 182, 184, 189, 200, 201, 217, 219, 226, 243
Theobald, Lewis 57, 67, 68
Theophrastus 6, 19
Thérèse Raquin 87, 106
There Shall Be No Night 183
Thesmophoriazusae 5
Thespis 129, 238
They Knew What They Wanted 177
Thomas, Augustus 110
Thomas, Kevin 223
Thompson, Alan R. 191
Thomson, James 57
Thorndike, Ashley 179
The Thunderstorm 122
Tieck, Ludwig 78, 79, 235
Tillich, Paul 163
Tocqueville, Alexis de 86
Toller, Ernst 82, 144
Tolstoy, Alexey 123
Tolstoy, Leo 65, 95, 124, 133, 152, 188, 205, 238
Tone, Franchot 198
Towse, John Ranken 111, 176
Toynbee, Arnold 247
Tractatus Coislinianus 11
Tracy, Spencer 177
tragedy 5, 6, 7, 8, 9, 10, 11, 12, 14, 15, 16, 18, 19, 22, 23, 24, 25, 26, 27, 28, 29, 30, 31, 32, 33, 34, 36, 38, 39, 43, 48, 50, 53, 56, 57, 58, 61, 63, 64, 68, 70, 71, 73, 74, 76, 77, 78, 79, 80, 81, 84, 85, 87, 92, 100, 116, 118, 120, 124, 129, 150, 151, 152, 154, 156, 159, 161, 165, 174, 180, 181, 186, 190, 192, 231, 232, 235, 237, 240, 242, 245
tragedy, domestic (*drame*) 63, 64, 65, 181
The Tragedy of Tragedies, or The Life and Death of Tom Thumb the Great 57
tragicomedy 10, 23, 24, 27, 28, 29, 31, 33, 37, 39, 42, 51, 56, 57, 59, 63, 89, 92, 116, 122, 143, 147, 160, 173, 232, 233

Trapp, Joseph 57
Tree, Ellen 100
Treplev 126
Trincaveli 22
Trissino, Giangiorgio 25
True West 199
Truffaut, François 221, 222, 223, 227, 244
Turgenev, Ivan 88, 131
Turia, Ricardo de 39
Tvardovsky, Alexander 137, 139
Twain, Mark 103, 113
Twining, Thomas 60
Tydeman, William 20
Tyler, Parker 208, 218, 223, 224, 244, 245
Tyler, Royall 98
Tynan, Kenneth 155, 156, 166, 167, 241
typage 210, 244
Tyrannical Love 43
Tyr et Sidon 28

Udall, Nicholas 32, 35
Ullman, Liv 218
Ulrici, H. 79
Uncle Tom's Cabin 103
Unities, Three (action, place, time) 7, 22, 25, 26, 27, 29, 31, 32, 42, 43, 44, 45, 48, 49, 51, 61, 62, 65, 68, 75, 84, 92, 112, 146, 151, 161, 217, 232, 234, 240
Upton, John 67, 70

Valentino, Rudolph 209
Valla, Giorgio 21
Vanbrugh, Sir John 55
Varchi, Benedetto 22
Variety 213
Vaughan, C.E. 149
Vega, Lope de 19, 38-39, 40, 41, 131, 132, 153, 233, 234, 245
Venus Observed 189
verisimilitude 13, 25, 28, 43, 44, 49, 99, 100, 119, 237
Vettori, Francesco 22
The Vietnamization of New Jersey 172-73
Vida, Marco Girolamo 21, 29, 46
Vigny, Alfred de 88
Villena, Enrique de 38

The Visit 154, 155
Vitaphone 209
Vitascope 203, 204
Vladimir 163, 164
Voice of America 187
Volkov, Feodor 116
Voltaire (François Marie Arouet) 61, 62, 63, 64, 66, 67, 69, 70, 72, 86, 179, 234
Vos, Nelvin 200

Wagner, Richard 79, 80, 87, 95, 100, 108, 146, 147, 148, 149, 152, 236, 240, 245
Wais, Kurt 65
Waiting for Godot 163-65, 241
Waiting for Lefty 183
Waley, Arthur 4
Walkley, A.B. 95
Warburton, William 57, 68
Ward, Artemus 102, 103
Warren, Austin 46
Warshow, Robert 224, 244
Warton, Joseph 58, 68
Water Engine 200
Watteau, Jean 246
The Weavers 82
Webster, John 52
The Wedding on the Eiffel Tower 147
Wedekind, Frank 82, 83
Weiss, Peter 139
Wellek, René 90
Welles, Orson 216
"well made" play 86, 88, 95, 96, 110, 123, 144, 166, 190, 199, 235, 237
Wells, H.G. 94
Wellwarth, George 158
Whalley, Peter 70
What Price Glory? 177
Whatley, Thomas 71
Wheeler, Andrew C. 107, 108, 109, 237
Whetstone, George 32
White, Richard Grant 101
The White Guard 195
Whitman, Alden 164
Whitman, Walt 100, 102, 103, 206, 237
Who's Afraid of Virginia Woolf? 172
Wickham, Glynne 17
Wienbarg, Ludolf 78
Wilcocke, Rev. T. 30
Wilde, Oscar 139, 178, 180
Wilder, Billy 225

Wilder, Thornton 79, 184, 200, 242
Wiles, Timothy 198
Wilkins, Edward G.P. 102, 103, 104, 237
William and Mary 55
Williams, Tennessee 154, 185, 186, 193, 242, 246
Williamson, James 204
Wilson, Garff 98
Wilson, J. Dover 151, 152
Wilson, Lanford 199
Wilson, Robert 197
Winckelmann, Johann 76
Winter, William 102, 104-06, 107, 108, 111, 237
Winters, Shelley 198
Winterset 182
wit 33, 48, 49, 50, 51, 53, 56, 59, 91, 118, 151, 191, 225
Witkiewicz, Stanislaw 149
Witkowski, Georg 78, 80, 82
Woe from Wit 117, 120
Wojtyla, Karol (Pope John Paul II) 195
Woodward, Joanne 198
Woollcott, Alexander 183, 188, 192
Worsley, T.C. 153
Wozzeck 81
Wycherley, William 90
Wyler, William 216

Yamamoto 218
Ye Beare and Ye Cubb 97
Yeats, William Butler 150, 159, 194, 240
Young, Edward 57
Young, Karl 18
Young, Stark 4, 180, 242
Young, Vernon 218, 225, 226, 229, 244
The Youngest 177
Young Germany 78
Yurev, S.A. 123

Zabeleta, Juan de 40
Zavadsky, Yuri 138, 139
Zen Buddhism 161
Zero, Mr. 177
Zesen, Philip von 73
Zhdanov, Andrei 134, 136
Zhukovsky, Vasily 117
Zola, Emile 82, 87, 89, 106, 236
The Zoo Story 198
Zorin, Leonid 137
Zucker, A.E. 4
Zukor, Adolph 204, 205